Handbook on
China's WTO Accession
And Its Impacts

Handbook on
China's WTO Accession And Its Impacts

Ching Cheong
Ching Hung Yee

World Scientific
New Jersey • London • Singapore • Hong Kong

Published by

World Scientific Publishing Co. Pte. Ltd.

5 Toh Tuck Link, Singapore 596224

USA office: Suite 202, 1060 Main Street, River Edge, NJ 07661

UK office: 57 Shelton Street, Covent Garden, London WC2H 9HE

British Library Cataloguing-in-Publication Data

A catalogue record for this book is available from the British Library.

HANDBOOK ON CHINA'S WTO ACCESSION AND ITS IMPACTS

ISBN 981-238-061-2

Printed by FuIsland Offset Printing (S) Pte Ltd, Singapore

Overview

China has taken 15 long years to accomplish the accession to the World Trade Organization (WTO). In the history of the People's Republic of China (PRC), it is the second longest international negotiation the country has ever experienced.

In the 1950's when the Cold War reigned and the world was divided into a capitalist and a socialist camp, China started the marathon Warsaw Talk with the United States in a bid to regain its seat in the United Nations (UN). China understood very well that the US held the key to its entrance into the UN. Hence the Warsaw Talk was initiated as an attempt to forge a cordial relation with the US.

Thirty years later in the mid 1980's China started another marathon talk to regain her seat in the General Agreement on Trade and Tariff (GATT), the forerunner of the WTO. Again, it is the US who holds the key to China's re-admission to the "Economic United Nations", the Chinese jargon for WTO.

Whether it is the political or economic UN, both took China more than a decade of tough negotiations, and the US calls the shots in both cases. This is the dire fact in China-US bilateral relations.

China's negotiation process for WTO accession is particularly difficult for two reasons. First, to gain admission China has to convert its own economic system from a centrally planned economy to a free market economy, in line with a WTO trade regime. This transition entails not just ideological difficulties but also actual hardships and hence it takes time to develop a domestic consensus.

Second, wary of China's potential growth made possible by WTO membership, the US and other developed countries are exacting exceptionally severe terms from China. For example it is denied "developing country" status although many economic indicators suggest that it still falls within that category. Treatment for the agriculture sector is a classic case. China is denied many of the protective measures that even Japan, a fully developed WTO member, is allowed to retain up to the present.

By becoming a full member of the WTO, China has in fact made three tiers of commitments.

The first tier is the commitment to the spirits of WTO, such as free trade, most favoured nations, national treatment and transparency, as expounded in the various documents setting up the organization and its predecessor, the GATT.[1]

The second tier is the commitment to the set of rules governing trade for specific sectors, whether agricultural and textile goods, or information technology and telecommunications. This is expounded in China's accession protocol.

The third tier is the commitment made in the bilateral agreements which China signed with her major trading partners. Their support is mandatory before China can be admitted to the WTO and therefore it has to satisfy each of them through elaborate bilateral negotiations.[2]

These three tiers of commitments constitute China's WTO accession package.

The complexity of the negotiating process, the economic and political balance sheets of WTO membership for China, as well as domestic supports and oppositions can hardly be adequately summarized in one book. This handbook does not attempt to do this job. Rather it tries to highlight the important commitments that China made to the international community and analyze the potential impacts of such commitments on China. Commitments and impacts will be the main theme of this handbook.

This handbook contains three Parts.

Part I outlines China's commitments to convert its economy from a centrally planned one to a free market one as far as cross border movements of goods, services and personnel are concerned. It reproduces China commitments in a tabular format to facilitate reading. The commitments are further supplemented with quick and brief references to WTO regulations where appropriate so that readers get to know how China's commitments relate to WTO obligations.

Part II examines the impacts on WTO membership on China as a whole and on its specific economic sectors.

Part III summarizes some of the main findings of the US Government General Accounting Office (GAO) Report to the US Congress on China's WTO accession. The Report identifies more than 600 commitments made by China. Part of the Report is included here to give an overall idea of the nature and types of commitments China made.

---

[1]See Appendix 1 for a full list of the various documents governing a WTO trade regime, and Appendix 2 for a list of legal documents specifically on China's commitments.
[2]China's main commitments to the WTO as stipulated in its protocol, is mostly a replica of its commitments to the US as stipulated in the Sino-US Bilateral Trade Agreement. In many instances, the two documents can be used almost interchangeably.

Appendix 1 lists all the legal instruments pertaining to China's accession to the WTO. Appendix 2 reprints the Protocol of China's accession but no attempt is made to summarize the schedules of tariff reduction because of its sheer size. However, China's schedule of commitments on services, re-arranged in a format more readable to the general reader, is included as Appendix 3 so that concerned readers could find out for themselves how their professions could be affected. Appendix 4 reprints the GATS Services Sectoral Classification GNS/W/120 and part of CPC Provisional Version. This appendix is attached to facilitate readers to check whether their specific professions, which are spelt out in three to six digital codes, are included in Chinese commitments.

December, 2002
Hong Kong

Acknowledgements

The editors would like to thank D&A Training Consultants company for the research assistance which they provided. Without their help it would be impossible for us to go through the mass of information within such a short time frame.

We would also like to thank the operators of a number of websites which provide very rich information on China's accession to the World Trade Organization (WTO). Apart from the WTO website, the sites which we most frequently consulted are:

Arbitration in China	www.arbitration.org.cn
CCPIT Patent and Trademark Law Office	www.ccpit-patent.com.cn
China Insurance Regulatory Commission	www.circ.gov.cn
China Law Web	www.qis.net/chinalaw
China Legal Change (operation ceased on 1 Oct 2002)	www.chinalegalchange.com
Chinaonline	www.chinaonline.com
China Patent Agent (HK) Ltd	www.cpahkltd.com
China Macroeconomic Information Network	www.macrochina.com.cn
China Economic Information Network	www.cei.gov.cn
Development and Research Centre of the State Council	drcnet.com.cn
European Commission's On Trade	http://europa.eu.int/comm/trade
Hongkong Trade Development Council	www.tdctrade.com
International Monetary Fund	www.imf.org
MOFTEC Ministry of Foreign Trade and Economic Cooperation	www.moftec.gov.cn (inception of new website on 13 Sept 2002: www.chinawto.gov.cn)
State Administration for Industry and Commerce	www.saic.gov.cn
State Economic and Trade Commission	www.setc.gov.cn
State Intellectual Property Office of China	www.sipo.gov.cn
UN Statistical Division	http://unstats.un.org/unsd/
US-China Business Council	www.uschina.org
White House Fact Sheets on US-China Bilateral Agreement	http://www.uschina.org/public/wto/factsheets
World Trade Organization	www.wto.org

ACKNOWLEDGEMENTS

Without these websites, it would be impossible to unravel the information maze associated with China's accession to the WTO.

Ching Cheong
Ching Hung-yee
Editors

Contents

CHINA'S COMMITMENTS ON ACCESSION TO THE WTO

Preface
(Part I)

Part I is essentially a re-organized presentation of China's commitments that were made upon China's accession to the World Trade Organizations.[1] The commitments made by China are contained in various accession documents. (*See Appendix 2 for a list of documents.*)

The Protocol on the Accession of the People's Republic of China signed at the Fourth Ministerial Conference of the WTO in Doha, Qatar on 11 November 2001 ("the Protocol") is the primary document on China's accession. Its annexes contain primarily schedules of specific commitments made by China for submission to WTO in respect of bound tariff rate, tariff concessions, preferential treatment, market access for goods and commitments in respect of market access for services. Timeframes for phasing in WTO obligations and for phasing out trade-restrictive policies are also given in detail.[2] The Report of the Working Party on China's Accession ("the Working Party Report") is another prime document. It contains conclusions of the final negotiations between China and members of the WTO in respect of China's foreign trade regime. *The Protocol* stipulates in its section 1.2 that certain paragraphs of the Working Party Report are incorporated to form its integral part. These paragraphs contain some 140-odd specific commitments mady by China as a result of negotiations. By being incorporated into *the Protocol*, these commitments become binding on China. Some of these paragraphs in fact contain more than one pledge by China. So if these individual commitments are to be counted, together with the *Protocol*, there are close to 700 commitments, according to the tabulation by the US General Accounting Office in an analysis report on China's commitments (*see* Part III). It is on the basis of these paragraphs that Chapter 1 through

---

[1]The WTO framework takes a single undertaking approach in that the Agreement establishing the WTO encompasses the GATT, as modified by the Uruguay Round, all agreements and arrangements concluded under its auspices and the complete results of the Uruguay Round. Accession to WTO entails the acceptance of all the covered agreements without exception. See Appendix 1 for a full list of WTO agreements.

[2]Pursuant to Part II of *the Protocol*, the Schedules annexed to *the Protocol* shall become the "Schedule of Concessions and Commitments" annexed to the *General Agreement in Tariff and Trade ("GATT 1994")* and "the Schedule of Specific Commitments" annexed to the *General Agreement on Trade in Services* ("GATS") relating to China. The staging of concessions and commitments listed in these Schedules shall be implemented as specified in the relevant parts of the relevant Schedules. Pursuant to Article II:6(a) of the *GATT 1994*, the applicable date in respect of the Schedule of Concessions and Commitments annexed to *the Protocol* shall be the date of accession (ie. 11 December 2001).

Chapter 4 of this book is compiled. *The Protocol,* together with its nine annexes and relevant parts of the Working Party Report form a wide-ranging package of China's commitments in the form of literal commitments, data commitments and schedules of commitments.

As said, the commitments by China laid down in Chapters 1 to 4 are compiled from relevant parts of the Working Party Report. These commitments are reproduced in a table of two columns. For ease of reading, the editor had effected slight modifications as to the contents of the commitments, mostly by supplementing them with text of legal provisions or reducing some of the contents to footnotes so as to make the commitment more concise. The order of the commitments have been re-arranged (other than that which appeared in the Working Party Report) to suit topical arrangement. The editor also added sub-headings in each table of specific commitment.

For each subject in respect of which a commitment was made by China, the specific commitment or confirmation itself is entered under the column "China's commitments/ confirmations". Emphases are added to certain verbs to indicate China's determination. In some cases, the statement(s) by china explaining its standpoint or the consideration associated with the making of a commitment is also entered here. This column should be read along with the text in the neighbouring column titled "Current situation/concerns raised by other WTO members". Here, as the title suggests, it recorded the various concerns posed by other WTO members during the negotiation or the current situation prevailing in China with regard to the subject. It is against such background that China made its commitment in the subject concerned. Where issues had been discussed but no commitment or confirmation was made, the discussions are reproduced as statements of facts or statements of opinions and remain untabulated under a specific topic. This format intends to save the readers' time in sorting out what had been discussed, confirmed, committed or not committed. Since much of the text is extracted from the Working Party Report, it is presented in indirect speech.

The tabulated text in Chapters 1 to 4 are supplemented as much as possible with the titles and article numbers of relevant WTO rules and/or with very brief principles so that readers do not have to first dig into the mass of WTO documents to comprehend the commitment. Introductory materials on various trade topics obtainable from the WTO website and materials from the Working Party Report itself are also used to compile the explanatory text, unless otherwise specified from other sources. Where necessary, information pertaining to China laws is also supplemented. All these supplementary materials appear either as explanatory text or footnote references. Furthermore, the relevant section of *the Protocol* is quoted (denoted as Protocol Ref: Section XX) wherever applicable for ease of reference. (*See* Appendix 2(b) of this book for the full text of *the Protocol.*)

For commitments relating to government policies (Chapter 1) and trade in goods (Chapter 2), readers need to refer separately to the schedules in annexes 1 to 8 to *the Protocol* for specific data related to the commitments. Those annexes are however, not found in this book due to the huge amount of data. For trade in services (Chapter 3), readers are advised to read this in conjunction with Appendix 3 for a re-formatted copy of China's schedule of commitments in services (Annex 9 to *the Protocol*). For intellectual property rights, the commitments are fully laid out in Chapter 4. Chapter 5 gives a brief account of the principles underlying the disputes settlement system of the WTO and whether China would fit into the system. The rules and procedures of the disputes settlement system apply to the consultations and disputes settlement procedures of all covered agreements of the WTO. In this regard, the system is a central, indispensable element in providing security and predictability to the WTO multilateral trade regime.

The commitments, as presented in Part 1, are ultimate results of multi-round negotiations. These commitments, together with all supplementary information shall not be regarded as rendering readers the scenarios in China in respect of the subject negotiated. There are trade topics such as agriculture and intellectual property protection in which negotiations are far too complicated to merit discussion in one whole book. The objective of this part and the relevant appendixes is nothing more than telling what China's commitments are. Readers have to consult other reference to get a grasp of the whole picture.

Chapters 3, 4, and 5 have more to inform than just presenting commitments. The reason is that three important new agreements emerged as a core among the multilateral trade agreements ("MLA") concluded as a result of the Uruguay Round negotiations. They are the *General Agreement on Trade in Service* ('GATS'), the *Agreement of Trade-Related Intellectual Property Rights Including Trade in Counterfeit Goods* ('TRIPS') and the *Understanding on the Rules and Procedures Governing the Settlement of Disputes* ('Disputes Settlement Procedures'). They are not found under the old GATT but their emergence opened up new dimensions in the multilateral trade regime. Hence, a brief introduction to each of these agreements is given at the beginning of Chapters 3, 4 and 5 respectively.

One important feature of the WTO is the *review* on regular basis *of trade policies* implemented by members. The WTO General Council conducts the review in which its primary purpose is to ensure transparency of trade policies and practices. The *transitional review mechanism* relative to China's accession will come into play one year after China's accession. By then, the various subsidiary bodies of the WTO (see Section 18 of *the Protocol*) shall each review the implementation by China of the WTO agreements and of the related provisions of *the Protocol*. This subject is, for the time being, not introduced in detail in this book.

The WTO Agreement[3] to which China accedes shall be the WTO Agreement as rectified, amended or otherwise modified by such legal instruments as may have entered into force before the date of China's accession.[4] Obligations in the Multilateral Trade Agreements annexed to the WTO Agreement ("MLA") are to be implemented over a period of time starting with the entry into force of the MLA.[5] However, as far as implementation of such

---

[3]The "Multilateral Trade Agreements" that appear in the Final Act of the Uruguay Round of Multilateral Trade Negotiations signed in Marrakesh on 15 April, 1994 along with *GATT 1994* (Amended) form part of the treaty establishing the WTO, *also see* note 1.

[4]Section 1.2 of *the Protocol*.

[5]The WTO Agreement entered into force in the year of 1995.

WTO obligations is concerned, it should be noted that upon its accession to WTO, China would have to implement the residual years of implementation of various MLA as if it had accepted those agreements on the date of their entry into force, except as otherwise provided for in *the Protocol.*[6] That means where transition for implementation is still in force under a MLA, China would be left with a shorter period for transition to full WTO compliance.

Note that there are ongoing changes to the laws, rules and regulations and measures ever since China acceded to WTO on 11 December, 2001. Adjustments to China's legal regime have started even before China's accession. Following China's accession, amendments or modifications to existing laws, rules and regulations as committed have been undergoing and such reform is expected to take place actively within a year after accession to bring China law in line with WTO obligations. Recently effected modifications at the time of compiling this work cover joint-ventures laws, investment measures, market access and intellectual property (see Chapter 4 for recent changes in IP laws). Some of the changes are found in the footnotes of the text.

---

[6]Pursuant to section 1.3 of *the Protocol*

chapter 1

China: Adapting to the WTO Trade Regime

The commitments made by China in the Working Party Report concerning the foreign trade regime are incorporated under S1.2 in the "Protocol on the Accession of the People's Republic of China" dated 10 November, 2001 (hereunder "the Protocol"). Together with its annexes, which contain China's commitments in the form of schedules in respect of tariff concessions for goods, market access for services and various notifications pursuant to WTO requirements, *the Protocol* wraps up the whole of China's commitments. This chapter focuses on commitments made by China concerning the adaptation of government policies to the WTO trade regime.

A. ECONOMIC POLICIES   Protocol Ref: S3

A1. Non-Discrimination (Including National Treatment)

Current situation/concerns raised by other WTO Members	China commitments/confirmations
Discriminatory practice — Nationality of an entity	
It was concerned that there should be: 1. Non-discriminatory treatment accorded to all foreign individuals and enterprises and foreign-funded enterprises in respect of the procurement of inputs and goods and services necessary for production of goods. The conditions, under which their goods were produced, marketed or sold, in the domestic market and for export should be on non-discriminatory basis too;	Entity China *would provide* the same treatment to Chinese enterprises, including foreign-funded enterprises, and foreign enterprises and individuals in China. However, any commitment to provide non-discriminatory treatment to Chinese enterprises would be subject to other provisions of *the Protocol* and, in particular, would not prejudice China's rights under the *GATS*, China's Schedule of Specific Commitments or commitments undertaken in relation to trade-related investment measures.

2. Non-discriminatory treatment in respect of the prices and availability of goods and services supplied by national and sub-national authorities and public or state enterprises, in areas including transportation, energy, basic telecommunications, other utilities and factors of production. There were also concerns: 3. With China's practice of conditioning or imposing restrictions upon entering China market based upon the nationality of the entity concerned; and 4. Over such practices in relation to the pricing and procurement of goods and services, and the distribution of import and export licences. China was requested not to condition such practices on the nationality of the entity concerned.	Goods China *would eliminate* dual pricing practices as well as differences in treatment accorded to goods produced for sale in China in comparison to those produced for export. All WTO Members China *would provide* non-discriminatory treatment to all WTO members, including Members of the WTO that were separate customs territories.

Chinese legislation in contravention of "National Treatment"	
There were concerns that certain provisions of Chinese laws, regulations, administrative notices and other requirements which could directly or indirectly result in less favourable treatment of imported products in contravention of Article III of the *General Agreement of Tariffs and Trade* ("GATT 1994").[1] Such requirements included: 1. product registration and certification; 2. internal taxation; 3. price and profit controls; and	The full respect of all laws, regulations and administrative requirements with the principle of non-discrimination between domestically produced and imported products *would be ensured and enforced* by the date of China's accession unless otherwise provided in *the Protocol* or the Working Party Report. By accession, China *would repeal* and *cease* to apply all such existing laws, regulations and other measures whose effect was inconsistent with WTO rules on national treatment.[2] Measures *would be taken* at national and sub-national level, including repeal or modification of legislation, to provide full GATT national treatment

---

[1]Article III of *GATT 1994* concerns "National Treatment on Internal Taxation and Regulation".
[2]Clause 22 of the Working Party Report: "....This commitment was made in relation to final or interim laws, administrative measures, rules and notices, or any other form of stipulation or guideline."

4. all distinct forms of licensing for imports, and distribution or sale of imported goods; and also,

5. there existed the differential treatment of goods of Chinese origin and goods of non-Chinese origin.

Specific reference was made to the procedures, charges, conditions for granting importing business licence, whether to import, distribute, re-sell or retail goods of non-Chinese origin. Reference was also made to taxes and fiscal provisions whose impacts depended, directly or indirectly, upon the Chinese or non-Chinese origin of the goods imported or traded. China had the obligation to ensure that product testing and certification requirements posed no greater burden — whether financial or practical — on goods of non-Chinese origin than on domestic goods.

in respect of laws, regulations and other measures applying to internal sale, offering for sale, purchase, transportation, distribution or use of:

i) after sales services (repair, maintenance and assistance), including any conditions applying to its provision, such as the MOFTEC third Decree of 6 September 1993, imposing mandatory licensing procedures for the supply of after-sales service on various imported products;

ii) pharmaceutical products, including regulations, notices and measures which subjected imported pharmaceuticals to distinct procedures and formulas for pricing and classification, or which set limits on profit margins attainable and imports, or which created any other conditions regarding price or local content which could result in less favourable treatment of imported products;

iii) cigarettes including unification of the licensing requirements so that a single licence authorized the sale of all cigarettes, irrespective of their country of origin, and elimination of any other restrictions regarding points of sale for imported products, such as could be imposed by the China National Tobacco Corporation ("CNTC"). It was understood that in the case of cigarettes, China could avail itself of a transitional period of two years to fully unify the licensing requirements. Immediately upon accession, and during the two year transitional period, the number of retail outlets selling imported cigarettes would be substantially increased throughout the territory of China;

iv) spirits, including requirements applied under China's *Administrative Measures on Imported Spirits in the Domestic Market*, and other provisions which imposed distinct criteria and licensing for the distribution and sale of different categories of spirits, including unification of the licensing requirements so that a single licence authorized the sale of all spirits irrespective of their country of origin;

	v) chemicals, including registration procedures applicable to imported products, such as those applied under China's *Provisions on the Environmental Administration of Initial Imports of Chemical Products and Imports and Exports of Toxic Chemical Products*; vi) boilers and pressure vessels, including certification and inspection procedures which had to be no less favourable than those applied to goods of Chinese origin, and fees applied by the relevant agencies or administrative bodies, which had to be equitable in relation to those chargeable for like products of domestic origin. In the cases of pharmaceuticals, spirits and chemicals, China would reserve the right to use a transitional period of one year from the date of accession to amend or repeal the relevant legislation.

A2. Monetary and Fiscal Policy

Current Fiscal Policy

Through the reform and opening up in the last two decades, China had established a fiscal management system which was compatible with the principles of a market economy.

With respect to fiscal revenue, a taxation system with a value-added tax as the main element had been established since the taxation reform in 1994.

With respect to fiscal expenditure, over recent years, the government had, in line with the public fiscal requirement generally exercised by market economies, strengthened its adjustment of the structure of expenditure and given priority to public needs so as to ensure the normal operations of the government.

Current Monetary Policy

In recent years, while pursuing proactive fiscal policy, China had implemented proper monetary policy and had taken a series of adjusting and reform measures:

— lowering the interest rate for loans from financial institutions;
— improving the system of required deposit reserves;
— lowering the ratio of required reserves;
— positively increasing the input of base money
— encouraging the commercial banks to expand their credit.

China's Future Fiscal Policy

The government of China:

— would further improve its taxation system
— would continue to improve the efficiency of fiscal expenditures through measures such as:
  • sectoral budget,
  • centralized payment by the national treasure and zero base budget;
  • improving management of fiscal expenditure.

China's Future Monetary Policy

The central bank would continue to pursue a prudent policy and to:

— maintain the stability of RMB,
— promote interest rate liberalization and
— establish a modern commercial banking system.

There was no specific commitment made here.

A3. Foreign Exchange and Payments

Concerns raised by other WTO Members

There was the concern about China's use of forex controls to regulate the level and composition of trade in goods and services.

In response, China stated that it was now a member of the International Monetary Fund ("IMF") and that recently its system of forex had undergone rapid change. In early 1994, official RMB exchange rates were unified with the market rates. The banking exchange system was adopted and a nationwide unified inter-bank forex market was established, with conditional convertibility of the Renminbi on current accounts. Since 1996, foreign invested enterprises ("FIEs") were also permitted into the banking exchange system. On 1 December, 1996, China had formally accepted the obligations of Article VIII of the IMF's Articles of Agreement, removing exchange restrictions on current account transactions.[3] Since then, RMB had been fully convertible on current accounts. China was confirmed by IMF to have no existing forex restrictions for current account transactions.[4]

---

[3]One of the obligations for member country which had accepted Article VIII of the IMF's Articles of Agreement.
[4]*See* Press Release Number 96/58 dated 4 December 1996, IMF website; IMF also confirmed this in its Staff Report on Article IV Consultations with China in 2000, *see* clause 28 of the Working Party Report.

Current situation

Regulating Body

The State Administration of Foreign Exchange ("SAFE") was under the auspices of the People's Bank of China ("PBC"), and was the administrative organ empowered to regulate forex. Its main function were to monitor and advise on balance of payments and forex matters, and to draft appropriate regulations and monitor compliance. With the approval of the PBC, domestic and foreign banks and financial institutions could engage in forex business.

Forex Payments and Receipts

Currently, for forex payments under current accounts, domestic entities (including FIEs) could purchase forex at *market exchange rates* from designated banks or debit their forex accounts directly upon presentation of valid documents.

For payments such as pre-payment, commission, etc. exceeding the proportion or limit, the entities could also purchase forex from the banks upon meeting the *bona fide test* administered by SAFE.

Forex for personal use by individuals could be purchased directly from the banks upon presentation of valid documents (within a specified limit).

Current account forex receipts owned by domestic entities had to be repatriated into China, though some of which could be retained and some sold to the designated banks at market rates. A verification system for forex payment (imports) and forex receipt (export) had also been adopted.

Exchange Rate Regime

Since the unification of exchange rates on 1 January, 1994, China adopted a single and managed floating exchange rate regime based on supply and demand. PBC published the reference rates of RMB against the US dollar, the HK dollar, and Japanese yen based on the weighted average prices of forex transactions at the interbank forex market during the previous day's trading. The buying and selling rates of RMB against the US dollar or other currencies were allowed to fluctuate within a prescribed range.

Designed forex banks had become major participation in forex transactions since 1 January 1994. On 1 April, 1994, the China Foreign Exchange Trading System was set up in Shanghai and branches were opened in dozens of cities. The Foreign Exchange Trading System had adopted a system of membership, respective quotation, concentrated trading and forex market settlement. Designated forex banks dealt on the inter-bank market according to the turnover position limit on banking exchange stipulated by SAFE and covered the position on the market. Depending on its macro-economic objectives, the PBC could intervene in the forex open market in order to regulate market supply and demand, and maintain the stability of the RMB exchange rate.

Forex Dealings of the FIEs

Since 1 July 1996, forex dealings of the FIEs was carried out through the banking exchange system.

China had granted national treatment to FIEs in exchange administration to encourage foreign direct investment. Accordingly FIEs were allowed to open and hold forex settlement accounts to retain receipts under current accounts, up to a maximum amount stipulated by the State Administration of Foreign Exchange. Receipts in excess of the maximum amount were required to be sold to designated forex banks.

No restrictions were maintained on the payment and transfer of current transactions by FIEs.

FIEs could also purchase forex from designated forex banks or debit their forex accounts for any payment under current transactions, upon the presentation of valid documents to the designated forex banks or SAFE for the bona fide test.

FIEs could also open forex accounts to hold foreign-invested capital, and they could sell from these accounts upon approval of SAFE.

FIEs could also borrow forex directly from domestic and overseas banks, but were required to register with SAFE afterwards, and obtain approval by SAFE for debt repayment and services.

FIEs could make payments from their forex accounts or in forex purchased from designated forex banks after liquidation, upon approval by SAFE according to law.

Governing Laws

The laws and regulations governing the forex activities of FIEs are:

— *Law of the People's Republic of China on Chinese-Foreign Equity Joint Venture*
  [adopted on 1 July 1979 by the National People's Congress, amended on 4 April 1990 and on 15 March 2001];
— *Law of the People's Republic of China on Chinese-Foreign Contractual Joint Venture*
  [adopted on 13 April 1988 at the seventh National People's Congress, amended on 31 October 2000];
— *Regulations on the Foreign Exchange Control of the People's Republic of China*
  [promulgated on 29 January 1996 as Directive No. 193 of the State Council, amended on 14 January 1997];
— *Regulations on Foreign Exchange Settlements, Sales and Payment in Foreign Exchange*
  [promulgated on 20 June 1996 by the People's Bank of China]

China's commitments/confirmations

China *would implement* its obligations with respect to forex matters in accordance with the provisions of the *WTO Agreement* and related declarations and decisions of the WTO that concerned the IMF. By accepting Article VIII of the IMF's Articles of Agreement, China cannot impose restrictions on the making of payments and transfers for current international transactions.[5] Unless otherwise provided for in the IMF's Articles of Association, China *would not* resort to any laws, regulations or other measures[6] that would restrict the availability to any

---

[5]Article VIII of *IMF's Articles of Agreement* stipulates"...no member shall, without the approval of the Fund, impose restrictions on the making of payments and transfers for current international transactions."
[6]This includes: any requirements with respect to contractual terms, according to clause 35 of the Working Party Report.

14

individual or enterprise of forex for current international transactions within its customs territory to an amount related to the forex inflows attributable to that individual or enterprise.

China *would provide* information on exchange measures as required under Article VIII, Section 5 of the IMF's Articles of Agreement and the transitional review mechanism.

A4. Balance-of-Payments Measures

Countries facing balance-of-payment difficulty, for instance, in the process of economic development or economic transition, may apply import restrictions under provisions in the *GATT 1994 Agreement* and under *the General Agreement on Trade in Services (GATS)*. Use of the balance of payments provisions in the WTO is governed by the following agreements:

1. **Articles XII and XVIII:B of** *GATT 1994*
2. **The** *Understanding on the Balance-of-payments Provisions of the GATT 1994 ("the BOPs Understanding")*
3. **Article XII of the** *GATS*

Under the *BOPs Understanding*,[7] WTO Members confirm that restrictive import measures taken for balance-of-payments purposes may only be applied to control the general level of imports and may not exceed what is necessary to address the balance-of-payments situation. In order to minimize any incidental protective effects, a Member shall administer restrictions in a transparent manner. Members may restrict the quantity and value of merchandise permitted to be imported. In curing BOPs situation, Members confirm to give preference to those measures with the least disruptive effect on trade. Such measures are referred to as price-based measures, which include import surcharges, import deposits requirements or other equivalent trade measures with an impact on the price of imported goods. Price-based measures taken for BOPs purposes may be applied by a Member in excess of the bound duties inscribed in the Schedule of that Member that are attached to *GATT 1994*.

Current situation/concerns raised by other WTO Members	China commitments/confirmations
BOP measures	
As regards with concern that: China should apply balance-of-payments ("BOPs") measures only under the circumstances provided for in the *WTO Agreement* and not as a justification for imposition of restrictions on imports for other protectionist purposes for specific	China considered that it should have the right to make full use of the provisions of WTO's *BOPs Understanding* to protect, if necessary, its BOPs situation. China *would fully comply* with the provisions of the *GATT 1994* and the *BOPs Understanding*.

---

[7]Paragraph 4, *BOPs Understanding*.

sectors, industries or products. These measures should have the least trade disruptive effect possible and should be limited to temporary import surcharges, import deposit requirements or other equivalent price-based trade measures.

Any such measures should be notified to the General Council together with a time schedule for their elimination and a programme of external and domestic policy measures to be used to restore BOPs equilibrium.

China should enjoy the same rights as those accorded to other developing country WTO Members, as provided in *GATT* Article XVIII:B and the *BOPs Understanding*.

Preference *would be given* to application of price-based measures as set forth in the *BOPs Understanding*. If China resorted to measures that were not price-based, it would transform such measures into price-based measures as soon as possible. Any measures taken *would be maintained* strictly in accordance with the *GATT 1994* and the *BOPs Understanding*, and *would not exceed* what was necessary to address the particular BOPs situation.

China further *confirmed* that measures taken for BOPs reasons would only be applied to control the general level of imports and not to protect specific sectors, industries or products, except for "essential products"[8] which were available under *BOPs Understanding*.

A5. Investment Regime
(*read also* Section D5, Chapter 2)

Protocol Ref: S7(3)

Current situation/concerns raised by other WTO Members	China commitments/confirmations
Opening up of a market-oriented environment for investments	
Since the opening up policy in the late 1970's, China had carried out a series of reforms of its investment regime. The government of China encouraged foreign investment into the Chinese market and had uninterruptedly opened and expanded the scope for investment. The government also encouraged the development of the non-state-operated economy and was speeding up the opening of areas for non-state investment.	China had promulgated investment guidelines and that the Government of China was in the process of revising and completing these guidelines. These guidelines and their implementation *would be* in full conformity with the *WTO Agreement*.

---

[8]ibid. "'essential products'... shall be understood to mean products which meet basic consumption needs or which contribute to the Member's effort to improve its balance-of-payments situation, such as capital goods or inputs needed for production."

With China's programme in the establishment of its market economy, enterprises with construction projects decided its own capital arrangement. Commercial banks' credit activities to all kinds of investors would be based on their own evaluation and decision-making, and would be at their own risk.

Intermediate investment agencies would break up their administrative relations with government agencies and operated in accordance with market force. Government-financed service activities would also be subject to contractual terms and conditions.

A6. State-Owned and State-Invested Enterprises   Protocol Ref: S6

Nature of Activities of State or State-owned Enterprises

Current situation/concerns raised by other WTO Members	China commitments/confirmations
Operating According to Market Forces In China's opinion, the state-owned enterprises of China basically operated in accordance with rules of market economy. The government would no longer directly administer the human, finance and material resources, and operational activities such as production, supply and marketing. Market forces decided the prices of commodities produced by state-owned enterprises and resources in operational areas were fundamentally allocated by the market. The state-owned banks had been commercialized and lending to state-owned enterprises took place exclusively under market conditions. China was furthering its reform of state-owned	China *would ensure* that all state-owned and state-invested enterprises would make purchases and sales based solely on commercial considerations, e.g., price, quality, marketability and availability, and that the enterprises of other WTO Members *would have* an adequate opportunity to compete for sales to and purchases from these enterprises on non-discriminatory terms and conditions. In addition, the Government of China *would not influence*, directly or indirectly, commercial decisions on the part of state-owned or state-invested enterprises, including on the quantity, value or country of origin of any goods purchased or sold, except in a manner consistent with the *WTO Agreement*. China *confirmed* that, without prejudice to China's rights in future negotiations in the *Government Procurement Agreement* of WTO, all laws,

enterprises and establishing a modern enterprise system.

Government's Role in Purchases and Sales

In light of the role that state-owned and state-invested enterprises played in China's economy, there were concerns about the continuing governmental influence and guidance of the decisions and activities of such enterprises relating to the purchase and sale of goods and services. Such purchases and sales should be based solely on commercial considerations, without any governmental influence or application of discriminatory measures.

There was the need for China to clarify its understanding of the types of activities that would not come within the scope of Article III:8(a) of *GATT 1994* [government procurement activities].[9] For example, any measure relating to state-owned and state-invested enterprises importing materials and machinery used in the assembly of goods, which were then exported or otherwise made available for commercial sale or use or for non-governmental purposes, would not be considered to be a measure relating to government procurement.

regulations and measures relating to the procurement by state-owned and state-invested enterprises of goods and services for commercial sale, production of goods or supply of services for commercial sale, or for non-governmental purposes *would not be considered* to be laws, regulations and measures *relating to government procurement*. Thus, such purchases or sales *would be subject* to the provisions of Articles II (most-favoured-nation treatment), XVI (market access) and XVII (national treatment) of the *General Agreement on Trade in Services ("GATS")*[10] and Article III of the *GATT 1994.*[11]

b. Government Procurement

In most countries the government, and its various agencies are, together, the biggest purchasers of goods and services of all kinds, ranging from basic commodities to high-technology

---

[9]Article III:8(a) of *GATT 1994* states that the provisions of Article III (national treatment on internal taxation and regulation) shall not apply to laws, regulations or requirements relating to government procurement.
[10]*See* Chapter 3.
[11]National treatment on internal taxation and regulation.

equipment. At the same time, the political pressure to favour domestic suppliers over their foreign competitors can be very strong.

The relative WTO Agreement regulating government procurement is the **Agreement on Government Procurement** *("GPA")*. It was first negotiated during the Tokyo Round of *GATT* and entered into force on 1 January 1981. Its purpose is to open up as much of this business as possible to international competition. It is designed to make laws, regulations, procedures and practices regarding government procurement more transparent and to ensure they do not protect domestic products or suppliers, or discriminate against foreign products or suppliers.

Current situation/concerns raised by other WTO Members	China commitments/confirmations
In order to promote China's government procurement regime, China was formulating its Government Procurement Law in addition to the *Interim Regulations on Government Procurement* promulgated by the Ministry of Finance in April 1998. There was the concern that China should become a party to *GPA* and that prior to its accession to the *GPA*, China should conduct all government procurement in a transparent and non-discriminatory manner. Public entities engaged exclusively in commercial activities would not be conducting procurement and thus laws, regulations and other measures regulating these entities' procurement practices would be fully subject to WTO requirements.	China stated that it intended to become a Party to the *GPA* and that until such time, all government entities at the central and sub-national level, as well as any of its public entities other than those engaged in exclusively commercial activities, *would conduct* their procurement in a transparent manner, and provide all foreign suppliers with equal opportunity to participate in that procurement pursuant to the principle of MFN treatment, i.e., if a procurement was opened to foreign suppliers, all foreign suppliers *would be provided* with equal opportunity to participate in that procurement (e.g., through the bidding process). Such entities' procurements *would be subject* only to laws, regulations, judicial decisions, administrative rulings of general application, and procedures (including standard contract clauses) which had been published and made available to the public. China *would become* an observer to the *GPA* upon accession to the *WTO Agreement* and initiate negotiations for membership in the *GPA* as soon as possible.

c. Transfer of Technology in Particular Those Related to Investment

Current situation/concerns raised by other WTO Members	China commitments/confirmations
There were concerns that laws, regulations and measures affecting the transfer of technology, in particular in the context of investment decisions. There were measures conditioning the receipt of benefits, including investment approvals, upon technology transfer. There was further concern that parties to an investment agreement should agree on the terms and conditions of technology transfer without government interference. The government should not, for example, condition investment approval upon technology transfer.	China *would only impose, apply or enforce* laws, regulations or measures relating to the transfer of technology, production processes, or other proprietary knowledge to an individual or enterprise in its territory that were *not* inconsistent with the *WTO Agreement on Trade-Related Aspects of Intellectual Property Rights* ("TRIPS Agreement") and the *Agreement on Trade-Related Investment Measures* ("TRIMs Agreement"). The terms and conditions of technology transfer, production processes or other proprietary knowledge, particularly in the context of an investment, *would only* require agreement between the parties to the investment.

A7. Pricing Policies   Protocol Ref: S6(2), S9, Annex 4

Concerns raised by other WTO Members
It was noted that China had made extensive use of price controls, for example, in the agricultural sector, and there existed multi-tier pricing practices for goods and services. There was concern that China expected to maintain price controls on the goods and services listed in Annex 4 to *the Protocol*[12] and that any such controls should be maintained in a manner consistent with the WTO Agreement, in particular Article III of the *GATT 1994* [national treatment] and Annex 2, paragraphs 3 and 4, of the *Agreement on Agriculture*.[13] The list of goods and services subject to state pricing and changes thereto should be published by China in the appropriate official journal.

---

[12]Titled "Products and Services Subject to Price Control".

[13]Annex 2 of the *Agricultural Agreement* is titled: "Domestic Support: The Basis for Exemption from the Reduction Commitments"; paragraph 3 concerns public stockholding for food security purpose, it is stated: ".....Food purchases by the government shall be made at current market prices and sales from food security stocks shall be made at no less than the current domestic market price for the product and quality in question." Paragraph 4 concerns domestic food aid, it is stated: ".....Food purchases by the government shall be made at current market prices and the financing and administration of the aid shall be transparent." *See also* section D9, Chapter 2 of this book on "Agricultural Policies" on "Domestic Support".

Price controls and state pricing in China also encompassed "guidance pricing" and regulation of the range of profits that enterprises could enjoy. There were concerns that price controls should be adopted only in extraordinary circumstances, must notify to the WTO Secretariat and should not be extended to goods and services beyond those listed in Annex 4. Those controls should also be removed as soon as the circumstances justifying their adoption were addressed.

There were further concerns that China could maintain prices below market-based ones in order to limit imports.

Current situation

China currently applied a mechanism of market-based pricing under macro-economic adjustment. There were presently three types of prices: government price, government guidance price and market-regulated price.

The *government price* was set by price administration authorities and could *not* be changed without the approval of these authorities. Products and services subject to government pricing were those having a direct bearing on the national economy and the basic needs of the people's livelihood, including those products that were scarce in China.

When setting prices for public utilities, important public welfare services and goods subject to natural monopolies and services which were of vital interest to the general public, government pricing authorities would hold public hearings and invite consumers, operators and other concerned parties to comment and debate on the necessity and impact of a price adjustment. The prices of important services were subject to the approval of the State Council. Government pricing was product- or service-specific, regardless of the ownership of the enterprises concerned.

The *government guidance price mechanism* was a more flexible form of pricing. The price administration authorities stipulated either a basic price or floating ranges of generally 5 per cent to 15 per cent. Enterprises could, within the limits of the guidance and taking into account the market situation, make their own decisions on prices. With *market-regulated prices*, enterprises were free to set prices in accordance with supply and demand to the extent permitted by generally applicable laws, regulations and policies concerning prices.

Due to the continued reform of China's price system, the share of government prices had dropped substantially and that of market-regulated prices had increased.[14] Annex 4 of *the Protocol* contained a comprehensive listing of all products and services presently subject to

---

[14]Clause 55 of the Working Party Report: "…of social retailing products, the share of government prices was about 4 per cent, that of government guidance prices 1.2 per cent, and that of market-regulated prices 94.7 per cent. For agricultural products, the share of government prices was 9.1 per cent, government guidance prices 7.1 per cent, and market-regulated 83.3 per cent. For production inputs, the share of government prices was 9.6 per cent, that of government guidance prices 4.4 per cent, and market-regulated prices 86 per cent…." [Note: The year of reference to which these statistics relate was not given in the Working Party Report].

government guidance pricing and government pricing. The services subject to price controls were listed by their respective CPC codes.[15]

Specific Activities Subject to Government Pricing or Government Guidance Pricing

(1) Intermediate Services — "*The Administrative Rules on Intermediate Services*" promulgated in 1999 by six central government agencies led by the State Development and Planning Commission ("SDPC") dealt with government pricing on intermediate services such as inspection authentication, notarization and arbitration and services which were in limited supply due to their special requirements.

(2) For legal services, the *Interim Regulation on Charges and Fees of Legal Services*, jointly promulgated by the SDPC and the Ministry of Justice stipulated that for law firms practising Chinese law, charges and fees for the following activities were subject to the approval of the SDPC: (i) representing a client in a civil case, including an appeal; (ii) representing a client in a case contesting an administrative agency's decision; (iii) providing legal advice to criminal suspects, acting for a client in connection with an appeal or prosecution, applying for bail, representing a defendant or victim in a criminal case; and (iv) representing a client in an arbitration.

(3) For foreign legal service providers engaged in activities such as those listed in China's GATS schedule [see Appendix 3 of this book], the foreign legal service providers *would determine* the appropriate charges and fees which would not be subject to government pricing or guidance pricing.

(4) Regulations also existed for the other services included in Annex 4. Government pricing and guidance pricing covered auditing services.

(5) For architectural services, advisory and pre-design architectural services and contract administration activities were subject to government pricing or government guidance pricing.

(6) For engineering services, advisory and consultative services, engineering design services for the construction of foundations and building structures, design services for mechanical and electrical installations for buildings, construction of civil engineering works, and industrial processes and production were subject to government pricing or government guidance pricing.

(7) Primary, secondary and higher education services were subject to government pricing.

(8) Charges for settlement, clearing and transmission services of banks referred to in Annex 4 related to the charges and fees collected by banks for the services provided to enterprises and individuals when the banks conducted currency payments and transmission and fund settlements by using clearance methods such as bills and notes, collections and acceptances. These mainly included commission charges of bills, cashier's cheques, cheques, remittances, entrusted collections of payment, and collections and acceptances of banks.

China's commitments/confirmations

(1) To Publish List of Goods and Services Subject to State Price

China *would publish* in the official journal the list of goods and services subject to state pricing and changes thereto, together with price-setting mechanisms and policies.

---

[15]Stands for UN Central Product Classification, the provisional version was updated as CPC Version 1.0, Series M, No. 77 (New York) in 1998, and was further updated as Version 1.1 on 21 February 2002.

(2) Monthly Pricing Information and Price Reform

China *confirmed* that the official journal providing price information was the *Pricing Monthly* of the People's Republic of China, published in Beijing. It was a monthly magazine listing all products and services priced by the State. China *would continue* to further its price reform, adjusting the catalogue subject to state pricing and further liberalize its pricing policies.

(3) Price Controls Not for Protection of Domestic Industries and Service Providers

China *confirmed* that price controls *would not be* used for purposes of affording protection to domestic industries or services providers.

(4) Price Controls to be WTO-consistent

As to the concern that China maintained prices below market-based ones to limit imports, China *confirmed* that it *would apply* its current price controls and any other price controls upon accession in a WTO-consistent fashion, and *would take* account of the interests of exporting WTO Members as provided for in Article III:9 of the *GATT 1994*.[16] Also, price controls *would not have* the effect of limiting or otherwise impairing China's market-access commitments on goods and services.

A8. Competition Policy

Work in the WTO on investment and competition policy issues so far has largely taken the form of specific responses to specific trade policy issues, rather than a look at the broad picture. New decisions reached at the 1996 ministerial conference in Singapore change the perspective. The ministers decided to set up two working groups to look more generally at the relationships between trade, on the one hand, and investment and competition policies, on the other.

The Government of China stated that it encouraged fair competition and was against acts of unfair competition of all kinds. *The Law of the People's Republic of China on Combating Unfair Competition*, promulgated on 2 September 1993 and implemented on 1 December 1993, was the basic law to maintain the order of competition in the market. In addition, the *Price Law*,[17] the *Law on Tendering and Bidding*,[18] the *Criminal Law*[19] and other relevant laws also

---

[16]Which says that internal maximum price control measures can have effects prejudicial to interests of contracting parties supplying the imported products. Accordingly, contracting parties applying such measures shall take account of the interests of the exporting member to avoid such prejudicial effects. [*Ed. Note*: the term "contracting parties" instead of "Members" was used in the original text of *GATT 1947* since GATT is an agreement, not an organization. After the establishment of WTO in 1995, by adopting WTO Agreement, contracting parties to GATT became members of WTO].

[17]Issued on 29 December, 1997 by President's decree of PRC (No. 92); adopted at the 29th Meeting of the Standing Committee of the Eighth National People's Congress and effective as of 1 May 1998.

[18]"*The Tendering and Bidding Law of the People's Republic of China*" was enacted and adopted by the Ninth National People's Congress on 1 January 2000.

[19]Adopted by the Second Session of the Fifth National People's Congress on 1 July 1979 and amended by the 5th Session of the Eighth National People's Congress on 14 March 1997, effective as of 1 October 1997.

contained provisions on anti-monopoly and unfair competition. China was *now* formulating the Law on Anti-Monopoly. There was no commitment made under this topic.

A9. Special Trade Arrangements

Protocol Ref: S4

Current situation/concerns raised by other WTO Members	China commitments/confirmations
There were specific concerns that China's special trade arrangements with third countries and separate customs territories were not in conformity with WTO requirements.	China's committed in *the Protocol*[20] that upon accession, China *shall eliminate* or *bring into conformity* with the *WTO Agreement* all special trade arrangements, including barter trade arrangements, with third countries and separate customs territories, which are not in conformity with *WTO Agreement*.

B. FRAMEWORK FOR MAKING AND ENFORCING POLICIES

B1. Structure and Powers of the Government

In accordance with the *Constitution* and the *Law on Legislation of the People's Republic of China*,[21] the National People's Congress was the highest organ of state power. Its permanent body was its Standing Committee. The National People's Congress and its Standing Committee exercised the legislative power of the State. They had the power to formulate the Constitution and laws. The State Council, i.e., the Central People's Government of China, was the executive body of the highest organ of state power. The State Council, in accordance with the Constitution and relevant laws, was entrusted with the power to formulate *administrative regulations*. The ministries, commissions and other competent departments (collectively referred to as "departments") of the State Council could issue *departmental rules* within the jurisdiction of their respective departments and in accordance with the laws and administrative regulations. The provincial people's congresses and their standing committees could adopt *local regulations*. The provincial governments had the power to make *local government rules*. The National People's Congress and its Standing Committee had the power to annul the administrative regulations that contradicted the Constitution and laws as well as the local regulations that contradicted the Constitution, laws and administrative regulations. The State Council had the power to annul departmental rules and local government rules that were inconsistent with the Constitution, laws or administrative regulations. In China's opinion, these features of the Chinese legal system would ensure an effective and uniform implementation of the obligations after China's accession.

---

[20]Section 4 of the *Protocol*.

[21]Adopted by the 3rd Session of the Ninth National People's Congress on 15 March 2000 and became operative on 1 July 2000.

a. Laws and Regulations Pertaining to or Affecting Trade

According to the Constitution and the *Law on the Procedures of Conclusion of Treaties*, the *WTO Agreement* fell within the category of "important international agreements" subject to the ratification by the Standing Committee of the National People's Congress.[22]

China *would ensure* that its laws and regulations pertaining to or affecting trade were in conformity with the *WTO Agreement* and with its commitments so as to fully perform its international obligations. For this purpose, China had commenced a plan to systematically revise its relevant domestic laws and enact new ones fully in compliance with the *WTO Agreement*.

b. Administrative Regulations, Rules and Measures of the Executive Branch

Current situation/concerns raised by other WTO Members	China commitments/confirmations
Administrative regulations, departmental rules and other central government measures.	China *confirmed* that administrative regulations, departmental rules and other central government measures *would be promulgated* in a timely manner so that China's commitments *would be* fully implemented within the relevant time frames. If these were not in place within such timeframes, authorities *would* still honour China's obligations under the *WTO Agreement* and *the Protocol*. The central government *would undertake* in a timely manner to revise or annul administrative regulations or departmental rules if they were inconsistent with China's obligations under the *WTO Agreement* and *the Protocol*.

B2. Authority of Sub-National Governments   Protocol Ref: S2(A)

Current situation/concerns raised by other WTO Members	China commitments/confirmations
The conformity of trade-related measure at sub-national level with WTO obligations	
There were concerns: 1. That multiple trade instruments were used by different levels of government	China *confirmed* that sub-national governments had no autonomous authority over issues of trade policy

---

[22]Article 7, *Law on the Procedures of Conclusion of Treaties*. The Law was adopted on 28 December 1990 at the 17th Session of the Standing Committee of the Seventh National People's Congress.

within China resulted in a lessening of the security and predictability of access to Chinese market; 2. With authority of sub-national governments in fiscal, financial and budgetary activities in respect of subsidies, taxation, trade policies and other issues covered by the *WTO Agreement* and *the Protocol*; 3. Whether the central government could effectively ensure that trade-related measures introduced at sub-national level conform to China's commitments in *WTO Agreement* and *the Protocol*.	to the extent that they were related to the *WTO Agreement* and *the Protocol*. China *would* in a timely manner *annul* local regulations, government rules and other local measures that were inconsistent with China's obligations. The central government *would ensure* that China's laws, regulations and other measures, including those of local governments at the sub-national level *(see* B3 *below)* conformed to China's obligations undertaken in the *WTO Agreement* and *the Protocol*.

B3. Uniform Administration of the Trade Regime   Protocol Re: S2(A)

Current situation/concerns raised by other WTO Members	China commitments/confirmations
The uniform application of WTO's obligations and China's commitment throughout the entire customs territory	
There were concerns: — if China would apply the requirements of the *WTO Agreement* and its other accession commitments throughout China's entire customs territory; — whether China's central government would be sufficiently informed about non-uniform practice and would take necessary enforcement actions. A mechanism should be established by which any concerned person could bring to the attention of the central government cases of non-uniform application of the trade regime and receive prompt and effective action to address such situations.	The provisions of the *WTO Agreement*, including *the Protocol, would be applied* uniformly throughout its customs territory, including in SEZs and other areas where special regimes for tariffs, taxes and regulations were established and at all levels of government. China *confirmed* that **laws, regulations and other measures** included decrees, orders, directives, administrative guidance and provisional and interim measures. **Local regulations, rules and other measures** were issued by local governments[23] at the provincial, city and county levels acting within their respective constitutional powers and functions and applied at their corresponding local level. Townships were only authorized to implement measures. Special economic areas were also

---

[23]In China, local governments included provincial governments, including autonomous regions and municipalities directly under the central government, cities, counties and townships, *see* clause 74 of the Working Party Report.

	authorized to issue and implement local rules and regulations. China *confirmed* that the mechanism established pursuant to Section 2(A) of the Protocol[24] *would be* operative upon accession. All individuals and entities could bring to the attention of central government authorities cases of non-uniform application of China's trade regime, including its commitments under the *WTO Agreement* and *the Protocol*. Such cases would be referred promptly to the responsible government agency, and when non-uniform application was established, the authorities would act promptly to address the situation utilizing the remedies available under China's laws, taking into consideration China's international obligations and the need to provide a meaningful remedy. The individual or entity notifying China's authorities would be informed promptly in writing of any decision and action taken.

B4. Notifications **Protocol Ref: S18.1, Annex 1A**

Current situation/concerns raised by other WTO Members	China commitments/confirmations
China was requested to submit notification required in *the Protocol* and Working Party Report to the WTO body with a mandate covering the subject of the notification.	China *would submit* its notifications required in *the Protocol* and the Working Party Report to the WTO body, consistent with Section 18.1 and Annex 1A of *the Protocol*.[25]

---

[24]Concerning the uniform administration of the trade regime.

[25]Section 18.1 of the *Protocol* stipulates that those subordinate bodies of WTO which have a mandate covering China's commitments under the WTO Agreement or *the Protocol* shall, within one year after China's accession, review the implementation by China of *the WTO Agreement* and of the related provisions of *the Protocol*. Annex 1A to the *Protocol* is titled "Information to be provided by China in the context of the Transitional Review Mechanism".

B5. Transparency

Concerns raised by other WTO Members
There were concerns about the lack of transparency regarding the laws, regulations and other measures that applied to matters covered in the *WTO Agreement* and *the Protocol*, in particular, the difficulty in finding and obtaining copies of regulations and other measures undertaken by various ministries as well as those taken by provincial and other local authorities.   There was the need to receive such information in a timely fashion so that governments and traders could be prepared to comply with such provisions and could exercise their rights in respect of implementation and enforcement of such measures. Emphasis was stressed on the importance of such pre-publication to enhancing secure, predictable trading relations. It was also noted that the development of the Internet and other means was able to ensure that information from all government bodies at all levels could be assembled in one place and made readily available.   The creation and maintenance of a single, authoritative journal and enquiry point would greatly facilitate dissemination of information and help promote compliance.

Current situation
China noted that: 1. The Government of China regularly issued publications providing information on China's foreign trade system, such as: — the "Almanac of Foreign Economic Relations and Trade" and "The Bulletin of MOFTEC" published by MOFTEC;   — "Statistical Yearbook of China", published by the State Statistical Bureau;   — "China's Customs Statistics (Quarterly)", edited and published by the Customs.   2. China's laws and regulations of the State Council relating to foreign trade were all published, as were rules issued by departments. Such laws, regulations and rules were available in: — the "Gazette of the State Council",   — the "Collection of the Laws and Regulations of the People's Republic of China" and   — the "MOFTEC Gazette".   3. The administrative regulations and directives relating to foreign trade were also published on MOFTEC's official website (http://www.moftec.gov.cn) and in periodicals.   4. There were no forex restrictions affecting import or export. Information on forex measures was published by the SAFE ("State Administration of Foreign Exchange) and was available on SAFE's website (http://www.safe.gov.cn) and via the news media.   5. Information concerning the administration of imports and exports would be published in the "International Business" newspaper and the "MOFTEC Gazette".   6. Information on China's customs laws and regulations, import and export duty rates, and customs procedures was published in the "Gazette of the State Council" and in the press media, and was available upon request. The procedures concerning application of duty rates, customs value and duty determination, drawback and duty recovery, as well as the

procedures concerning duty exemptions and reduction, were also published. Customs also published monthly customs statistics, calculated according to country of origin and final destination, on the basis of eight-digit HS levels.

7. Concerning foreign trade
   — any bilateral trade agreements concluded between China and its trading partners, and protocols on the exchange of goods negotiated under them were published in "The Treaty Series of the PRC".
   — the "Directory of China's Foreign Economic Relations and Trade Enterprises" and "China's Foreign Trade Corporations and Organizations" were two publications which identified foreign trade corporations and other enterprises in China engaged in foreign trade.

The full listing of official journals was as follows

— Gazette of the Standing Committee of the National People's Congress of the People's Republic of China;
— Gazette of the State Council of the People's Republic of China;
— Collection of the Laws of the People's Republic of China;
— Collection of the Laws and Regulations of the People's Republic of China;
— Gazette of MOFTEC of the People's Republic of China;
— Proclamation of the People's Bank of the People's Republic of China; and
— Proclamation of the Ministry of Finance of the People's Republic of China.

China commitments/confirmations

China *confirmed*:

A. That publication of all laws, regulations and other measures pertaining to or affecting trade in goods, services, *TRIPS* or the control of forex *would include* the effective date of these measures. It *would also include* the products and services affected by a particular measure, identified by appropriate tariff line and CPC classification.[26]
B. That China *would publish* in the official journal, by appropriate classification and by service where relevant, a list of all organizations, including those organizations delegated such authority from the national authorities, that were responsible for authorizing, approving or regulating services activities whether through grant of licence or other approval. Procedures and the conditions for obtaining such licences or approval *would also be published*.
C. That *none* of the information required by the *WTO Agreement* or *the Protocol* to be disclosed *would be withheld* as confidential information except for those reasons identified in Section 2(C) of *the Protocol*[27] or unless it would demonstrably prejudice the legitimate commercial interests of particular enterprises, public or private.

---

[26]*supra* note 15.

[27]Confidential information can be withheld by China in circumstances described under S2(C) (2) as "….for those laws, regulations and other measures involving national security, specific measures setting foreign exchange rates or monetary policy and other measures the publication of which would impede law enforcement." *See* also provision under Art X.1 of *GATT 1994*.

D. That China *would make available* to WTO Members translations into one or more of the official languages of the WTO all laws, regulations and other measures pertaining to or affecting trade in goods, services, *TRIPS* or the control of forex, and to the maximum extent possible *would make* these laws, regulations and other measures available before they were implemented or enforced, but in no case later than 90 days after they were implemented or enforced.

B6. Judicial Review

Protocol Ref: S2(D)

Current situation/concerns raised by other WTO Members	China commitments/confirmations
Independent tribunals and enquiry point	
There were concerns from some WTO Members that China should designate independent tribunals, contact points, and procedures for the prompt review of all administrative actions. And that such review procedures should include the opportunity for appeal, without penalty, by individuals or enterprises affected by any administrative action subject to review.	China *would revise* its relevant laws and regulations so that its relevant domestic laws and regulations would be consistent with the requirements of *the WTO Agreement* and *the Protocol* on procedures for judicial review of administrative actions.
	The tribunals responsible for such reviews *would be* impartial and independent of the agency entrusted with administrative enforcement, and *would not have* any substantial interest in the outcome of the matter.
Administrative actions that should be subject to review include those relating to the implementation of laws, regulations, judicial decisions, import or export licences, non-tariff measures and tariff-rate quota administration, conformity assessment procedures and other measures, and also any actions required to be reviewed under the relevant provisions of the *TRIPS Agreement* and the *GATS*. Certain types of measures, such as decisions relating to standards and chemical registration, would be subject to judicial review.	Administrative actions related to the implementation of laws, regulations, judicial decisions and administrative rulings of general application (including those relating to the implementation of national treatment, conformity assessment, the regulation, control, supply or promotion of a service, including the grant or denial of a licence to provide a service and other matters.)[28]
	Such administrative actions *would be subject to* the procedures for prompt review under Section 2(D)(2) of *the Protocol* [an opportunity for appeal to a

[28]Those laws, regulations, judicial decisions and administrative rulings of general application referred to in Article X:1 of *GATT 1994,* Article VI of the *GATS* and relevant provisions of *TRIPS*, according to clause 79 of the Working Party Report.

The tribunals should be independent of the agencies entrusted with administrative enforcement of the matter and should not have any substantial interest in the outcome of the matter.	judicial body].[29] Information on such procedures would be available through the enquiry point that China *would establish* upon accession (*see below*).

B7. Enquiry Point   Protocol Ref: S2(C)(3)

Current situation/concerns raised by other WTO Members	China commitments/confirmations
China was requested to set up an enquiry point where information relating to all laws, regulations and other measures, judicial decisions and administrative rulings of general application and other measures pertaining to or affecting trade in goods, services, *TRIPS* or the control of forex could be obtained.	China *would establish* or designate one or more enquiry points where all information relating to the laws, regulations and other measures pertaining to or affecting trade in goods, services, TRIPS or the control of forex, as well as the published texts, could be obtained and *would notify* the WTO of any enquiry point and its responsibility. The information *would include* the names of national or sub-national authorities (including contact points) responsible for implementing a particular measure.

---

[29]Section 2(D)(2) of *the Protocol*: "Review procedures shall include the opportunity for appeal, without penalty, by individuals or enterprises affected by an administrative action subject to review. If the initial right of appeal is to an administrative body, there shall in all cases be the opportunity to choose to appeal the decision to a judicial body. Notice of the decision on appeal shall be given to the appellant and the reasons for such decision shall be provided in writing. The appellant shall also be informed of any right to further appeal."

chapter 2

Commitments Made by China on Trade in Goods

For every Member of the WTO there is a Schedule of Concessions on Goods which forms an integral part of *GATT 1994*. Each schedule incorporates all the concessions made by the Member concerned in the Uruguay Round or in earlier negotiations. In the case of China, the results of its negotiations with WTO Members on customs tariff and other trade barriers are included in its Schedule of Concessions and Commitments on Goods which is attached as Annex 8 to the *Protocol*. This Schedule is also attached to *GATT 1994* (WTO document no. WT/ACC/CHN/49/Add. 1) and became effective on the day on which the *WTO Agreement* came into force for China, i.e. 11 December 2001.

PRINCIPLES OF WTO'S TRADING SYSTEM

The WTO agreements cover goods, services and intellectual property. They spell out the principles of liberalization, and the permitted exceptions. They included individual countries' commitments to lower customs tariffs and other trade barriers for trade in goods, which is the focus of this chapter that is relative to China. The agreements also include the individual countries' commitments to open and keep open services markets, Chapter 3 deals with this topic that is relative to China.

A number of simple, fundamental principles run throughout all of WTO agreements that deal with a wide range of trade activities in goods. These principles also apply to services and intellectual property. They include:

1. The trading system should be *without discrimination*. A country should not discriminate between its trading partners, who are all, equally, granted the "most-favoured-nation" or MFN status; and it should not discriminate between its own and foreign products, services or nationals (they are given "national treatment").
2. *Freer trade* is encouraged, with barriers gradually coming down through negotiations. Lowering trade barriers is one of the most obvious means of encouraging trade. The barriers concerned include customs duties (or tariffs) and non-tariff measures such as import quotas that restrict quantities selectively. Since 1947, negotiations focused on lowering tariffs on imported goods.

Negotiations had also expanded by the 1980s to cover non-tariff barriers on goods and to the new areas such as services and intellectual property.

3. *Predictability* and *stability* of the multilateral trade system encouraged trade and investment since foreign companies, investors and governments should be confident that trade barriers (including tariffs, non-tariff barriers and other measures) should not be raised arbitrarily. More and more tariff rates and market-opening commitments are "bound" in the WTO. In WTO, when countries agree to open their markets for goods (or services), they "bind" their commitments. For goods, these bindings amount to ceiling on customs tariff rates. The use of quotas and other measures to set limits on quantities of imports are discouraged. Another way to increase predictability is to make countries' trade rules as clear and public ("transparent") as possible. Many WTO agreements require governments to disclose their policies and practices by notifying the WTO.

4. By discouraging "unfair practices" such as export subsidies and dumping products at below cost to gain market share, trade is made *more competitive.*

5. The multilateral system is *more beneficial for less developed countries* by giving them more time to adjust, greater flexibility, and special privileges.

The General Agreement on Tariffs and Trade (GATT) always dealt with trade in goods, though its key principles such as "non-discrimination", "transparency" and "predictability" have been adopted by the agreements on services and intellectual property. The old GATT 1947 has been amended and incorporated into the new WTO agreements. The updated version is "GATT 1994". It deals with specific sectors or issues on trade in goods such as: agriculture, health regulations for farm products (SPS), textiles and clothing, product standards, investment measures, antidumping and countervailing measures, customs valuation methods, preshipment inspection, rules of origin, import licensing, subsidies and safeguards, state trading enterprises, information technology agreements.

A general interpretative note to Annex 1A to the *WTO Agreement*, which includes all the multilateral agreements related to trade in goods, provides that, in the event of conflict between a provision of *GATT 1994* and a provision of another agreement in Annex 1A, the provision of the other agreement shall prevail to the extent of the conflict.

A. TRADING RIGHTS

A1. General   Protocol Ref: S5, Annex 2(A)

Current Situation/Concerns Raised by Other WTO Members	China Commitments/Confirmations
Liberalization of Trading Rights	
Situation prior to accession: The right to import and export goods from China was only available to some Chinese enterprises.	**China *confirmed* that during the three years of transition after accession, China would progressively liberalize the scope and availability of trading rights.**

Foreign-invested enterprises had the right to trade, but were restricted to the importation for production purposes and exportation, according to the enterprises' scope of business.

Hence the linkage between an enterprise's scope of business or business licence and the right to trade effectively constitute a restriction on the right to import and export.

These restrictions contravene WTO requirements including Articles XI and III of *GATT 1994*.[1]

1. Upon accession, China *would eliminate* for both Chinese and foreign-invested enterprises any export performance, trade balancing, foreign exchange balancing and prior experience requirements, such as in importing and exporting, as criteria for obtaining or maintaining the right to import and export;

2. Wholly Chinese-invested enterprises are now required to apply for trading rights based on their approved scope of business, as with their foreign counterparts which had been subject to this requirement. The minimum registered capital requirement to obtain trading right for wholly Chinese-investment enterprises would be reduced from RMB Five Million in year one to RMB 1 million in year three. The examination and approval system would be eliminated at the end of the phase in periods for trading rights.

3. During the phase-in period, FIE ("Foreign Invested Enterprises") *would be granted* new or additional trading rights:

i) beginning one year after accession, joint venture enterprises with minority share foreign-investment would be granted full rights to trade; ii) beginning two years after accession, majority share foreign-invested joint ventures would be granted full rights to trade.

Within 3 years after accession, *all* enterprises in China *would be granted* the right to trade. Foreign-invested enterprises would not be required to establish in a particular form or as a separate entity to engage in importing and exporting nor would new business licence encompassing distribution be required to engage in importing and exporting.

[1]Article III of *GATT 1994* concerns "National Treatment of Internal Taxation and Regulation"; Articles XI concerns "General Elimination of Quantitative Restrictions".

Elimination of Examination and Approval system	
	China *would eliminate* its system of examination and approval of trading rights within three years after accession.
	At that time, China *would permit* all enterprises in China and foreign enterprises and individuals, including sole proprietorships of other WTO Members, to export and import all goods throughout the customs territory of China.
	Exception: the share of products listed in *Annex 2A to the Protocol*[2] reserved for importation and exportation by state trading enterprises.
	Such trading right, however did not permit importers to distribute goods within China. The provision of distribution services would be done in accordance with China's Schedule of Specific Commitments under the *General Agreement of Trade in Services ("GATS")*[3]. (*See* Chapter 3)
	Trading rights *would be* granted to foreign enterprises and individuals, including sole proprietorships of other WTO Members in a non-discriminatory and non-discretionary way. Any requirements for obtaining trading rights would be for customs and fiscal purposes only and *would not* constitute a barrier to trade.
	China emphasized that foreign enterprises and individuals with trading rights had to comply with all WTO-consistent requirements related to importing and exporting, such as those concerning import licensing, technical barriers to trade and sanitary and phytosanitary measures, [*see* sections B9, D3 and D4 below respectively] but *confirmed* that requirement relating to minimum capital and prior experience *would not apply*.

---

[2]*Annex 2A to the Protocol* refers to importation and exportation of products subject to state trading.
[3]*Annex 9 to the Protocol*; see Chapter 3.

A2. Designated Trading   Protocol Ref: S5, Annex 2(B)

Designated trading is a practice that provides the right to import certain products to certain entities designated by the government. Many of such rights are geographically restricted trading rights.

Current Situation/Concerns Raised by Other WTO Members	China Commitments/Confirmations
Currently, there are criteria for enterprises permitted to trade under the designated trading regime. Criteria included registered capital, import and export volume and the import volume of products subject to designated trading in the previous year, bank credit rating and profits and losses.	**To Expand List of Enterprises** China *would adjust and expand* its list of enterprises under its designated trading regime annually during the transition period, leading up to full implementation of the commitment contained in Annex 2B of *the Protocol*.[4]
Examples of products subject to designated trading are: natural rubber, plywood, timber, wool, acrylic, steel.	**To phase out limitation on Grant of Trading Rights** China *would phase out* the limitation on the grant of trading rights for goods specified in Annex 2B of the *Protocol* within 3 years after accession. China *would progressively liberalize the right to trade* in such goods by increasing the number of designated entities permitted to import goods in each of the 3 years of transition period specified in Annex 2B. [Such additional enterprises would *not* be disadvantaged in the allocation of Tariff Rate Quotas ("TRQs") (see B7 below on allocation of TRQ)]
	Measures by China to remove restrictions in **designated goods** 1. China *would eliminate* import and export volume as a criterion for obtaining the right to trade these designated products; 2. Reduce minimum capitalization requirements; and 3. Extend the right to register as designated importing and exporting enterprises to — enterprises that used such goods in the production of finished goods; — enterprises that distributed such goods in China.

---

[4]*Annex 2B to the Protocol* concerns products subject to designated trading.

| | At the end of 3 years, *all* enterprises in China and all foreign enterprises and individuals *would be permitted* to import and export such goods throughout the customs territory of China. |
| | During the transition period, *none* of the criteria applicable under the designated trading regime would constitute a quantitative restriction on imports or exports. |

B. Import Regulations

(Protocol Ref: S2(C), S7(1)(2)(4), S8, S11(1),(2)(4), Annex 2, Annex 3, Annex 8)

B1. Ordinary Customs Duties

The applicable WTO provision is ***Article XXVIII bis of GATT 1994 on Tariff Negotiations***. Contracting parties [became 'Members' upon the establishment of WTO—*see* note 16 of Chapter 1, same below] recognize that customs duties often constitute obstacles to trade. Negotiations that are directed to the substantial reduction of the general level of tariffs and other charges on imports and exports and in particular, to the reduction of high tariffs are of great importance to the expansion of international trade. Members may therefore sponsor such negotiations from time to time on a reciprocal and mutually advantageous basis and may conduct such negotiations with due regard to the objectives of *GATT* and the varying needs of individual Members.

China undertook bilateral market access negotiations on goods with Members of the Working Party.[5] The results of those negotiations were contained in the Schedule of Concessions and Commitments on Goods and formed *Annex 8 to the Protocol*.[6] ("Schedule on goods").

China decided to *bind* tariffs for *all* products in its schedule on market access for goods.

---

[5]The Working Party on the Accession of China to WTO was established in a Council's meeting on 4 March 1987 to examine the request of the Government of the People's Republic of China ("China") (L/6017, submitted on 10 July 1986) for resumption of its status as a GATT contracting party, and to submit to the Council recommendations which may include a draft Protocol on the Status of China. In a communication dated 7 December 1995, the Government of China applied for accession to the *Marrakesh Agreement Establishing the World Trade Organization* ("WTO Agreement") pursuant to Article XII of the *WTO Agreement*. Following China's application and pursuant to the decision of the General Council on 31 January 1995, the existing Working Party on China's Status as a GATT 1947 Contracting Party was transformed into a WTO Accession Working Party, effective from 7 December 1995. The terms of reference and the membership of the Working Party are reproduced in document WT/ACC/CHN/2/Rev.11 and Corr.1. *See* Introduction to Working Party Report.

[6]*China's Schedule of Concessions and Commitments on Goods, Annex 8 to the Protocol* (WTO document no. WT/ACC/CHN/49/Add.1). This Schedule is also attached to *GATT 1994*. *See* note 2, Preface of Part 1 of this book.

Current Situation/Concerns Raised by Other WTO Members	China Commitments/Confirmations
Situation prior to accession	Uniform Rate for wood and paper products
In recent years, China had effected substantial unilateral tariff reductions in many sectors.	The *same rates* of duty, including the rates applied under a preference programme, customs union or free-trade area, *would be applied* to all imports of wood and paper products.
China's tariff policy was to promote economic reform and opening of the economy. The basic principles for establishing duty rates were:	Elimination of tariff, duty charges of Information
	Technology Products
1. Duty-free or low duty rates were applied to imported goods which were needed for the national economy and the people's livelihood but which were not produced sufficiently domestically.	Upon accession, China *would participate* in the *Information Technology Agreement* ("ITA") and would eliminate tariffs on all information technology products as set out in its Schedule on goods.[8] Furthermore, upon accession, China *would eliminate* all other duties and charges for ITA products.
2. Import duty rates on raw materials were generally lower than those on semi-manufactured or manufactured products.	Tariff treatment in the auto sector for kits for
	motor vehicles
3. For parts or components of machinery, equipment and instruments which were not produced domestically, or at a sufficiently high standard, the import duty was lower than the duty on finished products.	China *confirmed* that China had no tariff lines for completely knocked-down [CKDs] kits for motor vehicles or semi-knocked down [SKDs] kits for motor vehicles. If China created such tariff lines, the tariff rates *would be* no more than 10 per cent.
4. Higher duty rates were applied to products which were produced domestically or which were considered non-essential for the national economy and the people's livelihood.	Tariff Liberalization Proposal
	China *committed* to support the tariff liberalization proposal outlined in WT/GC/W/138/Add.1 (22 April, 1999) and would participate fully in any tariff liberalization initiative based on this proposal that WTO Members might accept for implementation.
5. A higher duty was applied to imported products, the equivalent of which were produced domestically and the local manufacturer of which needed protection.	
China had adopted the Harmonized Commodity Description and Coding System ("HS") as from 1 January 1992.[7]	

---

[7]China also joined the *International Convention on the Harmonized Commodity Description and Coding System* in the same year. There were 21 sections, 97 Chapters and 7062 eight-digit tariff headings based on the six-digit HS'96 version in the Customs Tariff for the year 2000, according to clause 89 of the Working Party Report.

[8]*See* Attachment B, Annex 8 to *the Protocol* for list of information technology products.

Tariff rates were fixed by the State Council. The simple average of China's import duties in 2000 was 16.4 per cent. Currently there were two columns of import duty rates: the *preferential rates* applied to imports originating in countries and regions with which China had concluded reciprocal tariff agreements, whereas the *general rates* applied to imports from other sources.	

B2. Other Duties and Charges   Protocol Ref: S11(1)

The relevant WTO provisions include *Article II:1(b) of GATT 1994 on Schedules of Concessions* and *Understanding on the Interpretation of Article II:1(b) of GATT 1994 ("on other duties and charges")*. Article II:1(b) stipulates that imported foreign goods are not merely exempted from ordinary customs duties in excess of those set forth in the importing Member's Schedule of concessions[9], but are also exempted from all other duties and charges.[10]

Current Situation/Concern Raised by Other WTO Members	China Commitments/Confirmations
	China *had agreed to bind at zero* other duties and charges in its Schedule on goods[11] pursuant to *GATT* requirement.

B3. Rules of Origin

The relative WTO agreement is *Agreement on Rules of Origin* ("*the Agreement*"). Rules of origin are the criteria used to define where a product was made. They are an essential part of trade rules because a number of policies discriminate between exporting countries: quotas, preferential tariffs, anti-dumping actions, countervailing duty (charged to counter export subsidies), and more. *The Agreement* is the first-ever agreement on the subject requiring WTO Members to ensure that their rules of origin are transparent; that they do not have restricting, distorting, or disruptive effects on international trade; that they are administered in a consistent, uniform, impartial and reasonable

---

[9]Schedules of Concessions of Members are attached to *GATT 1994*.

[10]Article II:1(b) of the *GATT 1994* states that "The products....which are the products of territories of other Members....shall also be exempt from all other duties and charges of any kind imposed on or in connection with importation in excess of those imposed on the date of this Agreement or those directly and mandatorily required to be imposed thereafter by legislation in force in the importing territory on that date."

[11]*Supra* note 6.

manner; and that they are based on a positive standard (in other words, they should state what does confer origin rather than what does not).

For the longer term, *the Agreement* aims for common ("harmonized") rules of origin among all WTO Members, except in some kinds of preferential trade.[12] The agreement establishes a harmonization work programme to be completed by July 1998 but is still underway. The outcome will be a single set of rules of origin to be applied under non-preferential trading conditions by all WTO Members in all circumstances.

Current Situation/Concerns Raised by Other WTO Members	China Commitments/Confirmations
There were questions on how the rules of origin in China were adopted and applied: whether it was applied in the context of free trade agreements or otherwise; whether the rules of origin of China for both preferential and non-preferential trade complied fully with WTO's *Agreements on Rules of Origin*.	**Non-Preferential rules of origin** China *confirmed* that the rules of origin for import and export were *non-preferential* rules of origin. Once the international harmonization of non-preferential rules of origin was concluded, China *would fully adopt and apply* the internationally harmonized non-preferential rules of origin. By the date of accesssion, China *would,* in its legal framework, *establish* a mechanism providing an assessment of the origin of an import or an export and outlining the terms under which it would be provided. **Application of Rules of Origin** China *would not use* the rules of origin as an instrument to pursue trade objectives directly or indirectly. China *would apply* rules of origin equally for all purposes. **Conformity with WTO obligations** From the date of accession, China *would ensure* that: — its laws, regulations and other measures relating to rules of origin would be in full conformity with *WTO Agreement on Rules of Origin*; — it *would implement* such laws, regulations and other measures in full conformity with that Agreement.

---

[12]For example, countries setting up a free trade area are allowed to use different rules of origin for products traded under their free trade agreement.

B4. Fees and Charges for Services Rendered   Protocol Ref: S11(1)

The relevant WTO provision is **Article VIII of *GATT 1994 on Fees and Formalities connected with Importation and Exportation.*** Article VIII:1 stipulates that Members shall limit all fees and charges (other than import and export duties, and other taxes within the purview of Art III-National Treatment on Internal Taxation and Regulation) imposed on or in connection with importation (or exportation) to the approximate cost of services rendered. Members also recognize the need to reduce the diversity of such fees and charges, to minimize the incidence and the complexity of import and export formalities and to simplify import and export formalities. Article VIII:4 stipulates that the fees, charges, formalities and requirements imposed by governmental authorities in connection with importation and exportation shall include those relating to consular transactions, quantitative restrictions, licensing, exchange control, documents and certification, analysis and inspection, quarantine, sanitation and fumigation.

Current Situation/Concerns Raised by Other WTO Members	China Commitments/Confirmations
There was concern that as a condition of accession, China should undertake a commitment to ensure conformity of customs fees and charges with Article VIII of the *GATT 1994*.	Conformity with WTO obligations China *undertook* that China *would comply* with Article VIII of *GATT 1994* to ensure conformity of customs fees and charges.

B5. Application of Internal Taxes to Imports   Protocol Ref: S11(2)

The relevant WTO provision is ***Article III of GATT 1994 on National Treatment on Internal Taxation and Regulation***.

Current Situation/Concerns Raised by Other WTO Members	China Commitments/Confirmations
There was concern that some internal taxes applied to imports, including a value-added tax ("VAT"), were not administered in conformity with the requirements of the *GATT 1994*, particularly with the principle of national treatment on internal taxation and	Conformity with WTO obligations China *confirmed* that from the date of accession, China *would ensure* that its laws, regulations and other measures relating to internal taxes and charges levied on imports would be in full conformity with its WTO obligations.

regulation[13]; and that China appeared to permit the application of discriminatory internal taxes and charges to imported goods and services, including taxes and charges applied by sub-national authorities.

There were three major types of taxes levied on products and services:

(a) VAT levied on goods and services for processing, maintenance and assembling;

(b) the Consumption Tax on some selected consumer products; and

(c) the Business Tax on providing services, transferring intangible assets and selling real estate.

Both the VAT and the Consumption Tax were applicable to entities importing goods, and were collected by General Customs Administration ("Customs") at the point of entry. VAT was reimbursed once goods were exported. Exported goods were exempted from the Consumption Tax.

China *would implement* such laws, regulations and other measures in full conformity with those obligations.

B6. Tariff Exemptions and Reductions

The relative WTO provisions include *Article I (General Most-Favoured Nation Treatment), Article II (Schedules of Concessions) of GATT 1994*.

Under Article II of *GATT 1994* Members are obliged to accord to the trade of other Members treatment "no less favourable than that provided for in the appropriate Part of the appropriate Schedule" annexed to *GATT*.

Article II:1(b) of the *GATT 1994* states that "The products …. which are the products of territories of other Members, shall, on their importation into the territories to which the schedule relates, and subject to the terms, conditions or qualifications set forth in that schedule, be exempt from ordinary customs duties in excess of those set forth and provided therein….."

---

[13]Article III of *GATT*.

Current Situation/Concern Raised by Other WTO Members	China Commitments/Confirmations
Principle of MFN Treatment	
Currently, in accordance with international practices and provisions of China's *Customs Law,*[14] import duty reductions or exemptions were available for twelve types of goods.[15] Goods so imported were required to be put under Customs supervision and control. The customs duty was required to be recovered if such goods were sold, transferred or used for other purposes during the time period for supervision and control. There were concerns over: i) the availability and application of reductions and exemptions of tariff, other duties, taxes and charges, for a variety of enterprises and other entities, including state trading enterprises, state-owned enterprises, foreign-invested enterprises and not-for-profit entities; ii) the negative effect that such reductions or exemptions could have	China stated that the tariff exemption policy of China was developed and implemented in accordance with the *Customs Law* and the *Regulations of the PRC on Import and Export Duties.*[16] The State Council provided for the coverage of specific tariff reduction and exemption. China is of the opinion that all tariff reductions and exemptions were applied on a most-favoured-nation basis. Upon accession, China *would adopt and apply* tariff reductions and exemptions so as to ensure MFN treatment for imported goods.

[14]Adopted at the 19th Meeting of the Standing Committee of the Sixth National People's Congress on 22 January 1987, promulgated by Order No. 51 of the President of the People's Republic of China on 22 January 1987 and effective as of 1 July 1987, amended on 8 July 2000.

[15]According to clause 109 of the Working Party Report, these are:

(a) A consignment of goods, on which customs duties were estimated below RMB 10 yuan;

(b) advertising articles and samples, which were of no commercial value;

(c) goods and materials, which were rendered gratis by international organizations or foreign governments;

(d) fuels, stores, beverages and provisions for use en route loaded by any means of transport, which were in transit across the border;

(e) exported goods being replaced;

(f) goods damaged prior to Customs release;

(g) goods covered by international treaties providing for tariff reductions and exemptions which China had entered into or acceded to;

(h) goods temporarily imported;

(i) goods imported under inward processing programmes;

(j) goods imported at zero cost for replacement purposes;

(k) domestic- or foreign-funded projects encouraged by the government;

(l) articles for scientific research, education and the disabled.

[16]Promulgated by the State Council of the People's Republic of China on 7 March 1985, amended and promulgated by the State Council on 12 September 1987.

on revenues and predictability and certainty in application of tariff and other trade measures.	

B7. Tariff Rate Quotas ("TRQ") Protocol Ref: S2(C), S5, S7(3), S8, Annex 2
[See also chapter 8] Annex 8, Part 1, Section 1-B, Part III, Section A

The relevant WTO provisions include *Article XI (General Elimination of Quantitative Restrictions) and Article XIII (Non-discriminatory Administration of Quantitative Restrictions) of GATT 1994.*

China uses a tariff-rate quota system to control market access of some products such as wheat, corn, rice, soybean oil, palm oil, rapeseed oil, sugar, wool and cotton. Such system, also employed by other WTO Members for sensitive products, is a trade barrier whereby a specified quantity or quota of certain products are allowed to be imported at a lower tariff rate (in-quota rate), imports above that quota amount will be subject to higher tariffs (out-of-quota rate). China is prepared to increase tariff-rate quota amount and at the same time reduce the share of imports by state-trading enterprises of certain products over an implementation period of up to 2005. Such TRQ concessions and the TRQ system are described in Section 1-B, Part 1 and Section A, Part III of Annex 8 to *the Protocol.*

Current Situation/Concerns Raised by Other WTO Members	China Commitments/Confirmations
Administration of China's Tariff Rate Quota Regime and the practice of state enterprises in relation to importing such products	
There were general concerns that currently the operation of TRQ regime lacked the transparency, uniformity and predictability of the administration of its tariff quota regime. These concerns included: — the current lack of transparent regulations for administrating TRQs; — failure to establish and publish annual TRQ quantities; — use of administrative guidance; — distortions introduced into the market due to allocations based on determinations of governments at sub-national or provincial level of supply and utilization rather than commercial market criteria such as consumer preferences and end-user demand;	(1) Upon accession, China *would ensure* that TRQs were adminstrated on a transparent, predictable, uniform, fair and non-discriminatory basis using clearly specified timeframes, administrative procedures and requirements that *would* — *provide effective* import opportunities; — *reflect* consumer preferences and end-user demand; — *not inhibit* the filling of each TRQ. (2) Conformity with WTO. China *would apply* TRQs fully in accordance with WTO rules and principles and with the provisions set out in its Schedule of Concessions and Commitments on goods. (3) Import of goods subject to TRQ i) For the goods listed in *Annex 2 to the Protocol*[17] (under state trading or designated

---

[17]Those goods which importation and exportation were subject to state trading (Annex 2A) or designated trading (Annex 2B); *see* A2 under Section *"Trading Rights"*.

— general uncertainty, inconsistency and discrimination in trade of bulk commodities;
— trade-restrictive and non-competitive practices of state trading enterprises;
— similar concern existed in regards of the operation of China's TRQ system for products subject to "designated trading".

Concerned WTO Members requested China to:

— reduce tariffs for commodities subject to TRQs;
— enter into access commitments for these commodities;
— improve the administration of the TRQ Regime;
— ensure that trade would not be distorted by unjustified government regulation;
— to remove a number of specified products from China's TRQ system and that upon import, these products be subject only to tariff.

China was requested to commit itself to administer TRQs in a simple, transparent, timely, predictable, uniform, non-discriminatory, and non-trade restrictive manner, and in a way that would not cause trade distortions. Concerned WTO Members also requested China to ensure that its TRQ arrangements be no more administratively burdensome than absolutely necessary, and it was hoped that China would move as quickly as possible to a market-based TRQ allocation process.

trading) that were subject to a TRQ, China *would also apply:*

— the provisions of its Schedule relating to TRQ administration; and
— related commitments in the *Protocol*, including the grant of trading rights to non-state trading entities to import the TRQ allocations set aside for importation by such entities.

ii) For products in *Annex 2 to the Protocol* that were subject to designated trading, China *would ensure* that additional enterprises granted trading rights[18] would not be disadvantaged in the allocation of TRQ

(4)   Right to Import Goods subject to TRQ Granted to Non-Trade Enterprises

China confirmed that it would grant to any enterprise possessing the right to trade any product (pursuant to Section 5 of *the Protocol*[19]), the right to import:

i) goods subject to "state trading" and "designated trading"[20] that were also subject to a TRQ or to an agreed volume of imports by non-state trading enterprises. Such goods would be permitted to be imported at the out-of-quota rate.

Such right to import would not extend to the quantity of goods specifically reserved for importation by state trading enterprises.

ii) that portion of a TRQ reallocated to non-state trading enterprises pursuant to the agreed rules on TRQ administration.

---

[18]In accordance with China's commitments to phase out designated trading.

[19]Section 5 of the *Protocol* stipulates the "right to trade". As China progressively liberalize the availability and scope of the right to trade, so that, within 3 years after accession to WTO, all enterprises in China shall have the right to trade all goods throughout the customs territory of China, except for those goods which continue to be subject to state trading in accordance with the *Protocol; also see* the first section of this Chapter of "Trading Rights".

[20]As listed in Annex 2A to *the Protocol*.

Current imports subject to TRQ and Agricultural Products

Current/situation prior to accession

China explained that in 1996, for the first time, China published a list of import products subject to TRQs, together with the tariff rates applicable to imports both in and out of quota. Allocation of TRQ was based on historical performance and administration of the state trading regime, China was trying to simplify the TRQ administration regime and procedures in a bid to facilitate use, enhance efficiency and implement further reform.

The agricultural sector as an example of reform

In undertaking market-oriented reform in the agricultural sector, China had made progress in freeing agricultural products from state pricing and in guiding farmers to adjust the structure of agricultural production based on the demands of the market.

(1) Elimination of TRQ on certain products

In connection with the market-oriented reform process, China *committed* to Members of WTO in the bilateral negotiations with Members that, upon accession, it *would eliminate* TRQs on a number of products and subject these *only* to tariffs.

The products concerned *were barely, soybeans, rapeseed, peanut oil, sunflower seed oil, corn oil, and cottonseed oil.*

(2) TRQs were to replace quantitative import restrictions *on sugar, cotton and three types of fertilizers (DAP, NPK and urea).*

Allocation of TRQ via sub-national authorities

There was concern that to allocate TRQ to end-users via sub-national authorities would make it burdensome, creating an unnecessary separate process and reduce the likelihood that quotas would be filled. These TRQ procedures would not be consistent with China's commitment to uniform administration of its trade regime.

Concerned WTO Members sought confirmation from China that it would not establish a separate process of allocation to sub-national authorities, as well as confirmation that all allocation and reallocation decisions would be made by a single, central authority in China.

(1) Role of Sub-national bodies

China *confirmed* that the role of sub-national bodies *would be* limited to purely administrative operations. These bodies act as intermediaries between end-users and central authority with regard to TRQ applications and queries. They reported on allocation and reallocation decisions made by the central authority and provided information regarding such allocations and reallocations upon request. After the central authority decided on allocations of quota to end-users, the sub-national bodies would issue TRQ certificates accordingly.

(2) Consistent national allocation policy

China *would administer* a consistent national allocation (and reallocation) policy for TRQs, that it *would not establish* a separate process of allocation to sub-national authorities and that decisions regarding all allocations and reallocations to end-users *would be made* by a single, central authority.

B8. Quantitative Import Restrictions, Including
Prohibitions And Quotas   Protocol Ref: S7(1)(2)(3)(4), S8, Annex 3

The relevant WTO provisions are *Article XI (General Elimination of Quantitative Restrictions) and Article XIII (Non-discriminatory Administration of Quantitative Restrictions) of GATT 1994.*

Article XI of *GATT* generally provides that: no prohibitions or restrictions other than duties, taxes or other charges, whether made effective through quotas, import or export licenses or other measures, shall be instituted or maintained by any Member on the importation of any product of the territory of any other Member or on the exportation or sale for export of any product destined for the territory of any other Member. Certain prohibitions or restrictions are, however, not subject to the provision. For example, import restrictions on any agricultural or fisheries product, imported in any form, which are necessary to the enforcement of governmental measures under justifiable circumstances prescribed under the Article.

Article XIII of *GATT* generally provides that: no prohibition or restriction shall be applied by any Member on the imports originated from other Member or on the exports to any other Member, unless the importation of like product of all third countries or the exportation of the like product to all third countries is similarly prohibited or restricted.

a. Non-Tariff Measures in General

Non-tariff measures are measures other than tariff measures taken by a WTO Member that could hinder trade, such as technicalities, red tapes etc. A number of WTO agreements deal with non-tariff measures such as technical regulations and standards, import licencing, rules for the valuation of goods at customs, preshipment inspection (further checks on imports), rules of origin and investment measures.

Current Situation/Concerns Raised by Other WTO Members	China Commitments/Confirmations
Current situation with non-tariff measures: 1. *Trade-distorting effect*—There were a large number of non-tariff measures (such as licenses and quotas) in existence in China, both at the national and sub-national levels, which appeared to have a trade restrictive or trade distorting effect. 2. *Measures imposed at sub-national level without transparency*—Many	China *would not introduce, re-introduce* or apply non-tariff measures other than listed in Annex 3 to the *Protocol* unless justified under the *WTO Agreement.* That *only* the central government could issue regulations on non-tariff measures and that these measures would be implemented or enforced only by the central government or sub-national authorities with authorization from the central government. Sub-national authorities had no right to formulate non-tariff measures.

such measures were imposed by sub-national authorities in China in a non-transparent, discretionary and discriminatory basis. There were concerns that actions lacking authorization from the national authorities should not be implemented or enforced.

3. *Not to expand scope of non-tariff measures*—China had provided a list of non-tariff measures in respect of which China was prepared to commence phased elimination as contained in *Annex 3 to the Protocol*.[21] There were concern that for measures subject to phased elimination, China should provide for growth in the quota over the relevant period specified in Annex 3 and that protection afforded by such measures should not be increased or expanded in size, scope or duration unless justified under WTO provisions. No new measures should be applied unless justified under WTO provisions.

4. *Administration*—there was concern that all non-tariff measures administered by China that were applied after China's accession should be allocated and otherwise administered in strict conformity with WTO provisions.[22]

China *confirmed* that only the machinery and electronic products listed in *Annex 3 to the Protocol* were subject to specific tendering requirements and that these requirements would be administered pursuant to Chapter III of the *"Interim Measures for Import Administration of Machinery and Electronics Products"*.[23]

Annex 3 to the Protocol contained all of the products subject to quotas, licences and such tendering requirements in China and that, during the relevant phase-out period, China would implement the growth rates for quotas as indicated.

---

[21]*Annex 3 to the Protocol* concerns "Non-Tariff Measures Subject to Phased Elimination", there are two tables. Table One lists out 'Products subject to import licence, import quota and import tendering', Table Two is 'Products Quota' tabulated with initial quota volume/value and annual growth rate.

[22]Including Article XIII of *GATT 1994* ("Non-Discriminatory Administration of Quantitative Restrictions") and *Agreement on Import Licensing Procedures*, including notification requirements, according to clause 125 of the Working Party Report. *Read also* B9 on Import Licencing.

[23]Approved by the State Council on 22 September 1993 and promulgated in Order No. 1 by the State Economic and Trade Commission and Ministry of Foreign Trade and Economic Cooperation on 7 October 1993.

b. Quota Administration

Current Situation/Concern Raised by Other WTO Members	China Commitments/Confirmations
There were concern over: 1. obtaining information on how China would implement the quota and licencing requirements for products listed in Annex 3 of *the Protocol*, in particular the procedures and criteria for grant of quota allocations and licensing during the phase-out period for these restrictions; 2. requirements for obtaining a licence or quota allocation which often required multiple approvals from various authorities and at both the central and sub-national level. It was further concerned that a transparent, streamlined system that would issue quota allocations and licences through a simple, consolidated approval process that would ensure full use of the quota and its equitable distribution among importers, is required. 3. how China would establish the value of imports for those products whose quota was established in terms of value of imports.	**Conformity with WTO obligations** China confirmed that the administration of quotas and import licences would be consistent with the WTO Agreement, including Article XIII of the *GATT 1994*[24] and *the Agreement on Import Licensing Procedures.*[25] Procedure in obtaining ────────────── The allocation of quotas and issuance of import licences would go through a simple and transparent procedure, so as to ensure the full utilization of quota. Determining Value of Imports ────────────── The establishment of value of imports would be based on the information collected by the Customs authorities and provisions of the WTO *Customs Valuation Agreement*. For quota quantities specified interms of value, China would determine the value of any shipment based on the c.i.f. ship value listed on the bill of lading. No more products subject to quota unless justified ────────────── Also, China confirmed that the products currently covered under the HS categories listed in Annex 3 of *the Protocol*[26] as of the date of accession were the only products that would be subject to these quotas during the agreed phase-out periods. Any non-tariff measures covering additional products would need to be justified under the *WTO Agreement*. For products listed in Anned 3 that are subject to quota and licencing requirement, any entity that will possess the right to trade in the quota year[27] *could apply* for a quota allocation and licence to import such products.

---

[24]*Supra* note 22.

[25]*See* Section B9 for *Agreement in Import Licencing Procedures.*

[26]*Supra* note 21.

[27]Including enterprises possessing trading rights to import such products or inputs for production purposes under a particular quota category, according to Clause 128 of the Working Party Report.

c. Quota allocation with necessary import licence

Those allocated with quota would also obtain necessary import licence

China Commitments/Confirmations

China further *confirmed* that for products listed in Annex 3, China's system for quota allocation and licencing would ensure that those entities with quota allocations would also receive any necessary import licence.

This system *would conform* to WTO rules, including the WTO *Agreement on Import Licensing Procedures,* and *would be* transparent, timely, responsive to market conditions and *would minimize* the burden on trade.

Applications for a quota allocation would need to be submitted to *only one organization, at one level* (central or sub-national) for approval. The relevant organization would then issue an import licence based on the quota allocation, in most cases within 3 working days and, in exceptional cases, within a maximum of 10 working days after a request for the licence. A licence would be issued for the full amount of the quota and would be valid for the calendar year issued. Such licence would be extended once, upon request, for up to 3 months, if the request was made before 15 December of the current quota year. Imports occurring under an extended licence would be counted against the relevant quota amount for the year in which the allocation took place.

Publication of information

China Commitments/Confirmations

China further *confirmed* that the information relative to the issuance of quota allocations, and licenses, including:

1. the relevant issuing organizations;
2. the amount of quota, including growth in quota provided for in Annex 3;
3. descriptions and tariff codes of products covered by each quota and procedures and criteria for application;
4. beginning and end date of application periods;

would be published in the official journal[28] at least 21 days prior to the beginning of the application period.

Application period would be from 1–31 August. Quotas would be allocated to applicants no later than 60 days after closure of the application period.

---

[28]Referred to in Section 2(C)(2) of the *Protocol*, see Appendix 2 of this book.

d. Criteria for quota allocation

Criteria for quota allocation
China Commitments/Confirmations
These quota allocation would be: published in advance : applied in conformity with WTO requirements including *Agreements on Import Licencing*
In applying these criteria, China would consider: 1. the need to allow for *equitable participation* by procedures from WTO Members and 2. the need to maximize the potential for quota fill.
China Commitments/Confirmations:
(a) (i) If the relevant quota quantity exceeded total requests for quota allocation, all requests would be approved. (ii) In other cases, the criteria for allocation would be as follows: Historical performance of applicants where relevant (in cases in which average imports over the 3-year period immediately prior to the year of China's accession, for which data was available, amounted to less than 75 per cent of the relevant quota, it would be necessary to take into account other criteria *inter alia* as set for the below); — Production or processing capacity, in the case of intermediate products and raw materials; — Experience and ability in producing, importing, marketing, or servicing in international markets, in the case of finished products or products destined for wholesale or retail distribution;

(b)

(i) **Condition of allocation:**

Average imports over the 3-year period prior to China accession is > 75% of the relevant quota

	Amount of allocations	Qualification of applicatns
Year 1 —	10% of total quota to qualified Applicants	not previously been allocated quota
and in any subsequent years	the majority of any quota growth	

(ii) **In other cases:**

	Amount of allocations	Qualification of applicants
Year 1 —	25% of total quota to qualified applicants	not previously been allocated with quota
—	quota quantity at least equal to the absolute amount	applicants that had imported under a quota on the relevant products

	in the year prior to China's accession	in the year prior to China's accession
Year 2 —	the amount of quota growth + an amount equivalent to unfilled quota in Year 1	priority consideration given to requests from enterprises with = to or < 50% foreign ownership
Year 3 & 4	quota growth + an amount equivalent to unfilled quota of previous year	priority consideration to requests from enterprises with > 50% foreign ownership

(c) In all cases, a quota-holder that fully utilized its initial quota allocation would be guaranteed in the following year an allocation of quantity no less than the quantity imported in the previous year. A quota-holder that did not import its full allocation would receive a proportional reduction in its quota allocation in the subsequent year unless the quantity was returned for reallocation by 1 September. (*See below on "allocation"*)

e. Allocations and extended licences for unused allocations

Commercial terms of products subject to quota

China Commitments/Confirmations

China *confirmed* that all commercial terms of trade, including product specifications, product mix, pricing, and packaging, would be at the *sole discretion* of the quota holder, so long as the products are within the relevant quota category. Allocations would be valid for any article or mixure of articles subject to the same quota as specified in *Annex 3 of the Protocol*.

Allocations

China Commitments/Confirmations

Allocations *would be valid* for a period of one calendar year from the opening of the quota import period. However, if the allocated quota was not used up by 1 September, the holder of a quota allocation was to immediately return the unused portion of an allocation to the relevant authority for reallocation. Notice would be published on availability of unused allocations.

Licences

China Commitments/Confirmations

Licences for goods imported under *reallocated quota would be extended* once, upon request, for up to 3 months, if the request was made before 15 December of the current quota year. Imports occuring under an extended licence would be counted against the relevant quota amount for the year in which the re-allocation took place.

B9. Import Licencing   **Protocol Ref: S7(2)(3)(4), S8**

The relative WTO provisions include ***Articles XI and XIII:3(a) of GATT 1994*** and **the**
Agreement on Import Licensing Procedures ("the Agreement"). The Agreement says
import licensing should be simple, transparent and predictable. For example, the Agreement
requires governments to publish suffcent information for traders to know how and why the
licences are granted. It also describes how countries should notify the WTO when they
introduce new import licensing procedures or change existing procedures. The Agreement
offers guidance on how governments should assess applications for licences.

Some licences are issued automatically if certain conditions are met. The Agreement sets
criteria for automatic licensing so that the procedures used do not restrict trade.

Other licences are not issued automatically. The Agreement tries to minimize the importers'
burden in applying for licences, so that the administrative work does not in itself restrict or
distort imports. The Agreement says the agencies handling licensing should not normally take
more than 30 days to deal with an application—60 days when all application are considered
at the same time.

Current Situation/Concerns Raised by other WTO Members	**China Commitments/Confirmations**
List of entities responsible for authorization and approval of imports	
On request for additional information about China's system of import licensing: China claimed that its import licensing system was administered without discrimination among countries or regions; and that regulations of its import licensing system for import commodities were uniformly implemented throughout China.[29] In 1999, of the total import value of US$ 165.7 billion, imports *subject to licensing* represented 8.45 per cent, covering US$ 14 billion. MOFTEC ("Ministry of Foreign Trade and Economic Co-operation") determined	China *confirmed* that the list of all entities responsible for the authorization or approval of imports *would be updated and republished* in the official journal, the MOFTEC Gazette, within one month of any change thereto.

---

[29]Such as the "*Interim Regulations of Licensing System for Import Commodities*" promulgated by the State Council
in 1984 and the detailed rules for its implementation issued by MOFTEC and Customs.

which products should be subject to import licensing according to the relevant provisions of the *"Foreign Trade Law"*.[30]

Further, in 1993, China had applied import restrictions to 53 product categories. By 1999, the number had been reduced to 35.[31] In the same year, there were 13 commodity categories which were imported by the foreign trade companies designated by MOFTEC.[32]

Currently, applications for import licences could be submitted to the Quota and Licence Administrative Bureau of MOFTEC or Special Commissioner Offices in 16 provinces, or Commissions of Foreign Economic Relations and Trade at their offices at provincial level. The examination and approval of the licence took two to three working days.

Import of Special Commodities

There was concern that provisonal procedures for registration for the import of special commodities[33], in particular	China exphasized that the purpose of the registration system for the import of special commodities was only to gather statistical information.

[30]Adopted at the Seventh Meeting of the Standing Committee of the Eighth National People's Congress on 12 May 1994, promulgated by Order No. 22 of the President of the People's Republic of China on 12 May 1994 and effective as of 1 July 1994.

[31]Products covered were (1) Processed oil; (2) Wool; (3) Polyester fibre; (4) Acrylic fibres; (5) Polyester fillet; (6) Natural rubber; (7) Vehicles tyres; (8) Sodium cyanide; (9) Sugar; (10) Fertilizer; (11) Tobacco and its products; (12) Acetate tow; (13) Cotton; (14) Motor vehicles and their key parts; (15) Motorcycles and their engines and chassises; (16) Colour television sets and TV kinescope; (17) Radios, tape recorders and their main parts; (18) Refrigerators and their compressor; (19) Washing machines; (20) Recording equipment and its key parts; (21) Cameras and their bodies (without lenses); (22) Watches; (23) Air conditioners and their compressor; (24) Audio and video tape duplication equipment; (25) Crane lorries and their chassises; (26) Electronic microscopes; (27) Open-end spinning machines; (28) Electronic colour scanners; (29) Grain; (30) Vegetable oil; (31) Wine; (32) Colour sensitive material; (33) Chemical under supervision and control that were used for chemical weapon; (34) Chemicals used to produce narcotics; and (35) Laser disc production facilities; *see* clause 134 of the Working Party Report.

[32]These categories were as follows: (1) Processed oil; (2) Fertilizer; (3) Tobacco; (4) Vegetable oil; (5) Grain; (6) Natural rubber; (7) Wool; (8) Acrylic fibers; (9) Sugar; (10) Cotton; (11) Crude oil; (12) Steel; and (13) Plywood, *see* clause 134 of the Working Party Report.

[33]*China's Provisional Procedures for the Administration of Automatic Registration for the Import of Special Commodities (13 Aug 1994) see* clause 136 of Working Party Report.

the criteria for approval of registration would act as a restraint on imports.	China *confirmed* that upon accession, China *would bring* its automatic licensing system into conformity with Article 2 of the *Agreement on Import Licensing Procedures*.[34] [This provision requires a Member to ensure that the administrative procedures used to implement import licencing regimes conform with relevant *GATT* provisons with a view to preventing trade distortions that may arise from an inapporpriate operation of those procedures.]
Multiple requirements for imports subject to tariff quota administration	
Current requirements include: — importation of products subject to tariff quota administration requirements had to go through extensive procedures to receive a quota allocation; (the quota certificate would indicate whether the subject good was to be imported through a state trading enterprise or a non-state trading enterprise and would be valid for a certain period of time); — the entity importing the good would need trading rights. It was concerned that in light of these multiple requirements, a quota allocation certificate should satisfy any import licensing requirement that might apply.	China *confirmed* that China would *not* require a separate import lcence approval for goods subject to a TRQ allocation requirement but would provide any necessary import licence in the procedure that granted a quota allocation. (Also *see* B7 on "TRQ" above)

B10. Customs Valuation   Protocol Ref: S7(2)

The relative WTO provisions include **Article VII of GATT 1994** and the **Agreement on Implementation of Article VII of the GATT ("Customs Valuation Agreement")**. It aims for a fair, uniform and neutral system for the valuation of goods for customs purposes — a system that conforms to commercial realities, and which outlaws the use of arbitrary or fictitious customs values.

---

[34]Article 2 of the WTO's *Agreement on Import Licensing Procedures* specifies that "Mambers shall ensure that the administrative procedures used to implement import licencing regimes are in conformity with relevant provisions of *GATT 1994* including annexes and protocols...... with a view to preventing trade distortions that may arise from an inappropriate operation of those procedures, taking into account the ...... needs of developing country member".

The *Customs Valuation Agreement* provides a set of valuation rules, expanding and giving greater precison to the provisions on customs valuation in the original GATT.

A related Uruguay Round ministerial decision gives customs administrations the right to request further information in cases where they have reason to doubt the accuracy of the declared value of imported goods. If the administration maintains a reasonable doubt, despite any additional information, it may be deemed that the customs value of the imported goods cannot be determined on the basis of the declared value.

Current Situation/Concerns Raised by Other WTO Members	China Commitments/Confirmations
Determination of customs value	
There was concern regarding the methods used by China to determine the customs value of goods, in particular regarding the practice of using minimum or reference prices for certain goods, which would be inconsistent with the *Customs Valuation Agreement* of WTO. Current situation in China: The overwhelming majority of China's customs duties were *ad valoren* duties. The customs value of imported goods was assessed according to the c.i.f. price based on the transaction value, as defined in the *Customs Valuation Agreement*.[35] The *Customs Law* of China also provided for appeal procedures. If the appeal was rejected, the importer could sue at the People's Court.	China *had ceased* to use and would not reintroduce minimum or reference prices as a means to determine customs value. China *confirmed* that, upon accession, China *would apply* fully the *Customs Valuation Agreement*, including the customs valuation methodologies set forth in Articles 1 trhrough 8 of the Agreement. In addition, China *would apply* as soon as practicable, but in any event no later than *two* years from the date of accession the provision of: — the *Decision on Treatment of Interest Charges in Customs Value of Imported Goods,* and — the *Decision on the Valuation of Carrier Media Bearing Software for Data Procession Equipment of WTO.*[36]

[35]If the transaction value of imported goods could not be determined, the customs value was determined based on other means provided for in *Customs Valuation Agreement* of WTO. China's *Customs Law* provides for appeal procedures. In the event of a dispute over calculation of duty paid or payable with the Customs, the dissatisfied importer could apply to Customs for a reconsideration of the case. If the appeal was rejected the importer could sue at the People's Court. *See* clause 142 of Working Party Report.

[36]Adopted by the WTO Committee on Customs Valuation (G/VAL/5), *see* clause 143 of the Working party Report.

B11. Other Customs Formalities

China joined the *International Convention on the Simplication and Harmonisation of Customs Procedures* in 1988 and on 15 June 2000 signed *the Draft Protocol on the Amendment of the International Convention on the Simplification and Harmonisation of Customs Procedures*. The Customs authorities of China had only adopted such customs formalities as declaration, examination, levying of duties and release which were *consistent* with international practices.

B12. Preshipment Inspection   Protocol Ref: S7(2)

Preshipment inspection – further checks on imports could be a form of non-tariff barrier to trade.

The relative WTO agreement is *the **Agreement on Preshipment Inspection** ("the Agreement")*. Preshipment inspection is the practice of employing specialized private companies (or "independent entities") to check shipment details — essentially price, quantity and quality — of goods ordered overseas. Used by governments of developing countries, the purpose is to safeguard national financial interests (prevention of capital flight and commercial fraud as well as customs duty evasion, for instance) and to compensate for inadequacies in administrative infrastructures.

The Agreement recognizes that *GATT* principles and obligations apply to the activities of preshipment inspection agenceis mandated by governments. The obligations placed on governments which use preshipment inspections include non-discrimination, transparency, protection of confidential business information, avoidance of unreasonable delay, the use of specific guidelines for conducting price verification and the avoidance of conflicts of interest by the inspection agenceis. The obligations of exporting Members towards countries using preshipment inspection include non-discrimination in the application of domestic laws and regulations, prompt publication of those laws and regulations and the provision of technical assistance where requested.

The Agreement establishes an independent review procedure which purpose is to resolve disputes between an exporter and an inspection agency.

Current Situation/Concerns Raised by Other WTO Members	China Commitments/Confirmations
Currently, there were trade and commercial inspection agencies (including joint-venture agencies) engaged in preshipment inspection.	China *would:* i. *comply* with the *Agreement on Preshipment Inspection;*

There was concern whether China would use the services of a private preshipment inspection entity.	ii. *regulate* the existing trade and commerce inspection agencies; and
	iii. *permit* the qualified agenceis to be engaged in preshipment inspection line with the government mandate or the terms and conditions of commercial contracts.
	
	Conformity with WTO obligations
	
	i. China *would ensure* that, upon accession, any laws and regulations relating to preshipment inspection by any inspection agency, inlcuding private entities, *would be consistent* with relevant WTO agreements, in particular:
	
	   a. the *Agreement on Preshipment Inspection* and
	   b. the *Customs Valuation Agreement*.
	
	ii. Any fees charged in connection with such preshipment inspection would be commensurate with the service provided, in conformity with Article VIII:1 of *GATT 1994*.[37]

B13. Anti-Dumping, Countervailing Duties   Protocol Ref: S15

The relative WTO provisions include *Article VI, GATT Agreement*, *the Agreement on Implementation of Article VI of GATT 1994 ("Anti-Dumping Agreement")* and *Agreement on Subsidies and Countervailing Measures ("SCM Agreement")*. Anti-Dumping and Subsidies and Countervailing Measures are among the exceptions to the principles of binding tariff and MFN upheld by WTO Agreeement. The other exception is *safeguards (see B14 below)*.

If a company exports a product at a price lower than the price it normally charges on its own home market, it is said to be "dumping" the product. The WTO agreement does not pass judgement whether dumping is unfair competition. Its focus is on how governments can or cannot react to dumping — it disciplines anti-dumping actions by the *Anti-dumping Agreement*.

Anti-dumping Agreement allows governments to act against dumping where there is genuine ("material") injury to the competing domestic industry of the importing country. In order to do that the government had to be able to show that dumping is taking place, calculate the extent of dumping (how much lower the export price is compared to the exporter's home market price), and to show that dumping is causing injury.

---

[37]*See* Section B4 for explanation of Article VIII: 1 of *GATT 1994*.

Typically anti-dumping action means charging extra import duty on the particular product from the particular exporting country in order to bring its price closer to the "normal value" or to remove the injury to domestic industry in the importing country.

The principle of price comparability in determining what is "normal value" and hence margin of dumping becomes very important. Investigations must be carried out by the affected domestic industry of the importing country before an action can be taken and whereby a determination in "dumping" can be reached. It must be proved with evidences that there exist a causal link between the dumped imports and the alleged injury caused to the domestic market for such products in the importing country.

The *SCM Agreement* addresses two separate but closely related topics: multilateral disciplines regulating the provision of subsidies' by a Member, it also regulates the actions a Member can take, after investigation, to counter the effects of subsidies. The definition of "subsidy" contains three elements: (i) a financial contribution (ii) by a government or any public body within the territory of a Member (iii) which confers a benefit. All three of these elements must be satisfied in order for a subsidy to exist. A subsidy is not subject to the *SCM Agreements* unless it has been specifically provided to an enterprise or industry or group of enterprises or industries. The basic principle is that a subsidy that distorts the allocation of resources within an economy should be subject to discipline.

Two basic categories of subsides under the Agreement are 'prohibited subsidies'and 'actionable subsidies'. 'Prohibited subsidies' consist of "export subsidies" and "local contents subsidies" [*see* section C3 of this Chapter]. 'Actionable subsidies' are not prohibited. Most subsidies, such as production subsidies, fall into the "actionable" category. Actionable subsidies are subject to challenge in the WTO through multilateral dispute settlement mechanism or to countervailing measures, in the event that they cause adverse effects to the interests of another Members. A Member importing subsidized goods can launch its own investigation and ultimately charge extra duty ("countervailing duty") on such subsidized imports that are found to be hurting domestic producers. It can use the WTO's dispute settlements procedure to seek the withdrawal of the subsidy or the removal of its adverse effects.

The *SCM Agreement* also establishes the substantive and procedural requirements that must be fulfilled before a Member may apply a countervailing measure against subsidized imports.

Current Situation/Concerns Raised by Other WTO Members	China Commitments/Confirmations
China promulgated regulations and procedures on anti-dumping and countervailing duties in1997 with reference to the WTO's *Anti-Dumping Agreement* and *Agreement on Subsidies and Countervailing Measures*.	Conformity with WTO obligations China *committed* to revise China's current regulations and procedures prior to its accession in order to fully implement China's obligations under the *Anti-Dumping* [*see* note 47] and *SCM Agreements*.

There were **concerns****** that Chinese anti-dumping duties rules need to be brought into compliance with WTO's provisions substantially because:	Members of the Working Party[38] and China *agreed* that the term "national law" in Section 15(d) of the Protocol, should be interpreted to cover *not only* laws but also decrees, regulations and administrative rules.
i) the current investigations by the Chinese authority were judged to be inconsistent with *Anti-Dumping Agreement*;	
ii) in certain cases, the basis for calculating dumping margins for a preliminary affirmative determination was not disclosed to interested parties.	
iii) the determination of injury and causation did not appear to have been made on an objective examination of sufficient evidence.	

***In turn, China had the same concern when its products were subject to investigation by other WTO Members.

Alternate Methodology for Price Comparison and Unfair Treatment to China

It was noted that China was continuing the process of transition towards a full market economy. It was noted that under those circumstances, in the case of imports of Chinese origin into a WTO Member, special difficulties could exist in determining cost and price comparability in the context of anti-dumping investigations and countervailing duty investigations.[39] In such cases, the importing WTO Member might find it necessary to take into account the possibility that a strict comparison with domestic costs and prices in China might not always be appropriate.

China expressed concern with regard to past measures taken by certain WTO Members which had treated China as a non-market economy and imposed anti-dumping duties on Chinese companies without identifying or publishing the criteria used, without giving Chinese companies sufficient opportunity to present evidence and defend their interests in a fair manner, and without explaining the rationale underlying their determinations, including with respect to the method of price comparison in the determinations. In response to these

---

[38]*supra* note 5.
[39]*See* Part V of the *SCM Agreement* on procedures of investigations and Articles 2,3,5,6,7 of the *Anti-dumping Agreement* on procedures of dumping investigations.

concerns, *members of the Working Party confirmed that* in implementing subparagraph (a)(ii) of Section 15 of *the Protocol*[40], WTO Members would comply with certain obligations.

Obligations of WTO Members

When determining price comparability in a particular case in a manner not based on a strict comparison with domestic costs or prices in China, WTO Member importing goods of Chinese origin was to establish and publish in advance criteria for:

i)   establishing whether market economy conditions prevailed in the industry or company that produce the like product and

ii) methodology for determining price comparability.

Notification of such criteria must be made to the Committee on Anti-Dumping Practices before they were applied.

The process of investigation should be transparent. Ample opportunity should be given in a particular case to Chinese producers or exporters:

a.   to make comments on application of the methodology for determining price comparability;

b.   to present evidence on information required by the importing WTO Member;

c.   to defend their interest.

Also, the importing WTO Member should provide a sufficiently detailed reasoning of its determinations in a particular case.

Current Situation/Concerns Raised by other WTO Members	China Commitments/Confirmations
Application of the Anti-Dumping Agreement	
	China stated that determinations made by China during investigations initiated pursuant to applications made before accession should be free from challenge under the *Anti-Dumping Agreement* by the Members of the WTO. China *confirmed* that notwithstanding Article 18.3 of the *Anti-Dumping Agreement* [which concerns that provisions of the Agreement shall apply to investigations, and reviews of existing measures initiated on or after

---

[40]Section 15(a)(ii) of *the Protocol*: *"The importing WTO Member may use a methodology that is not based on a strict price comparison with domestic prices or costs in China if the producers under investigations cannot clearly show that market economy conditions prevail in the industry producing the like product with regard to manufacture, production and sale of that product."*

the date of entry into force for a Member of the *WTO Agreement*],

(a) China *would apply* the provisions of the Anti-Dumping Agreement to:

(i) proceedings in determining final liability for payment of anti-dumping duties, any refund or reimbursement.[41] Such proceedings include the calculation of margins of dumping, in connection with anti-dumping measures adopted before accession ("existing measures"); and

(ii) reviews of existing measures initiated pursuant to requests made following accession. [Reviews that may be initiated are: reviews for determining individual margins of dumping for exporters or producers who claimed they are not related to dumping;[42] review to determine if there is the need to continue with the imposition of anti-dumping duty;[43] and review on the duration of anti-dumping duty.[44]]

Any review of an existing measure including those made on the own initiative of authorities of importing country[45] would be initiated no later than five years from the date of its imposition.

(b) China *would also provide* the type of judicial review described in the *Anti-Dumping Agreement*[46] with regard to proceedings in subparagraph (a) (i) and reviews under subparagraph (a) (ii) above.

---

[41]*Anti-Dumping Agreement*, Article 9.3
[42]*ibid*, Article 9.5
[43]*ibid*, Article 11.2
[44]*ibid*, Article 11.3
[45]*ibid*
[46]*ibid*, Article 13

Government Bodies Responsible for Anti-Dumping Duties and Countervailing Duty Investigations

Pursuant to the provisions of *"Regulation on Anti-dumping and Countervailing Measures of the People's Republic of China"*, promulgated by the State Council on 25 March 1997,[47] there were four Chinese government bodies responsible for anti-dumping and countervailing duty investigations:

(a)   Ministry of Foreign Trade and Economic Cooperation ("MOFTEC")
(b)   State Economics and Trade Commission ("SETC")
(c)   General Customs Administration ("Customs")
(d)   Tariff Commission of the State Council ("TCSC")[48]

B14. Safeguards for Increased Imports

The relative WTO Agreement is **Agreement on safeguards**. A WTO Member may restrict imports of a product temporarily (take "safeguard" actions) if its domestic industry is injured or threatened with injury caused by a surge in imports. The injury has to be serious. Safeguard measures were always available under *GATT* (Article 19). However, safeguards

---

[47]A new *Anti-Dumping Regulations* was promulgated by the State Council on 26 November 2001 and effective as of 1 January 2002. Many provisions of the new *Regulations* follow the terminology of the WTO *Anti-Dumping Agreement* closely, and there are many new details that have been added that are also drawn from that Agreement; *see* analysis in "China's New Anti-dumping Rules: Battleground for a New protectionism?", China Law & Practice, February 2002 pp. 79-83.

[48]*See* clause 153 of the Working Party Report—The respective responsibilities of these bodies are:

(a)   Ministry of Foreign Trade and Economic Cooperation ("MOFTEC")—Receiving anti-dumping and countervailing petitions; Conducting investigations on foreign subsidies and on dumping and dumping margins and issuing relevant preliminary determination decisions and notices; Negotiating with foreign interested parties on "Price Undertaking" if necessary; Providing proposal on imposition of definitive anti-dumping or countervailing duties or proposals on duty refund, etc. There was an Anti-dumping Division established under the Department of Treaties and Law of MOFTEC, with responsibility to handle anti-dumping and countervailing investigations on alleged imports.

(b)   State Economics and Trade Commission ("SETC")—Responsible for the investigation of injury caused to the domestic industry by the dumped or subsidized imports, the extent of such injury and making injury findings. There was a non-permanent decision and policy-making body in SETC, named the Injury Investigation and Determination Committee ("IIDC"), which was composed of six commissioners from the relevant departments of SETC. There was a permanent executive office in charge of the investigation of injury to the industry and submitting its findings to the IIDC for approval.

(c)   General Customs Administration ("Customs")—Coordinating anti-dumping investigations with MOFTEC; enforcing anti-dumping measures such as collecting cash deposits and dumping duties, enforcing countervailing measures by collecting countervailing duties, and monitoring implementation.

(d)   Tariff Commission of the State Council ("TCSC")—Making final decisions on whether or not to levy the anti-dumping or countervailing duties based on the suggestions by MOFTEC with regard to imposing anti-dumping or countervailing duties and reimbursing excess amount of duties, respectively.

are "contingent trade barriers", a safeguard measure should not last more than four years, although this can be extended up to eight years.[49] Examples of safeguard measures are tariff increase and exercising of import quotas. Safeguard measures shall be applied to a product being imported irrespective of its source, that is, indiscriminately to all member countries supplying the same product.

Current Situation/Concerns Raised by Other WTO Members	China Commitments/Confirmations
Consistency with WTO obligations	
	Upon accesssion, China *would implement* its Regulation on Safeguard by which the future safeguard measures would be regulated. The contents of this new regulation would be fully consistent with the *Agreement on safeguards*. China was in the process of drafting safeguard legislation in accordance with Article 29 of the *Foreign Trade Law*[50] and the *Agreement on Safeguards*.

C. EXPORT REGULATIONS
Protocol Ref: S2(C), S7(1) (2) (4), S8, S10, S11, S15, ANNEX 5B, ANNEX 6

C1. Customs Tariffs, Fees and Charges for Services Rendered, Application of Internal Taxes to Exports (Protocol Ref: S11, Annex 6)

The relevant WTO provision is **Article VIII of *GATT 1994 on Fees and Formalities connected with Importation and Exportation***.

There were concerns whether taxes and charges applied exclusively to exports should be eliminated unless applied in conformity with *Article VIII of GATT*[51] or listed in *Annex 6 to the Protocol* (produces subject to export duty).

In China, the majority of products were free of export duty, although 84 items, including *tungsten ore, ferrosilicon and some aluminum products*, were subject to export duties. The customs value of exported goods was the F.O.B. price of the goods. No specific commitment was made here.

---

[49]Article 7(1) of *Agreement on Safeguards* stipulates safeguard measures shall not exceed four years; Article 7(3) says the total period of application of safeguard measures including extension shall not exceed eight years; two more years for developing countries under Article 9(2).

[50]Article 29 of the *Foreign Trade Law* stipulates "Should the normal production of some of the domestic goods be in great harm or under great threat of such harm due to the increasing import of same kinds of goods or similar goods that are in severe competition with the domestic ones, the State may take any counter measures to expel or mitigate such harm or threat".

[51]*See* Section B4 and B8 of this Chapter for explanation of Article VIII of *GATT*

C2. Export Licensing and Export Restrictions   Protocol Ref: S7(4), S8

The relevant WTO provisions include **Article XI** *of GATT 1994 on General Elimination of Quantitative Restrictions,* **Article XIII** *Non-Discriminatory Administration of Quantitative Restrictions* and **Article XX of** *GATT 1994 on General Exceptions.*

Current Situation/Concerns Raised by Other WTO Members	China Commitments/Confirmations
List of entities for the authorization or approval of exports to be published	
	China *confirmed* that the list of all entities responsible for the authorization or approval of exports would be updated and republished in the official journal, the MOFTEC Gazette, within one month of any change thereto.
Conformity with WTO obligations	
China applied its export licence system to certain agricultural products, resource products and chemicals. China's export licencing system was administered in accordance with the *Interim Procedures for the Export Licencing System.*	China *would abide by* WTO rules in respect of non-automatic export licensing and export restrictions. The *Foreign Trade Law would* also *be brought* into conformity with *GATT* requirements. Moreover, export restrictions and licensing *would only be applied,* after the date of accession, in those cases where this was justified by *GATT* provisions.
By 1999, the total number of products subject to export licensing had been reduced to 58 categories and 73 items with an export value of US$ 18.5 billion, taking up only 9.5 per cent of total exports, down from 143 categories in 1992 taking up 48.3% of total exports then. However, the remaining number was still considered to be high and that there was request that they be either reduced further or eliminated by the date of accession in order to achieve full compatibility with *GATT* requirements.	
The main criteria used in determining whether a product was subjet to export licensing, as set down in *the Foreign Trade Law* were: (1) maintenance of national security or public interests; (2) protection against shortage of supply in the domestic market or exhaustion of natural resources; (3) limited market	

capacity of importing countries or regions; or (4) obligations stipulated in international treaties.[52] Export licensing was also used for statistical purposes.

An application for an export licence had to be submitted to the licence issuing institutions authorized by MOFTEC. The procedures were the same for all export destinations. A decision on the request for an export licence normally took three working days.

Incompatibility with *GATT 1994*

There was conern that some of the criteria of *the Foreign Trade Law* referred to above did not at present meet the specific conditions laid down in Articles XI and XX of the *GATT 1994*.

The conditions in the Article XI of *GATT 1994* in regard to non-automatic licensing and export restrictios are such that: export prohibitions, restrictions and non-automatic licensing could only temporarily be applied to prevent or relieve critical shortages of foodstuffs or other products essential to an exporting WTO Member.

Article XX of the *GATT 1994* also allowed for restrictive export measures, *but only* if such measures were made effective in conjunction with restrictions on domestic production or consumption.

Non-Automatic Export Restrictions On Silk And Other Products

There was concern about China's restrictions on exports of silk and about export restrictions on other goods, in particular raw materials or intermeidate products that cound be subject to further processing, such as tungsten ore concentrates, rare earths and other metals.	Upon accession, remaining non-automatic restrictions on exports *would be notified* to the WTO annually and *would be eliminated* unless they could be justified under the *WTO Agreement* or *the Protocol*.

---

[52]The criteria is set out under Article 16, Ch.3 of *Foreign Trade Law*.

C3. Export Subsidies   Protocol Ref: S10, S12(1), Annex 5B

The relevant WTO provisions include the *Subsidies and Countervailing Measures ("SCM Agreement") (see Section B13* of this Chapter) *and Article XVI of GATT 1994 (on "Subsidies")*

Prohibited subsidies Two categories of subsidies are prohibited by Article 3 of the *SCM Agreement*. The first category consists of subsidies contingent, in law or in fact, whether wholly or as one of several conditions, on export performance ("export subsidies"). A detailed list of export subsidies is annexed to the *SCM Agreement*. The second category consists of subsidies contingent, whether solely or as one of several other conditions, upon the use of domestic over imported goods ("local content subsidies"). These two categories of subsidies are prohibited because they are designed to directly affect trade and thus are most likely to have adverse effects on the interests of other Members.

Current Situation/Concern Raised by other WTO Members	China Commitments/Confirmations
List of prohibited subsidies	
Incomplete list of prohibited subsidies	Export Subsidies
China provided a list of prohibited subsidies and a timetable for their elimination in *Annex 5B to the Protocol*.[53] The subsidies so listed fall within the scope of *the SCM Agreement*[54] but the list was considered to be incomplete by some WTO Members.	China *confirmed* that as provided in *the Protocol*,[55] it *would eliminate* all export subsidies, within the meaning of the *SCM Agreement*[56], by the time of accession.
	To this end, China *would*, by accession, *cease* to maintain all pre-existing export subsidies programmes and, upon accession, *make no* further payments or disbursements, nor forego revenue or confer any other benefit, under such programmes.
	This commitment covered subsidies granted at all levels of government which were contingent, in law or in fact, upon an obligation to export.

---

[53]In *Annex 5B to the Protocol* titled "Subsidies to be Phased Out".

[54]*See* section B13 of this Chapter on *SCM Agreement*; Article 3 of *SCM Agreement* concerns "prohibition" of subsidies

[55]Section 10.3 of *the Protocol*.

[56]Aritcle 3.1(a) of the *SCM Agreement* stipulates that subsidies contingent, in law or in fact, whether solely or as one of several other conditions, upon export performance are prohibited ("export subsidies"). Annex 1 to the *SCM Agreement* illustrates a list of such export subsidies which includes for instance, the provision by governments of direct subsidies to a firm or an industry contingent upon export performance; currency retention schemes which involve a bonus on exports; allowance of special deductions directly related to exports or export performance etc.

	Local contents subsidies
	On the same basis, China *would eliminate,* upon accession, all subsidies contingent upon the use of domestic over imported goods, within the meaning of the *SCM Agreement.*[57]

D. INTERNAL POLICIES AFFECTING FOREIGN TRADE IN GOODS

D1. Taxes and Charges Levied on Imports and Exports

Protocol Ref: S2(c), S3(a), S11

The relevant WTO provisions include *Article I, Articles III:2, III:4, Article XI:1* of *GATT 1994*.

Current Situation/Concern Raised by other WTO Members	China Commitments/Confirmations
Confirmity with Non-Discriminatory Obligations	
There was concern that the application of the VAT and additional charges levied by sub-national governments on imports should be on non-discriminatory basis.	China *confirmed* that upon accession, China *would ensure* that its laws and regulations relating to all fees, charges or taxes levied on imports and exports would be in full conformity with its WTO obligations, including obligations under *GATT 1994* such as[58]:
	— most-favoured-nation treatment;
	— national treatment afforded to imported goods in respect of internal taxes and charges, and national treatment in respect of all laws, regulations and requirements affecting the internal sale, purchase, transportation, distribution and use of imported goods;
	— no prohibitions or restrictions shall be instituted or maintained on importation of any product or on exportation, whether made effective through quotas, import or export licences or other measures.
	And that China would also *implement* such laws and regulations in full conformity with these obligations.

---

[57]Article 3.1(b) of the *SCM Agreement* concerns subsides contingent upon the use of domestic over imported goods ("local contents subsidies").

[58]Articles I, III:2 and III:4, and XI:1 of the *GATT 1994* respectively.

D2. Industrial Policy including Subsidies

Protocol Ref: S10, S15 (b)(c), Annexes 5A and 5B

The relevant WTO agreement is *SCM Agreement*.[59]

There are transition rules and special and differential treatment available in the Agreement. Developed countries Members not otherwise eligible for special and differential treatment are allowed three years from the date on which for them the *SCM Agreement* enters into force to phase out "prohibited subsidies" [*see* section C3]. Such subsidies must be notified within 90 days of the entry into force of the WTO Agreement for the notifying Member.

Members in transformation to a market economy are given a seven-year period to phase out prohibited subsidies. These subsidies must, however, have been notified within two years of the date of entry into force of the WTO Agreement (i.e., by 31 December 1996 for those Members upon whom WTO Agreement came into force on 1 January 1995) in order to benefit from the special treatment. Members in transformation also receive preferential treatment with respect to actionable subsidies. Article 25 of the *SCM Agreement* requires that Members notify all specific subsidies (at all levels of government and covering all goods sectors, including agriculture) to the SCM Committee. New and full notifications are due every three years with update notifications in intervening years.

China's notification of subsidies is included in Annexes 5A and 5B of the *Protocol*.

Current Situation/Concerns Raised by Other WTO Members	China Commitments/Confirmations
Some Members are still skeptical about the potential for certain level of trade-distorting subsidization despite of the reform undergoing in China.	China explained it had exerted much effort in its ongoing reform process to reduce the availability of certain types of subsidies, and that certain provisions under Article 27 should be available to it.
These subsidies could have an impact not only on access to China's domestic markets, but also on the performacne of Chinese exports in the markets of other WTO Members and should be subject to effective *SCM Agreement* disciplines.	China was *committed to implementing* the *SCM Agreement* in a manner that was fair and equitable to China and to other WTO Members. In line with this approach, China intended to reserve the right to benefit from certain provisions [on special and differential treatment of developing member countries] under Article 27 of the *SCM Agreement*,[60]

---

[59]*See Section B13* for *Agreement on Subsidies and Countervailing Measures*.

[60]These are mainly benefits relating to developing member countries under Article 27 of the *SCM* Agreement, which include: Article 27.10 concerns developing member country treatment—countervailing duty investigation shall terminate where overall level of subsidies granted upon the product in question does not exceed 2 per cent of its value calculated on a per unit basis etc; Article 27.11 more preferential treatment for those developing countries where export subsidies have been eliminated prior to the expiry of 8 years requirements under the Agreement, and for those developing countries listed in Annex 2 of this *SCM Agreement*, the number in Article 27.10 shall be 3 per cent rather than 2 per cent; Article 27.12 relates to Articles 27.10, 27.11; Article 27.15 allows developing country member to request for a review to determine if a specific countervailing measure is consistent with the provisions of Articles 27.10 and 27.11."

Also, it would be inappropriate for China to benefit from certain provisions of Article 27 of the Agreement. [Those provisions concern benefits to developing country members.]	while confirming that China *would not* seek to invoke certain provisions under the same article of the *SCM Agreement*.[61]

Concern whether State-Owned Enterprises are Government Actors in providing Financial Contributions

In view of the special characteristics of China's economy, it has to be clarified that when state-owned enterprises (including banks) provided financial contributions, they were doing so as government actors within the scope[62] of the *SCM Agreement*.	China however, was in the opinion that such financial contributions would not necessarily give rise to a benefit within the meaning of the *SCM Agreement*.[63] China's objective was that state-owned enterprises, including banks, should be run on a commercial basis and be responsible for their own profits and losses.

Notification to WTO on subsidies was not made comprehensively

Certain types of subsidies identified with state support did not appear in *Annexes 5A and 5B to the Protocol*[64], which was last modified on 31 May 2000. Examples are those with state support	China explained it had experienced difficulty in obtaining accurate data about all types of subsidies and was attempting to reduce the availability of certain types of subsidies, in particular by reforming its tax system and making government-owned banks operate on a commercial basis.

---

[61]Treatment relating to developing member countries under Article 27 of the *SCM Agreement* that would not be invoked by China include: Article 27.8, Members shall not presume that a subsidy granted by a developing country member results in serious prejudice; positive evidence for such presumption shall be demonstrated; Article 27.9 concerns that remedies may not be sought on some actionable subsidies maintained by developing countries unless inconsistency with *GATT* obligations such as nullification or impairment of tariff concessions is found to exist as a result of the subsidy or unless injury to a domestic industry in the market of importing member occurs; Article 27.13 concerns that actionable subsidies shall not apply to certain subsidies granted within and directly linked to a privatization programme of a developing country member, such as direct forgiveness of debt, subsidies to cover social costs in whatever form etc.

[62]Article 1.1 (a)(1) of the *SCM Agreement* defines certain circumstances wherein a financial contribution by a government or any public body within the territory of a Member (referred to as "government" under the Agreement) constitutes the existence of a subsidy; for instance, a government practice involves a direct transfer of funds (e.g. grants, loans, and equity infusion); government revenue that is otherwise due is foregone or not collected etc. or, Article 1.1.(a)(2) states that there is any form of income or price support in the sense of Article XVI ('subsidies') of *GATT 1994*, and, according to Article 1.1(b), a benefit is thereby conferred.

[63]*ibid*.

[64]*Annex 5A to the Protocol* concerns "Notification pursuant Article 25 of SCM Agreement" which lists out various types of subsidies in China including different preferential policies and tax treatments; and *Annex 5B* concerns "Subsidies to be Phased Out".

through the banking system, notably government-owned banks, in the form of: — policy loans; — the automatic roll-over of unpaid principal and interest; — forgiven and non-performing loans — the selective use of below-market interest rates. There were also: — unreported tax subsidies; — investment subsidies and subsidies provided by sub-national governments, some of which favoured exporting firms; — subsidies granted to the telecommunications, footwear, coal and shipbuilding sectors.	China *confirmed* that it *would progressively work* towards a full notification of subsidies, as contemplated by the *SCM Agreement*.[65]
Concerning subsidies provided to SEZs	
Some of the subsidies that China provided in connection with *SEZs* and other special economic areas appeared to be contingent upon export performance or on the use of domestic goods.	China expressed that the main purpose of such subsidies was to promote regional development and foreign investment. China *confirmed* that it *would,* upon accession, *eliminate* any such subsidies which were inconsistent with the *SCM Agreement.*

Two clarifications made by China and these are not commitments:

(1) VAT on Steel
In response to comment that the Steel Import Substitution Programme appeared to provide export subsidies to the big four steel groups in China, China clarified that China did not collect VAT on imported and domestically produced steel used as raw material for the processing trade. Such a policy was consistent with WTO rules and the practices of many WTO Members, and thus should not be considered as subsidies.

(2) VAT Rebate Treatment
Regarding information on the "China High-Tech Product Export Catalogue" which set forth central government export policies for the *telecommunications, computer software, aviation and aerospace, lasers, pharmaceuticals, medical equipment, new materials and energy industries.*

---

[65]Article 25 of the *SCM Agreement* on "notification".

China clarified that products listed in the Catalogue would enjoy full VAT rebated treatment, while other exported products would only be given partial VAT rebate treatment. Such a policy was consistent with Article XVI of the *GATT 1994*[66] and relevant Annexes of the *SCM Agreement*. And that the VAT rebates were applied only to exported products and not to domestically consumed products.

D3. Technical Barriers to Trade ("TBT")   Protocol Ref: S7(2), S13

Technical regulations and industrial standards vary from country to country. If the standards are set arbitrarily, they could be used as an excuse for protectionism. Standards can become obstacles to trade.

The relative WTO Agreement is the *Agreement on Technical Barriers to Trade* ("*TBT Agreement*"), one of the Uruguay Round multilateral trade negotiations with a purpose to further objectives of *GATT 1994*. *The TBT Agreement* sets out a *Code of Good Practice* for the preparation, adoption and application of standards by central government bodies.[67] It also includes provisions describing how local government and non-governmental bodies should apply their own regulations – normally they should use the same principles as apply to central governments. The Agreement sets the procedures used to decide whether a product conforms with national standards have to be fair and equitable. It discourages any methods that would give doemstically produced goods an unfair advantage. It encourages countries to recognize each other's testing procedures. *TBT Agreement* does not apply to Sanitary and Phytosanitary Measures (*see* Section D4 below).

a. TBT Administration and Publication

Current Situation/Concern Raised by Other WTO Members	China Commitments/Confirmations
China had set up a TBT notification authority and two enquiry points which had been notified to the TBT Committee[68].	Upon accession, notices of adopted and proposed technical regulations, standards and conformity assessment procedures *would be published*. The names of the publications where this information could be found *would be included* in China's Statement of Implementation and Administration under Article 15.2 of the *TBT Agreement*, which would be submitted upon accession.

---

[66]Article XVI of *GATT 1994* on "Subsidies".

[67]*Annex 3 to the TBT Agreement.*

[68]A committee was established pursuant to Article 13 of the *TBT Agreement* composing of representatives from each of the Members for the purpose of affording Members the opportunity of consulting on any matters relating to the operation of the *TBT Agreement* or the furtherance of its objectives, and shall carry out such responsibilities as assigned to it under the *TBT Agreement* or by the Members.

b. Technical Regulations and Standards[69]

Current Situation/Concern Raised by Other WTO Members	China Commitments/Confirmations
Internal Mechanisms	
Technical Regulations and Standards	Further to China's implementation of WTO provisions, internal mechanisms *would exist*, upon accession, to inform and consult with, on an ongoing basis, government agencies and ministries (at national and sub-national levels), and private sector interests on the rights and obligations under the *GATT 1994* and the *TBT Agreement*.
Opportunity for public consultation and comment on proposed standards and technical regulations	
	Upon accession, China's procedures *would clearly indicate* that opportunity for public consultation and comment existed and that comments would be given due consideration regardless of origin.
	Also upon accession, China *would have in place* minimum timeframes for allowing public comment on proposed technical regulations, standards and conformity assessment procedures as set out in the *TBT Agreement* and relevant decisions and recommendations adopted by the TBT Committee.
Harmonization Of Existing Standards With International Technical Standards	
There were concerns in obtaining information on: i. the extent to which international standards were used as the basis for existing Chinese standards as well as the basis for new standards; and	With China's efforts in restructuring government agencies, China *would*, not later than four months after accession, *notify* acceptance of the Code of Good Practice.[70] For government standardizing bodies, a clear policy existed to periodically review existing standards,

---

[69]*Annex 1* to the *TBT Agreement* defines, for the purpose of the agreement: "Technical Regulation" as '*Document which lays down product characteristics or their related processes and production methods, including the applicable administrative provisions, with which compliance is mandatory. It may also include or deal exclusively with terminology, symbols, packaging, marking or labelling requirements as they apply to a product, process or production method*'; and "Standard" as '*Document approved by a recognized body, that provides, for common and repeated use, rules, guidelines or characteristics for products or related processes and production methods, with which compliance is not mandatory. It may also include or deal exclusively with terminology, symbols, packaging, marking or labelling requirements as they apply to a product, process or production method.*'
[70]*Supra* note 67

ii. details on China's plans for reviewing existing standards so as to harmonize them with relevant international standards. Current situation: China is a full member of ISO, IEC and ITU and China actively participated in the development of relevant international standards.	*inter alia,* to harmonize them with relevant international standards where appropriate. Furthermore, China *would speed up* its process of revising the current voluntary national, local and sectoral standards so as to harmonize them with international standards.

The Use Of Relevant International Standards as Basis of Existing Standards

There were concerns: 1. that China did not use relevant and available international standards as the basis for some of its existing technical regulations; and also 2. on whether China has any plans for using international standards as the basis for new technical regulations and whether there are plans to review existing standards for purpose of harmonization with international standards. Current situation: Since 1980, as a basic policy of accelerating industrial modernization and promoting economic growth, China had been actively adopting international standards as the basis for technical regulations. As a result of China's efforts in the past 20 years, the use of international standards as the basis for technical regulations had increased from 12 per cent to 40 per cent.	China *confirmed* that: under the policy of active adoption of international standards as basis for technical regulations, technical regulations were reviewed every five years, *inter alia,* to ensure that international standards were used in accordance with the provision of *TBT Agreement* (except when such international standards or relevant parts would be ineffective or inappropriate means for fulfilling the legitimate objectives pursued, according to Article 2.4 of the Agreement). China *would provide* this policy as part of its notification under the *TBT Agreement.*[71] China had begun formulating a standardization development programme to meet the requirements of the *TBT Agreement* and had undertaken to further increase the use of international standards as the basis for technical regulations by 10 per cent in five years. China *would also make publicity available* procedures to implement the obligations under the Agreement as to the acceptance of equivalent technical regulations of other Member.[72]

---

[71]The *TBT Agreement*, Article 15.2: Each Member shall, promptly after the date on which the WTO Agreement enters into force for it, inform the Committee [of TBT] of measures in existence or taken to ensure the implementation or administration of this Agreement. Any changes of such measures thereafter shall also be notified to the Committee on TBT.

[72]The *TBT Agreement,* Article 2.7: Members shall give positive consideration to accepting as equivalent technical regulations of other Members, even if these regulations differ from their own, provided that they are satisfied that these regulations adequately fulfill the objectives of their own regulations.

Government Bodies in-charged	
China was requested to identify local government bodies, directly below the central government level, and non-governmental organizations, that were authorized to adopt techinical regulations or conformity assessment procedures.	Upon accession, china *would provide* a list of relevant local governmental and non-governmental bodies that were authorized to adopt technical regulations or conformity assessment procedures as part of its notification under Article 15.2 of the *TBT Agreement.*[73]
Terminology of "Technical Standards"	
There was concern that China's use of the terms "technical regulations" and "standards" was not always consistent with the definitions found in the *TBT Agreement,*[74] e.g., China sometimes used the word "standards" to refer to mandatory requirement that fell within the definition of "technical regulations". Also, China had developed a number of different types of measures, referred to as "standards", at levels other than the central government, in particular, regional, sectoral, and enterprise levels.	China would use the terms "technical regulations" and "standards" according to their meanings under the *TBT Agreement*[75] in its notifications under *TBT Agreement* and in publications referenced therein.

c. *Conformity Assessment Procedures*[76]

Current Situation/Concern Raised by Other WTO Members	China Commitments/Confirmations
Information on Conformity Assessment Procedures	
China was asked for information about: 1. The extent to which international guides and recommendations were	China *would use* relevant guides or recommendations issued by international standardizing bodies as the basis for new conformity

---

[73]*supra note* 71.

[74]*supra* note 69 for definitions.

[75]*ibid.*

[76]*ibid, Annex 1*, defines "Conformity assessment procedures" as '*Any procedure used, directly or indirectly, to determine that relevant requirements in technical regulations or standards are fulfilled.*'

used as the basis for existing conformity assessment procedures;

2. details on China's plans for using such guides and recommendations as the basis for new conformity procedures; and

3. details on China's plans for reviewing existing conformity assessment procedures so as to harmonize them with relevant international guides and recommendations. Current situation: China stated that it played a full part in the preparation by appropriate international standardizing bodies of guides and recommendations for conformity assessment procedures, e.g., as a full member of ISO CASCO. [ISO Committee on Conformity Assessment]

assessment procedures in accordance with the *TBT Agreement*.[77]

Existing conformity assessment procedures were reviewed concurrently with and under the same policy as related technical regulations, *inter alia*, to ensure the use of relevant international guides or recommendations in accordance with the *TBT Agreement*.

Upon accession, China *would ensure* that the *same* conformity assessment procedures were applied to both imported and domestic products.

Duplicative or multiple conformity assessment procedures

Concerning about the complexity and inconsistency of China's conformity assessment regime with *TBT Agreement* requirements, in particular, conformity assessment on imported and domestic products was not performed by the same governmental entities and that this situation could result in less favourable treatment for imports.

China stated that:

The State General Administration of the People's Republic of China for Quality Supervision and Inspection and Quarantine ("AQSIQ") was responsible for all policies and procedures related to conformity assessment in China. Other government ministries and agencies developed conformity assessment policies and procedures but that these had to be authorized by AQSIQ before they could be enacted.

China *would not maintain* multiple or duplicative conformity assessment procedures, nor would it impose requirements exclusively on imported products.

---

[77]The *TBT Agreement*, Article 5.4: Member to ensure central government bodies use them [relevant guides and recommendations issued by international standardizing bodies] as a basis for their conformity assessment procedures, unless they are inappropriate for the Members concerned for reasons such as national security requirements, protection of human health or safety etc.

Inconsistency of Chinese law with WTO obligations	
There was concern about the consistency of the *Law of the People's Republic of China on Import-Export Commodity Inspection*[78] and its implementing regulations with the *TBT Agreement*. In particular, provisions for technical regulations and conformity assessment procedures did not adequately address fundamental obligations such as transparency, non-discrimination, national treatment, and the avoidance of unnecessary barriers to trade. For example, the 'Statutory Inspection', and the 'Safety Licence System for Import Commodities' ("the System")[79] described under the above-mentioned laws and the implementing regulations, were inconsistent with the principle of national treatment and constituted an unnecessary obstacle to international trade. For instance, frequent plant inspections are required under the System for imports.	China *would bring* the Law and Implementing Regulations, as well as other relevant legislation and regulations, into conformity with the *TBT Agreement* by the date of accession. For technical regulations and conformity assessment procedures related to goods currently subject to the Safety Licence System for Impoprt Commodities, relevant legislation and regulations *would be brought* into full conformity with *the TBT Agreement* by the date of accession. China *confirmed* to eliminate unnecessary barriers to trade, again, China *committed* that it *would not maintain* multiple or duplicative conformity assessment procedures, nor would it impose requirements exclusively on imported products.
Confidentiality of Information	
With respect to the confidentiality of information in connection with conformity assessment procedures undertaken by China	China *would fully implement* the obligations of the *TBT Agreement* in the confidentiality of information in connection with conformity assessment procedures; and *would also respect* in the same way as for domestic products the confidentiality of

[78]First adopted at the Sixth Meeting of the Standing Committee of the Seventh National People's Congress on 21 February 1989 and promulgated by Order No 14 of the President of the People's Republic of China on 21 February 1989 and effective as of 1 August 1989; amendment to the law was adopted and promulgated by the Decision of the Standing Committee of the National People's Congress on 28 April 2002 and will come into force on 1 October 2002.

[79]Articles 4,5,6 of the *Law of the People's Republic of China on Import-Export Commodity Inspection* and Articles 4,5,9 of its implementation regulations concern "statutory inspection"; Articles 22 of the law concerns "safety licence system for import commodities", and Articles 38 of its implementation regulations concern "safety and hygiene". *See* clauses 188, 189 of the Working Party Report. [*Ed note:* the Articles number quoted in the Working Party Report for the *Law of the People's Republic of China on Import-Export Commodity Inspection* refers to the law enacted in 1989].

	information about products from WTO Members arising from or supplied in connection with such conformity assessment procedures.[80]

Accepting Results of Conformity Assessment by Other WTO Members

There was concern about China's practice of not accepting the results of conformity assssment by bodies in other WTO Members.	Products certified by bodies recognized by China *would require* no additional conformity assessment procedures in China, except for random sampling of said products.
It was noted that Article 6.1 of the *TBT Agreement* describes the obligation of unilateral acceptance of the results of conformity assessment. China was requested to make public and update on an ongoing basis information on conformity assessment bodies that were recognized by China.	Furthermore, where random sampling was undertaken and China's test results differed from the test results of competent bodies in other WTO Members, China *would act* in accordance with existing international guidelines and recommendations, or *would provide* a process of review with the objective of resolving such differences.
	China *would provide* on an ongoing basis information on conformity assessment bodies that were recognized by China.

Operation of foreign-invested conformity assessment bodies

There was concern that China should not maintain requirements for foreign and joint-venture conformity assessment bodies that had the effect of acting as barriers to their operations. All such conformity assessment bodies that met China's requirements should be eligible for accreditation and accorded national treatment.	As for foreign and joint-venture conformity assessment bodies, China *would not maintain* requirements which had the effect of acting as barriers to their operation, unless otherwise specified in China's Schedule of Specific Commitments.[81]
	China *confirmed* that the accreditation requirements *would be* transparent and provide national treatment to foreign conformity assessment bodies.

Specific Concerns

Regarding such matters as:	China *would implement* the following measures *prior to* accession *unless* otherwise indicated:
(a) registration of initial imports of chemical products,	(a) Registration of Initial Imports of Chemical Products

---

[80]The *TBT Agreement*, Article 5.2.4: "the confidentiality of information about products originating in the territories of other Members arising from or supplied in connection with such conformity assessment procedures is respected in the same way for domestic products and in such a manner that legitimate commercial interests are protected;"

[81]*See Chapter 3* and *Appendix 3 of this book* for *China's Schedule.*

(b) procedures to obtain and apply "CCIB" safety mark and the "Great Wall" mark, (c) automobiles and parts, and (d) the safety and quality licence system for boilers and pressure vessels.	New law and regulations *would be enacted and implemented one year after accession* regarding assessment and control of chemical for the protection of the environment to ensure complete national treatment and full consistency with international practice. "Inventory chemicals" (annexed to the new law and regulations) *would be exempted* from a registration obligation. A unified assessment procedure *would be established* for domestic and imported products. (b) CCIB safety Mark and the "Great Wall" Mark *Unify* the existing certification marks, i.e., the "CCIB" mark and the "Great Wall" mark into a new certification mark. Simplify the procedures for obtaining such a mark. For like imported and domestic goods, all bodies and agencies *would issue* the same mark and charge the same fee. Importers *would require* no more than three months to obtain both marks regarding the same products. *Accepting* testing reports for products subject to the Internationsal Electrotechnical Commission's System for Conformity Testing to Standards for Safety of Electrical Equipment ("IECEE CB Scheme"). (c) Automobiles and Parts *Unify* its laws, regulations and standards applied to domestic and imported automobiles and parts. To establish a transparent system of laws, standards and implementation regulations to ensure that national treatment be accorded to imported products. (d) Safety and Quality Licence System for Boilers and Pressure Vessels Imported products are accorded with same treatment as domestic products in conformity assessment procedure and inspection requirement. Internaional standards are adopted as the basis for technical regulations.

Conformity with TBT *Agreement*	
	All in all, China *confirmed* that, except as otherwise specified in *the Protocol*, China would apply all obligations under the *TBT Agreement* from the date of accession.

D4. Sanitary and Phytosanitary Measures ("SPS") Protocol Ref: S7(2), S14

The relative WTO Agreement is *the **Agreement on the Application of Sanitary and Phytosanitary Measures** ("SPS Agreement")* which entered into force with the establishment of the WTO on 1 January 1995. The *SPS Agreement* is part of the agricultural agreement package. It sets out the basic rules for food safety and animal and plant health standards. It allows Member countries to set their own standards. But it also says regulations must be based on science. The regulations should be applied only to the extent necessary to protect human, animal or plant life or health. And they should not arbitrarily or unjustifiably discriminate between countries where identical or similar conditions prevail. Members countries are encouraged to use international standards, guidelines and recommendations where they exist. The Agreement still allows countries to use different standards and different methods of inspecting products.

Current Situation/Concern Raised by Other WTO Members	China Commitments/Confirmations
The use of sanitary and phytosanitary procedures as non-tariff barriers	
In relation to the use by China of sanitary and phytosanitary procedures as non-tariff barriers and in some specific instances China's measures were not consistent with the *SPS Agreement of* WTO. WTO Members sought assurance from China that it would only use SPS measures to the extent necessary to protect human, animal or plant life or health, and that such measures would be based fully on scientific principles.	China stated that pursuant to the provisions of the *SPS Agreement,* China applied SPS measures only to the extent necessary to protect the life and health of human beings, animals and plants. Most of China's SPS measures were based on international standards, guidelines and recommendations. China *would not apply* SPS measures in a manner, which would act as a disguised restriction on trade. In accordance with the *SPS Agreement*, China *would ensure* that SPS measures would not be maintained without sufficient scientific evidence.
Conformity with WTO Obligations	
There was the opinion that China should comply with the *SPS Agreement* from the date of its accession, and should ensure	China *would fully comply* with the *SPS Agreement* and *would ensure* the conformity with *the SPS Agreement* of all of its laws, regulations,

conformity with the *SPS Agreement* of all its laws, regulations, decrees, requirements and procedures relating to SPS measures.	decrees, requirements and procedures relating to SPS measures from the date of accession. China had set up an SPS notification authority and an SPS enquiry point[82] which would be notified to the SPS Committee.[83] SPS measures, including those relating to inspection, had been published in publications such as the MOFTEC Gazette. Information could also be gathered from the SPS notification authority or from China's SPS enquiry point.

D5. Trade-Related Investment Measures ("TRIMs")   Protocol Ref: S7(3)

The *Agreement on Trade-Related Investment Measures* was one of the multilateral agreements on trade in goods negotiated in the Uruguay Round and applies only to measures that affect trade in goods. It prohibits trade-related investment measures that have trade-restrictive and distorting effects. It states that no Member shall apply a measure that is prohibited by the provisions of national treatment or quantitative restrictions under *GATT 1994*. Examples of inconsistent measures include local content, or trade balancing requirements etc. The Agreement contains transitional arrangements allowing Members to maintain notified TRIMs for a limited time following the entry into force of the WTO (which shall be eliminated within 2 years for developed countries, 5 years for developing countries and seven years for least-developed countries.) The Agreement also establishes a Committee on TRIMs to monitor the operation and implementation of these commitments.

a. Compliance with Agreement on TRIMs

China's Commitments/Confirmations
Upon accession, China *would comply* fully with the *TRIMs Agreement,* without recourse to Article 5 [84] thereof:

---

[82]Both SPS notification authority and SPS enquiry point are requirement under *Annex B* of the *SPS Agreement.*
[83]The SPS Committee was established pursuant to Article 12 of the *SPS Agreemennt* to provide a regular forum for consultations. It carries out functions necessary to implement the provisions of the *SPS Agreement* and the furtherance of its objectives, in particular to harmonization [of Members' sanitary or phytosanitary measures with international standards, guides or recommendations.]
[84]Article 5 of *TRIMs* on "Notification and Transitional Arrangements": Article 5.1 concerns notification of trade-related investment measures that are inconsistent with *TRIMs Agreement;* Article 5.2 concerns transitional period to eliminate inconsistent measures; Article 5.3 concerns possible extension of transitional period for developing country to be considered by the Council For Trade in Goods; Article 5.4 precludes Members from modifying the terms of measures as notified under 5.1; Article 5.5 is a standstill requirement, Member may apply *TRIMs* to new investment during the transitional period under Article 5.2.

A) China *would eliminate*:
  i) foreign-exchange balancing requirements;
  ii) trade balancing requirements;
  iii) local content requirements;
  iv) export performance requirements.

Chinese authorities *would not enforce* the terms of contracts containing such requirements.

B) Also, the allocation, permission or rights for importation and investment *would not be*:
  i. *conditional* upon performance requirements set by national or sub-national authorities; or
  ii. *subject to* secondary conditions covering, for example, the conduct of research, the provision of offsets or other forms of industrial compensation,[85] the use of local inputs or the transfer of technology.
C) China *would grant* permission to invest, import licences, quotas and tariff rate quotas without regard to the existence of competing Chinese domestic suppliers.

China *would respect* the freedom of contract of enterprises, consistent with its obligations under the *WTO Agreement* and *the Protocol*.

b. Commitments in the Automotive Industry

China Commitments/Confirmations

1. China *confirmed* that the government's Industrial Policy for the Automotive Sector *would be amended* to ensure compatibility with WTO rules and principles.

2. Amendments *would be made to ensure* that all measures applicable to motor vehicle producers restricting the categories, types or models of vehicle permitted for production, *would* gradually *be lifted*. Such measures *would be* completely *removed* two years after accession, thus ensuring that motor vehicle producers *would be free* to choose the categories, types and models they produced.[86]

3. China also *agreed to raise* the approval limit at level of provincial governments in approving investments in motor vehicle manufacturing:

Time frame	Limit
Current	US$30 million
one year after accession	US$60 million
two years after accession	US$90 million
four years after accession	US$150 million

4. With respect to the manufacture of motor vehicle engines, China *agreed to remove* the 50 per cent foreign equity limit for joint-ventures upon accession.

---

[85]Including specified types or volumes of business opportunities, paragraph 201 of the Working Party Report.
[86]However, it was understood that category authorizations by the government could continue to distinguish between trucks and buses, light commercial vehicles, and passenger cars (including multi-purpose vehicles and sport utility vehicles), *see* clause 203 of the Working Party Report.

D6. State Trading Entities   Protocol Ref: S6, Annex 2A

Article XVII of the GATT 1994 is the principal Article dealing with state trading enterprises (referred to as "STEs") and their operations.[87] It sets out that such enterprises – in their purchases or sales involving either imports or exports – are to act in accordance with the general principles of non-discrimination, and that commercial considerations only are to guide their decisions on imports and exports. It also instructs that Members are to notify their state trading enterprises to the WTO annually. Paragraph 1 of *the **WTO Understanding on the Interpretation of Article XVII*** gives working definition of a state trading enterprise as the following:

"Governmental and non-governmental enterprises, including marketing boards, which have been granted exclusive or special rights or privileges, including statutory or constitutional powers, in the exercise of which they influence through their purchases or sales the level or direction of imports or exports."

Particularly important in this definition is the phrase "in the exercise of which they influence … the level or direction of imports or exports", as this goes to the heart of what the regulation of state trading in the WTO is aimed at – that is, the potentially distorting effects on trade of the operations of state trading enterprises. Conversely, the WTO does not seek to prohibit or even discourage the establishment or maintenance of state trading enterprises, but merely to ensure that they are not operated in a manner inconsistent with WTO principles and rules.

Notification requirement does not apply to what is termed "government procurement", i.e. imports of products for immediate or ultimate consumption in governmental use, and this is specified in both of the above legal texts. (Government procurement is regulated by the Agreement on Government Procurement for those Members which are parties to it.)

The substantive obligations of Members under the rules governing state trading can be summarized in the following four points: (1) non-discrimination, commonly referred to as "most favoured naion" or "MFN" treatment; (2) no quantitative restrictions; (3) preservation of the value of tariff concessions; and (4) transparency.

---

[87]In addition to the core provisions in Article XVII of *GATT 1994* and *the WTO Understanding on the Interpretation of Article XVII,* a number of other GATT Articles deal with state trading in one way or another: The Interpretative Note to Articles XI (General Elimination of Quantitative Restrictions), XII (Restrictions to Safeguard the Balance of Payments), XIII (Non-discriminatory Administration of Quantitative Restrictions), XIV (Exceptions to the Rule of Non-discrimination) and XVIII (Governmental Assistance to Economic Development) states that throughout these Articles, the terms "import restrictions" of "export restrictions" include restrictions made effective through state trading operations.

a. Non-transparent activities of State Trading Enterprises

Current Situation/Concern Raised by Other WTO Members	China Commitments/Confirmations
Examples of such activities that were not in accordance with WTO obligations: — the import purchasing practices and procedures of state trading enterprises were not fully transparent and in compliance with the requirements of the *WTO Agreement*; — measures were taken to influence or direct state trading enterprises as to quantity, value, or country of origin of goods purchased or sold; these measures should only be taken in accordance with WTO requirements; — in case of exported goods [under state trading], the domestic procurement prices, contract terms for delivery and financing terms and conditions were not sufficiently disclosed. China should notify such information pursuant to *GATT 1994* and the *Understanding on the Interpretation of Article XVII of GATT 1994*. China should also undertake to ensure all state enterprises complied with the requirements of *WTO Agreement*.	China stated that its state trading enterprises had full management autonomy and reaponsibility for their own profits and losses. China had notified by providing a list of products subject to state trading in *Annex 2A of the Protocol*.[88] Information on state trading enterprises, as required to be disclosed under WTO Agreement or *the Protocol*, *would be supplied,* and *would not be withheld* on grounds of confidentiality.[89]

---

[88]*supra* note 2.

[89]Clause 333 of the Working Party Report states China would not withhold information required to be disclosed under *WTO Agreement* or *the Protocol* on grounds of confidentiality unless in circumstances specified in *the Protocol*, for instance, for laws, regulations or other measures involving national security; or that disclosure would demonstrably prejudice the legitimate commercial interests of particular enterprises, private or public.

b. Non-State Traders

Current Situation/Concern Raised by Other WTO Members	China Commitments/Confirmations
Annual allocations of import quantities for fertilizers and crude and porcessed oil.	China *confirmed* that imports allocated to non-state traders of crude and processed oil, as specified in Annex 2A *of the Protocol,*[90] *would be carried over* to the next year if they were not fully utilized.
There are certain specific arrangements that applied differently to non-state traders for instance, state enterprises trading in fertilizers are obliged to carry over to the next year any unused import quantities.	In addition, China *would publish,* on a quarterly basis, the requests for imports that had been made by non-state traders, as well as the licences granted, and *would supply* information relevant to such traders upon request.
Also, China should assure that for oil products, quantities, reserved for non-traders would be allocated in such a manner that they would be fully utilized.	As to imports for production purposes, China *confirmed* that notwithstanding Section 5(1) of *the Protocol,*[91] non-state trading enterprises, including private enterprises, *would still be permitted* to import for production purposes, goods subject to state trading or designated trading, and that national treatment would be provided to such imports.
Import Goods for Production Purposes	
Prior to accession, some enterprises in China were permitted to import goods for their production purpose, included those products permissible under State Trading.	

c. Supplies of Raw Materials in the Textiles Sector

Current Situation/Concern Raised by Other WTO Members	China Commitments/Confirmations
There was concern about supplies of raw materials in the textiles sector, and particularly in regard to supplies of silk, in the light of China's position as the major world supplier of silk. Currently silk export is subject to state trading rights.	China *confirmed* that China *would progressively abolish* the system of state trading in respect of silk. Measures would be introduced to increase and extend trading rights, with the result that: 1. China *would remove* completely silk as set out in numbers 10 and 11 in the list of products subject to state trading on exports;[92] and

---

[90]*supra* note 2.

[91]Section 5(1) of *the Protocol* stipulates that China would progressively liberalize the availability and scope of the right to trade in all goods within 3 years after accession *except* for those goods subject to state trading.

[92]*Annex 2A2 to the Protocol* (list of products subject to state trading on exports).

	2. China *would grant* the right to trade in such products to all individuals and enterprises no later than *1 January 2005*. Pending the implementation of this right, China *undertook not to introduce* any changes of a more restrictive nature to the existing structures in place for the supply of silk. China further *confirmed* that the conditions for access to supplies of raw materials in the textiles sector *would be the same* for foreign and domestic users; access to supplies of raw materials as enjoyed under existing arrangements *would not be* adversely affected following China's accession.

d. Trade-Distorting Effect of Current Imports of Agricultural Commodities into China

Current Situation/Concern Raised by Other WTO Members	China Commitments/Confirmations
There was concern that domestic prices for most agricultural commodities in China were higher than world prices, and this differential allowed China's state trading enterprises to import at low prices and then mark up the price when selling the product to wholesalers and end-users. There was further concern that this practice could become more widespread when access opportunities were created under TRQ[93], hence resulting in a trade-distorting effect because mark-ups could be used to reduce the competitiveness of imported products and limit the range of qualities and grades available to end-users in China.	China stated that: currently state-trading enterprises did not mark up imported products; instead, they only charged a nominal transaction fee which limit was set under China's law. Consequently, China's practice was consistent with WTO obligations, did not result in any trade-distorting effect. China *would ensure* that no price increase in respect to imports, in particular by state trading enterprises, *would result* in protection beyond that allowed in its Schedule of Concessions and Commitments on Goods[94] or that was not otherwise justified under WTO rules.

[93]See B7 of this Chapter.
[94]*Supra* note 6.

D7. Special Economic Areas   **Protocol Ref: S2(A)(B)**

General situation:

China stated that since 1979 China had established a number of special economic areas where more open policies were applied. They included five SEZs, 14 open coastal cities, six open cities along the Yangtze River, 21 provincial capital cities and 13 inland boundary cities. Those special economic areas enjoyed greater flexibility in utilizing foreign capital, introducing foreign technology and conducting economic cooperation overseas. At present, foreign investors were entitled to certain preferential treatment.

FIEs located in SEZs or the Economic and Technical Development Zones of open coastal cities were entitled to a corporate income tax rate of 15 per cent (the normal tax was 33 per cent). Profits remitted abroad by foreign investors were exempted from income tax. The preferential income tax rate of 15 per cent was applicable to technology-intensive or knowledge-intensive items or projects with foreign investment of over US\$30 million, as well as enterprises that operated in the fields of energy, transport and port construction.

Throughout the customs territory of China, a socialist market economy system was applied. In 1999, the foreign trade volume of SEZs accounted for nearly one fifth of the nation's total. The national laws and regulations on taxation were applicable to SEZs in a uniform manner.

a. Non-discriminatory treatment in application of tax and import policies for goods imported from special economic areas

Current Situation/Concerns Raised by Other WTO Members	China Commitments/Confirmations
There were further requests for information on products imported from special economic areas into the other parts of the customs territory of China. And that China should take steps to ensure that all products so imported would be subject to the same normal customs duties and charges as any other product imported into the customs territory of China. There was also concern that China should notify the WTO of all the relevant laws, regulations and other measures relating to its special economic	1. China indicated that there was no plan to establish any new SEZs. *The special preferential tariff policies applied to SEZs had been eliminated.* With the development of China's economic reform and opening up, China *would implement* its tariff policy uniformly throughout its customs territory. For imported products introduced from these special economic areas into other parts of China's customs territory, China *undertake* to ensure non-discriminatory treatment in application of all taxes, import restrictions and customs duties and other charges as that normally applied to imports into the other parts of China's customs territory.

areas and any additions, modifications thereof. Notification should list and identify all those special economic areas.	2. China *would strengthen* the uniform enforcement of taxes, tariffs and non-tariff measures on trade between its special economic areas and the other parts of China's customs territory. Statistics on trade between China's special economic areas and the other parts of its customs territory *would be* maintained and improved, and would be notified to the WTO on a regular basis.
	3. China *would provide* information in its notifications describing how the special trade, tariff, and tax regulations applied were limited to the designated special economic areas, including information concerning their enforcement.
	4. Any preferential arrangements provided to foreign invested enterprises located within the special economic areas *would be provided* on a non-discriminatory basis.

b. Uniform Administration of the Trade Regime

Current Situation/Concern Raised by Other WTO Members	China Commitments/Confirmations
As to whether the assistance provided to minority autonomous regions and other areas of economic poverty was consistent with WTO requirements.	China *confirmed* that China had a clear commitment to uniform administration of the trade regime within each such area and that, upon acession, China *would ensure* that such assistance would be implemented consistent with WTO obligations.

D8. Transit

The current regulation of transit in China, *the Regulations of the Customs of the People's Republic of China on the Supervision and Administration of Transit Goods,* was consistent with Article V of the *GATT 1994*.[95] There was no specific commitment made here.

---

[95]Article V of *GATT 1994* concerns freedom of transit.

D9. Agricultural Policies   **Protocol Ref: S7(2), S12, Annex 8**

(also *see* D6.d Trade-Distorting Effect of Current Imports of Agricultural Commodities into China)

The relative WTO agreement concluded and included in the Final Act of the Uruguay Round of Multilateral Trade Negotiation is the ***Agreement of Agriculture*** ("*The Agricultural Agreement*"). The long term objective of *the Agricultural Agreement* is to establish a fair and market-oriented agricultural trading system. This objective is to provide for substantial progressive reductions in agricultural support and protection sustained over an agreed period of time, resulting in correcting and preventing restricting and distortions in world agricultural markets. This would improve predictability and security for importing and exporting countries alike.

The Agricultural Agreement includes specific commitments by WTO Member governments to improve market access and reduce trade-distorting subsidies in agriculture, such as domestic support through government measures ("domestic support measures") and export subsidies; and to reaching an agreement on sanitary and phytosanitary issues.

Tariff reductions for agricultural products are specified in the national schedule of a Member country forming part of the Member's schedule of concessions and commitments of goods. The committed tariffs and tariff quota covering all agricultural products took effect in 1995. It was agreed that developed countries would cut the tariffs (the higher out-of-quota rates in case of tariff-quotas) by an average of 36 per cent, in equal rates over six years (24 per cent cuts over 10 years.) These commitments are being implemented over a six-year period (10 years for developing countries) that began in 1995.

There were numerical targets for implementing the Agreement's objective in cutting subsidies and protection. Only the figures for cutting export subsidies in *the Agricultural Agreement.* As for domestic support, there are two categories—support of trade-distorting effect[96] or support that do not fit into any of the exempt categories are subject to the rules of *the Agricultural Agreement* and reduction commitments. On the other hand, support with no or minimal trade-distorting effect and those measures qualified for exemption are not subject to reduction.[97] The *Agricultural Agreement* sets out a number of general and measure-specific criteria which, when met, allow measures to be exempted from reduction commitments (so called "Green Box Measures"). Domestic support measures that have no, or minimal distorting effect on trade is one kind of such Measures. The reduction committed by Members are also

---

[96]Such as those favouring agricultural producers, say market price support measures, direct production subsidies or input subsidies.

[97]*See Annex 2* to the *Agricultural Agreement* on "Domestic Support: The Basis for Exemption from the Reduction Commitments".

specified in their national schedules and are expressed in terms of a 'Total Aggregate Measurement of Support' ("Total AMS").[98] These scheduled Total AMS limit are bound, i.e. cannot be exceeded. Members with a Total AMS have to reduce base period (1986-88) support by 20 per cent over 6 years starting in 1995 (developing countries members to reduce by 13 per cent over 10 years; least-developed countries do not need to make any cuts.)

The package on agricultural agreements also includes the **Agreement on Sanitary and Phytosanitary Measures** ("*SPS*" *Measures—see section D4*).

Current Situation/Concerns Raised by other WTO Members	China Commitments/Confirmations
Restrictive practices and policies for imports	
Nothing that China is a country with a vast agricultural base, as well as a vast population, agricultural security and food security in particular, was an issue of supreme importance. China based its policies on domestic agricultural supply, especially on balanced supply and demand of grains. Meanwhile, China actively sought internatinal resources as a necessary supplement. There were concerns about China's linkage of import policies for agriculture, including TRQ allocations, to domestic production policy and the sub-national supply and utilization situation. Those Members requested that China undertake an appropriate commitment to eliminate these practices.	China *confirmed* that China would base import policies for agriculture on commercial considerations only.
Removal of Restrictions on Imports	
There was concern in relation to administrative guidance provided at the national and sub-national level, which	Consistent with China's commitment to uniform administration, by the date of accession, China *would not maintain, resort or revert* to guidance

---

[98]*Total AMS* covers all support provided on either a product-specific or non-product specific basis that does not qualify for exemption and is to be reduced by 20 per cent (13.3 per cent for developing countries, with no reduction for least-developed countries) during the implementation period (six-year in the case of developed countries and over ten years in the case of developing countries. Least-developed countries are not required to reduce their tariffs). *See* note 100 for explanation of "Aggregate Measurement of Support (AMS)".

could have the effect of influencing the quantity and composition of agricultural imports. To ensure the creation of effective market access opportunities for imported agricultural goods, China was requested to assure that agricultural and trade policies would not discriminate against imported products.	plans or administrative guidance at the national or sub-national level that regulate the quantity, quality or treatment of imports, or constitute import substitution practices or other non-tariff measures, including those maintained through state trading enterprises at the national or sub-national level.

Export Subsidies

There claimed to be export subsidies on certain agricultural products such as large stocks of grain and cotton inconsistent with other WTO obligations. These stocks were procured at relatively high prices by state-trading enterprises and exported at prices lower than the comparable price charged for the like product to buyers in the domestic markets. China was requested to ensure that all entities, including state trading enterprises at the national or sub-national level, operated in accordance with China's obligations, including those on export subsidies.	All entities in China, including state trading enterprises and any other state-affiliated, state-run, or state-controlled entity at the national or sub-national level, *would operate* in accordance with China's WTO obligations, including those on export subsidies. Further, national and sub-national authorities *would not provide* fund transfers or other benefits to any entities in China that would be inconsistent with its WTO obligations, including to offset losses accrued through exports. By the date of accession, China *would not maintain* or *introduce* any export subsidies on agricultural products.

Domestic Support Measures

	China *confirmed* that while China could provide domestic support measures of the type of Article 6.2 of *the Agriculture Agreement*,[99] the amount of such support *would be* included in China's calculation of its Aggregate Measurement of Support ("AMS")[100].

---

[99]This is the type of domestic support measures that should have been subject to reduction commitments were they not measures of a developing country member; hence, domestivc support measures meeting the criteria set in this article shall not be required to be included in the calculation of a Member country's current Total AMS (*see* note 98 for Total AMS).

[100]Aggregate Measurement of Support ("AMS") means the annual level of support provided by a Member government, expressed in monetary terms, for an agricultural product in favour of the producers of the basic agricultural product ('product-specific support'), or non-product-specific support provided in favour of agricultural producers in general, other than support provided under programmes that are qualified for exemption from tariff reductions under the *Agricultural Agreement*; i.e. AMS are in general subject to reduction commitments. *Also See Annex 3, Agricultural Agreement* for calculation of AMS.

	China's Total AMS[101] Commitment Level was set forth in Part IV, Section 1 of China's Schedule.[102]*****
	China *would have recourse* to a *de minimis* exemption for product-specific support equivalent to 8.5 per cent of the total value of production of a basic agricultural product during the relevant year, and a *de minimis* exemption for non-product-specific support of 8.5 per cent of the value of China's total agricultural production during the relevant year. Accordingly, these percentages would constitute China's *de minimis* exemption under Article 6.4 of the *Agriculture Agreement*.[103]
Matter to be further clarified	
There was concern that the domestic support tables of China in document WT/ACC/CHN/38/Rev.3 did provide a basis for supporting the commitments in China's Schedule but it still contained issues which required further methodological clarification relating to policy classification.	China *confirmed* that this clarification would be addressed in the context of China's notification obligations under the *Agriculture Agreement*.

*****China's concessions on agricultural tariffs, and commitments on domestic support and on export subsidies for agricultural products were contained in the *Schedule of Concessions and Commitments on Goods* which was annexed to *the Protocol* as *Annex 8*.

D10. Trade in Civil Aircraft

The relative WTO agreement is *the **Agreement on Trade in Civil Aircraft** ("the Agreement")* which was originally negotiated in the Tokyo Round and entered into force on 1 January 1980. This agreement is one of the remaining two agreements ("known as "plurilateral agreement")

---

[101]*Supra* note 98.

[102]Pursuant to Article 6.1 of the *Agricultural Agreement*, the commitments are expressed in terms of Total AMS and "Annual and Final Bound Commitments Levels".

[103]De minimis exemption—under Article 6.4 of the Agreement, there is a 5 per cent threshold for exempting reduction of support. There is no requirement to reduce trade-distorting domestic support in any year in which the aggregate value of the product-specific support does not exceed 5 per cent of the total value of production of the agricultural product in question. Also, non-product specific support which is less than 5 per cent of the value of total agricultural production is also exempt from reduction. The 5 per cent threshold applies to developed countries (in the case of developing countries the de minimis ceiling is 10 per cent). China's 8.5 per cent threshold is a midway figure between that of developing and developed countries.

that were not joined by all WTO Members. (The other one is *Agreement on Government Procurement.*) It now has 26 signatories.

The Agreement eliminates import duties on all aircraft, other than military aircraft, as well as on all other products covered by *the Agreement* — civil aircraft engines and their parts and components, all components and sub-assemblies of civil aircraft, and flight simulators and their parts and components. It contains disciplines on government-directed procurement of civil aircraft and inducements to purchase, as well as on government financial support for the civil aircraft sector.

Current Situation/Concern Raised by Other WTO Members	China Commitments/Confirmations
As to whether China is to join the *Agreement on Trade in Civil Aircraft.*	China indicated that China was not in a position to commit to joining the *Agreement on Trade in Civil Aircraft* at the present stage. China *would not impose* any provisions of offsets or other forms of industrial compensation when purchasing civil aircraft, including specified types or volumes of business opportunities.

D11. Textiles

The relative WTO agreement is the **Agreement on Textiles and Clothing** *("ATC Agreement")*. Textiles, like agriculture, is one of the hardest fought issues in the WTO, as it was in the formern *GATT* system. Its objective is to secure eventual integration of the textiles and clothing sector into the *GATT* on the basis of strengthened *GATT* rules and disciplines. Much of the trade was previously subject to bilateral quota negotiated under the Miltifibre Arrangement ("MFA"). The quota conflicted with *GATTs* general preference for customs tariffs instead of measures that restrict quantities. They were also exceptions to the *GATT* principle of treating all trading partners equally because they specified how much the importing country was going to accept from individual exporting countries.

Since 1995, the *ATC Agreement* has taken over from the MFA. It is now going through fundamental change under a 10-year schedule of integration agreed in the Uruguay Round. By 1 January, 2005, the sector is to be fully integrated into normal *GATT* rules. Integration means that trade in textiles and clothing sector will be governed by the general rules of *GATT*. In particular the system of import quotas that has dominated the trade since the early 1960s is being phased out, and importing countries will no longer be able to discriminate between exporters. The *ATC* will itself no longer exist: it is the only WTO agreement that has self-destruction built in.

The agreement states the percentage of products that have to be brought under *GATT* rules at stages. If any of these products came under quotas, then the quotas must be removed at the same time. The percentages are applied to the importing country's textiles and clothing trade levels in 1990. The agreement also says the quantities of imports permitted under the quotas should grow annually, and that the rate of expansion should increase at each stage. How fast that expansion should be is set out in a formula based on the growth rate that existed under the old Multifibre Arrangement.

China Commitments/Confirmations

China *accepted* that:
The quantitative restrictions maintained by WTO Members on imports of textiles and apparel products originating in China that were in force on the date prior to the date of China's accession should be notified to the Textiles Monitoring Body ("TMB") as being the base levels for the purpose of application of Articles 2 and 3 of the *ATC Agreement*.[104]

For such WTO Members that maintain quantitative restrictions, the phrase "day prior to the date of entry into force of the *WTO Agreement*", contained in Article 2.1 of the *ATC*, should be deemed to refer to the day prior to the date of China's accession. To these base levels, the increase in growth rates provided for in Articles 2.13 and 2.14 of the *ATC*[105] should be applied, as appropriate, from the date of China's accession.

China *agreed to apply* seven provisions to trade in textiles and clothing products until 31 December, 2008 and be part of the terms and conditions for China's accession. These provisions mainly provide for measures to be taken by WTO Member in face of market disruption by Chinese imports of textile and apparel products, such as:

— A WTO Member could request consultations with China to resolve the issue. The WTO Member so request was to provide a detailed statement of reasons and justifications together with data showing: 1) the existence of or threat of market disruptions and 2) the role of Chinese imports in that disruption.
— Such consultation would be held within 30 days of receipt of the request and a mutually satisfactory solution should be reached within 90 days of the receipt of the request.
— China were to hold shipments to the requesting Member with specified quantities[106] and if no solution could be reached during the 90-day consultation period, consultations would

---

[104]Footnote 4 of *ATC* defines "Restrictions" as to denote all unilateral quantitative restrictions, bilateral arrangements and other measures having a similar effect, such as quota. Articles 2 of *ATC* concerns integration of textile and clothing products into *GATT* by stages; Article 3 concerns requirements of notifications by Member the maintenance of restrictions on such products.

[105]For products not yet integrated into *GATT* and are still subject to MFA restrictions, the level of restraint [quantities of products brought under restrictions or quota] should be increased in three stages and at such growth rates as stipulated in Articles 2.13, 2.14 of *ATC*. In the case of China, the stages are referenced to the date of China's accession to WTO instead of the date of entry into force of the *WTO Agreement* as stipulated under Articles 2.13 and 2.14 of *ATC*.

[106]Clause 242(c) of the Working Party Report," …. China agreed to hold its shipments to the requesting Member of textile or textile products in the category or categories subject to these consultations to a level no greater than 7.5 per cent (6 per cent for wool product categories) above the amount entered during the first 12 months of the most recent 14 months preceding the month in which the request for consultation was made."

> continue and the restraint limit of shipment continues for textiles or textile products in the category or categories subject to these consultations; but the term of such restraint would last no longer than 12 months after request for consultations.
> — No action taken under these provisions would remain in effect beyond one year.
> — Measures could not be applied to the same product at the same time under this provision and the provisions of Section 16 of the *Protocol* (transitional product-specific safeguard mechanism).

D12. Measures Maintained Against China   Protocol Ref: S17, Annex 7

Whether to eliminate non-tariff measures maintained against China
As to whether WTO Members should eliminate all discriminatory non-tariff measures maintained against Chinese exports from the date of China's accession. Some Members held the opinion that such measures did not need to be phased out until such time as China's foreign trade regime fully conformed to WTO obligations.
Agreement Among WTO Members
It was agreed that any prohibitions, quantitative restrictions or other measures maintained against imports from China in a manner inconsistent with the WTO Agreement would be listed in *Annex 7 to the Protocol*.[107] It was further agreed that all such measures *would be phased out* or otherwise dealt with in accordance with mutually agreed terms and timetables as specified in Annex 7.

D13. Transitional Product-Specific Safeguards   Protocol Ref: S16

A. Market Disruption

"Safeguards for increased imports" in B14 of this Chapter is one of the safeguard measures generally available under the *Agreement on Safeguards*. Under the agreement, any WTO Member (including China) may adopt such safeguard to restrict imports of a product when the Member faces the threat of a surge in imports (irrespective of the origin) causing injury to its domestic market. Transitional safeguards in this section and S16 of *the Protocol* refer specifically to measures that may be undertaken by any WTO Members against a surge of imports from China, including any measures available under the *Agreement on Safeguards*. China particularly concerned that WTO Members provide due process and use objective criteria in determining the existence of market disruption or trade diversion.

---

[107]"Reservations by WTO Members — Prohibitions, Quantitative Restrictions, Other Measures Against Imports from China".

Commitments by WTO Members in Implementing Transitional Safeguards against Chinese Imports

With respect to implementation of the product-specific safeguard, section 16 of *the Protocol* included specific requirements that WTO Members needed to follow in connection with an action under that Section. Members of the Working Party on china Accession *confirmed* that in implementing the provisions on market disruption[108], WTO Members *would comply* with those provisions and to take measures such as the following:

An action to address market disruption would be taken only after an investigation by the importing WTO Member pursuant to procedures previously established and made available to the public.

The competent authority of the importing Member would *publish notice* in each of such occasions as:

i)   the commencement of any investigation under the product-specific safeguard provisions of the *Protocol*;

ii) any measure proposed to be taken;

iii) the decision to apply a measure including an explanation on the basis, scope and duration of the measure;

iv) the commencement of any proceeding to consider any extension of duration of an action;

and to hold a public hearing on each of such occasions for importers and exporters and other interested parties to present evidence and their views as to the appropriateness of whether or not to take a measure and to respond to the presentations of other parties;

In determining whether market disruption existed, the competent authorities of the importing WTO Member would consider *objective factors*, including (1) the volume of imports of the product which was the subject of the investigation; (2) the effect of imports of such product on prices in the importing WTO Member's market for the like or directly competitive products; (3) the effect of imports of such product on the domestic industry producing like or directly competitive products.

Except for good cause, no investigation under Section 16 of the *Protocol* on the same subject matter could be initiated less than one year after the completion of a previous investigation;

and that a WTO member would apply a measure only for such period of time as was necessary to prevent or remedy market disruption.

---

[108]Section 16(4) of *the Protocol:* "Market disruption shall exist whenever imports of an article, like or directly competitive with an article produced by the domestic industry, are increasing rapidly, either absolutely or relatively, so as to be a significant cause of material injury, or threat of material injury to the domestic industry......".

B. Trade Diversion　　　　　　　　　　　　　　　　**Protocol Ref: S16(8)**

Commitments by WTO Members

Trade diversion referred to an increase in imports from China of a product into a WTO Member as the result of an action by China or *other* WTO Members pursuant to paragraphs 2, 3 or 7 of Section 16 of *the Protocol*[109] [i.e. actions addressing market disruptions]. *The Protocol* required a determination that any trade diversion was significant and that the action taken [by China or other WTO Members] to address market disruption had caused or threatened to cause significant diversion of trade [into the market of the importing WTO Member]. Members of the Working Party agreed that *objective criteria* had to be applied in such determination. Among the factors to be examined were:

(a)　the actual or imminent increase in market share of imports from China in the importing WTO Member;

(b)　the nature or extent of the action taken or proposed by China or other WTO Members;

(c)　the actual or imminent increase in the volume of imports from China due to the action taken or proposed;

(d)　conditions of demand and supply in the importing WTO Member's market for the products at issue; and

(e)　the extent of exports from China to the WTO Member(s) applying a measure pursuant to paragraphs 2, 3 or 7 of Section 16 of *the Protocol*[110] and to the importing WTO Member.

A measure taken to address significant diversions of trade would be terminated not later than 30 days after the expiration of the action [addressing market disruption] taken by the WTO Member or Members involved against imports from China.

If the WTO Member or Members taking an action to address market disruption notified the WTO Committee on Safeguards of any modification of an action, the competent authorities of the WTO Member addressing trade diversion would determine whether a significant diversion of trade continued to exist and determine whether to modify, withdraw or keep in place the action taken.

---

[109]Section 16(2) of *the Protocol* says if it is agreed that Chinese imports are a cause to market disruption in an importing WTO Member, China shall take such action to prevent or remedy the market disruption; Section 16(3) provides that if consultations fail, the importing WTO Member shall be free to withdraw concessions or to limit Chinese imports to the extent to prevent or remedy market disruption; Section 16(7) provides that in critical circumstances, the WTO Member affected may take a provisional safeguard measure pursuant to a preliminary determination on market disruption. Actions taken under these provisions shall be notified to the Committee on Safeguards under WTO organization [established under Article 13(1) of WTO's *Agreement on Safeguards* under the authority of the Council for Trade in Goods].

[110]*ibid.*

chapter 3

China's Commitments on Trade in Services

I. INTRODUCTION TO GATS

What is *GATS*?

The General Agreement on Trade in Services ("GATS") was the first ever set of multilateral, legally enforceable rules covering international trade in services. It was negotiated in the Uruguay Round and formed part of the covered agreements of WTO.

The *GATS* establishes a set of rules and disciplines governing WTO Member countries' use of trade measures in services. Such measures consist of laws, regulations, administrative actions and decisions affecting the purchase, payment, or use of a service or the presence of foreign service suppliers. The *GATS* disciplines extend across all government levels, including non-governmental bodies in the exercise of delegated powers.[1]

Purpose of *GATS*

GATS creates a credible and reliable system of international trade rules; ensures a fair and equitable treatment of all participants (principle of non-discrimination); stimulates economic activity through guaranteed policy bindings; and promotes trade and development through progressive liberalization.

Framework of *GATS*

GATS comprises of the following elements:

1. the main text containing general principles and obligations that all members have to apply;
2. supplementary agreements in the form of annexes dealing with rules for specific sectors[2];

---

[1]Page 25, *Manual of Statistics in International Trade in Service*, edited by UN Statistics Division, final draft 6 September 2001 (first sighted on 18 January 2002 at web site: http://esa.un.org/unsd/tradeserv/docs/msits_ unedited010906.pdf; second sight in November 2002 at web site: http://unstats.un.org/unsd/tradeserv/docs/msits_unedited010906.pdf).

[2]These include: *Annex on Article II (Most-favoured-Nation) Exemption; Annex on Movement of Natural Persons supplying services under GATS; Annex on Air Transport Service; Annexes on Financial Services; Annex on Negotiations on Maritime Transport Service and Annexes on Telecommunication.*

3. individual countries' specific commitments to provide access to their markets ("national schedules"), schedule of commitment for each WTO Member was submitted which sets out commitments not to impose greater restrictions on the supply of services by other Members than that specified;

4. Lists attaching to national schedules of Members showing where countries are temporarily not applying the "most-favoured-nation" principle of non-discrimination ("List of Article II exemptions")[3];

5. Protocols on post-Uruguay sectoral negotiations.

All of the above forms an integral part of the *GATS* Agreement.

Protocols on Sectoral Negotiations

The results of sectoral negotiations (post-Uruguay Round Negotiations) are new specific commitments and/or most-favoured-nation exemptions related to the sector of service concerned. The new commitments and MFN exemptions have been incorporated into the existing Schedules and Exemption Lists by way of separate Protocols[4] to the *GATS*.

Progressive Liberalization

GATS promotes the liberalization of international trade in service. The Uruguay Round was only the beginning. On-going negotiations on commitments have taken place since the Uruguay Round. The goal is to take the liberalization process further by increasing the level of commitments in schedules. A full new services round will start no later than 2000.

Total Coverage

GATS covers all internationally traded services. Services *not* covered under *GATS* are:

1 services supplied in the exercise of governmental authority, that is, service which is supplied neither on a commercial basis, nor in competition with one or more service suppliers[5], for instance, social security schemes and such public service as health or education; and

---

[3]Article II:2 of the *GATS*.

[4]They are: *Second Protocol on Financial Services* adopted 21 July 1995, entered into force 1 September 1996; *Third Protocol on movement of natural persons adopted 21 July 1995, entered into force 30 January 1996; Fourth Protocol on Basic Communications* adopted 30 April 1997 entered into force 5 February 1998; *Fifth Protocol on Financial Services* adopted 14 November 1997, entered into force 1 March 1999.

[5]Clause 3, Article I of the *GATS*.

2   measures affecting air-traffic rights, or services directly related to the exercise of traffic rights, with certain exceptions.[6]

Definition of "Services"

A country's market access commitments with respect to a particular service sector may vary depending upon how the service is delivered. *GATS* does not give an all-embracing definition for trade in services. However, *GATS* distinguishes between four modes of supplying services[7]: cross-border trade, consumption abroad, commercial presence, and presence of natural persons.

i.   **Cross-border supply** is defined to cover services flows from the territory of one Member into the territory of another Member (e.g. banking or architectural services transmitted via telecommunications or mail);

ii.   **Consumption abroad** refers to situations where a service consumer (e.g. tourist or patient) moves into another Member's territory to obtain a service;

iii. **Commercial presence** implies that a service supplier of one Member establishes a territorial presence, including through ownership or lease of premises, in another Member's territory to provide a service (e.g. foreign banks setting up operations in a country); and

iv.   **Presence of natural persons** consists of persons of one Member entering the territory of another Member to supply a service (e.g. accountants, doctors or teachers). *The Annex on Movement of Natural Persons Supplying Services Under GATS* specifies, however, that Members remain free to operate measures regarding citizenship, residence or access to the employment market on a permanent basis.

Members' Commitments on Market-opening: Schedule of Commitments

Each WTO Member is required to have a Schedule of Specific Commitments ("national schedule") which identifies the services for which the Member guarantees market access and national treatment and any limitations that may be attached.

The degree of opening up market for a given sector or mode of service varies from country to country. Some members offer full competition in the market while others may deny any degree of market access. Typical market access limitations include restrictions on the legal form of establishment or in capital participation, setting ceiling for the number of service suppliers and their employees, limiting geographical presence of establishments.

While *GATS* requires all Members countries to submit a schedule, it does not obligate them to assume commitments in any sector. Members are free, subject to the results of their

---

[6]These exceptions are (i) aircraft repair and maintenance services; (ii) the selling and marketing of air transport services; (iii) computer reservation system (CRS) services, *See* clauses 2 and 3, *Annex on Air Transport Service, Annex to GATS*.

[7]Article I of the *GATS*.

negotiations with other participants, to identify which sectors, sub-sectors or activities they will list in their schedules, and it is only to these that the commitments apply.

The *GATS* requires WTO Members to ensure that the relevant standards, requirements, and procedures do not constitute unnecessary barriers to trade and, in particular, that they are not more burdensome than is necessary to ensure the quality of service.

Classification of Services Sectors

In the great majority of schedules the order in which the sectors are listed corresponds to the GATT Secretariat classification[8] which lists twelve broad sectors. *(See* Appendix 4)

1. Business services;
2. Communication services;
3. Construction and Related Engineering services
4. Distribution services;
5. Educational services;
6. Environmental services;
7. Financial services;
8. Health-related and Social services;
9. Tourism and Travel-related services;
10. Recreational, Cultural, and Sporting services;
11. Transport services;
12. "Other services not included elsewhere".

These sectors are sub-divided into sub-sectors or separate service activities. As an example, the tourism category breaks down into sub-sectors for hotels and restaurants, travel agencies and tour operators, and tourist guide services.

In most cases, the sectoral entries are accompanied by numerical references to the Central Product Classification system of the United Nations** which gives a detailed explanation of the services activities covered by each listed sector or sub-sector.

All commitments in a schedule are *bound* unless otherwise specified. Members are free to tailor the sector coverage and substantive content of such commitments as they see fit.

---

[8]In the Uruguay Round of multilateral trade negotiations, the *Provisional Central Product Classification* (superceded by *CPC* version 1.0, 1998) was used as a source by the Secretariat of the GATT in the preparation of the *GATS*. Under the *GATS* agreements, texts which had legal standing and which embodied extensive references to CPC were drafted. These were referred to by *GATS* as the "GNS/120 list" [MTN.GNS/W/120 list dated 10 July 1991]. *See Appendix 4 for 'Provisional Central Product Classification', UN Statistics Division*, web-address http://unstats.un.org/unsd/cr/registry/regcst.asp? CI = 9 & Lg = 1; *also see* note 15 of Chapter 1 of this book.

Sample of a national schedule[9]:

Sector or sub-sector	Limitations on market access	Limitations on national treatment	Additional commitments
I. HORIZONTAL COMMITMENTS			
All Sectors included in this schedule	Entries by Member any limitations in respect of a particular mode of supply notably *commercial presence* and *the presence of natural persons*	In respect of commercial presence	Positive undertakings if any
II SECTOR-SPECIFIC COMMITMENTS			
e.g. Distribution Services c. Retailing services (**CPU 631)	Entries by Member any limitations or offers for opening market access if any, in respect of: — cross-border supply; — consumption abroad; — commercial presence; — presence of natural persons	Entries by Member any limitations in respect of: — cross-border supply; — consumption abroad; — commercial presence; — presence of natural persons	Positive undertakings, if any

General Obligations under GATS

1. Most-favoured-nation treatment ("MFN")

Favour one, favour all. MFN means treating one's trading partners equally. Under *GATS,* if a country allows foreign competition in a sector, equal opportunities in that sector should be given to service providers from all other WTO Members. This applies even if the country has made no specific commitment under the WTO to provide foreign companies access to its markets.

MFN applies to *all* services, but some special temporary exemptions have been allowed.

MFN Exemptions

A number of countries are given the right to continue giving more favourable treatment to particular countries in particular service activities by listing "MFN exemptions" alongside

---

[9]This sample is constructed based on a fictitious country's national schedule – the "Arcadia Schedule" which is an exemplary schedule illustrating how commitments are entered by a Member country, *see "Introduction to GATS",* WTO's website.

their first sets of commitments.[10] However, these exemptions could only be made once and temporary — in principle not more than ten years and are subject to review after not more than five years.

2. National Treatment

In services trade, it means that once a foreign country has been allowed to supply a service in one's country there should be no discrimination between the foreign and local companies. Under *GATS,* a country only has to apply this principle when it has made a specific commitment to provide foreigners access to its services market. It *does not* have to apply national treatment in sectors where it has made no commitment.

3. Other obligations under GATS

i. Transparency — *GATS* Members are required, inter alia:

   a) to publish promptly all measures of general application that significantly affect trade in services covered by specific commitments; or to make such information publicly available and notify to Council of Trade in Services of WTO promptly all introductions or changes in laws, regulations or administrative guidance;[11] and
   b) to establish national enquiry points mandated to respond to other Member's information requests.[12]

ii. Impartial Services Regulations vs National Policy Objectives

The *GATS* expressly recognizes the right of Members to regulate the supply of services in pursuit of their own policy objectives and does not seek to influence these objectives. *GATS* establishes a framework of rules to ensure that services regulations are administered in a reasonable, objective and impartial manner and do not constitute unnecessary barriers to trade.[13]

In sectors where members have committed, each Member must ensure that all measures of application affecting trade in services are administered in a reasonable, objective and impartial manner. Judicial, arbitral or administrative tribunals or procedures must exist that allow foreign service suppliers to obtain an impartial review.[14]

iii. Other generally applicable provisions: recognition by Members of the education, experience, licences or certifications as granted in a particular country; disciplines on the operation of monopolies

---

[10]List of Article II Exemptions
[11]Article III: 1,2,3 of the *GATS*
[12]*ibid* Article III:4
[13]*ibid* Article VI
[14]*ibid* Article VI:2(a)

and exclusive suppliers; emergency safeguards; subsidies; government such procurement; general and security exceptions. Exceptions to *GATS* obligations include such measures of Member government to: protect public morals and human, animal or plant life or health; maintain public order; prevent deceptive or fraudulent practices; protect individual privacy; provide for equitable taxation; safeguard forex balances when serious difficulties arise; protect national security.

Modification or Withdrawal of Commitments

No commitment can be modified or withdrawn until at least three years after they have entered into force. At least three months' notice must be given of the proposed change and the price to be paid is that compensatory adjustments are to be negotiated between the Member wishing to change with those affected Members.[15]

Disputes Settlement

Disputes settlement will take place under the central WTO rules and mechanisms.[16]

II. CHINA'S COMMITMENTS

Since the adoption of the open door policy from the early 1980s and up to recently, China had remained a closed market for trade in services. One of the main reasons was probably China was well aware that local services were unable to compete with foreign services supplies. National security is often employed as an excuse to block the entry of foreign investors in trading in services, in particular in the sector of telecommunication. In the last couple of years China had opened up part of her services trade. Since 1995, MOFTEC periodically reviewed the list of industries in which foreign investments is encouraged, restricted or prohibited. Readers are strongly recommended to consult the new list (including services industries), which was approved by the State Council on 4 March 2002 and which echoes the commitments made by China on WTO accession.[17] In recent years, MOFTEC has been working to amend China's laws relating to trading in services so as to prepare for the accession to WTO.

As with national schedules submitted by other WTO Members, China's commitments in trade in services (market access) are the result from the negotiations between China and WTO

[15]Article XXI of the *GATS*.

[16]*ibid*, Articles XXII, XXIII, also *see* Chapter 5 of this book.

[17]The post-WTO *"List for Guidance on Foreign Investment in Industries"* and annex was approved by the State Council on 4 March, 2002, jointly promulgated on 11 March 2002 by virtue of order No. 21 of the State Development Planning Commission of the People's Republic of China, The State Economic and Trade Commission of the People's Republic of China and the Ministry of Foreign Trade and Economic Cooperation of the People's Republic of China, implemented as from 1 April 2002, and which also repealed the list issued by the above-named authorities on 31 December 1997; *see* the new list in website of the State Economic and Trade Commission http://www.setc.gov.cn.

Members. These commitments are enumerated in a document titled "Part II-Schedule of Specific Commitments on Services and List of Article II MFN Exemptions" which is annexed to the Protocol of Accession of China as Annex 9. *(See Appendix 3 of this book for a copy of China's Schedule, which has been re-formatted for ease of reading.)*[18]

Evaluation of Commitments made by China

As with other national schedules, China's commitments in the schedule tend to reflect its national policy objectives and constraints, overall and in individual sectors.

In order to determine the real level of market access represented by China, as with all other WTO Members, it is necessary to examine:

(1) the range of activities covered in each service sector;
(2) the limitations on market access and national treatment pertaining to the different modes of supply; and
(3) a list of MFN exemptions to assess the extent to which China gives preferential treatment to, or discriminate against, one or more of its trading partners.

II.A. CHINA'S SCHEDULE OF SPECIFIC COMMITMENTS ON SERVICES
("CHINA'S SCHEDULE") [SEE APPENDIX 3 FOR A RE-FORMATTED COPY]

The entries in China's schedule constitute a legally binding commitment.

Services sectors committed for market opening

The markets opened up by China for various services sectors include the following (*refer* to Table 6 of Part III and *Appendix 3*, and also to *Appendix 4* for detailed classification of services sectors.):

Business sector: legal services; accounting, auditing and bookkeeping services; taxation services; architectural, engineering, urban planning services; medical and dental services; consultancy services related to computer hardware installation; software implementation services; data processing services; real estate services; advertising services; management consulting services; technical testing and analysis, and freight inspection services; services incidental to agriculture, forestry, hunting and fishing, related scientific technical consulting services; offshore oil-field services, geological, geophysical and other scientific prospecting services; sub-surface surveying services; onshore oilfield services; photographic services; packaging services; convention services; translation and interpretation services; maintenance and repair services, rental and leasing;

Communication services sector: courier services; telecommunications services (basic telecommunication services, value-added services, mobile voice and data services); audiovisual

---

[18]Attempt has been made by the editor to ensure that the re-arranged format of the Schedule has not altered or affected the contents and meanings of any of the commitments displayed in the original format.

services (videos including entertainment software and distribution services, sound recording distribution, cinema theatre services);

Construction and related engineering services sector;

Distribution services sector: commission agents' services; wholesale trade services; retailing services; franchising services, wholesale or retail trade services away from a fixed location;

Educational services sector: primary/secondary/higher education/adult education and other educational services including English training;

Environmental services sector;

Financial services sector: All insurance and insurance-related services; banking and other financial services; motor vehicle financing services by non-bank financial institutions; other financial services; securities;

Tourism and travel related services sector: hotels (including apartment buildings) and restaurants; travel agencies and tour operators;

Transport services sector: international maritime transport; maritime cargo handling services and customs clearance services for maritime transport; container station and depot services; maritime agency services; internal waterways freight transport; aircraft repair and maintenance services; air transport computer reservation system services; freight transportation by rail and by road in trucks or cars; storage and warehousing services; and freight forwarding agency services for all modes of transport.

China did not make commitments in respect of *health-related and social services (sector 8); recreational, cultural and sporting services (sector 10); other services not included elsewhere (sector 12)* and also certain sub-sectors.

Components of China's Schedule

The China's schedule is set out in the format *mandated* under *GATS*.[19] Commitments are split into two sections:

Section 1. **"horizontal" commitments** - which stipulate limitations that apply to *all* of the sectors included in the schedule; these often refer to a particular mode of supply, notably commercial presence and the presence of natural persons. Any evaluation of sector-specific commitments must therefore take the horizontal entries into account.

---

[19]*Refer to* note 9.

Section 2. **"sectoral" commitments** - commitments which apply to trade in services in a particular sector or sub-sector are listed.

The Underlying Principles (for both horizontal and sectoral commitments)

1. Limitations on Market Access[20]

— The commitments enumerated here are the conclusion of multilateral negotiations between China and her major trading partners.
— Entries against each specific sector guarantee access to China's market in the sectors listed and spell out any limitations on access.[21] For example, limitations may be imposed on the number of services suppliers, service operations or employees in the sector; the value of transactions; the legal form of the service supplier; or the participation of foreign capital.

2. Limitations on National Treatment[22]

— Commitment to national treatment implies that China does not operate discriminatory measures benefiting domestic services or service suppliers.
— The key requirement is *not to* modify, in law or in fact, the conditions of competition in favour of the Member's own service industry.
— The extension of national treatment in any particular sector may be made subject to conditions and qualifications.

3. Additional commitments[23]

i.   These are not obligatory but China may decide in a given sector to make additional commitments relating to measures other than those subject to scheduling under national treatment and market access, for example qualifications, technical standards and licensing requirements or procedures.
ii. Additional commitments are to be used to indicate *positive* undertakings, not the listing of additional limitations or restrictions.

Annexes to China's Schedule *(see <u>end of</u> Appendix 3 of this book)*

1. Annex 1 Reference Paper on the definitions and principles on the regulatory framework for the basic telecommunications services.

---

[20]Article XVI of *GATS*.
[21]*See* limitations permissible under *GATS*, Article XVI:2.
[22]*Also see* Article XVII of *GATS*.
[23]*Also see* Article XVIII of *GATS*.

These include competitive safeguards for the prevention of anti-competitive practices in telecommunications; interconnection rights to be provided under non-discriminatory terms and conditions and in a timely fashion at cost-based charges; transparent rules and procedures for interconnection negotiations, arrangements, disputes settlement and licensing requirements; the provision of an independent regulatory body etc.

2. *A Note by the Chairman of the Group on Basic Telecommunication*, which clarifies the scope of basic telecom service;

3. *A Note by the Chairman of the Group of Basic Telecommunication* on Market Access Limitations on Spectrum Availability;

4. *Annex 2 on Distribution Services* which defines four main sub-sectors:

i.   Commission agents services;
ii. Wholesaling;
iii. Retailing and
iv. Franchising

5. *Annex 3 on Insurance: Definition of "Master Policy"*

It gives the definition of a Master Policy (*see* "Highlighted Commitments by China" below). It also stipulates that the following types of insurance can not be underwritten or co-insured by insurers located other than where the subject-insured are located, or covered under a master policy:

i.   motor insurance;
ii. credit insurance;
iii. employer liabilities insurance;
iv. statutory insurance (see definition in "Highlighted Commitments by China" below) and
v.   other insurance business excluded by the CIRC (China Insurance Regulatory Commission).

II.B. CHINA'S COMMITMENTS IN THE PROTOCOL

The Working Party Report highlights discussion on certain issues in China services market indicating the intense interests and concerns of other WTO Members in such areas. One example of such particular concern is the insurance services sector. China has given elaboration, clarifications and explanations against these concerns in the form of confirmations and commitments in the Working Party Report (referred below as "highlighted commitments in trade in services"). As explained in preface to Part I of this book, these commitments are incorporated to form an integral part of *the Protocol*[24], thus adding weight to their significance in China's policy in the liberalization of services market. These should be read in conjunction with the specific commitments spelt out in the relevant sectors of China's Schedule. Among these elaboration or clarifications, the definition of "Distribution Services" and the definition of "Master Policy" of an insurance were drawn up in single document attaching to *China's Schedule* as *Annex 2* and *Annex 3* respectively.

II.C. HIGHLIGHTED COMMITMENTS IN CHINA'S PROTOCOL

A Licensing (required in services such as banking services in China's Schedule)

Issues concerned	China Commitments/confirmations
As regards with concern over: 1. the lack of transparency in China's current services regime, in particular with respect to obtaining, extending, renewing, denying and terminating licences and other approvals required to provide services in China's market and appeals of such actions (hereafter referred to as "China's licensing procedures and conditions"); and also 2. that China's licensing procedures and conditions should not in themselves act as a barrier to market access and should not be more trade restrictive than necessary. Upon accession, China should publish: (a) a list of authorities responsible for authorizing, approving or regulating those services sectors in which China made specific commitments; (b) China's licensing procedures and conditions.	Paragraph 332 of the Working Party Report *would apply*: China *would publish* a list of all organizations that were responsible for authorizing, approving or regulating service (whether through grant of licence or other approval) activities for each service sector, including those organizations delegated with such authority from the central government authorities; Upon accession, China *would ensure* that China's licensing procedures and conditions would not act as barriers to market access and would not be more trade restrictive than necessary. Upon accession, China *would publish* in the official journal all of China's licensing procedures and conditions. In accordance with China's commitments under *the WTO Agreement, the Protocol* and its *Schedule of Specific Commitments,* China *confirmed*[25] that for those services included in China's Schedule of Specific Commitments, China *would ensure* that: (a) China's licensing procedures and conditions were published prior to becoming effective;

---

[24]Paragraph 1.2 of *the Protocol.*

[25]In accordance with China's commitments under the *WTO Agreement, the Protocol* and its *Schedule of Specific Commitments.*

	(b) In that publication, China would specify reasonable time frames for review and decision by all relevant authorities in China's licensing procedures and conditions;
	(c) Applications would be able request licensing without individual invitation;
	(d) Any fees charged would be commensurate with the administrative cost of processing an application (excluded fees: fees determined through auction or a tendering process);
	(e) The competent authorities of China *would*, after receipt of an applications,:
	— *inform* the applicant whether the application was considered complete under China's domestic laws and regulations; and
	— in the case of incomplete applications, *identify* the additional information that was required to complete the application; and
	— *provide* the opportunity to cure deficiencies;
	(f) Decisions *would be taken* promptly on all applications;
	(g) If an application was terminated or denied, the applicant *would be informed* in writing and without delay the reasons for such action. The applicant would have the possibility of resubmitting, at its discretion, a new application that addressed the reasons for termination or denial;
	(h) If an application was approved, the applicant *would be informed* in writing and without delay. The licence or approval would enable the applicant to start the commercial operations upon registration of the company with SAIC[26] for fiscal and other similar administrative purposes. This registration would be completed within 2 months of the submission of a complete file, as required by public SAIC regulations, and in accordance with China's Schedule of Specific Commitments;
	(i) Where China required an examination to licence professionals, such examinations would be scheduled at reasonable intervals.

---

[26]State Administration of Industry and Commerce.

B The Independence of Regulators
(for almost all services included in China's Schedule)

Issues concerned	China's Commitments/confirmations
There was concern about maintaining the independence of regulators from those they regulated.	For the services included in China's Schedule of Specific Commitments, relevant regulatory authorities *would be separate from,* and *not accountable to,* any services suppliers they regulated, *Exception*: courier and railway transportation services. For these excepted sectors, China would comply with other relevant provisions of *the WTO Agreement* and *the Protocol*.

C Sales Away from a Fixed Location (Direct Sales)
(*see* Sector 4 "Distribution" of China's Schedule[27])

Issues concerned	China's Commitments/confirmations
Some WTO Members noted the World Code of Conduct proved a strong ethical basis for regulating sales away from a fixed location.	China *would consult* with WTO Members and develop regulations, consistent with China's Schedule of Specific Commitments and its obligations under *GATS*, on sales away from a fixed location.

D Insurance and Insurance-related Business
(under Sector 7 "Financial Services" of China's Schedule)

D1 Terms

Issues Concerned	China's Commitments/confirmations
Regarding certain terms in China's Schedule of Specific Commitments:	China *confirmed* the definition and scope of the following terms: (a) A **"master policy"**[28] was a policy that provided blanket coverage for the same legal person's property and liabilities located in different places. A master policy could only be issued by the business department of an

---

[27]Definition of "Distribution Trade Services" was given under *Annex 2* to China's Schedule. In this definition, distribution trade services are comprised of four main sub-sectors: commission agents services; wholesaling; retailing; and franchising.

[28]This full definition was given in *Annex 3* to China's Schedule, *see* Appendix 3 of this book.

insurer's head office or that of its authorized province-level branch offices. Other branches were not allowed to issue master policies.

(i)   For master policy business with the state key construction projects as its subject-matter insured.

If investors on the state key construction projects (i.e. projects that were so listed and annually announced by the State Development and Planning Commission) met either of the following requirements, they could purchase a master policy from insures that were located in the same place as the investors' legal persons were located.

1.   The investment on the subject-matter insured were all from China (*including* the reinvestment from the foreign-invested enterprises in China) and the sum of investment of the investor accounted for over 15 per cent of the total investment.

2.   The investment was partially from abroad, and partially from China (*including* the reinvestment from the foreign-invested enterprises in China) and the sum of investment of the Chinese investor accounted for over 15 per cent of the total domestic investment.

For those projects that drew all investment from abroad, every insurer could provide coverage in the form of a master policy.

(ii) A Master policy covering different subject-matters insured of the same legal person.

For those subject-matters insured located in different places and owned by the same legal person (*excluding* financial, railway, and post and telecommunications industries and enterprises), a master policy could be issued on the basis of either of the following conditions.

1.   For the sake of payment of the premium tax, insurance companies

incorporated where the legal person or accounting unit of the insurance applicant was located, were allowed to issue a master policy.

2. If over 50 per cent of the insurance amount of the subject-matter insured was from a larger or medium sized city, the insurers in that city were allowed to issue a master policy, no matter whether the insurance applicant's legal person or accounting unit was located in the city.

(b) **Large scale commercial risk** meant an insurance risk written on any large scale commercial enterprise if, upon accession, the aggregate annual premium exceeded 800 thousand RMB and the investment was more than 200 million RMB; one year after accession, if the aggregate annual premium exceeded 600 thousand RMB and the investment was more than 180 million RMB; two years after accession, if the aggregate annual premium exceeded 400 thousand RMB and the investment was more than 150 million RMB.

(c) **Statutory insurance** in China's Schedule of Specific Commitments[29] were limited to the following specific categories, and no additional lines or products would be added: third party auto liability insurance, and driver and operator liability for buses and other commercial vehicles.

China's commitment:
China *confirmed* that any changes to the definition of master policy and large scale commercial risk *would be consistent with* China's Specific Schedule of Commitments and

---

[29]*Annex 3* to China's Schedule specifies that: "Motor insurance, credit insurance, employer liabilities insurance, statutory insurance, and other insurance business that are excluded by the CIRC (China Insurance Regulatory Commission) cannot be underwritten or co-insured by insurers located other than where the subject-matter are located, or covered under a master policy".

	obligations under *GATS* so as to progressively liberalize access to this services sector.

D2 The qualifications for foreign insurance companies

Issues Concerned	China's Commitments/confirmations
China had scheduled certain qualifications as limitations under *GATS* Articles XVI and XVII[30] that foreign insurers had to meet to apply for a licence to provide services in China. These qualifications should not apply to those foreign insurance companies already established in China seeking authorization to establish a branch or sub-branch.	China *permitted* internal branching for insurance firms consistent with the phase-out of geographic restrictions. [*see* China's Schedule, Appendix 3 of this book] The qualifications for foreign insurers applying for a licence to enter China's market *would not apply* to foreign insurers already established in China that were seeking authorization to establish branches or sub-branches.[31] China also *confirmed* that a branch and a sub-branch were an extension of the parent enterprise and not a separate legal entity and that China *would permit* internal branching accordingly on that basis, and in compliance with China's schedule of Specific Commitments, including provisions on MFN treatment.

D3 Prior experience requirement for establishment in insurance sector

Issues Concerned	China's Commitments/confirmations
Prior Experience Requirement for Establishment in Insurance Sector	China *confirmed* that the merging, division, restructuring or other change of legal form of an insurance company *would not impact* the prior experience requirements included in China's Schedule of Specific Commitments if the new entity continued to supply insurance services.

---

[30]These qualifications relate to a minimum period of establishment in a WTO Member, total assets and maintenance of a representative office in China.

[31]The extension of grandfathered investments through branching, sub-branching or any other legal form.

E Choice of Partner
(concerns various sectors in China's Schedule where the incorporation of joint-ventures is mandated in specific sectors, for instance in insurance sector)

Issues Concerned	China's Commitments/confirmations
The existing practice of imposing conditions on the Chinese companies that were allowed to partner with foreign service suppliers could amount to *de facto* quotas, as the number of potential partners (Chinese companies) meeting those conditions might be limited.	A foreign service supplier *would be able* to partner with any Chinese entity of its choice, including outside the sector of operation of the joint venture, as long as the Chinese partner was legally established in China. The joint venture as such should meet the prudential and specific sectoral requirements,[32] on the same basis as those for domestic enterprises and which must be publicly available.

F Modification of the Equity Interest
(This concerns various services in China's Schedule where joint ventures are established)

Issues Concerned	China's Commitments/confirmations
Modification of the equity interest in joint ventures	The Chinese and foreign partners in an established joint venture *would be able to* discuss the modification of their respective equity participation levels in the joint venture and implement such modification if agreement was reached by both sides and also approved by the authorities. Such an agreement *would be approved* if consistent with the revelvant equity commitments in China's Schedule of Specific Commitments.

---

[32]As stipulated in China's Schedule of Services against each sector.

G Inspection Services
(Under 'Other Business Service' of sector 1–"Business Services" in China's Schedule)

Issues Concerned	China's Commitments/confirmations
There were requirements maintained by China on foreign and joint venture commodity inspection agencies with the effect as a barrier to trade.	China *would not maintain* requirements which had the effect of acting as barriers to the operation of foreign and joint venture commodity inspection agencies, unless otherwise specified in China's Schedule of Specific Commitments.

H Market Research
(Under sector 1—"Business Services" in China's Schedule)

Issues concerned	China's Commitments/confirmations
Market research activities	Upon accession, China *would remove* the prior approval requirement for market research services,[33] including market analysis (of the size and other characteristics of a market) and analysis of consumer attitudes and preferences. Market research firms registered in China, which were engaged in such services, *would only be required* to file the survey plan and the questionnaire form on record in the statistical agencies of government at or above the provincial level.

I Legal Service
(Under 'Professional Services' of sector 1—"Business Services" in China's Schedule)

This is *not* a commitment. China *clarified* that "Chinese national registered lawyers", as indicated in China's Schedule of Specific Commitments, were those Chinese nationals who had obtained a lawyer's certificate and were holding a Chinese practicing permit and were registered to practice in a Chinese law firm.

---

[33]Defined as "investigation services designed to secure information on the prospects and performance of an organization's products in the market", see clause 318 of the Working Party Report.

J Minority Shareholder Rights

(Under various services of China's Schedule where foreign investors are mandated to hold minority shareholdings such as telecommunication, securities, cinema theatre, advertising etc.)

Issues concerned	China's Commitments/confirmations
Foreigners holding minority shareholders rights due to limitation in market access	With respect to its Schedule of Specific Commitments, China *confirmed* that, while China had limited its market access commitments in some sectors to permit foreigners to hold only a minority equity interest, a minority shareholder could enforce rights in the investment under China's laws, regulations and measures. Moreover, WTO Members would have recourse to WTO dispute settlement to ensure implementation of all commitments in China's *GATS* schedule.

chapter 4

China's Commitments in Trade-Related Intellectual Property Regime

I. INTRODUCTION TO TRIPS (AGREEMENT ON TRADE-RELATED ASPECTS OF INTELLECTUAL PROPERTY RIGHTS INCLUDING TRADE IN COUNTERFEIT GOODS)

The TRIPS Agreement is Annex 1C of the Marrakesh Agreement Establishing the World Trade Organization, signed in Marrakesh, Morocco on 15 April 1994 ("the Agreement"). It is part of the package of agreements that has to be accepted by all members of the WTO. TRIPS marks the emergence of intellectual property rights as a fully fledged trade-related issue.[1]

Origins: Into The Rule-Based Trade System

The extent of protection and enforcement of intellectual property ("IP") rights varied widely around the world; and as intellectual property became more important in trade, these differences became a source of tension in international economic relations. New internationally-agreed trade rules for intellectual property rights were seen as a way to introduce more order and predictability, and for disputes to be settled more systematically. The 1986-94 Uruguay Round achieved that.[2]

---

[1]International Chamber of Commerce, *Intellectual Property & International Trade- A Guide to the Uruguay Round TRIPS Agreement, ICC Publication No. 522*, ICC Publishing S. A. Paris, 1996, p. 5.
[2]*supra* note 1, Chapter 2, by Lynne Saylor and John Beton, pp. 12-15, gives an account on the background and context how intellectual property rights emerged as a subject related to trade and became an agenda at the Uruguay negotiation the conclusion of which leads to *TRIPS Agreement*.

TRIPS is an attempt to narrow the gaps in the way these rights are protected around the world, and to bring them under common international rules.[3] Article 2 of TRIPS specifically provides that its main provisions, except those relating to dispute prevention and settlement, shall not derogate from existing obligations of member countries under conventions administered by World Intellectual Property Organizations (WIPO) such as the Paris Convention (Industrial Property), the Berne Convention (copyright), the Rome Convention (neighbouring rights, jointly administered by WIPO, UNESCO and ILO) and the Washington Treaty (Integrated Circuits).[4] Member countries must also comply with the substantive provisions of these conventions, which are used as a starting point for defining obligations under TRIPS.[5]

The TRIPS also complements the existing international conventions with "plus elements". Those international conventions did not provide sufficient protection against the adverse effects of trade distortion as they provide for neither enforcement nor dispute settlement mechanisms. The TRIPS Agreement was conceived to fill the gaps.[6] When there are trade disputes over intellectual property rights, the WTO's dispute settlement system is now available. The obligations under TRIPS to provide quick and efficient procedures will bring important changes in the laws of some industrialized countries.[7]

The Agreement covers five broad issues:

— how basic **principles** of the trading system and other international intellectual property agreements should be applied
— how to give adequate **protection** to intellectual property rights.

---

[3]*supra* note 1 Chapter 1, by Daphne Yong-d'Herve, pp.8-10, "Before the conclusion of TRIPS, the international legal framework for intellectual property rights was essentially structured by treaties administered by and negotiated under the auspices of the World Intellectual Property Organization (WIPO), the United Nations organization responsible for intellectual property matters. The principal WIPO treaties which concern areas also covered by TRIPS are the *Paris Convention on the Protection of Industrial Property of 1883 amended in Stockholm in 1967* ("the Paris Convention"), the *Berne Convention for the Protection of Literary and Artistic Works of 1996* ("the Berne Convention"), the *Rome Convention for the Protection of Performers, Producers of Phonograms and Broadcasting Organizations 1961* ('the Rome Convention"), the *Treaty on Intellectual Property in respect of Integrated Circuits of 1989* ("the Washington Treaty")." Other international agreements include: in the case of trademarks, *the Madrid Agreement concerning the International Registration of Marks (1891)* and *the Protocol relating to the Madrid Agreement (1989)*; in the case of geographical indications, the *Lisbon Agreement for the Protection of Appellations of Origin and their International Registration (1958)*, the *Madrid Agreement on the Repression of False or Deceptive Indications of Source on Goods (1891)*.
[4]*Ibid., the Rome Convention* was jointly administered by World Intellectual Property Organization, United Nations Educational Scientific Cultural Organization (UNESCO) and International Labour Organization (ILO), *op. cit. note 3,* p. 8.
[5]*ibid.,* p. 10.
[6]*supra* note 3, p. 10.
[7]*supra* note 1, Chapter 3, by Thomas Pletscher, p. 21.

— how countries should **enforce** those rights adequately in their own territories
— how to **settle disputes** on intellectual property between members of the WTO
— **special transitional arrangements** during the period when the new system is being introduced.

Basic principles: national treatment, MFN, and technological progress

As in GATT and GATS, the starting point of the intellectual property agreement is basic principles of non-discrimination: national treatment (treating one's own nationals and foreigners equally), and most-favoured-nation treatment (equal treatment for nationals of all trading partners in the WTO). National treatment is also a key principle in other intellectual property agreements outside the WTO.

Balance of interest

When an inventor or creator is granted patent or copyright protection, he obtains the right to stop other people making unauthorized copies. Society at large sees this temporary intellectual property protection as an incentive to encourage the development of new technology and creations, which will eventually be available to all. Innovation is an ongoing, cumulative and dynamic process. Strengthening the intellectual property rights can sometimes impede this process and become harmful to economic development.[8] The TRIPS Agreement recognizes the need to strike a balance. It says intellectual property protection should contribute to technical innovation and the transfer of technology. It also says both producers and users should benefit, and economic and social welfare should be enhanced.

How to Protect Intellectual Property: Common Ground-Rules

The second part of the TRIPS Agreement looks at different kinds of intellectual property rights and how to protect them. The purpose is to ensure that adequate standards of protection exist in all member countries. Here the starting point is the obligations of the main international agreements of the World Intellectual Property Organization (WIPO) that already existed before the WTO was created:

— the Paris Convention for the Protection of Industrial Property (patents, industrial designs, etc).
— the Berne Convention for the Protection of Literary and Artistic Works (copyright).

Some areas are not covered by these conventions. In some cases, the standards of protection prescribed were thought inadequate. So the TRIPS Agreement adds a significant number of new or higher standards.

---

[8]Pamela Samuelson, "Intellectual Property and Economic Development: Opportunities for China in the Information Age", http://www.sims.berkeley.edu/~pam/papers/chinaip.html, viewed on 19 February 2001.

Types of Intellectual Property

Intellectual property rights are customarily divided into two main areas:

(i) Copyright and rights related to copyright

The rights of authors of literary and artistic works (such as books and other writings, musical compositions, paintings, sculpture, computer programs and films) are protected by copyright, for a minimum period of 50 years after the death of the author.

Also protected through copyright and related (sometimes referred to as "neighbouring") rights are the rights of performers (e.g. actors, singers and musicians), producers of phonograms (sound recordings) and broadcasting organizations. The main social purpose of protection of copyright and related rights is to encourage and reward creative work.

(ii) Industrial property

Industrial property can usefully be divided into two main areas:
One area can be characterized as the protection of distinctive signs, in particular trademarks (which distinguish the goods or services of one undertaking from those of other undertakings) and geographical indications (which identify a good as originating in a place where a given characteristic of the good is essentially attributable to its geographical origin).

The protection of such distinctive signs aims to stimulate and ensure fair competition and to protect consumers, by enabling them to make informed choices between various goods and services. The protection may last indefinitely, provided the sign in question continues to be distinctive.

Other types of industrial property are protected primarily to stimulate innovation, design and the creation of technology. In this category fall inventions (protected by patents), industrial designs and trade secrets.

The social purpose is to provide protection for the results of investment in the development of new technology, thus giving the incentive and means to finance research and development activities.

A functioning intellectual property regime should also facilitate the transfer of technology in the form of foreign direct investment, joint ventures and licensing.

The areas covered by the TRIPS Agreement

— Copyright and related rights
— Trademarks, including service marks
— Geographical indications
— Industrial designs
— Patents

— Layout-designs (topographies) of integrated circuits
— Undisclosed information, including trade secrets

Among these, patents, and in many cases, industrial designs, integrated circuit designs, geographical indications and trademarks, have to be registered in order to receive protection. The registration includes a description of what is being protected — the invention, design, brand name, logo, etc — and this description is public information.

Copyright and trade secrets are, on the other hand, protected automatically according to specified conditions. They do not have to be registered.

Some Special Features in TRIPS

1) Copyright

The TRIPS Agreement ensures that computer programmes will be protected as literary works under the Berne Convention and outlines how databases should be protected.

It also expands international copyright rules to cover rental rights. Authors of computer programmes and producers of sound recordings must have the right to prohibit the commercial rental of their works to the public. A similar exclusive right applies to films where commercial rental has led to widespread copying, affecting copyright-owners' potential earnings from their films.

The Agreement says performers must also have the right to prevent unauthorized recording, reproduction and broadcast of live performances (bootlegging) for no less than 50 years. Producers of sound recordings must have the right to prevent the unauthorized reproduction of recordings for a period of 50 years.

2) Trademarks

The Agreement defines what types of signs must be eligible for protection as trademarks, and what the minimum rights conferred on their owners must be. It says that service marks must be protected in the same way as trademarks used for goods. Marks that have become well-known in a particular country enjoy additional protection.

3) Geographical Indications

Place names are sometimes used to identify a product. Well-known examples include "Champagne", "Scotch", "Tequila", and "Roquefort" cheese. Wine and spirits makers are particularly concerned about the use of place-names to identify products, and the TRIPS Agreement contains special provisions for these products. But the issue is also important for other types of goods.

The use of a place name to describe a product in this way — a "geographical indication"— usually identifies both its geographical origin and its characteristics. Therefore, using the place name when the product was made elsewhere or when it does not have the usual characteristics can mislead consumers, and it can lead to unfair competition. The TRIPS Agreement says countries have to prevent the misuse of place names.

For wines and spirits, the Agreement provides higher levels of protection, i.e. even where there is no danger of the public being misled.

Some exceptions are allowed, for example if the name is already protected as a trademark or if it has become a generic term. For example, "cheddar" now refers to a particular type of cheese not necessarily made in Cheddar. But any country wanting to make an exception for these reasons must be willing to negotiate with the country which wants to protect the geographical indication in question. The Agreement provides for further negotiations in the WTO to establish a multilateral system of notification and registration of geographical indications for wines.

4) Industrial Designs

Under the TRIPS Agreement, industrial designs must be protected for at least 10 years. Owners of protected designs must be able to prevent the manufacture, sale or importation of articles bearing or embodying a design which is a copy of the protected design.

5) Patents

The Agreement says patent protection must be available for inventions for at least 20 years. Patent protection must be available for both products and processes, in almost all fields of technology. Governments can refuse to issue a patent for an invention if its commercial exploitation is prohibited for reasons of public order or morality. They can also exclude diagnostic, therapeutic and surgical methods, plants and animals (other than microorganisms), and biological processes for the production of plants or animals (other than microbiological processes).

Plant varieties, however, must be protectable by patents or by a special system (such as the breeder's rights provided in the conventions of UPOV — the International Union for the Protection of New Varieties of Plants).

The Agreement describes the minimum rights that a patent owner must enjoy. But it also allows certain exceptions. A patent-owner could abuse his rights, for example by failing to supply the product on the market. To deal with that possibility, the Agreement says governments can issue "compulsory licences", allowing a competitor to produce the product or use the process under licence. But this can only be done under certain conditions aimed at safeguarding the legitimate interests of the patent-holder.

If a patent is issued for a production process, then the rights must extend to the product directly obtained from the process. Under certain conditions alleged infringers may be ordered by a court to prove that they have not used the patented process.

6) Integrated Circuits Layout Designs

The basis for protecting integrated circuit designs ("topographies") in the TRIPS Agreement is *the Washington Treaty on Intellectual Property in Respect of Integrated Circuits*, which comes under the World Intellectual Property Organization. This was adopted in 1989 but has not yet entered into force. The TRIPS Agreement adds a number of provisions: for example, protection must be available for at least 10 years.

7) Undisclosed information and trade secrets

Trade secrets and other types of "undisclosed information" which have commercial value must be protected against breach of confidence and other acts contrary to honest commercial practices. But reasonable steps must have been taken to keep the information secret. Test data submitted to governments in order to obtain marketing approval for new pharmaceutical or agricultural chemicals must also be protected against unfair commercial use.

Curbing Anti-Competitive Licensing Contracts

The owner of a copyright, patent or other form of intellectual property right can issue a licence for someone else to produce or copy the protected trademark, work, invention, design, etc. The Agreement recognizes that the terms of a licensing contract could restrict competition or impede technology transfer. It says that under certain conditions, governments have the right to take action to prevent anti-competitive licensing that abuses intellectual property rights. It also says governments must be prepared to consult each other on controlling anti-competitive licensing.

Enforcement: Tough But Fair

Having intellectual property laws is not enough. They must be enforceable. This is covered in Part 3 of TRIPS. The Agreement says governments have to ensure that intellectual property rights can be enforced under their laws, and that the penalties for infringement are tough enough to deter further violations. The procedures must be fair and equitable, and not unnecessarily complicated or costly. They must not entail unreasonable time-limits or unwarranted delays. People involved should be able to ask a court to review an administrative decision or to appeal a lower court's ruling.

The Agreement describes in some detail how enforcement have to be handled, including rules for obtaining evidence, provisional measures, injunctions, damages and other penalties.

It says courts must have the right, under certain conditions, to order the disposal or destruction of pirated or counterfeit goods. Wilful trademark counterfeiting or copyright piracy on a commercial scale must be criminal offences. Governments have to make sure that intellectual property rights owners can receive the assistance of customs authorities to prevent imports of counterfeit and pirated goods.

Transition Arrangements: 1, 5 Or 11 Years To Fall Into Line

When the WTO agreements took effect on 1 January 1995, developed countries were given one year to ensure that their laws and practices conform with the TRIPS Agreement. Developing countries and (under certain conditions) transition economies are given five years. Least developed countries have 11 years.

If a developing country did not provide product patent protection in a particular area of technology when the TRIPS Agreement came into force (1 January 1995), it has up to 10 years to introduce the protection. But for pharmaceutical and agricultural chemical products, the country must accept the filing of patent applications from the beginning of the transitional period, though the patent need not be granted until the end of this period. If the government allows the relevant pharmaceutical or agricultural chemical to be marketed during the transition period, it must — subject to certain conditions — provide an exclusive marketing right for the product for five years, or until a product patent is granted, whichever is shorter.

Subject to certain exceptions, the general rule is that obligations in the Agreement apply to intellectual property rights that exist at the end of a country's transition period, as well as to new ones.

Regulating Body

A Council for Trade-Related Aspects of Intellectual Property Rights monitors the working of the Agreement and governments' compliance with it.

Significance of TRIPS

The TRIPS Agreement represents an instructive and contemporary case study of what can be achieved through close multi-industry collaboration and government-private sector cooperation.[9] It represents a major step forward in establishing transparent rules and disciplines to facilitate the management of intellectual property.[10]

---

[9]*supra* note 2, p. 12.
[10]ibid., p. 15.

All business sectors will benefit from the Agreement, in particular those sectors investing heavily in research and development. Beneficiaries of TRIPS will not only be large multinational companies but also small and medium enterprises, which have been prevented by the deficiencies in the existing system from enjoying reasonable protection at fair costs on a worldwide basis. The TRIPS Agreement will therefore generally improve the investment climate.[11]

Special acknowledgement for materials in Section 1:

1. "Trading into the Future", 2nd Edition, Revised April 1999; "TRIPS: What are intellectual property right?", WTO website.
2. International Chamber of Commerce, *Intellectual Property & International Trade- A Guide to the Uruguay Round TRIPS Agreement, ICC Publication No. 522,* ICC Publishing S. A. Paris, 1996.

II. CHINA AND TRIPS

Since 1980, China had taken numerous steps towards bringing its intellectual property legislation into compliance with international standards. Take copyright law as an example, despite China's unfamiliarity with the concept of copyright, China managed to build up a treaties-based regime of law that closely modeled on western and US Laws.[12] If an international treaty concluded or acceded to by China contains provisions that differ from provisions of Chinese laws, the provisions of the international treaty shall apply, except those on which China has made reservations.[13]

TRIPS, after going into effect, has been accepted universally as a multilateral protective regulation for IP. It will therefore become an important condition for China to enhance the protection of intellectual property when it joins the WTO.

"Universal implementation of IP laws was the main task the Chinese government need to perform in order to satisfy international concerns and to comply with the requirements of the TRIPS, a prerequisite for WTO admission."[14] By acceding to WTO, China must observe the TRIPS Agreement.

---

[11]*supra* note 7.

[12]The legal regime for copyright protection in China during 1990s: The *Copyright Law,* promulgated on 7 September 1990, [recently amended on 27 October, 2001, *see* notes 20, 27]; *The PRC Copyright Law Implementing Regulation* promulgated by the State Council on 24 May 1991 and effective on 1 June 1991; *The Computer Software Protection Regulations,* effective 1 October 1991; *the Computer Software Copyright Registration Procedures,* effective 18 April 1991; the *Implementation of International Copyright Treaties Provisions,* effective 30 September 1992; the *Resolution on Punishment of Crimes of Copyright Infringement adopted by the Standing Committee of the National People's Congress* on 5 July 1994; Article 217 of the *Amended Criminal Law* effective 1 October, 1997 stipulated a fixed-term sentence of up to seven years for copyright infringement.

[13]*See* Article 142 of the *General Principles of Civil Law* and Article 238 of *the Civil Procedure Law.*

[14]said by Todd Dickinson, former director of the USPTO (United States Patent and Trademark Office), when he was in Beijing to meet with Chinese IP chiefs in late 2000 as director of USPTO. "IP Concerns threaten passage to the WTO", *IP Asia* November 2000.

China has made much progress in the protection of intellectual property. Changes initiated by China in enhancing its laws on IP protection were driven both by the internal needs and international pressure. Since China clearly intends to participate in the information age, it will need to have in place the legal infrastructure necessary to protect intellectual property, and encourage creation, research and development.[15] Prosperity in the emerging global information economy depends in substantial part on the strength of information industries which, in turn, depends on respect for intellectual property rights.[15a] Intellectual property law can help fulfil China's further aspirations for growth of its economy. This is especially true for the information sector of China's economy because markets for information products and services can only thrive when intellectual property rights are secured.[16]

In recent years, as China has developed, local companies and individuals have been lobbying government to protect their intellectual property rights. *"We are not afraid of Microsoft, but of piracy"*[17] exclaimed by some IT personages in China. International pressure has also been continually exerted since 1990s, typically in the several rounds of Sino-US bilateral negotiations on China's intellectual property protection.[18]

Recent Efforts In Living Up To TRIPS, Standards

In order to meet China's internal requirements to improve the system of intellectual property protection and align China's intellectual property laws with TRIPS and other international treaties to which China is a party, such as the WIPO treaties[19], the Madrid Agreement Concerning International Registration of Marks, the Patent Cooperation Treaty, China has stepped up with reforms in the protection of IP rights. *(See* Part III, Section E of this Chapter for the list of laws to be revised in the attached Table B).

The most recent important changes at the time of compiling this book are amendments to three major laws in intellectual property: the *PRC Copyright Law* and the *PRC Trademark Law* were amended on 27 October, 2001 by virtue of the decisions of the Standing Committee of the National People's Congress. Both amendments effected numerous changes to the

---

[15]*supra* note 8.

[15a]*ibid.*

[16]*ibid.*

[17]reported by Xiao Hai in "Not Afraid of Microsoft, But of Piracy—China to create Anti-Piracy Alliance" that rampant copyright infringement acts and piracy have been causing tremendous impairment of the national industry in China and also dampening the enthusiasm for creation. *China Patents & Trademarks*, No. 2, 2000 p 21.

[18]*See* discussions by Julia Cheng, "China's Copyright System: Rising to the Spirit of TRIPS requires an Internal Focus and WTO Membership", *Fordham International Law Journal,* 21 Fordham Int'l L.J. 1941, Fordham University School of Law, June 1998; *also see* Assafa Endeshaw's commentary: "A Critical Assessment of the U.S.-China Conflict on Intellectual Property", *Albany Law Journal of Science & Technology,* 6 Alb. L.J. Sci. & Tech. 295, 1996.

[19]*supra* note 3.

existing laws.[20,21] Their implementation rules have also been amended subsequently in August 2002. The *Patent Law* and its implementation rules have also been amended prior to China's accession. *(See* section B5 in Part III of this Chapter).

Other recent modifications to IP regime include:[22]

The Notice Concerning Several Issues on Applying for Recognition of Well-Known Trademarks by the State Administration for Industry and Commerce (on 28 April 2000); this Notice was issued to further standardize well-known trademark application procedures and to address the problem of overcharging by agencies and individuals for helping enterprises making such applications.

The Royalty Standards for Copyright in the Production of Digital Products (for Trial Implementation) (1 July 2000) set forth prescribed forms of royalty payments for the use of works protected by copyright law in digital products.

An Interpretation of Several Issues Relating to Adjudication of and Application of Law to Cases of Copyright Disputes on Computer Network issued by the Supreme People's Court on 22 November 2000 and became effective 21 December 2000. It deals with infringement of copyrighted work over computer network.

The Interpretation of the Supreme People's Court Concerning Implementing Preservation of Assets by People's Courts with Regard to Registered Trademark Rights (2 January 2001) provides guidance on the operation of the "preservation of assets" enforcement mechanism in China's Civil Procedure Law when it is sought to preserve registered trademark assets.

---

[20]Major amendments to the *Copyright Law* include: incorporating to copyright the right of rental and right of information dissemination on internet; providing the protection on databases etc; expanding the performer's right to authorize others to reproduce and distribute sound/video recording products including their performance, and the right to receive remuneration etc; adding the right of sound/video recording producers to authorize others to rent or distribute their products through information network; providing more legal remedies for copyright infringees such as the specifying of methods for calculating the amount of compensation for damages; adopting the pre-trial injunction for suspension of alleged infringement and property preservation measure; limiting the scope of "statutory licenses"; adding the evidence preservation measure; adding the provision for legal liabilities of publishers, producers, distributors and renters of reproduction of works etc.; adding the requirement for concluding a written contract for assignment of copyright. *See* web site of China Patent Agent (H.K.) Ltd. http://www.cpahkltd.com.

[21]Major amendments to the *Trademark Law* include: enlarging the elements that form a trademark from words, devices, or their combinations to words, devices, characters, figures, three-dimensional signs, combination with colours and combination of the above elements; enlargement of the range of objects to be protected including Collective Marks, Certification Marks; adding provision on protecting well-known trademarks; adding the provision on claiming priority of a trademark; adding provision on preventing prior registration in bad faith; adding provision of judicial trial procedure for administrative decisions; adding provision of pre-litigation injunction and provisional measures. *See* web site of CCPIT Patent and Trademark Law Office, http://www.ccpit-patent.com.cn.

[22]information available from website of China Legal Change, http://www.chinalegalchange.com.

The Regulations on Protection of the Layout-Designs of Integrated Circuits (28 March 2001) appear to be an effort to bring China's intellectual property legislation in line with section 6 of the Agreement on Trade-Related Aspects of Intellectual Property Rights.

The Notice of the State Administration of Taxation Concerning the Issue of Collecting Business Tax on the Assignment of Copyright (16 April 2001) was issued to standardize Business Tax policies involved in the assignment of copyright.

The Detailed Implementing Rules for the Law of the People's Republic of China on Patents was issued by the State Council on 15 June 2001 and became effective as of 1 July 2001. It introduces numerous changes from the 1992 implementing rules.

Judicial Interpretation by the Supreme People's Court on Several Issues Relating to Application of Law in Adjudication of Cases of Civil Disputes over Domain Names on Computer Network, adopted on 26 June, 2001 and became effective on 24 July, 2001. The purpose of the Interpretation is to properly adjudicate cases of civil disputes over acts of registration and use of domain names on the computer network.

The Detailed Implementing Rules for the Regulations on Protection of the Layout-Designs of Integrated Circuits (18 September 2001) provide the detailed rules on how to implement the Regulations on Protection of the Layout-Designs of Integrated Circuits which came into force on October 1, 2001.

The Measures of the People's Republic of China for Administration of the Registration of Technology Import/Export Contracts (issued on 16 November 2001) set forth the rules governing registration of technology import and export contracts for technology that may be freely imported or exported. The technology importer or exporter must carry out online registration on the China International E-Commerce Network.

The Regulations of the People's Republic of China on Administration of Technology Import and Export was promulgated on 10 December 2001. It introduces an approval system for restricted technology. Licensing administration is implemented for such technology. The technology import contract will come into force on the day on which the technology import license is issued.

The Interpretation on the Issue of the Law Applicable to Stopping the Infringement of Exclusive Rights in Registered Trademarks and Preservation of Evidence Prior to Litigation (promulgated on 9 January 2002). It gives guidance on implementation of the new provisions in China's *Trademark Law* on preliminary injunctions to stop infringement of trademarks and preserve evidence.

China's system of intellectual property protection is plagued by a number of shortcomings: weakness in the enforcement system, low administrative penalties, inadequate damages[23],

---

[23]*see* detailed discussions in the issue by Xiaoqing FENG and Fang LIAO, "Copyright Damages in the People's Republic of China", *the Journal of World Intellectual Property*, volume 3, September 2000 No. 5.

local protectionism. Some say social and cultural factors are also key reasons for the high levels of intellectual property infringement in China. Confucianism and the notion of sharing creative works and ideas have inclined resistance adherence to intellectual property laws in China.[24]

It appears though the changes brought China's intellectual property regime more in line with that of TRIPS, however, serious enforcement measures have to be taken. China seems very determined to abide by WTO rules in this regard. Long Yongtu, China's chief negotiator on WTO accession said: *enforcement of the IP commitments will "apply from day one" from the date the laws and regulations are revised, and that China will ensure that its practices are in line with the WTO's Agreement on Trade-Related Aspects of Intellectual Property Rights (TRIPS) from the date that China joins the global trade body.*[25]

Despite China's determination, whether IP owners would rest assured remains to be seen. China's accession to WTO has at least provided them with one more alternative in enforcing their rights through their own government — the WTO mechanism of settling disputes among members.[26]

III. CHINA COMMITMENTS

A. GENERAL

A1. Overview

Current Situation/Concerns Raised by Other WTO Members	China Commitments/Confirmations
Since late 1970s, China had made tremendous efforts in the internationalization of its laws and regulations for the protection of intellectual property right ("IPRs"). As a result, notwithstanding the initial stage of	For accession to the *WTO Agreement* and compliance with the *TRIPS Agreement*, further amendments had been made to the *Patent Law*. The amendments to the *Copyright Law* and the *Trademark Law*, as well as relevant implementing rules covering different areas of the *TRIPS Agreement, would* also be accomplished upon China's accession. Laws adopted by the National People's Congress and administrative

---

[24]Carolyn Morton, "The Accession of the People's Republic of China to the WTO and Protection of Intellectual Property", presented at Session S26/SU7 in Law Conference 2001, www.conference.co.nz/law2001/pdf%20files/MortonSa27andSu7.pdf viewed on 12 Feb 02; *also see* analysis of all these issues by Julia Cheng, *op cit* note 18.

[25]Long Yongtu told reporters this when asked about details on how China planned to enforce its IP commitments in a wrap-up meeting of the WTO's working party on Chinese accession in December 2000 in Geneva. Long also said the Agreement reached with WTO on intellectual property was 'the most comprehensive description of China's plan to protect intellectual property rights.' *"China's WTO Accession", World Intellectual Property Report*, Vol 15, No. 1, Jan 2001.

[26]Disputes prevention and settlement are also provided under Articles 63~64 of *TRIPS*.

its development, China's IPR protection system aimed at achieving world dimension and world standards. [*See* end of this Chapter Table A for lists of administrative rules concerning intellectual property rights currently in force in China.] The status of ongoing reforms and other relevant information was presented in Table B.	regulations, including implementing rules, issued by the State Council were applied and enforced by the people's courts. Other laws, regulations and measures relating to the implementation of the *TRIPS Agreement* had been or would be notified to the WTO and would be made available upon request.

A2. Responsible agencies for policy formulation and implementation

Current situation:

At present, different agencies were responsible for IPR policy formulation and implementation:

— The State Intellectual Property Office ("SIPO") was responsible for patent approval;
— The Trademarks Office under the State Administration for Industry and Commerce ("SAIC") was responsible for trademarks registration;
— The Copyright Office was responsible for copyright policy making;
— SAIC was responsible for anti-unfair competition, including the protection of trade secrets;
— The State Drug Administration ("SDA") was responsible for administrative protection of pharmaceuticals;
— The General Customs Administration was responsible for border measures;
— The Ministry of Agriculture and the State Administration of Forestry were responsible for protection of plant varieties;
— The Ministry of Information Industry was responsible for the protection of layout designs of integrated circuits;
— and the State General Administration of the People's Republic of China for Quality Supervision and Inspection and Quarantine and SAIC were responsible for combating counterfeiting activities.

Other agencies like the agency for press and publications, the people's courts and police were also involved in the protection of IPR in China.

A3. Participation in international intellectual property agreements

China had joined relevant international conventions and had actively participated in the activities sponsored by relevant international organizations.

— China became a member of the World Intellectual Property Organization in 1980.

— In 1985, China became a member of the *Paris Convention for the Protection of Industrial Property*. China was one of the first countries that signed the *Treaty on Intellectual Property in Respect of Integrated Circuits*, the negotiation of which was concluded in 1989.

— In 1989, China became a member of the *Madrid Agreement Concerning the International Registration of Marks* and in 1992, China became a member of the *Berne Convention for the Protection of Literary and Artistic Works*.

— In 1993, China became a member of the *Convention for the Protection of Producers of Phonograms Against Unauthorized Duplication of Their Phonograms*.

— In 1994, China became a member of the *Patent Cooperation Treaty* and a member of the *Nice Agreement Concerning the International Classification of Goods and Services for the Purposes of the Registration of Marks*.

— In 1995, China became a member of the *Budapest Treaty on the International Recognition of the Deposit of Microorganisms for the Purposes of Patent Procedure* and applied for membership in the *Protocols of the Madrid Agreement Concerning the International Registration of Marks*.

— In 1996, China became a member of the *Locarno Agreement on Establishing an International Classification for Industrial Designs*;

— and in 1997, China became a member of the *Strasbourg Agreement Concerning the International Patent Classification*.

— Besides the above efforts, China participated in the *TRIPS* negotiations during the Uruguay Round and initialled the Final Act.

A4. Application of national and MFN treatment to foreign nationals

The relevant *TRIPS* provisions are: **Articles 3 and 4 of part I**

Current Situation/Concerns Raised by other WTO Members	China commitments/confirmations
National Treatment was not provided in China's Copyright and Trademark Laws	
There were certain provisions of China's copyright and trademark laws, as well as *China's Rules on Banning the Infringement of Business Services (23 November 1995)* that did not provide national treatment to foreign right-holders. And that such treatment should be fully applied so that copyright enforcement action by local copyright bureaux involving foreign right-holders would no longer require clearance by the National Copyright Administration in Beijing.	China's IPR laws provided that any foreigner would be treated in accordance with any agreement concluded between the foreign country and China, or in accordance with any international treaty to which both countries were party, or on the basis of the principle of reciprocity. China *would modify* relevant laws, regulations and other measures so as to ensure national and MFN treatment to foreign right-holders regarding all intellectual property rights across the board in compliance with the *TRIPS Agreement*.

B. SUBSTANTIVE STANDARDS OF PROTECTION, INCLUDING PROCEDURES FOR THE ACQUISITION AND MAINTENANCE OF INTELLECTUAL PROPERTY RIGHTS

B1. Copyright protection

The relevant *TRIPS* provisions are: **Section 1 of Part II (Article 9 ~ 14)** which concerns the relation of *TRIPS* to the *Berne Convention;* computer programs and compilations of data; rental rights; term of protection; limitations and exceptions; protection of performers; producers of phonograms (sound recording) and broadcasting organizations.

Current situation:

The *Copyright Law*, which was promulgated in 1990,[27] established the basic copyright protection system in China together with the Implementing Rules of the *Copyright* Law (30 May 1991), the *Provisions on the Implementation of the International Copyright Treaty* (25 September 1992) and other related laws and regulations. In principle, this system was in compliance with the international IPR treaties and practices. For the protection of copyright and neighbouring rights, not only civil and criminal liabilities but also administrative liabilities, were provided for in this system. According to China's statement, the infringing activities could be curbed in a timely and effective manner and the legitimate rights of the right-holders could be protected. [Note that on 27 October, 2001, China had just amended the *Copyright Law* for the first time since its enactment.[28]]

Current Situation/Concerns Raised by Other WTO Members	China Commitments/Confirmations
Amendments to be made to conform with TRIPS	
There was still inconsistency of China's current law on the protection of copyright and related rights with the *TRIPS Agreement*. For instance, the rights of performers and producers need to be clarified in order to bring them into conformity with Article 14 of *TRIPS*. The law should also provide expressly for provisional measures to preserve	Realizing that there were some existing differences between China's copyright laws and the *TRIPS Agreement,* the amendment to the *Copyright Law* had been accelerated. The proposed amendments would clarify the payment system by broadcasting organizations which use the recording products and also include: — rental rights in respect of computer programs and movies, — mechanical performance rights,

[27]First adopted at the Fifteenth Session of the Standing Committee of the Seventh National People's Congress on 7 September 1990, and revised in accordance with the *Decision on the Amendment of the Copyright Law of the People's Republic of China* adopted at the 24th Session of the Standing Committee of the Ninth National People's Congress on 27 October 2001.

[28]*ibid., also see* note 20 for main points of amendments.

evidence including documentary evidence in the enforcement of copyright and to provide for remedies sufficient to deter further infringements.	— rights of communication to the public and related protection measures, — protection of database compilations, — provisional measures, — increasing the legitimate compensation amount and — strengthening the measures against infringing activities. China's copyright regime including Regulation for the Implementation of the *Copyright Law* and the *Provisions on the Implementation of the International Copyright Treaty* would be amended so as to ensure full consistency with China's obligations under the *TRIPS Agreement*.

B2. Trademarks, including services marks

The relevant *TRIPS* provisions are: **Section 2 of Part II (Articles 15 ~21)** regarding protectable subject matter; rights conferred; exceptions; term of protections; requirement of use; other requirements; and licensing and assignment.

Current Situation/Concerns Raised by Other WTO Members	China Commitments/Confirmations
National Treatment/the Registrability of a non-distinctive trademark/well-known trademarks etc.	
There were concerns: i) whether certain provisions of China's *Trademark Law* provided national treatment to foreign owners of trademarks, including well-known trademarks. Foreign owners of	China's legislative and law enforcement bodies had realized that the existing *Trademark Law*[29] fell somewhat short of fulfilling the requirements of the *TRIPS Agreement* and the *Paris Convention* in a few aspects and were therefore preparing to amend the existing *Trademark Law* to fully meet the requirements of the *TRIPS Agreement*.

[29]*Note that as with the Copyright Law, the Trademark Law of China had just been amended. The Trademark Law was* first adopted at the 24th Session of the Standing Committee of the Fifth National People's Congress on 23 August 1982; revised the first time according to the *Decision on the Amendment of the Trademark Law of the People's Republic of China,* adopted at the 30th Session of the Standing Committee of the Seventh National People's Congress, on 22 February 1993; and revised for the second time according to the *Decision on the Amendment of the Trademark Law of the People's Republic of China* adopted at the 24th Session of the Standing Committee of the Ninth National People's Congress on 27 October 2001; *see* note 21 for main points of amendments.

trademarks are required to use designated trademark agents while Chinese nationals were permitted to file directly with China's trademark office; ii) that certain signs are not eligible for protection as required under the *TRIPS Agreement*. These include names, letters, numerals and colours capable of distinguishing goods and services; iii) the qualification for registrability of a non-distinctive trademark when it has acquired distinctiveness based on use; it was not clear if under China's law that actual use of a mark was not required before a party could file for registration. iv) about the protection of well-known trademarks in China, in particular those not registered in China. China's laws and regulations did not specifically state the criteria for determining whether a mark was well-known and therefore [WTO] members could not determine if it conformed to the requirements of Article 16 of the *TRIPS Agreement*. Moreover, China had provided protection to "well known" trademarks owned by nationals, but such protection had not yet offered to the well-known trade marks of foreigners.	Modifications *would* mainly *be made* to the following aspects:[30] — to include the trademark registration of three-dimensional symbols, combinations of colours, alphabets and figures; — to add the content of collective trademark and certification trademark (including geographical indications); — to introduce official symbol protection; — to protect well-known trademarks; — to include priority rights; — to modify the existing trademark right confirmation system and offer interested parties the opportunity for judicial review concerning the confirmation of trademark rights; — to crack down on all serious infringements; and — to improve the system for providing damages for trademark infringement.

B3. *Geographical indications, including appellations of origin*

The relevant *TRIPS* provisions are: **Section 3 of Part II (Articles 22~24)** regarding protection of geographical indications; additional protections for geographical indications for wines and spirits; international negotiations and exceptions;

---

[30]*See* second revision made to *Trademark Law* by China adopted on 27 October, 2001, *also see* note 21.

Current Situation/Concerns Raised by Other WTO Members	China Commitments/Confirmations
Compliance with TRIPS	
The importance of China's legislation complying with the obligations under the *TRIPS Agreement* was stressed.	The relevant rules of the SAIC and the State General Administration of PRC for Quality Supervision and Inspection and Quarantine partly provided protection for geographical indications, including the appellations of origin. The amendments to the *Trademark Law* would have a specific provision on the protection of geographical indications. China *reiterated* China's intention to *fully comply with* relevant articles in the *TRIPS Agreement* on geographical indications.[31]

B4. Industrial designs

The relevant *TRIPS* provisions are: **Section 4 of Part II (Articles 25~26)** concerning requirements for protection; and protection.

The industrial design provisions of China's patent law appeared to implement substantial portions of the *TRIPS Agreement* requirements relating to industrial designs. One notable exception was the area of textile designs which could be protected under *China's Provisions on the Implementation of the International Copyright Treaty* as works of applied art. China was requested to incorporate this protection into its law and to provide such protection to domestic textile designs. There was no specific commitment made in respect of this.

---

[31] In the second revision to the *Trademark Law,* its Article 16 states: "*Where a trademark contains a geographic indication of the goods in respect of which the trademark is used, the goods is not from the region indicated therein and it misleads the public, it shall be rejected for registration and prohibited from use; however, any trademark that has been registered in good faith shall remain valid. The geographic indications mentioned in the preceding paragraph refer to the signs that signify the place of origin of the goods in respect of which the signs are used, their specific quality, reputation or other features as mainly decided by the natural or cultural factors of the regions.*"; *see* the translation of this law at http://www.cpahkltd.com.

[32] The *Patent Law* was adopted at the 4th Session of the Standing Committee of the Sixth National People's Congress 12 March 1984; revised for the first time by the "*Decision Regarding the Amendment of the Patent Law of the PRC*" at the 27th Session of the Standing Committee of the Seventh National People's Congress on 4 September 1992; revised for the second time by the "*Decision Regarding the Amendment of the Patent Law of the PRC*" at the 17th Meeting of the Standing Committee of the Ninth National People's Congress on 25th August 2000, effective as of 1 July 2001.

B5. Patents

The relevant *TRIPS* provisions are: **Section 5 of Part II (Articles 27 ~34)** regarding patentable subject matter; rights conferred; conditions on patent applicants; exceptions to rights conferred; other use without authorization of the right holder; revocation and forfeiture; term of protection; process patents: burden of proof.

Current Situation:

China had amended its *Patent Law* twice, the first time in 1992, the second time in 2000.[32] The latest revised version took effect on 1 July 2001 which included the following elements:

(1) patent owners would have the right to prevent others from offering for sale the patented product without their consent (Article 11);

(2) for utility model and design applications or patents, the final decision on re-examination and invalidation would be made by the people's courts other than for inventions that were patented prior to the amendment (Articles 41 and 46);

(3) patent owners could, before instituting legal proceedings, request the people's court to take provisional measures such as to order the suspension of infringing acts and to provide property preservation (Article 61); and

(4) conditions for granting a compulsory licence would be further clarified and made consistent with the *TRIPS Agreement.*

China's statement:

Since its establishment, SIPO had paid great attention to strengthening its contacts and coordination with relevant departments and ministries in the field of IPR law enforcement, especially in the areas of settling inter-agency problems and resolving key cases. At the same time, SPO had taken appropriate measures to improve the performance of local patent authorities in law enforcement. In China's opinion, the *Patent Law* is largely complaint with *TRIPS*.

The Patent Law is compliant with TRIPS agreement in the following aspects:

1. The range of patent protection and protection for new plant varieties

The relevant *TRIPS* provision is **Article 27** "Patentable Subject Matter".

Current Situation/Concern Raised by Other WTO Members	China Commitments/Confirmations
China had already met the requirements of **Article 27 of the *TRIPS Agreement*** (patentable subject matter) [**expect** that a	To bridge the gap in literal interpretation, China *would amend* the *Implementing Rules of the Patent Law* to ensure that Article 5 of China's *Patent Law*

slight discrepancy in literal interpretation need to be clarified.]

When amending the Patent Law in 1992, China modified Article 25 therein with reference to the relevant stipulations in the draft of the *TRIPS Agreement* and expanded the coverage of patent protection to food, beverages, flavourings, pharmaceuticals and materials obtained by chemical methods. The scope of patent exclusions would be limited to "*scientific discoveries, rules and methods of intellectual activities, diagnostic and therapeutic methods for the treatment of diseases, animals and plant varieties, as well as materials obtained by the change of nucleus*".

There appeared to be a literal difference between Article 5 of China's *Patent Law* with *TRIPS* provision [Article 27.2] in interpreting inventions that "violate laws of China".[33]

Article 5 of China's *Patent Law* stipulated that inventions that violate laws of China or social morality or prejudice public interest would not be entitled to patent right.

would be implemented in full compliance with Article 27.2 of the *TRIPS Agreement*,[34] which stipulated that:

"*Members may exclude from patentability inventions, the prevention within their territory of the commercial exploitation of which is necessary to protect* ordre public *or morality, including to protect human, animal or plant life or health or to avoid serious prejudice to the environment, provided that such exclusion is not made merely because the exploitation is prohibited by their law*." [ie. Members may not exclude inventions from patentability merely because the law prohibits the exploitation]

---

[33]The meaning of "violating laws of China" should be restricted. If the *sale is* prohibited of a certain patented product or products manufactured by a patented method, the granting of patent right cannot be denied to this product invention or invention of product manufacturing method by relying on Article 5 of the *Patent Law. See* clause 270 of the Working Party Report.

[34]*Note* that the *Implementing Rules of the Patent Law* was amended on 26 June 2001 to comply with Article 27.2 of *TRIPS, its* Rule 9 stipulates: "*The invention-creations contrary to the laws of the State referred to in Article 5 of the Patent Law do not include invention-creations the exploitation of which is prohibited under the laws of the State.*" The amendment to the *Implementing Rules of the Patent Law* was approved by the State Council on 26 June, 2001 and promulgated by the State Intellectual Properly Office of the People's Republic of China on 1 July 2001, effective 1 July 2001. *See* the translation of the Rules at http://www.cpahkltd.com.

2. Right of Patentee

The relevant *TRIPS* provision is **Article 28** "Rights Conferred".

China stated that its *Patent Law* had fully accommodated the requirement of Article 28 of *TRIPS*.

2.1 First, in the 1992 amendment to the *Patent Law,* Article 11 was modified (prior licence required for use of patent).[35] This modification expanded the scope of patentees' right, namely the new content of "the right to prohibit import" and "the effect of patented processes is extended to: products directly obtained by patented processes".

2.2. Second, the second amendment made to the *Patent Law,* Article 11 was once again modified. A new stipulation was introduced granting patentees the right to prohibit others from offering for sale the patented products or products directly obtained by patented processes *without* the consent of patentees.

3. Compulsory Licensing

The relevant *TRIPS* provision is: Article 31 concerning other use without authorization of the right holder.

3.1 Conditions of compulsory licensing for dependent patents

With regard to the conditions of compulsory licences for dependent patents, *China adopted the relevant expressions* of Article 31(1) of *TRIPS* concerning the exploitation of a patent. In the second amendment to the *Patent Law* in 2000, Article 53 of the *Patent Law* was modified to read: "a later invention or utility model is an important technical progress with striking economic significance as compared to the earlier invention or utility model".[36] The regulations on time, scope and termination of compulsory licensing enforcement were laid down in Article 52 of the amended *Patent Law*, for instance, when the circumstances which led to such compulsory licence ceased to exist and were unlikely to recur, SIPO could, upon request of the patentee, terminate the compulsory licence after examination. As such, China claimed that its *Patent Law* had regulations on compulsory licensing with clearer structure and improved content. These regulations were fully consistent with the *TRIPS Agreement.*

---

[35]Article 11 of the *Chinese Patent Law* was modified as follows: "any entity or individual is, without prior licensing from the patentee, prohibited from making, using or selling patented products or patented processes, or using or selling products directly obtained by the patented processes for the purpose of production and operation". It was also prohibited for any entity or individual to import patented products or products directly obtained by patented processes for the purpose of production and operation. *See* clause 271 of the Working Party Report.

[36]*compare* with the description under Article 31(1)(i) of TRIPS, which reads *"the invention claimed in* the second patent shall involve an important technical advance of considerable economic significance in relation to the invention claimed in the first patent".

3.2 Clarification of the subject matter

Current Situation/Concerns Raised by Other WTO Members	China Commitments/Confirmations
As to further concerns requesting for clarification of the subject matter that would be subject to compulsory licensing under the *Patent Law*.	China agreed that still not all the requirements of Article 31 of the *TRIPS Agreement* had been incorporated into Chinese law, and that the *Implementing Rules of the Patent Law would* therefore *be modified* so as to ensure that: (1) use without authorization of the right-holder would only be permitted if, prior to such use, the proposed user had made efforts to obtain authorization from the right-holder on reasonable commercial terms and conditions, on the understanding that this requirement could be waived in the case of a national emergency or other circumstances of extreme urgency or in cases of public non-commercial use.[37] (2) the right-holder would be paid adequate remuneration in the circumstances of each case, taking into account the economic value of authorization;[38] (3) any such use would be authorized predominantly for the supply of the domestic market,[39] and (4) in the case of semi-conductor technology, the scope and duration of such use would only be for public non-commercial use or to remedy a practice determined after judicial or administrative process to be anti-competitive.[40]

---

[37]The *Implementing Rules of the Patent Law* was amended and effective 1 July 2001 to include such requirement under its Rule 72 to comply with Article 31(b) of *TRIPS*.

[38]The *Implementing Rules of the Patent Law* was amended and effective 1 July 2001 to include such requirement under its Rule 76 to comply with Article 31(h) of *TRIPS*.

[39]The *Implementing Rules of the Patent Law* was amended and effective 1 July 2001 to include such requirement under its Rule 72 to comply with Article 31(f) of *TRIPS*.

[40]The *Implementing Rules of the Patent Law* was amended and effective 1 July 2001 to include such requirement under its Rule 72 to comply with Article 31(c) of *TRIPS*.

4. Administrative Decisions Subject to Judicial Review

The relevant *TRIPS* provision is: **Article 32** "Revocation/Forfeiture"—which says an opportunity for judicial review of any decision to revoke or forfeit a patent shall be available [in the legislation of Members].

Regarding this provision, in light of Articles 41 and 46 of the amended *Patent Law,* patent applicants or patentees of inventions, as well as applicable utility models and designs, could institute legal proceedings in the people's court if they were not satisfied with the review or nullity decisions made by the Patent Review Board. According to China, this modification enabled China's *Patent Law* to be fully consistent with *TRIPS* regarding administrative decisions which were subject to judicial review.

5. Duration of patent right protection

The relevant *TRIPS* provisions are: **Articles 26 and 33** regarding protection and term of protection.

Article 42 of the *Patent Law* reads: "the duration of inventions patent right is 20 years and the duration of patent right for applicable utility model and designs is 10 years, counted as of the date of application". This complies with Articles 26 and 33 of the *TRIPS Agreement* concerning the duration of patent rights.

6. Process Patents

The relevant *TRIPS* provision is: **Article 34** concerning process patents: burden of proof.

Regarding this provision, China's *Patent Law* was modified in 1992 and 2000, and was now in full conformity with the *TRIPS Agreement.* The amended paragraph 2 of Article 57 reads: "when any infringement dispute relates to a process patent for the manufacture of a new product, any entity or individual manufacturing the identical product shall furnish proof to the effect that a different process is used in the manufacture of its or his product".

B6. Plant variety protection

The relevant *TRIPS* provision is **paragraph 3 of Article 27** "Patentable Subject Matter".

An account was given on the current situation. No commitment was made.

China *confirmed* that China was a party to the 1978 text of the *Universal Convention on the Protection of Plant Varieties ("UPOV")*. In March 1997, the State Council formulated and promulgated the *Regulation on the Protection of New Plant Varieties,* thus offering protection for new plant varieties in a *sui generis*[41] form consistent with the requirements of

---

[41]Of its own nature, altogether unique; sui generis rights refer to the protection of certain categories of rights outside the traditional scope of copyright, *consider* compilation of databases and semi-conductor topography makers' rights.

the *TRIPS Agreement*. A unit or an individual that had accomplished the breeding enjoyed an exclusive right in their right-granted variety. No unit or individual could, without permission from the owner of the variety rights (referred to as "the variety rights owner"), produce or market for commercial purposes the propagation material of the rights-granted variety, or repeatedly use for commercial purposes the propagation material of the rights-granted variety in the production of the propagation material of another variety. The conditions of non-voluntary licensing were set out in the regulation. The period of protection of variety rights, from the date of grant of the rights, would be 20 years for vines, forest trees, fruit trees and ornamental trees and 15 years for other plants.

B7. Layout designs of integrated circuits

The relevant *TRIPS* provisions are: **Section 6 of Part II (Articles 35 ~ 38)** regarding layout designs (topographies) of integrated circuits.

China was one of the first countries to sign the *Treaty on Intellectual Property in Respect of Integrated Circuits* in 1989. The specific *Regulation on the Protection of Layout Designs of Integrated Circuits,* which *would implement* China's obligations under Section 6, Part II of the *TRIPS Agreement,* was issued in April 2001 and *had been effective* on 1 October 2001.

The Regulation provided protection to layout-designs, according to which the following acts if performed without authorization of the right-holder were unlawful: importing, selling or otherwise distributing for commercial purposes a protected layout-design, an integrated circuit in which a protected layout-design was incorporated, or an article incorporating such an integrated circuit only in so far as it continued to contain an unlawfully reproduced layout-design. The exception clause and non-voluntary licensing clause were in conformity with Article 37 of *TRIPS*.[42] The term of protection was 10 years counted from the date of filing an application for registration or from the first commercial exploitation wherever in the world it occurred. In addition, the protection to the layout-design of integrated circuits was in accordance with Article 2 through 7 (other than paragraph 3 of Article 6), Article 12 and paragraph 3 of Article 16 of the *Treaty on Intellectual Property In Respect of Integrated Circuits.*

B8. Requirements on undisclosed information, including trade secrets and test data

The relevant *TRIPS* provision is: **Section 7 of Part II (Articles 39)** concerning protection of undisclosed information)

---

[42]Concerns "acts not requiring the authorization of the right holder" of layout designs.

Current Situation/Concern Raised by Other WTO Members	China Commitments/Confirmations
There was concern about China's protection against unfair commercial use and disclosure of undisclosed test and other data submitted to authorities in China to obtain marketing approval for pharmaceuticals and agricultural chemicals. China stated that Article 10 of the *Anti-unfair Competition Law*[43] provided that a business operator must not infringe upon trade secrets. Trade Secrets refer to any technology information or business operation information which was unknown to public, could bring about economic benefits to the obligee, had practical utility and about which the obligee had adopted secret-keeping measures. Article 219 of the *Criminal Law*[44] had similar definitions on trade secrets.	China *confirmed* that China *would*, in compliance with Article 39.3 of the *TRIPS Agreement, provide* effective protection against unfair commercial use of undisclosed test or other data submitted to authorities in China as required in support of applications for marketing approval of pharmaceutical or of agricultural chemical products which utilized new chemical entities, except where the disclosure was for public's interests, or where steps were taken to ensure that the data are protected against unfair commercial use. This protection *would include* enactment of laws and regulations to make sure that no person could rely on such data without the permission of the person who submitted the data in support of an application for product approval. The protection lasts for a period of at least six years from the date on which China granted marketing approval to the person submitting the data. During this period, any second applicant for market authorization would only be granted market authorization if he submits his own data. This protection of data *would be available* to all pharmaceutical and agricultural products which utilize new chemical entities, irrespective of whether they were patent-protected or not.

C. MEASURES TO CONTROL ABUSE OF INTELLECTUAL PROPERTY RIGHTS

The relevant *TRIPS* provision is: **Section 8 of Part II (Article 40)** regarding control of anti-competitive practices in contractual licences.

According to *TRIPS,* Members agree that some licensing practices or conditions pertaining to intellectual property rights which restrain competition may have adverse effects on trade and may impede the transfer and dissemination of technology.[45] *TRIPS* does not prevent Members from specifying in their legislation such licensing practices or conditions that may

---

[43]Or translated as *The Law of the People's Republic of China for Countering Unfair Competition*. The law was adopted on 2 September 1993 at the Third Session of the Standing Committee of the Eighth National People's Congress and became effective on 1 December 1993.

[44]*The Criminal Law* was first adopted by the Second Session of the Fifth National People's Congress on 1 July 1979 and amended by the 5th Session of the Eighth National People's Congress on 14 March 1997, effective as of 1 October 1997.

[45]*TRIPS*, Article 40(1).

in particular cases constitute an abuse of intellectual property rights. A Member may adopt appropriate measures to prevent or control such practices, and that they shall be consistent with other provisions of *TRIPS*.[46] Opportunities for consultations between and among Members should be considered and granted on alleged violation of laws and regulations of any Member in this subject matter.[47]

Current Situation/Concerns Raised by Other WTO Members	China commitments/confirmations
There were provisions relating to compulsory licenses in the *Patent Law* to prevent abuse of patent right. The *Trademark Law* provided that the trademark registrant may, by concluding a trademark licensing contract, authorize another person to use its registered trademark. The licensor would supervise the quality of the goods on which the licensee used the licensor's registered trademark and the licensee would guarantee the quality of the goods on which the registered trademark was to be used.	China's legislation *would comply* with *TRIPS* obligations, notably as to the request for consultations with other Members. These rules *would apply* across the board to all intellectual property rights.
There were some concerns as to be compatibility of China's rules on control of anti-competitive licensing practices or conditions with the corresponding obligations under Article 40 of the *TRIPS Agreement*.	

D. ENFORCEMENT

D1. General

The relevant *TRIPS* provisions is: **Section 1 of Part III (Article 41)** on general obligations of enforcement of intellectual properly rights.

---

[46]*ibid*, Article 40(2), measures to prevent or control practices of abuse may include for example, exclusive grantback conditions, conditions preventing challenges to validity and coercive package licensing in the light of the relevant laws and regulations of a Member.

[47]*ibid*, Articles 40 (3) (4).

Members shall ensure that enforcement procedures as specified under Part III of *TRIPS* are available under their law so as to permit effective action against any act of infringement of intellectual property rights covered by *TRIPS*, including expeditious remedies to prevent infringements and remedies which constitute a deterrent to further infringements. The procedures shall be applied in such a manner as to avoid the creation of barriers to legitimate trade and to provide for safeguards against their abuse.[48]

Procedures concerning the enforcement of intellectual property rights shall be fair and equitable. They shall not be unnecessarily complicated or costly, or entail unreasonable time-limits or unwarranted delays.[49] Decisions on the merits of a case shall preferably be in writing and reasoned, based only on evidence in respect of which parties were offered the opportunity to be heard.[50] Parties to a proceeding shall have an opportunity for review by a judicial authority of final administrative decisions.[51] A Member's judicial system for the enforcement of intellectual property rights need not be distinctive from that for the enforcement of law in general.[52]

Current Situation/Concerns Raised by Other WTO Members	China Commitments/Confirmations
The strengthening of legislative framework for the Enforcement of Intellectual Property	
It was concerned that there was a continued need for additional enforcement efforts by the government of China; and that China should strengthen the legislative framework for the enforcement of IPR to the benefits of all right holders. The vigorous application of the enforcement legislation could also considerably reduce the existing high level of copyright piracy and trademark counterfeiting. Action should include closure of manufacturing facilities as well as markets, retail shops that had been the object of administrative convictions for infringing activities.	China stated that the measures for cracking down on intellectual property piracy were always severe in China. In judicial aspects, courts at all levels were continuously paying attention to the trial of IPR cases. As for administration aspects, the administrative authorities at all levels were putting emphasis on strengthening anti-piracy work. In addition, the administrative authorities were also enhancing the legal publication and education of the general public in a bid to ensure that the legal environment of China *would be able to meet* the requirements for enforcing the *TRIPS Agreement*.

[48]*ibid* Article 41(1)
[49]*ibid* Article 41(2)
[50]*ibid.* Article 41(3)
[51]*ibid.* Article 41(4)
[52]*ibid.* Article 41(5)

Currently, where an infringement of intellectual property rights was found in China, the person concerned could bring a lawsuit to a court. Since 1992, special IPR courts have been set up in major cities such as Beijing and Shanghai on the basis of their specialized collegial panels. According to China's legislation, individuals and enterprises would be held responsible for all their IPR infringing activities and subject to civil and/or criminal liabilities. If found guilty under *Criminal Law*, the person directly responsible could be sentenced to a fixed-term imprisonment of no more than seven years[53] or be subject to detention or a fine.	

D2. Civil and administrative procedures and remedies

The relevant *TRIPS* provisions are: **Section 2 of Part III (Articles 42-49)** concerning fair and equitable procedures; evidence; injunctions; damages; other remedies; right of information; indemnification of the defendant; and administrative procedures.

Current Situation/Concerns Raised by Other WTO Members	China Commitments/Confirmations
Costly judicial actions and inadequate damages to compensate injury of infringement	
There were concern that certain practices relating to the filing of civil judicial actions that made it difficult for intellectual property right-holders to pursue their rights in China courts. China's system of basing filing fees on the amount of damages requested makes large-scale infringement actions unnecessarily costly. Also, there was the practice of calculating damages based on the	China stated that Article 118 of the *General Principles of the Civil Law* provided that if the rights of authorship (copyrights), patent rights, rights of exclusive use of trademarks, rights of discovery, rights of invention or rights for scientific and technological research achievements of citizens or juridical persons were infringed upon by such means as plagiarism, alteration or imitation, they had the right to demand that the infringement be stopped, its ill effects be eliminated and the damages be compensated for. The *Trademark Law*, the *Patent Law* and the *Copyright Law* had similar provisions.

---

[53]Article 213 of the *Criminal Law*.

infringer's profits. This combined with China's rules on establishing the level of profits which require evidence of actual sale and which disregard inventory and past activity, often resulted in inadequate damage amounts to compensate for the injury that the right-holder has suffered.	China *confirmed* that Articles 42 (fair and equitable procedures) and 43 (evidence) of the *TRIPS Agreement* would be effectively implemented under the judicial rules of civil procedure. The relevant implementing rules *would be amended* to ensure full compliance with Articles 45 (damages) and 46 (other remedies) of the *TRIPS Agreement* to the effect that damages paid by the infringer to the right-holder would be adequate to compensate for the injury suffered because of an infringement of that person's intellectual property right by an infringer who knowingly engaged in infringing activity.

The inadequate levels of administrative sanctions in China

Most intellectual property right (IPR) enforcement in China was done through administrative actions. As such, the inadequate levels of administrative sanctions in China which, when coupled with the high threshold for initiating criminal prosecutions, made IPR enforcement in China difficult. Administrative sanctions generally amounted to small fines and the loss of infringing inventory. There was the need for administrative authorities to refer more cases to the appropriate authorities for initiation of criminal actions, including those repeated offenders and willful piracy and counterfeiting. At present, the *Trademark Law,* the *Patent Law* and the *Copyright Law* all contain provisions on administrative sanctions on infringement of holders' rights.	China stated that most IPR enforcement actions in China resulted in administrative measures to address the infringement. There were ongoing efforts to strengthen the sanctions that were available to administrative authorities and the increased attention given to enforcement of IPRs. The government *would continue* to enhance its enforcement efforts, including through the application of more effective administrative sanctions. Relevant agencies, including the State Administration for Industry and Commerce, the State General Administration of the People's Republic of China for Quality Supervision and Inspection and Quarantine and the Copyright Office, now had the authority to confiscate equipment used for making counterfeit and pirated products and other evidence of infringement. These relevant agencies *would be* encouraged to exercise their authority to seize and preserve evidence of infringement such as inventory and documents. Administrative authorities *would have* the authority to impose sufficient sanctions to prevent or deter further infringement and would be encouraged to exercise that authority. Appropriate cases, including those involving repeat offenders and willful piracy and counterfeiting *would be* referred to relevant authorities for prosecution under the criminal law provisions.

D3. Provisional measures

The relevant *TRIPS* provision is **Section 3 of Part III (Article 50)**.

Article 50(1)(2) stipulates that judicial authorities have the authority to order prompt and effective provisional measures to (a) prevent an infringement of intellectual property from occurring, in particular to prevent entry into the channels of commerce in their jurisdiction of goods including imported goods immediately after customs clearance, and (b) to preserve the evidence of alleged infringement. The judicial authorities shall have the authority to adopt provisional measures where appropriate, in particular where any delay is likely to cause irreparable harm to the right holder, or where there is a demonstrable risk of evidence being destroyed.

TRIPS also stipulates that the judicial authorities shall order such measures against any reasonably available evidence in order to satisfy themselves with a sufficient degree of certainty that the applicant for such measure is the right holder, and that the applicant's right is being infringed or that such infringement is imminent. A review of such measure shall take place upon request of the defendant with a view to deciding whether these measures shall be modified, revoked or confirmed.[54]

Current Situation/Concerns Raised by Other WTO Members	China Commitments/Confirmations
In order to enhance the deterrent power of law against infringements and to guarantee that the legitimate rights and interests of patentees would not suffer from irreparable harm as well as to comply with the *TRIPS Agreement*, China, when amending the *Patent Law* for the second time in 2000, introduced Article 61 to regulate provisional measures, which provided as follows: *"where a patentee or any interested party who can provide any reasonable evidence that his right is being infringed or that such infringement is imminent, and any delay in stopping the acts is likely to cause irreparable harm to his or its legitimate rights and interests, he or it may, before instituting legal proceedings,*	Article 61 of the *Patent Law would be implemented* in a way fully consistent with Article 50.1~4 of the *TRIPS Agreement.* "Reasonable evidence" in Article 61 of the *Patent Law would be*, through its implementing rules, clarified to mean "any reasonably available evidence in order to satisfy with sufficient degree of certainty that the applicant is the right-holder and that the applicant's right is being infringed or that such infringement is imminent, and to order the applicant to provide a security or equivalent assurance sufficient to protect the defendant and to prevent abuse".

---

[54]*TRIPS,* Article 50(3)(4).

request the people's court to order the suspension of related acts and to provide property preservation....." It was still unclear whether holders of IP rights other than patents could rely on a similar procedure.	

D4. Special border measures

The relevant *TRIPS* provisions are: **Section 4 of Part III (Articles 51~60)**.

Current Situation/Concerns Raised by Other WTO Members	China Commitments/Confirmations
According to the *Regulations of the People's Republic of China Governing Customs Protection of Intellectual Property Rights*,[55] China's Customs offices must take measures to intercept importation or exportation of goods that were proved to be infringing the rights of trademarks, patents or copyrights legally protected in China. China's Customs offices were granted authority to investigate any suspected shipment and confiscate the goods in case infringement was proved. There were concerns as to the compatibility of existing border measures with Articles 51-60 of *TRIPS*.	China *would provide* holders of intellectual property rights with procedures related to borders measures that complied fully with the relevant provisions of the *TRIPS Agreement*. Procedures under Articles 51 to 60 of the *TRIPS Agreement* are: Right holder to apply for suspension of release into free circulation by customs authorities (Article 51), rules on evidence for initiating this procedure (Article 52), requirements on the security and assurance to be provided by the applicant needed to protect the defendant and to prevent abuse (Article 53), rules on notice of the suspension (Article 54) and its duration (Article 55), rules on indemnification of the importer in case of wrongful detention by customs authorities (Article 56) and opportunity for the right-holder to have the goods detained inspected [goods means any suspected importation of counterfeit trademark or pirated copyright goods] (Article 57); compatibility of rules on action ex-officio by competent authorities and the conditions attached (Article 58), the remedies provided against infringing goods (Article 59) and the quantities subject to the *de minimis* rules (Article 60).

---

[55]Promulgated by Decree No. 179 of the State Council of the People's Republic of China on 5 July 1995 and effective 1 October 1995.

D5. Criminal procedures

The relevant *TRIPS* provision is: **Section 5 of Part III (Article 61)**.

Current Situation/Concerns Raised by Other WTO Members	China Commitments/Confirmations
Article 213 to 220 *of the Criminal Law (Crimes of Infringing on Intellectual Property Rights)* provided that whoever seriously infringes the right-holders' rights of registered trademarks, patents, copyrights or trade secrets would be sentenced to fixed-term imprisonment and would also be fined. As regards with concerns that criminal procedures could not be used effectively to address piracy and counterfeiting, in particular, the monetary thresholds for bringing a criminal action, as currently applied, were very high and seldom met. Those thresholds should be lowered so as to permit effective action that would deter future piracy and counterfeiting.	China's administrative authority *would recommend* that the judicial authority make necessary adjustments to lower the thresholds so as to address these concerns. Noting the advanced state of protection for intellectual property rights in China, China *confirmed* that upon accession China *would fully apply* the provisions of the *TRIPS Agreement*.

E. ADMINISTRATIVE RULES AND REVISIONS OF IPR LAWS OF PRC

Table A: The Administrative Rules of China Concerning Intellectual Property Rights

The following three parts were the administrative rules regarding protection of intellectual property right, which were still in force in China. As an important part of China's IPR legal system, these rules had a great effect on IPR protection, enforcing the IPR law, etc.

Part I List of Administrative Rules Regarding Protection of Patent Right
Part II List of Administrative Rules Regarding Protection of Trademark
Part III List of Administrative Rules Regarding Protection of Copyright

Part I List of Administrative Rules Regarding Protection of Patent Right

(i) Methods on the Showing the Identification of Right of Priority to Applicant made by Patent Office of China (1 March 1988)
(ii) Opinions of the Patent Office of China concerning the Implementation of the Regulations on Patent Commissioning (19 April 1991)
(iii) Explanation of the Patent Office of China on Certain Matters Relating to the Commissioning Involving Foreign Interests (16 November 1987)
(iv) Decree of Patent Office of China (No.26) (20 November 1989)

(v) Decree of Patent Office of China (No.27) (21 December 1989)

(vi) Decree of Patent Office of China (No.31) (14 March 1991)

(vii) Procedures for Administrative Reconsideration of Patent Office of the People's Republic of China (for Trial Implementation) (21 December 1992)

(viii) Methods of Handling the Patent Disputes by the Administrative Authorities for Patent Affairs (4 December 1989)

Part II List of Administrative Rules Regarding Protection of Trademark

(i) Circular on the Commodities Demanded to Use Registered Trademark made by the State Administration for Industry and Commerce (14 January 1988)

(ii) Circular on the Prohibition from Registering the Other Person's Trademark Abroad without Being Authorized made by State Administration for Industry and Commerce and the Ministry of Foreign Economy and Trade (19 November 1990)

(iii) Interim Provisions on Claims for Priority in Applying for Registration of Trademarks made by State Administration for Industry and Commerce (15 March 1983)

(iv) Methods of the Application International Registration of Trademark of Madrid made by the State Administration for Industry and Commerce (2 March 1989)

(v) Circular on the Stopping Using the Literal of "Xiang Bin" or "Champagne" in Varieties of Commodities of Alcohol made by the State Administration for Industry and Commerce (26 October 1989)

(vi) Circular on Printing and distributing "the Rules regarding the Question of Using Trademark in Can Food for Export" (15 October 1991)

(vii) Provisions on the Control over the Surrogate of Trademark

(viii) Provisions on the Registration of and the Control over the Collective Trademark and Certified Trademark (issued on 30 December 1994, revised on 3 December 1998)

(ix) Provisions on the Control over the Printing of Trademark (issued on 5 September 1996, revised on 3 December 1998)

Part III List of Administrative Rules Regarding Protection of Copyright

(i) Opinions of the National Copyright Administration on Questions Relating to Reprinting the Programs in Advance in Broadcast and Television (12 December 1987)

(ii) Circular of the National Copyright Administration of Printing and Distribution "Report Relating to Appropriate Handling the Copyright Question in the Process of Culture Communication with Taiwan" and "Interim Provisions Relating to the Copyright Question of Pressing the Works Written by Taiwan Compatriots" (8 February 1988)

(iii) Circular of National Copyright Administration regarding the Points for Attention of Transferring Copyright to Taiwan's Press Person (26 December 1987)

(iv) Opinions of National Copyright Administration on Matters Relating to Local Work on Copyright Management (May 1988)

(v) Circular of the National Copyright Administration concerning Procedures of Examining and Verifying the Copyright Trading Contract Between the Mainland and Hong Kong, Macao and Taiwan (2 November 1988)

(vi) Opinions on Certain Matters of the National Copyright Administration concerning Handling Copyright Cases (27 December 1988)

(vii)   Circular of the National Copyright Administration concerning the Standard of Paying Author's Remuneration When the Press Reprint and Extract the Published Works at Present (27 August 1991)

(viii)   Interim Provisions of the Standard of Paying Author's Remuneration When the Press Reprint and Extract the Published Works with the Consent by Law (1 August 1993)

(ix)   Interim Provisions of the Standard of Paying Author's Remuneration When Perform the Published Works with the Consent by Law (1 August 1993)

(x)   Interim Provisions of the Standard of Paying Author's Remuneration When Record the Published Works with the Consent by Law (1 August 1993)

(xi)   Direction of the Chinese Center of Receiving and Transmitting Author's Remuneration concerning Receiving and Transmitting Remuneration About the Press Extract the Published Works

(xii)   Circular of the National Copyright Administration concerning Enforcing "the Memorandum of Understanding between the Government of the People's Republic of China and the Government of thc United States of America on the Protection of Intellectual Property" (29 February 1992)

(xiii)   Urgent Circular concerning Strengthening Administration of Reproducing Compact Discs and Laser Discs (12 April 1994)

(xiv)   Circular of Enforcing "Urgent Circular concerning Strengthening Administration of Reproducing Compact Discs and Laser Discs" (12 May 1994)

(xv)   Cooperate Circular of the Ministry of Judicial and National Copyright Administration concerning Bringing Notary Office into Play in Dealing with the Infringing Copyright Cases (29 August 1994)

(xvi)   Measures of the Registration of Copyright of Computer Software (4 June 1992)

(xvii)   Guide to Classified Coding of Software in Computer Software's Registration

(xviii)   The Item and Standard of Registration Expenses of Computer Software (18 April 1992)

Table B: Revision of China's IPR Laws in Conformity with the TRIPS Agreement

The People's Republic of China had conducted an intensive work programme to examine and revise the IPR laws, administrative regulations and department rules relating to the implementation of the *WTO Agreement* and China's accession commitments. A list of China's IPR laws, administrative regulations and department rules to be revised and abolished was hereby notified to the Working Party. Part I of the list contained eight laws and regulations. Part II of the list contained four department rules to be revised or abolished for the same reason. This list included the names of laws, regulations and department rules, reasons for revision or abolishment, and dates of implementation.

Part I. Laws and Administrative Regulations

Laws and Regulations	Date of Implementation
1. *Copyright Law* of the People's Republic of China	Upon accession
2. Regulations for the implementation of the *Copyright Law* of the People's Republic of China	Upon accession

3.	Regulations for the Protection of Computer Software	Upon accession
4.	*Trademark Law* of the People's Republic of China	Upon accession
5.	Detailed Rules for the Implementation of the *Trademark Law* of the People's Republic of China	Upon accession
6.	Regulations of the People's Republic of China on the Protection of New Varieties of Plants	Effective as of 1 October 1997
7.	Law of the People's Republic of China Against Unfair Competition	Effective as of 1 December 1993
8.	Regulations on the Implementation of the Integrated Circuit Layout Design	To be effective as of 10 October 2001

Part II. Department Rules

Department Rules	Date of Implementation
1. Interim Rules on the Administration of Patents in Agriculture, Animal Husbandry and Fisheries	To be abolished upon accession
2. Notice on the Interim Regulation on the Protection of Copyright of Books and Magazines	To be abolished upon accession
3. Notice on the Issuance of the "Detailed Rules of Interim Regulations on the Protection of Copyright of Books and Magazines", "Publication Intention Contracts" and "Publication Contracts"	To be abolished upon accession
4. Interpretation of Article 15(4) of the "Interim Regulation on the Protection Copyright of Books and Magazines"	To be abolished upon accession

chapter 5

China and WTO Dispute Settlement Mechanism

Disputes settlement under WTO is governed by the rules and procedures contained in the *Understanding on Rules and Procedures Governing the Settlement of Disputes ("the Understanding").* The *Understanding* is a Uruguay Round agreement[1] which came into effect on 1 January 1995.

The dispute settlement procedures laid down in the *Understanding* apply to the disputes brought pursuant to consultation and dispute settlement provisions of most of the covered agreements of WTO. These procedures also apply to consultation and settlement of disputes between Member countries concerning their rights and obligations under the provisions of the Agreement Establishing the WTO.[2] A dispute arises when one Member country adopts a trade policy measure or takes some actions that one or more fellow-WTO Members considers to be breaking WTO agreements or to be a failure to live up to obligations under an WTO agreement. Dispute settlement under WTO is the first system available for the multilateral resolution of disputes in respect of various agreements between states and with enforceable decisions.

I. REGULATORY BODY[3]

Settling disputes is the responsibility of a sole body, the **Dispute Settlement Body (DSB, the General Council in another guise),** which administers the dispute settlement procedures. DSB has the sole authority to establish "panels" of experts to consider the case, and to accept

---

[1]Annex 2 to the *WTO Agreement.*

[2]*See* Appendix 1 of the *Understanding* "Agreements covered by the Understanding". These include: (a) Agreement Establishing the WTO; (b) Multilateral Trade Agreements: Annex 1A Multilateral Agreements on Trade in Goods, (see list of agreements in Appendix 1 of this book); Annex 1B *General Agreements on Trade in Services*, Annex 1C *Agreement on Trade-Related Aspects of Intellectual Property Rights*, Annex 2 *Understanding on Rules and Procedures Governing the Settlement of Disputes; (c)* Plurilateral Trade Agreements, Annex 4: *Agreement on Trade in Civil Aircraft, Agreement on Government Procurement, International Dairy Agreement, International Bovine Meat Agreement.*

[3]the *Understanding*, Article 2 "Administration" [of the Dispute Settlement Procedures].

or reject the panels' findings or the results of an appeal. It monitors the implementation of the rulings and recommendations, and has the power to authorize retaliation (sanctions) when a Member country does not comply with a ruling.

II. MEMBER'S UNDERTAKING TO EMPLOY THE PROCEDURES

WTO Members have committed pursuant to Article 23 of the *Understanding* that if they believe fellow-members are violating trade rules, they will make use of the multilateral system of settling disputes instead of taking action unilaterally. They committed to abide by agreed procedures and respect judgments given in the panel or appellate body reports adopted by DSB or an arbitration award rendered pursuant to the *Understanding*. Jurisdiction over trade-related disputes by the DSB shall be exclusive, mandatory and binding upon all WTO Members. The *Understanding* also stresses that prompt compliance with recommendations or rulings of the DSB by disputing parties is essential in order to ensure effective resolution of disputes to the benefit of all Members.[4]

III. AIM AND PROCEDURES OF THE DISPUTE SETTLEMENT PROCEDURES[5]

The aim of the dispute settlement mechanism is stated to be to secure "a positive solution to the dispute" and preferably "a solution mutually acceptable to the parties".

The procedures comprise of five main stages:

Stage 1 – *Consultation*[6] failing which, dispute settlement shall proceed to next stage;
Stage 2 – *Establishment of Panels* by DSB;[7]
Stage 3 – *Panel Proceedings*[8]: these include written presentations by both sides; first hearing; rebuttals; the engagement of expert review group; first draft of report; interim report; review; final report; report becomes a ruling;
Stage 4 – *Appeal*[9]: only issues of law will be dealt with in this stage;
Stage 5 – *Implementation of Recommendations and Rulings*[10]: prompt compliance with DSB recommendations and rulings in order to ensure the effective resolution of disputes. Should Member country concerned not comply with the DSB recommendations and rulings, it must negotiate with the complainant for a compensation agreement, failing which, complainant may request the DSB to implement sanctions on the party violating trade rules.

(See a flow chart illustrating a typical panel process and proposed timetable for panel work at the end of this chapter)

---

[4]*Ibid.*, Article 21(1).
[5]*Ibid.*, Appendix 3 "Working Procedures".
[6]*Ibid.*, Article 4.
[7]*Ibid.*, Article 7 "Terms of Reference of Panels".
[8]*Ibid.*, Articles 12~16, 18~20.
[9]*Ibid.*, Articles 17~20.
[10]*Ibid.*, Articles 21, 22.

It is not the scope of this handbook to give an in-depth discussion on the procedures whereby a dispute in a trade matter between or among Member countries is handled or resolved. An attempt however, is made to highlight the special features and strengths of the disputes settlement procedures that make it the central pillar of WTO.

IV. STRENGTHS OF THE DISPUTES SETTLEMENT PROCEDURES (MAIN PRINCIPLES: EQUITABLE, FAST, EFFECTIVE, MUTUALLY ACCEPTABLE)

Well-defined Stages and Timeframe

WTO's dispute settlement procedures is a more structured process with more clearly defined stages than that existed under the old *GATT*. The old *GATT* had no fixed timetables for handling disputes in reaching a final ruling; rulings were easier to block then, and many cases were dragged on for a long time inconclusively. WTO's procedures introduced greater discipline for the length of time a case should take to be settled and sets out in considerable detail the procedures and timetable to be followed. It is therefore more secured and predictable.

Prompt Settlement

WTO's dispute settlement procedures were set to emphasize prompt settlement that is essential if the WTO is to function effectively. In particular, a timeframe is set for compliance with panel recommendations and rulings.[11] If a case runs its full course to a first ruling, it should not normally take more than about one year to 15 months if the case is appealed.[12]

Flexibility

The agreed time limits are flexible, and if the case is considered urgent, for example if perishable goods are involved, then the case should take three months less.

Panel Rulings are adopted automatically- a mechanism with teeth[13]

It is made impossible for the Member country losing a case to block the adoption of the ruling. Under the previous *GATT* procedures, rulings could only be adopted by consensus, meaning that a single objection could block the ruling (*positive consensus rule*). A country with overwhelming influence could easily block a *GATT* ruling making it virtually unworkable. Now under WTO's disputes settlement procedures, rulings of the panels or appellate reports are automatically adopted

---

[11]*Ibid.*, Article 21(3).

[12]*Ibid.*, Article 21(4).

[13]*See* analysis by Sean Leonard, *"When China joins: The Power of WTO Dispute Resolution"*, <u>China Law & Practice</u>, July/August 2000, p. 37.

unless there is a consensus to reject a ruling (*negative consensus rule*)[14]— any country wanting to block a ruling has to persuade all other WTO Members (including its adversary in the case) to share its view. Thus, trade disputes resolutions between WTO Members have become greatly de-politicized.[15]

Consultation and Conciliation throughout

The underlying principle of the *Understanding* is the call for good faith negotiations between the WTO Members to resolve disputes before resorting to the establishment of panels pursuant to the provisions in the *Understanding*.[16] The priority is to settle disputes, through consultations if possible. Consultation between the parties in dispute is the very first stage of the entire procedure. Even when the case has progressed to other stages, consultation and mediation are still always possible. At all stages, the Director General of WTO may be asked to intervene by providing his good offices, conciliation or mediation to help the Members achieve settlement of disputes.[17] At all stages Members in disputes are encouraged to consult each other in order to settle 'out of court'. That is the preferred solution.

Built-in mechanism and Arbitration

Apart from consultation and mediation, mechanisms for appeal, expert advice and enforcement are built in the system. Additionally, Article 25 of the *Understanding* provides expeditious arbitration within the WTO that may be used as an alternative means of disputes settlement subject to the mutual agreement of the parties.

Transparency and Impartiality

A final report by the panel is circulated to all WTO Members before a ruling is made during the panel process. While facts and evidences of the case in dispute are being considered, expert advice are invited or adopted if necessary, points of law are considered in the appeal stage.

DSB has the sole authority to establish a panel or experts to consider a dispute. Panels are like tribunals. A panel should make an objective assessment of the matter before it, and make such other findings as will assist the DSB in making the recommendations or in giving the rulings provided for in the covered agreements.[18] Panelists serve in their individual capacities. They must disclose their interests if any, in the case in question. They cannot receive instructions from any governments nor receive influence from politicians. The panel may seek for information from any

---

[14]*the Understanding*, Article 2, footnote 1, Articles 16.4, 17.14.
[15]*Supra* note 13.
[16]*the Understanding*, Article 4.
[17]*Ibid.*, Article 5.
[18]*Ibid.*, Article 11.

source. It consults experts or appoints an expert review group to prepare an advisory report with respect to a factual issue concerning a scientific or other technical matter raised by a party to a dispute.[19]

Effect of Sanctions not to Spill Over

If a Member country that is the target of a complaint loses and eventually fails to comply with the recommendations of the panel report or the appeal report to negotiate with the complaining country for a determination of compensation, the complaining side may ask the DSB for permission to impose limited trade sanctions (by way of suspending the application of concessions, [for example tariff reduction] or obligations under the covered agreements).

Concessions or obligations suspended pursuant to the disputes settlement procedures would first be imposed in the same sector as the subject of dispute. This is the general principle. If this is not practical or effective, concessions or obligations may be suspended with respect to a different sector of the same agreement. For example, an obligation of copyright protection under *TRIPS* may be suspended in retaliation of a patent infringement under *TRIPS*. In turn, if this is not effective or practicable and if circumstances are serious enough, the action can be taken under another agreement. For example, a concession in the *Agreement on Textiles and Clothing* may be suspended in retaliation for a violation of *TRIPS*. Thus, the chance of actions spilling over into unrelated sectors is minimized while allowing actions to be effective.

Closing Remarks: China and WTO's Disputes Settlement System

It appears China would adapt amenably to WTO's dispute settlement system. The emphasis on mutual agreement in settling disputes throughout the conduct of WTO's procedures closely resembles Chinese mentality in working for peace in mediating disputes. This can be seen in that China's civil litigation procedure provides for a mediation mechanism ("the court conciliation"[20]) which operates to reconcile differences of opposition parties; failing which the parties then go to court, i.e. to continue with legal proceedings.[21] The Chinese court does not hear cases where the

---

[19]*Ibid.*, Article 13(1)(2), Appendix 4 "Rules and Procedures for Expert Review Groups".

[20]*See* article by Professor Tang Houzhi, Vice Chairman, China International Economic and Trade Arbitration Commission (CIETAC), China Council for the Promotion of International Trade (CCPIT) Conciliation Centre, in "*CONCILIATION IN CHINA, Explore and Research—Conciliation*," 2001 No. 1, (website of Arbitration in China, www.arbitration.org.cn). "*Conciliation (mediation) in China falls into five categories, i.e. People's Conciliation; Administrative Conciliation; Court Conciliation; Conciliation by Conciliation Institutions; and Conciliation by Arbitration Organizations. The last three categories involve international (foreign-related) elements*".

[21]Article 9 of the *Civil Procedure Law of the People's Republic of China* provides that in trying civil cases, the people's courts shall conduct conciliation for the parties on a voluntary and legal basis. If conciliation fails, judgments shall be rendered without delay; Article 16 provides that the people's conciliation committees shall be mass organizations to conduct civil disputes under the guidance of the grass-roots level as well as the basic people's courts. Articles 85 through 91 of the same law stipulates the procedures for conciliation conducted by the people's courts.

parties only apply for conciliation, but always conciliates litigation cases during court proceedings.[22] This is one of the important characteristics of the Chinese litigation procedure, known as the "Combination of Litigation with Conciliation".[23] A court Conciliation Statement has the same legal effect as a court judgment [but is just that] no appeal against it is allowed.[24]

Resolving commercial and civil disputes by conciliation is a good Chinese tradition.[25] The remarkably good record of settling commercial disputes through arbitration in China illustrated her adherence to the spirit of conciliation.[26] And of course, those who do business with

---

[22]*Supra* note 20, "...*4. conciliation procedure can be conducted separately or in combination with arbitration proceedings and litigation proceedings*".

[23]*Supra* note 20.

[24]*ibid.*

[25]*ibid.*

[26]*Op cit* note 20 By the end of 1999, the conciliation network of China Council for the Promotion of International Trade (CCPIT) had had an accumulative caseload of more than 2000 cases with a successful rate of 80% and up. Parties involved spread over more than 30 countries and regions in the world. CCPIT is also called the China Chamber of International Commerce (CCOIC).

Since 1992 the CCPIT has set up more than 30 local conciliation centres within its Sub-councils in various provinces, municipalities and major cities in China. These conciliation centres have formed a conciliation network all over the country. The network chiefly deals with international (foreign-related) cases. It handles some domestic cases as well. The network uses a set of uniform conciliation rules, i.e. the CCPIT Conciliation Rules. Before the establishment of the CCPIT Conciliation Centre, all applications for conciliation of international commercial and maritime disputes were submitted to the two international arbitration commissions (China International Economic and Trade Arbitration Commission (CIETAC and China Maritime Arbitration Commission (CMAC). Now, applications can be submitted to the CCPIT Conciliation Centre or to the above-said two arbitration commissions.

Also see article by Yu Xiaosong, President of CCPIT/CCIC, CIETAC/CCOIC Court of Arbitration and CMAC, in '*Foreword*' of '*Let China Arbitration Advance Towards the World Further and Let the World Understand China Better*', 2001, No. 1, web site of Arbitration in China, www.arbitration.org.cn, states that: Arbitration in China has developed a great deal as the same as that of China economy since China has adopted the open and reform policy in 1979, especially in the mid of 1990th, China International Economic and Trade Arbitration Commission (CIETAC, established in 1956) as well as China Maritime Arbitration Commission (CMAC, established in 1959), the first arbitration institutions dealing with the international commercial and maritime arbitration in China, have already become one of the main and important international arbitration institutions in the world, with CIETAC accepting 238 cases in 1990, 274 cases in 1991, and 633 cases in 2000, already holding a lead of the world arbitration institutions in taking cognizance of cases, parties coming from more than 40 countries and districts, most of which are Hong Kong SAR, United States, Singapore, Korea, Japan, Taiwan region, Australia, German, Canada, Swiss, Russia, Italy and New Zealand and the claiming amount up to RMB 74.8 billion in 2000.

From Oct. 1, 2000, CIETAC also accepts domestic arbitration cases in accordance with Arbitration Rules of CIETAC 2000 in order to adapt to the new development of arbitration in China since the implementation of *Arbitration Law of PRC* in 1995. At the same time, CIETAC also has its name as the Court of Arbitration of China Chamber of International Commerce (CCOIC Court of Arbitration).

China is a Member state of *New York Convention on Recognition and Enforcement of Foreign Arbitral Award, 1958*, therefore, the arbitral awards on international commercial and maritime disputes made by CIETAC and CMAC can be enforced by the Member States of New York Convention through out the world. China has a good outside judicial environment to the development of arbitration.

Chinese are aware that often, commercial contracts and joint venture contracts with the Chinese bear an opening remark as "Based on the spirit of mutual cooperation and friendly consultation...."

"The Disputes Settlement Procedures was ... ... WTO's most individual contribution to the stability of the global economy. ... ... The system is working as intended-as a means above all for conciliation and for encouraging resolution of disputes, rather than just for making judgements. By reducing the scope for unilateral actions, it is also an important guarantee of fair trade for [less powerful countries]."[27] This was perhaps one of the main reasons China strove to accede to WTO.[28] Under WTO's disputes settlement mechanism, China would no longer subject itself to unilateral actions imposed or threatened to be imposed on it as in many occasions in trade-related bilateral negotiations where China found itself in an inferior position; in particular when the subject matter of negotiation was brought into association with political issues. China would feel comfortable subjecting herself to a rules-based system that deals with a dispute impartially irrespective of the size and power of the disputing countries. In fact, it did not hesitate to do so. China had, for the first time since it became Member of WTO in December, 2001, appealed to the WTO's dispute settlement mechanism and employed the WTO regulations to defend its interests. On 26 March 2002, China submitted to DSB a Request for Consultation[29] with the US government on the issue concerning US's imposing definitive safeguard measures in the form of an increase in import duties of certain steel products.[30] The request was made on grounds that US's measures were in breach of its obligations under *GATT 1994* and the *Agreement on Safeguards*. The matter is still under processing by WTO at the time of compiling this book.

While on the one hand China started putting on test this multilateral system, WTO Members having disputes with China could also put forth their case for hearing following the procedures in the *Understanding*. For example, foreign investors holding a minority equity interest in a joint venture in China in certain services sectors could enforce their rights in the investments through venue available under China's laws, regulations and measures. Moreover, their own government, acting on their behalf, would have recourse to WTO dispute settlement to ensure implementation of all commitments in China's *GATS* schedule.

---

[27]By Renato Ruggiero, former WTO Director-General, in a speech given in Seoul on 17 April 1997, *"The Future Path of the Multilateral Trading System"* WTO News, WTO website.

[28]*See* other possible advantages when China joins WTO, *supra* note 13.

[29]China's Request for Consultation (Document no. 02-1629, Document symbol WT/DS252/1, dated 2 April 2002) http://www.wto.org.

[30]On 5 March 2002, US declared to impose definitive safeguard measures in the form of an increase in duties (of up to 30 percent) on a wide range of steel imports. This measure was considered by US's trading partners as an act of trade protectionism that went against WTO rules. The US decision encountered serious protests from EU, Japan, Korea, Brazil an China etc., and triggered retaliatory measures.

Flow Chart of Panel Procedure

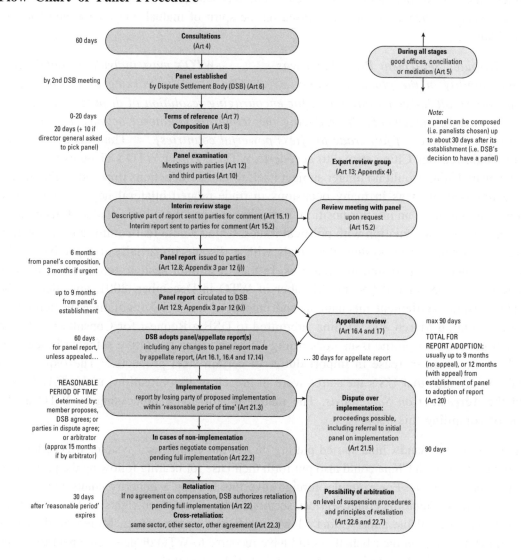

Some specified times are maximums, some are minimums, some binding, some not

Source: WTO website

Proposed Timetable for Panel Work:

(a) Receipt of first written submissions of the parties	3-6 weeks
(1) complaining Party:	2-3 weeks
(2) Party complained against:	
(b) Date, time and place of first substantive meeting with the parties; third party session:	1-2 weeks
(c) Receipt of written rebuttals of the parties:	2-3 weeks
(d) Date, time and place of second substantive meeting with the parties:	1-2 weeks
(e) Issuance of descriptive part of the report to the parties	2-4 weeks
(f) Receipt of comments by the parties on the descriptive part of the report:	2 weeks
(g) Issuance of the interim report, including the findings and conclusions, to the parties:	2-4 weeks
(h) Deadline for party to request review of part(s) of report:	1 week
(i) Period of review by panel, including possible additional meeting with parties:	2 weeks
(j) Issuance of final report to parties to dispute:	2 weeks
(k) Circulation of the final report to the Members:	3 weeks

The above calendar may be changed in the light of unforeseen developments. Additional meetings with the parties shall be scheduled if required.

(Source: WTO website)

ACKNOWLEDGEMENTS AND BIBLIOGRAPHY FOR THIS CHAPTER

Intellectual Property & International Trade – A Guide to the Uruguay Round TRIPS Agreement, International Chamber of Commerce, 1996, p. 75–79.

WTO web site: *"Trading into the future", 1999 version, "The introduction to the WTO", "The WTO's 'most individual contribution"*.

Web site of Arbitration in China, sponsored by China International Economic and Trade Arbitration Commission and China Maritime Arbitration Commission etc. web address: www.arbitration.org.cn.

PART II

IMPACTS OF WTO ACCESSION ON CHINA

Preface
(Part II)

Part II deals with the impacts of WTO accession on China.

In this Part, we shall quote the findings of researchers and views of industry experts on the likely impacts of WTO accession on China. The sources from which we extract information are clearly annotated at the very beginning of each chapter or section.

Chapter 6 outlines the economic impacts. It presents the findings of various scholars and officials on the economic consequences of WTO membership. Chapter 7 deals with socio-political impacts. Seven commentaries from the media are included to illustrate the political costs and benefits of WTO membership.

Chapter 8 through 15 deals with specific sectors. Each chapter begins with a brief summary of China's commitments, followed by an analysis of their impacts on the sector concerned.

To navigate through the information maze, we rely heavily on the series of fact sheets issued by a number of institutes like the US-China Business Council and the Hongkong Trade Development Council (HKTDC). They provide succinct summaries of the complicated commitments.

Most of these fact sheets were based on the 1999 US-China Bilateral Agreement, not the official accession document itself. This is understandable since the US-China Bilateral Agreement was published almost two years ahead of the official release of China's accession document. Besides, since the US-China Bilateral Agreement is the most significant bilateral agreement that determined China's accession, it can be used *almost* interchangeably with the official accession document itself.

Nevertheless, there are still minor discrepancies, due to China's willingness to speed up the market liberalization process after they signed the US-China Bilateral Agreement. Where discrepancies are sufficiently obvious, these will be denoted by a square bracket containing information drawn from the accession documents.

We also rely much on Chinaonline.com for providing panoramic views of the WTO impacts on China, from scholars, officials and industry leaders.

chapter 6

Economic Impacts of WTO Membership

In Chapters 6 and 7 we shall deal briefly with the economic and socio-political impacts respectively of WTO membership on China. The fierce and prolonged debate in China about the pros and cons of WTO membership and its overall desirability reflects a different understanding of how membership is going to affect the country. However we shall not venture into these territories. Instead we shall present as many salient facts as possible without indulging into the debate itself. Our approach will be strictly factual.

A. MACROECONOMIC IMPACTS

Many Chinese and foreign scholars have tried to measure the impact of WTO accession on China's economy. Their methodologies are similar, using a "computable general equilibrium" (CGE) model and its variants but with different assumptions and base periods.

This section presents the findings of several studies, both by the Chinese and foreign economists. So far the most comprehensive one by the Chinese is done by Dr Yu Yongding and Zheng Binwen of the Chinese Academy of Social Sciences (CASS) entitled *The Research Report on China's Entry into WTO — The Analysis of the China's Industries* first published in 2000 by the Social Sciences Documentation Publishing House (thereafter referred to as "the CASS Report by Yu and Zheng 2000").

1. Impact on the Overall Economy

The CASS Report by Yu and Zheng 2000 concludes that WTO membership will boost China's gross domestic product (GDP) by RMB 195.5 billion (US$ 23.64 billion) by 2005, or 1.5% higher than if China remained out of WTO.

WTO membership will also increase China's social welfare revenues by RMB 159.5 billion (US$19.29 billion) by 2005, accounting for 1.2% of the total GDP that year.

The GDP and welfare revenue estimates for 2005 are at 1995 price levels and presume that China fulfills its market concessions by that year.

The rise in GDP and welfare are the results of greater efficiency brought by redistribution of resources according to comparative advantages, said the Report.

However, the benefits will not be evenly distributed from sector to sector. Output will fall in the protected cotton and wheat sectors and the capital-intensive sectors of automobiles, instruments and meters, while labor-intensive sectors such as textiles and garments will benefit from China's WTO entry, the Report said.

What is likely to be a major cost of the economic readjustment resulting from WTO entry is the transfer of the labor force between sectors; about 9.6 million agricultural workers would have to switch sectors, according to the Report.

The overall impacts on the economy is set out in Table 6.1 comparing the situation in 2005 when China fully implements its WTO obligations against 2000 when it was not WTO member yet.

The table shows that there are positive gains for all GDP components, i.e. consumption (0.58%), investment (1.75%), government expenditure (3.51%), export (26.93%) and imports (25.79%).

In terms of income, urban income is expected to make a 4.56% gain but the rural income will suffer a 2% loss. The agricultural sector is the most obvious sufferer after WTO accession, with both farm income (−2.05%) and factor price of arable land (−18.38%) experience a worsening off.

Table 6.1 Impact of WTO Membership on China's Economy

Indicator	Gain/Loss in % By 2005 Due to WTO Accession
Gross Domestic Product (GDP)	1.53
Social Welfare (as % of GDP)	1.24
Consumption	0.58
Investment	1.75
Export	26.93
Import	25.79
Terms of Trade	−1.57
Real Exchange Rate	1.85
Government Revenue	3.51
Urban Income	4.56
Rural Income	−2.05
Factor Prices:	
agricultural labour	2.19
manufacturing labour	2.19
Professional	6.05
agricultural land	−18.38
Food Self-sufficiency	0.923

Source: Extracted from Table 1–10, the CASS Report by Yu and Zheng, 2000

2. Impact on Employment

According to the CASS Report by Yu and Zheng 2000, WTO membership will create 12 million jobs, but also reduce 10.95 million in the next five years.

Between 1998 and 2005 the following industries (in decreasing order of magnitude) will see an increase in job opportunities:[1]

Textiles: 2.83 million;
Wholesale and retail: 2.62 million;
Apparel: 2.61 million;
Construction: 928,000;
Chemicals: 589,000;
Infrastructure: 416,000;
Food processing: 316,000;
Leather products: 219,000;
Stationery: 145,000;
Building materials: 57,000;
Metal products: 49,000; and
Services: 49,000.
These add up to 12 million new jobs being created.

However, some industries will see a decrease in employment opportunities over the same period. They are:

Agriculture: 9.6 million
Auto: 498,000;
Machinery: 298,000;
Grain and edible oil processing: 133,000;
Electronics and communications equipment: 109,000;
Electric machinery: 97,000;
Instrument making: 78,000;
Metallurgy: 42,000;
Oil and natural gas: 38,000;
Oil processing: 31,000; and
Coal mining: 22,000.
The combined number of reduced job opportunities will reach 10.95 million.

The CASS Report is a bit over optimistic as it predicts that new jobs created (12 million) will be more than offset old jobs lost (10.95 million).

In Chapters 7 and 8, we shall present some less optimistic views.

---

[1]Extracted from Table 1–11, CASS Report by Yu and Zheng, 2000

3. Impact on Foreign Trade

Two World Bank economists, Elena Ianchovichina and Will Martin, have conducted a study to measure the impact of WTO accession on China's foreign trade pattern ("Ianchovichina and Martin 2001")[2]. There are several interesting conclusions.

a. WTO membership increases China's share of world trade rather than output.

Their study finds that even in the absence of WTO accession there will be rapid growth in China's shares of world output.

Without accession China's share of world output is projected to increase between 1995 and 2005 from 3.4 to 5.3 percent and its share of exports from 3.7 to 4.8 percent. While WTO membership has almost no impact on the share of output, it has a significant impact on the share of trade. With WTO membership, China's share of world export markets rises to 6.8 percent, and of world import markets, to 6.6 percent.

b. At the sectoral level, the most important impact of accession is on China's output of apparel, which rises by 263 percent over the ten-year period, compared with only 57 percent in the absence of WTO membership. It results in an increase in China's share of world output of apparel from 8.84 percent (absence of WTO membership) to 20.1 percent with accession. This share rises dramatically because of the lifting of the burdens imposed by the *Multi-fibre Agreement* (MFA) on China's exports.

China's export of apparel also increases dramatically, rising by 375 percent over the decade, compared to 45 percent in the absence of WTO membership. As a result China's share of world export markets for apparel also increases substantially, to over 47 percent. The expansion of the apparel sector stimulates input demand for imported textiles, which increase by 272 percent by 2005.

c. The automobile sector, and a number of high-tech sectors, experience very substantial increases in their exports under the accession scenario, as their costs are reduced following liberalization.

The output growth of the high-tech sector (electronics) is export driven with the export share growing from 7.8 percent to almost 10 percent. The export shares of all manufacturing sectors grow under WTO accession due to a rapid increase in intra-industry trade.

d. On the import side China becomes a much bigger market for its trading partners following accession to the WTO.

China increases its agricultural imports of oilseeds, meat, and various food products. This

---

[2]Elena Ianchovichina and Will Martin, *"Trade Liberalization in China's Accession to the WTO"*, The World Bank, (June 2001), retrievable at http://www.econ.worldbank.org/files/2228_wps2623.pdf

increase in the importance of agricultural imports reflects the strong shift in comparative advantage away from agriculture.

e. With accession to the WTO, China is expected to continue being a powerful driver of growth, especially in East Asia.

The study suggests that China's joining the WTO will provide the greatest mercantilist benefits to exporters in Taiwan, Japan and other newly industrializing countries (NICs) in the region. Imports from these regions to China are estimated to increase by 83, 47 and 83 percent respectively as a consequence of WTO membership. While intra-regional trade in North East Asia will increase as a result of China's accession to the WTO, ASEAN countries might not benefit as much, about 14 percent.

Table 6.2 WTO membership and China's share in world economy

	China's Output, Exports and Imports as a Share of World Total (in %)								
	Output			Export			Import		
	1995	2005		1995	2005		1995	2005	
		no WTO	with WTO		no WTO	with WTO		no WTO	with WTO
Foodgrains	14.29	19.59	19.39	0.3	0.06	0.06	6.45	16.35	16.02
Feedgrains	8.33	10.55	10.43	0.72	0.12	0.12	3.2	9.18	9.13
Oilseeds	5.13	6.22	6.34	4.05	0.76	0.7	1.15	3.94	4.04
Meat & Livestock	6.7	11.62	12.12	3.51	0.51	0.46	2.02	8.88	9.63
Dairy	0.75	1.34	1.42	0.08	0.03	0.02	0.17	0.61	0.62
Other agriculture	10.58	15.65	15.42	2.32	0.36	0.35	2.74	9.62	9.8
Other food	2.27	3.15	3.15	2.61	1.21	1.27	3.1	6.39	6.15
Beverage/tobacco	4.89	7.02	4.37	2.42	1.03	0.99	0.89	1.29	16.24
Extractive industries	8.07	12.29	11.88	1.69	0.12	0.14	1.55	9.09	8.5
Textiles	10.79	13.88	14.16	8.43	8.84	10.6	13.35	17.96	25.47
Wearing apparel	7.02	8.84	20.1	19.58	18.54	47.14	1.04	1.09	3.69
Wood & paper	2.41	3.67	3.35	2.19	2.59	3	2.57	3.86	4.64
Petrochemicals	5	7.57	7.06	2.56	3.06	3.42	4.02	5.76	6.33
Metals	5.45	8.99	8.4	3.38	5.47	6.48	4.23	5.77	6.62
Automobiles	1.91	3.76	1.1	0.13	0.69	2.16	1.95	1.81	4.83
Electronics	2.63	4.53	4.81	4.97	7.79	9.79	3.57	5.25	5.72
Other manufactures	6.4	10.41	9.81	5.49	8.05	9.86	4.23	5.89	7.45
Utilities	2.69	3.9	3.79	5.82	6.7	7.51	1.2	1.73	1.46
Trade/transport	2.55	3.73	3.69	1.7	2.79	3.07	2.03	2.41	2.19
Construction	3.29	6.22	6.07	0	0	0	1.82	2.81	2.69
Business/finance	0.89	1.34	1.31	1.92	2.5	2.68	1.49	1.95	1.82
Government services	1.58	2.37	2.34	1.01	0.62	0.65	0.72	1.31	1.22
Total	3.38	5.26	5.13	3.71	4.78	6.76	3.36	5.34	6.61

Source: Table 6, Ianchovichina & Martin (June 2001)

4. Impact On Different Sectors

Using different criteria and base year, the CASS Report by Yu and Zheng 2000 provided another estimate of the impact of WTO membership on China's primary, secondary and tertiary sectors, which is summarized in Table 6.3.

5. Impact on Different Regions

Two other Chinese scholars, Fan and Zheng (2001), tried to measure the differential impact of WTO membership on China's different provinces and their results are presented in Table 6.4.[3]

According to them, some regions have better aggregate response than others because the industrial mix in these regions are relatively favoured by the trade liberalization and the trade liberalization has greater impacts on the industrial mix.

B. IMPACT ON THE WORLD

In their joint study, Ianchovichina & Martin (2001) of the World Bank find that the world as a whole will gain by China's accession to the WTO, with the largest gain going to China.

Table 6.5 shows regional income and welfare change due to China's WTO accession. It shows that China will be the biggest beneficiary of the accession, followed by the industrialized countries and the newly industrialized economies in East Asia.

While the world as a whole also benefits from China becoming a more open economy as a result of WTO membership, most developing countries competing with China in third markets will lose from China's accession to the WTO. India and Indonesia are expected to be hurt most, mainly because of the removal of *Multi-Fibre Agreement* (MFA) restrictions on China's apparel exports.

Another study by Wang (2001)[4] however, finds that the world as a whole gains more than China as a result of China's WTO accession. He finds an increase in China's real income of US$ 188 billion over the ten years 2000 to 2010, or $19 billion per year, against an increase in world income of $89 billion per year.

---

[3]Extracted from *"The Impact of China's Trade Liberalization for WTO Accession-A Computable General Equilibrium Analysis"* by Fan Mingtai and Zheng Yuxin. Fan, Associate Professor of Institute of Quantitative & Technical Economics, Chinese Academy of Social Sciences ("CASS") and Zheng, Deputy Director, Institute of Quantitative & Technical Economics, CASS. The Paper was for presentation to the international conference "Greater China and the WTO", City University of Hong Kong, 22–24 March 2001, retrievable from *http://www.cityu.edu.hk/ef/ conference/ChinaWTO/papers.htm*

Table 6.3 Impact of WTO on China's Economic Sectors

Products	Output Billion RMB	%	Employment 10,000	%	Import Billion RMB	%	Export Billion RMB	%
Rice	−4.6	−1.4	−246.1	−2.8	5.6	300.1	0	12
Wheat	−17.2	−9	−540.3	−14.2	26.8	205.5	0	73.3
other cereals	0.3	0.1	1.6	0	10.4	226.1	0	0.2
Cotton	−11.7	−12.6	−498.2	−22.6	45	426.6	0	209.4
other non-food crops	11.3	1.8	151.1	1.9	0.7	10.9	0.1	1.1
Forestry	1.3	1.1	5.4	1.4	1.1	10.7	0	−2.2
Fleece	−3	−37	−10	−37.5	5.1	86.6	0	−15.4
other animal products	73.7	5.7	104.1	5	1	77.1	2.8	13
all other agr products	7.8	5.2	57.2	5.1	0.1	19.4	0	4.6
Fishery	4.2	1	9	1.3	0.6	55.8	2.3	6.1
Coal	−2.9	−1.2	−2.2	−0.3	0.1	4.5	−0.5	−4.3
petroleum & gas	−11.6	−4.8	−3.8	−2.9	2.2	4.9	−2.5	−10
Metal	−2.5	−1.7	−1.1	−0.8	0.2	0.6	−0.2	−3.9
non-metal	1.6	0.4	5.3	1.4	0.8	6.7	−0.4	−2.2
food processing	−18.7	−5.8	−13.3	−8	45.8	260.2	0.3	126.6
sugar refinery	−1.7	−2.1	−1.5	−1.6	3.8	83.8	0.3	18.5
other food industries	74.8	5.3	31.6	5.9	8.5	16.1	24.2	31.7
Textile	390.1	25.5	282.5	23.6	158.5	85.7	183.1	63.8
Apparel	522.3	74	261	52.3	6.3	124.4	491.6	214.1
leather goods	26.8	5.9	21.9	7.6	43	124.1	8.8	6.6
wood & furniture	−2	−0.6	2.1	0.6	1.3	5.6	−1.5	−2.1
paper & stationery	10.2	1.1	14.5	2.1	9.8	13	1.9	1.2
electricity generation	−8.4	−1.4	−0.1	0	0	5.6	−0.4	−0.72
petroleum refinery	−16.7	−3.5	−3.1	−2.6	11.1	35.1	−1.6	−6.8
coal & natural gas	−1.5	−1.6	−0.3	−1.2	0	1.7	−0.6	−4.3
Chemical	95	3.8	58.9	4.2	92.5	26.8	32.7	14.4
construction materials	−11.3	−0.8	5.7	0.3	0.8	2.8	−4	−4.2
Metallurgy	−28.9	−1.7	−4.2	−0.5	3.1	1.6	−5.2	−5.7
metal goods	−3.4	−0.4	4.9	0.9	2.9	8	−3.5	−3.8
Machinery	−51	−3.1	−29.8	−2.2	49.3	10.2	−8.6	−4.4
Automobile	−81.2	−15.1	−49.8	−14.5	41.8	105.1	−0.9	−7.8
other transport vehicle	−0.6	−0.2	2.5	0.8	2.3	4.8	−1.6	−4
electrical machinery	−28.6	−3.2	−9.7	−1.8	11.1	12	−5.6	−4.9
telecom & electronic goods	−43.8	−4.7	−10.9	−3.3	12.9	5.2	-13.4	−5.2
meters & instruments	−4.5	−5.8	−7.8	−5	3.1	9.7	−0.7	−6.4
machinery repair	1	0.9	2.4	1.5	0	0		
other industries not classified	1	1.2	9.7	2.2	4.5	60.2	0.1	1.7
construction	33.1	1.2	92.8	2.2	0.5	3.6	0	−0.3
infrastructure	2.8	0.2	41.6	1.1	2.1	3.4	−1.7	−1.3
commerce	45.4	1.8	261.5	3.3	3.3	4	−0.3	−0.8
services	−3.5	−0.1	4.9	0.1	4.9	3.8	−2.1	−2
Total	943.4		0		622.9		692.9	

Source: Table 1–11, The CASS Report by Yu and Zheng, 2000

Table 6.4 Differential impacts of WTO on the provinces

Impact of WTO Membership on China's Economy (Effects on Regional Outputs in %)	
Provinces	Impact (+/−) in % of WTO on Output
Beijing	1.05
Guangdong	0.91
Zhejiang	0.85
Fujian	0.83
Tianjin	0.78
Chongqing	0.78
Shanghai	0.77
Jiangsu	0.66
Shaanxi	0.61
Tibet	0.58
Hainan	0.57
Sichuan	0.57
Hubei	0.56
Shanxi	0.51
Hunan	0.48
Jinin	0.47
Anhui	0.47
Inner Mongolia	0.46
Guizhou	0.46
Jiangxi	0.45
Hebei	0.44
Guangxi	0.43
Yunnan	0.43
Shangdong	0.42
Liaoning	0.41
Henan	0.39
Ningxia	0.32
Qinghai	0.17
Gansu	0.14
Heilongjiang	0
Xinjiang	−0.01

Source: "*The Impact of China's Trade Liberalization for WTO Accession-A Computable General Equilibrium Analysis*" by Fan Mingtai, Zheng Yuxin, 2001

Thus perhaps the findings of both Wang and Ianchovichina & Martin serve as a ceiling and floor estimate of the effect of China's membership in the WTO on the world as a whole.

---

[4]Wang, Zhi, "*The Impact of China's WTO Accession on Patterns of World Trade*", paper prepared for the International Agricultural Trade Research Consortium, 18–20 May 2001, quoted in Ianchovichina & Martin 2001.

Table 6.5 Global welfare changes due to China's WTO accession

Global Welfare Changes Due to China's WTO Accession				
Countries/Regions	Income in Billion US$			
	Base Year	Changes w/o WTO		Change due to WTO	% change due to WTO as a share over
	1995	1995-2005	2005		2005
China	714	577	1291	28.6	2.22
Developed Countries	22141	5240	27381	19.7	0.07
a. North America	7976	2561	10537	9.5	0.09
b. West Europe	8650	1828	10478	7.1	0.07
c. Japan	5095	724	5819	2.9	0.05
d. Australia & New Zealand	420	127	547	0.2	0.04
Developing Countries	5465	1935	7400	7.8	0.11
a. East Asia	1448	582	2030	12.5	0.62
of which: Taiwan	281	177	458	5.2	1.14
b. Southeast Asia	343	118	461	−0.4	−0.09
of which: Indonesia	200	50	250	−0.2	−0.08
c. South Asia	441	249	690	−0.4	−0.06
of which: India	331	188	519	−3.2	−0.62

Source: Adapted from Table 10, Ianchovichina & Martin (2001).

Socio-political Impacts

The impact of China's WTO membership extends far beyond the economic realm and affects the political and social spheres as well. In fact an important reason for China to take 15 years to negotiate the accession terms, apart from the US exacting a high price, is the difficulty of developing a domestic consensus over an issue that promises to bring tremendous changes to the country.

It is not feasible in a short chapter to list out all the political and social implications of WTO membership for China. Hence in this chapter, the analysis of selected China watchers or journalistic commentaries will be reprinted to give a glimpse of the nature and complexity of problems involved. Section A will focus on risks and opportunities while Section B will attempt to explain why from both China and the US point of view the WTO membership is desirable.

Section A: Risks and Opportunities – This section presents the views on the "Risks and Opportunities" of WTO membership for China. It reprints three articles illustrating the economic, social and political risks of WTO membership. Since most Chinese experts considered the financial and agricultural sectors as the two most vulnerable upon WTO accession, they will be used as case study.

On the plus side, China is hopeful that WTO membership will lead to a gradual economic integration with Taiwan which hopefully would lead to eventual political union. It also hopes that with China, Taiwan, Hong Kong and Macao in the WTO, a Greater China Free Trade Area will emerge as a major economic bloc in the world. Two articles covering these issues are reprinted.

The five articles selected are:

1. *The Straits Times*, Singapore: "WTO puts China at risk of major financial crisis", 4 December 2001
2. *The Straits Times,* Singapore: "Tough Challenges for China upon WTO entry", 12 November 2001
3. Business Asia, Economic Intelligent Unit: "China and the WTO, living on a volcano", 11 February 2002, as quoted by Chinaonline.com in "WTO entry could weaken Beijing"
4. *The Straits Times*, Singapore: "Beijing sees a first step towards unification", 10 November 2001
5. *The Straits Times*, Singapore: "China FTA could be engine of growth for Asia", 10 December 2001

Section B: Why WTO for China – This section presents the views on why China wants WTO membership despite of great inherent risks, and why the US wants China in the WTO, included here are two articles:

1. Business China, Economic Intelligent Unit: "China: Good Intention", 3 December 2001, as quoted by Chinaonline.com in "China's motives and fears"
2. Joseph Fewsmith, "The Impact of WTO on Chinese politics", a National Bureau of Asian Research publication, vol. 11, Essay 2, 2000.

We believe that these selected articles give a fair idea of the complexity of the issue of WTO membership for China.

A. RISKS AND OPPORTUNITIES

1. RISKS

a. Economic Risk: the financial sector: a case study

(*The following article appeared on 04 December 2001, The Straits Times, Page: 14 "WTO puts China at risk of major financial crisis" by Ching Cheong, East Asia Correspondent.*)

Most Chinese experts concur that China is exposed to potential financial insecurity on joining the World Trade Organisation (WTO) while government officials admit that the financial sector faces greater risks than opportunities in the short run.

The risks stem from the fact that the financial sector is grossly unprepared for the drastic changes mandated by the commitments China made to align its economic operations with WTO norms and standards.

In its bilateral agreement with the United States, China undertook to open, after five years, its entire financial sector to foreign competitors.

This would mean transforming the sector from an essentially command-type operation to a market-type one within a short period.

A paper, *Chinese Financial Stability And Development Upon WTO Accession*, noted: "This is demanding too much of the Chinese financial sector and is sure to brew crisis."

The paper's co-authors are International Monetary Fund economist Huang Haizhou and an economist at the department of economics at the University of California at Berkeley, Dr Qian Ying-yi.

In the paper, they predicted that the probability of having a major financial crisis within the next few years after WTO accession is unity statistical jargon for certainty. The Chinese financial sector, because of its sensitive nature, is the least touched by reform. This is why it still has most of the essential features of an archiac planned economy.

For example, it still assumes both the fiscal and monetary roles of the state: Appropriating resources to state-owned enterprises (SOEs) and bailing them out should they fail. This accounts for its intrinsic weaknesses.

The biggest weakness is the insolvency of the whole banking system. None of the "Big Four" meets the stringent standard for prudential banking, set by the Bank of International Settlement (BIS), of maintaining a capital-adequacy ratio of 8 per cent.

The "Big Four" refers to the four largest state-owned banks in China – the Industrial and Commercial Bank of China, the Bank of China, the China Construction Bank and the Agricultural Bank of China.

By BIS standard, technically all of them are bankrupt. They are kept afloat, however, by sheer administrative forces.

Insolvent Banking System

For example, the government floated a special bond in 1998 to raise RMB 270 billion (S$61.7 billion/US$35.31 billion) to supplement their capital and raise their capital-adequacy ratio by two percentage points.

The government is aware that insolvency of the banking system is likely to stay for some time and it is, therefore, prepared to accept a lower-than-BIS standard.

For example, the Centre of Economic Security Research (CESR) of Qinghua University uses a capital adequacy ratio of 6 per cent as a benchmark to measure the security of the financial system, instead of the BIS standard of 8 per cent.

Even so, the CESR concludes that the financial sector is insecure, suggesting that the overall ratio for the banking system still falls below 6 per cent, or well below the BIS standard.

Another weakness of the sector is the mammoth non-performing loans (NPLs) which, according to central banker Dai Xianglong, stands at RMB 1.8 trillion [US$217.4 billion], or 26 per cent of their total loans of RMB 6.8 trillion [US$821.4 billion] by the end of October [2001] - a staggering figure.

The government has already set up four asset-management corporations (AMCs) - Huarong, China Orient, China Cinda and the Great Wall - to take bad loans off the books of the Big Four state banks.

From 1999 till the end of June this year [2001], they had already absorbed a combined RMB 1.4 trillion [US$169.1 billion] of bad loans and driven the NPL ratio down by 10 per cent.

If the latest NPL ratio remains as high as 26 per cent, it confirms previous private-sector estimates, for example by Ernest & Young, an international accounting firm, that as high as 40 per cent of the loan portfolios of major Chinese banks are NPLs.

At 26.6 per cent, it is still way above the CESR's benchmark of 18 per cent for security, indicating a potentially risky financial sector.

The AMCs is no solution to the NPL issue unless two conditions are fulfilled. First, they must have a greater ability than the banks to recover loans from debtors.

Secondly, once they take the NPLs off the balance sheets of the state-owned banks, those banks must alter their behaviour to prevent the creation of new NPLs in the future.

Structural Weakness

According to the International Risk and Payment Review published by international management consultant firm Dun and Bradstreet, neither of these two conditions are in place.

On the first condition, the review said that since mass bankruptcies have been frowned upon, creditors - banks and AMCs alike - are unable to seize assets by making bankruptcy petitions to the court.

"With little prospect of being paid in the future and with no access to debtor assets, the AMCs have justified their existence by negotiating a number of debt-for-equity swaps," it said.

"In economic terms, such actions are meaningless: Worthless loans assets are swopped for worthless equity."

On the second condition, it observed: "There is little evidence that the banks are acting according to commercial criteria.

"Since the provision of working capital to SOEs remained a core responsibility of the commercial banks, and since the provision of such capital keeps the majority of such enterprises afloat and the failure of SOEs is still politically unacceptable, the commercial banks, in effect, retain a social welfare role."

Hence, the whole financial sector, plagued by insolvency and huge NPLs, is structurally weak, giving rise to fears that it may not be able to handle the pressure of global competition on China's accession to the WTO.

Economists Huang and Qian warned that given the multiplying effect of a financial crisis, the damage to the economy could be much more serious than failure in any other sector.

China should, therefore, double its efforts to reform the financial sector over the next five years so as to prepare for the tough competition arising from WTO membership.

b. Social Risk: the plight of the agricultural sector: a case study

(*This article appeared on 12 November 2001, The Straits Times, Page: 14, "Tough challenges for China upon WTO entry", by Ching Cheong, East Asia Correspondent.*)

China formalised its accession to the World Trade Organisation (WTO) in Qatar yesterday [11 November 2001], ending a 15-year marathon negotiation to gain admission to the so-called economic United Nations.

China has strong political and economic reasons for wanting to be part of the WTO.

Membership will raise its gross domestic product by about 2 per cent, going by the most optimistic estimates; expand its global reach for resources and markets; secure its place as a major power in the international community; and create a favourable environment for an eventual peaceful unification with Taiwan.

Yet, in the short run, it will have to brace itself for the huge political risks that WTO membership entails, thanks to the colossal concessions it made to the United States during bilateral negotiations.

A headline on the website of the New York-based US-China Trade Council reads: "*USA: All the Great Benefits. China: All the Tough Challenges.*" The article said that the US had to do only one thing - say yes to the agreement - leaving all the tough things to China.

It highlights vividly the extremely asymmetrical nature of the bilateral agreement between the two countries.

The arrangement for agricultural goods is the most uneven part of the agreement and, as a result, that sector is exposed to great risk.

Even Chinese Premier Zhu Rongji admitted, at the recent "ASEAN plus three" meeting in Brunei, that he was most worried about this sector.

Under the framework agreed upon with the US, China would have to reduce its agricultural tariffs from the current overall average of 22 per cent to 17.5 per cent by 2004.

For products the US has placed priority on, they will go down further – to 14 per cent. In the most extreme case, tariffs on US corn, a high-priority product, have to be cut to 3 per cent.

In addition, China would have to adopt a tariff-rate quota system under which a specific quantity of imports will be allowed in at a low duty (10 per cent or less), while imports above that level will face a higher duty.

China promises to increase vastly imports at lower duty. It also undertakes to remove sanitary/ phytosanitary barriers to US exports of citrus fruits, meat and grains by accepting the lower US standards for inspection.

American companies will be granted trading and distribution rights for agricultural products in China. Now, such rights are monopolised by state trading firms.

According to Dr Weng Tie-jun, senior fellow at the Agriculture Research Centre, the research arm of the Ministry of Agriculture, the sum effect of the arrangements will mean that by 2006, imports for soya bean, wheat, corn, rice and cotton will see astronomical increases, and a substantial part of the trade will be handled by foreign firms.

While the bilateral agreement provides for a surge of American products into the Chinese market, the US did not commit itself to open up its own market to Chinese products.

Instead, it maintains a 15-year-long anti-dumping and a safeguard clause as cushions against any import surges from China.

The asymmetrical nature of the agreement is just too obvious. As a result of the bilateral agreement, the Centre for Development Research – a think-tank which comes directly under the State Council - said that a substantial number of rural labourers would be displaced.

It estimated that a total of 12.8 million jobs from the rice, wheat and cotton sectors would be lost as a result of the agreement.

It warned that between now and 2010, at least 9.6 million of the displaced peasants will have to find jobs in the cities, compounding the already serious unemployment problems there.

Yet this is just the tip of the iceberg, as this analysis looks at the direct impact on only three major products. Another study by the same centre revealed even more startling findings.

If the entire agricultural sector is considered, and indirect impacts are also counted, then the total size of displaced labour migrating to the cities in the next 10 years will reach a staggering 176 million, almost ten times more.

Currently, surplus labour in the urban area has already reached 40 million, while surplus population in the rural area has reached 200 million.

If another 176 million members of the rural population are displaced in the next 10 years, the task of creating jobs becomes a "mission impossible".

The most optimistic forecast of the job-creating effect of WTO membership is seven million annually, based on the assumption that WTO membership will bring about two additional percentage points in GDP growth, and that every percentage-point increase in GDP will generate 3.5 million new jobs.

In other words, 70 million new jobs will be created over a 10-year period.

Clearly, this falls far too short of meeting the target of 176 million jobs in the worst-case scenario. This can have grave social, economic and political consequences.

And this is what worries Premier Zhu most.

c. Political Risk: the stability of the government — WTO entry could weaken Beijing

(The piece is from an article "China and WTO, living on a volcano", 11 February 2002, Business Asia, the Economist Intelligence Unit (EIU), a U.K.-based information provider, retrieved from the archives of Chinaonline.com, in "WTO entry could weaken Beijing", 2002, and reproduced with the permission of the EIU.)

Of late, it seems China can do no wrong. Its strong economic growth — at least, if you believe official numbers — has offered rare cause for optimism while most of the world suffers an economic slowdown. Its leadership has played ball in the struggle against terrorism, and seems intent on keeping relations with the US on an even keel. And then there is China's WTO entry, which has released a torrent of hyperbole and expectations, and ensured the country's continuing appeal to foreign investors — 2001's US$47 billion inflow of FDI (Foreign Direct Investment) was a record; the figure is forecast to rise past US$50 billion this year, to its highest level ever.

If assurance were needed that China is becoming more of a global player — and that policies of engagement rather than confrontation are needed — then what better evidence, surely, than China's entrance to the world's premier trade club, and agreement to play by its rules?

That may be so. But China's accession to the WTO also needs to be viewed as a consequence of change, not just as a cause. Complying with WTO requirements will force many changes. But WTO membership has been sought and acquired precisely because of changes that have already taken place. This fact explains why China's leadership is so keen on submitting to WTO rules.

A tectonic shift

Underlying China's development over the last couple of decades has been the government's conviction — driven initially by Deng Xiaoping, and now accepted as a matter of fact — that China can become a modern, powerful state by reforming its economy, but not its political structure. That thinking has allowed the leadership to favour reforms that appear to foster the creation of wealth over those that allow for the popular selection of the government.

Indeed, the Chinese government has consistently acted as if the country's economic structure and political system can be separated. If the government is competent at managing the economy, then the government's constitution, and how it is selected, ought to be no business of most citizens. By the same token, people can be left largely free to enrich themselves — provided they don't challenge political authority.

That is why the government has been willing to run China's economy along what are, at least nominally, rules-based lines. Indeed, a market-based system is now accepted by the leadership as the best way of increasing China's economic muscle. Key to this is taking the government out of day-to-day involvement in business and economic management.

Since the mid-1990s the government has moved to hand over control of the economy to corporations, and then to float some of these companies on international stockmarkets — as has happened to the telecom operators China Mobile and China Unicom, and the petroleum corporation, SINOPEC.

In 1998, it took this process a step further when it reorganised the central government, slashing the number of ministries and ministry-level bodies from 40 to 29. Among the casualties were the most of the industry-related ministries.

While the state remains heavily entangled in the operations of the economy, there is little doubt about its long-term goal. This is to move towards a model where the government mainly exercises economic control indirectly, through its regulatory functions.

It is tempting to see these changes as a part of a bigger trend: a reworking of the methods of government to make government more efficient. It is in fact the other way round: the government is being re-worked to deliver greater economic efficiency — not by making it more efficient, but by lessening its ability to play a role in day-to-day economic management (though that does not mean it is prepared to lose control altogether).

WTO entry is part of the move towards greater economic efficiency. But it is by no means an isolated move — it is one of a generally coherent package of reforms that have been driven forward in a surprisingly consistent manner over the past few years. The main elements are:

- reform of state-owned industry, including semi-privatisation of major corporations;
- banking and financial reform;
- housing reform;
- and pension and social-security reform.

These reforms are often presented as an attempt by the Chinese state to relieve itself of the cradle-to-grave welfare responsibilities it has held until recently. This is only partly true: what the government is attempting to do is pass these responsibilities on to other bodies — ultimately businesses — who can make decisions on pricing them on the basis of a market.

The force behind these reforms — and the drive to maintain their momentum — can be broadly attributed to the prime minister, Zhu Rongji. But the changes have been accepted by all leaders and are supported by an almost universal consensus.

Faultlines

To advocates of market economics — and even many who are more neutral — getting the government out of business is a good thing. The emergence and rapid growth of a private sector, plus the sizeable role played by the foreign-invested sector (especially for exports), have helped let loose the country's economic potential over the past two decades.

But, at the same time, power is being concentrated in fewer hands at the centre. This may or may not be a bad thing; what is almost certainly a bad thing is that the government's ability to monitor what is happening is weakening as the economy and the country become ever more complex.

This lessening ability to monitor can in large part be attributed to the government's move away from a command economy. But there are also other factors. Since the Communist Party took power in 1949, it has relied on varying techniques to exercise its power over the country. Economically, it used a planned economy, whose agents — first the urban people's communes and street committees, then state-owned enterprises — it used to manage the lives of its urban population.

The rest of the population (as well as the urban population) was controlled through the household registration or hukou system, which forces everyone to live where they were registered, and until recently has prevented people from moving around. Information was controlled by the state's monopoly of the media. Lastly, there was the state's internal security apparatus.

Of this quartet of control measures, only the security apparatus remains intact. The population is moving in ever greater numbers as un-or under- employed rural workers head to the coast in their tens of millions looking for work; moves to ease the hukou system announced last year will only increase this internal migration.

The media are growing freer — despite clampdowns — while the Internet and telecoms offer a huge proportion of the population ways of communicating with each other freely that would have been unthinkable even a decade ago.

A new, ungovernable China?

The state which emerges from these changes appears weaker, and with fewer tools with which it can directly control the economy and society. The hope is that market mechanisms will play the principal disciplining role — hence the importance of the rules being introduced via China's WTO membership. But the problem here will not be whether WTO regulations can be implemented, but whether the steps the government has taken to free the economy will result in the country becoming ungovernable.

A slimmed-down bureaucracy might be good in principle. But, for example, the US$480 million now believed to have been taken from a Bank of China branch in Guangdong between 1992 and 2001 points to a need for more, not less oversight. And here is the crux: the government is freeing the economy at a time when it has removed its old methods of monitoring and control — the command economy — without having installed adequate new mechanisms. The outcome is a system in which a weakened state is finding itself powerless to control those who decide to take advantage of its inability.

As a result, corruption has become an entrenched part of the Chinese system. High-level instances have surfaced from one end of the country to the other in the last few years: Beijing (the former mayor, Chen Xitong), Shenyang (the mayor, Mu Suixin, and deputy mayor, Ma Xiangdong), Xiamen (the deputy mayor, who was party to a RMB 23 billion [US$2.77 billion] smuggling operation), Shantou (a multi-billion-renminbi tax fraud), Zhanjiang (the Communist Party head) and Jiangxi (the vice-governor).

On top of these instances are cases where money has simply disappeared. The Guangdong International Trust and Investment Corporation (GITIC) closed with debts of more than US$4 billion — money that had been borrowed and spent. As with the Bank of China's missing US$480 million, someone discovered it had gone, but only well after the event.

For all the talk of WTO bringing in profound reforms, there is much that its rules will get nowhere near touching. The fear of WTO entry should not be that the much-vaunted "rules-based" era it is supposed to usher in will fail to be implemented, nor that opening China's markets to international competition will lead to the closure of thousands of inefficient local companies or allow cheap food imports to undermine rural incomes.

Instead, the chief reason for worry over China's WTO entry must be that it will contribute to a weakening of the centre's ability to exercise control, leaving a vacuum in which corruption and regionalism can flourish. The tale that must surely worry the Chinese government most is that of Indonesia, and how its opened markets, weak government and endemic corruption led to that country falling off the economic map following Asia's economic crisis of 1997-99.

2. OPPORTUNITIES

a. Economic Integration Leading to Political Unification

(*This article appeared on 10 November 2001, The Straits Times, Page: A1, "Beijing sees a first step towards unification" by Ching Cheong, East Asia Correspondent.*)

ENTRY OF CHINA AND TAIWAN INTO WTO

With the admission of China and Taiwan into the World Trade Organisation (WTO), Beijing hopes that this one event will bring about the conditions for a peaceful unification.

This was one of the reasons cited by Beijing to justify the immense concessions it made during negotiations with the United States.

China and Taiwan are expected to be approved for WTO entry at a five-day meeting, which started yesterday [9 November 2001], of the 142-member global trading body in Doha, Qatar.

China said that WTO membership is needed as a first step towards economic integration with Taiwan.

Since 1979, Beijing has been pushing for "three direct links" in trade, sea and air transportation, as well as telecommunication between the two sides of the Taiwan Strait as a first move towards unification.

Direct cross-strait ties were severed in 1949 when the Kuomintang forces lost a civil war to the communists in China and fled to Taiwan.

The timing to push for greater economic integration between China and Taiwan has never been better.

US support for Taiwan has slackened due to the Sept 11 terrorist attacks.

As the Bush administration now needs Chinese support for its campaign against terrorists in Afghanistan, it is prepared to shelve the Taiwan card for the time being.

Weakened US support was evident during last month's [Oct 2001] Asia Pacific Economic Cooperation (APEC) summit where Taiwan suffered a major diplomatic debacle.

For the first time in APEC history, Taiwan was not represented at the leaders' summit because China objected to the choice of Taipei's representative.

The US, distracted by its anti-terrorism agenda, was unwilling to support a subtle Taiwanese attempt to break APEC norms.

There was therefore no US lobbying throughout the episode.

With the APEC rout in mind, Taiwan is no longer insisting that upon entry to the WTO, cross-strait trade be treated as country-to-country trade.

Instead, it now defines trade between the two sides as a "special case" to be governed by "special rules".

Taiwan's dependence on China is exacerbated by the anticipated recession in the US following the terrorist attacks.

In recent years, China has replaced the US as Taiwan's No 1 source of trade surplus.

The terrorist attacks have further shrunk the American economy and its ability to absorb Taiwanese exports, thereby increasing its dependence on China.

Politically, China's WTO membership would enhance Sino-US relations.

Former US President Bill Clinton said that it was in America's interest to have China in the WTO as it restrains Chinese international behaviour, integrates it with the Western world, promotes trade with the US and makes it politically more open and tolerant.

It follows that Chinese WTO membership would lead to more stable and interdependent Sino-US relations, and this would curtail the separatist movement in Taiwan.

Economically, WTO membership would turn China into the world's second largest market after the US for both consumption and investment.

While the US is undoubtedly the world's No 1 market, China, Japan and the European Union (EU) have been vying to become the world's second largest market.

With WTO membership for both sides of the Taiwan Strait, China stands a good chance of becoming the world's second largest market.

This would be the strongest incentive for Taiwan to further integrate with the mainland.

With Taiwan's separatist movement kept at bay while economic forces work towards closer integration, Beijing hopes to create an environment conducive to peaceful unification.

If it achieves this goal, the huge concessions that China made to gain WTO accession would be well worth its while.

b. Creation of a Greater China Free Trade Area

(This article appeared on 10 December 2001, The Straits Times, Page 12, "China FTA could be engine of growth for Asia" by Ching Cheong, East Asia Correspondent.)

Shortly after launching the China-Asean free trade area last month [November 2001], Beijing took another major step towards exerting its economic influence by announcing plans to create a China Free Trade Area (CFTA) comprising mainland China, Taiwan, Hongkong and Macau.

Mr Long Yongtu, chief negotiator on China's accession to the World Trade Organisation (WTO), said at an economic conference in Hongkong late last month [November 2001] that the central government had given the green light for the creation of a CFTA.

"We have received similar suggestions in the past, and the time is ripe now that the four entities are members of the WTO," he said, arguing that a CFTA is consistent with WTO rules.

"The fact that a country has four seats is extremely unique and it provides rare opportunities for greater integration among the four."

China hopes that the CFTA will be launched successfully in less than 10 years.

When realised, it will become the fourth-largest economic entity in the world after the United States, Japan and Germany. Currently, China ranks seventh in the world league.

In Asia, with a combined gross domestic product last year [2000] of US$1.53 trillion (S$2.8 trillion), it is second only to Japan, and surpasses all the other Asian countries combined (US$1.42 trillion).

Its total trade has also reached US$1 trillion, again surpassing all other Asian nations combined (except Japan).

These figures point to the CFTA becoming a huge economic bloc with tremendous potential to energise growth in Asia and the world at large.

A good indicator of this potential is the combined size of foreign-exchange (forex) reserves held by the CFTA.

Of the world's top five forex reserves owners, three belong to CFTA members.

Their aggregate forex reserves exceed US$380 billion, or 38 per cent of the total held by the top 10 forex reserves owners, estimated to be about US$1 trillion as at the end of last year [2000].

Prudently deployed, this huge pool of reserves can be translated into capital exports to other parts of Asia and provide a measure of currency stability for the region.

The downside, from its neighbours' point of view, would be even tougher competition for them in the years to come.

China has mapped out a three-stage approach towards building up the CFTA.

Stage one, to be achieved by 2003, would be the integration of the economies of mainland China, Hongkong and Macau.

Stage two aims to incorporate Taiwan by 2005.

Stage three aims to further expand the economic bloc to tie up with the development of other FTAs, such as the China-Asean FTA scheduled to be operational by 2010.

In the short-term, the emphasis will be on regional cooperation in developing tourism, harnessing human resources and promoting cooperation in information technology.

In the medium-term of five to 10 years, the CFTA hopes to eliminate tariff and non-tariff barriers completely by adopting a general preferential system among members, although each of them will still be free to set their own policies vis-à-vis third parties.

In line with the system, the grouping would also try to develop its own consensus on rules of origin to identify CFTA from non-CFTA products, consistent with the non-discrimination principle of the WTO.

Another medium-term target is to facilitate the trade in services. In accordance with China's accession commitment, trading in the services sectors will be liberalised by 2005-2006.

Taiwan and Hong Kong have a definite edge over China in services such as finance, law, accountancy, consultancy and trade facilitation.

By liberalising trade in these sectors within the CFTA first, China could shorten substantially its learning curve so that it would be better equipped to face the stiff competition in 2005-2006.

In the long-term, China hopes to realize full economic integration among the four entities so that Taiwan will be bonded to the mainland and thus greatly reduce the risk of its breaking away.

Mr Chi Fulin, deputy chairman of the China Institute of Structural Reform, who has been influential in promoting the CFTA concept, said:

"If the Taiwan Strait, now a political divide with little commercial value, could be turned into a golden waterway carrying goods and personnel across the strait, or if a Hongkong-Shanghai-Taipei triangle could be turned into a centre of capital, human resources and technology for the Greater China economic zone, then the issue of political unification would be more easily solved."

B. WHY WTO FOR CHINA

1. CHINA'S WTO MOTIVES AND FEARS

(This article is from "China: Good Intention", dated 4 December 2001, Business China, the Economist Intelligence Unit, retrieved from the archives of Chinaonline.com, in "China's WTO motives and fears" and reproduced with the permission of the EIU.)

(4 December 2001) China's motives for joining the World Trade Organisation (WTO) are probably not as simple as is often made out. It is not solely about opening the country's markets. After all, market liberalisation in China will not begin with accession to the world trading body. Since 1979, the nation's economic expansion has been nothing short of startling, and for many years explosive. China has received record amounts of foreign direct investment and achieved exponential growth in its export sector. In return, it has opened its markets only partially to foreign participation, keeping foreign investors champing at the bit for over two decades.

Despite this progress, the leadership's desire to join the grouping (and thus open further) has proved unyielding and strong — enough so that China has agreed to meet quite stringent demands. Had it been included in the General Agreement on Trade and Tariffs (GATT), predecessor to the WTO, China would not have been compelled to liberalise some of its more sensitive sectors, including telecommunications and financial services, and IT. But China missed that chance and by 1995 the WTO had replaced GATT and expanded membership requirements to include all of those sectors. Even compared with countries that have joined since 1995, China's accession was won on significantly more exacting terms.

Partly behind the government's eagerness to enter the WTO may be a belief that globalisation is an irresistible trend and that China has far more to gain by taking part than by watching from the sidelines. But this is likely to have played a relatively minor role in the government's decision to join the WTO. Probably more influential is that for the Chinese Communist Party (CCP), WTO membership forms part of a wider political agenda. This includes the advancement of its overall economic reform programme, the maintenance of social stability in the face of a vastly increased number of unemployed, and most importantly, cementing its own position in China's political future.

The next step

The Chinese economy is now in the throes of a major restructuring quite independent of the WTO. In particular, this involves the country's transition from a predominantly agrarian society to an industrialised one. Although other Asian countries have experienced the same transformation, nowhere has it occurred on a scale as huge as that in China. While the change is economic in nature, it is defined largely in human terms — a mass migration that will see hundreds of millions of rural workers move to the country's ever-growing urban areas.

This is occurring for two major reasons. First, the agriculture sector is dreadfully overmanned. It employs about half (some 350 million people) of China's labour force, although it represents only one-fifth of the overall economy. The land/labour ratio in the countryside is simply too high to allow farmers' incomes to keep pace with those of urban workers, as farms are small and productivity limited. Second, China's agricultural products — especially its staple crops such as wheat — cannot remain profitable in a market where foreign imports keep prices low.

With 60-70% of rural workers already unemployed or underemployed, the sector may ultimately support only about 100 million. Farm workers are now expected to move to urban areas in search of employment at a rate likely to exceed 10 million people per year, or 5% of the urban labour force. This migration will be facilitated by the gradual dismantling of the household registration (or hukou) system, through which the government has limited worker mobility.

Urban stress

Urbanisation will mean a dislocation of grand proportions — China has four times the population of the US and half the inhabitable land — and is likely to lead to the creation of mega-cities with some 30 million inhabitants each. Infrastructure, already reaching its maximum capacity in many cities, will be overwhelmed if the government cannot keep up with urban expansion. Similarly, the number of those dependent on the state will surely rise and the government will need to fund a national welfare system.

Compounding this labour translocation is continuing retrenchment in the state sector, where in the last three years some 30 million workers have been let go. Not only does the government face a large population displacement, but also the daunting task of creating some 20 million jobs annually for the next 20 years to soak up the nation's labour surplus.

The government recently announced that due to liberalisation under the WTO, China could expect some 12 million jobs to be created and another 11 million eliminated. These figures are highly optimistic. They also ignore the fact that workers being put out of work are not likely to be easily re-employable, as many new jobs will require some skills.

Should unemployment soar, the potential for unrest is real. The government is deeply anxious at the prospect of millions of displaced workers demonstrating — or worse — outside government offices across the country. Labour strikes, often held by unpaid state-sector employees, are already a common occurrence and becoming more so. The government, recognising this threat, has made the maintenance of social and political stability a central driving force shaping China's economic policy.

Do or die

Initially, China's WTO accession will worsen the risk to government and the rule of the CCP, serving both to increase the number of unemployed and accelerate worker migration. But if China can hang on, its long-term prospects are better in the WTO than out of it. But in the meantime will the central government maintain the resolve to implement its new-found obligations? The answer: it will have to.

The current wave of economic reform, initiated by Deng Xiaoping in the late 1970s, has served its purpose. Now political factionalism, local protectionism and bureaucratic inertia have all combined to slow the progress of liberalisation. Beijing is now banking on WTO membership to break through the logjam and allow the economy to continue growing fast enough — it hopes — to soak up the jobless hoards.

In the central government, concessions made as part of the WTO negotiating process will allow China's economic reformists to push ahead, despite the opposition to free-market practices posed by influential political factions and government ministries, such as those controlling the agriculture and telecoms sectors.

In local governments, where barriers to reform are arguably more serious, WTO membership also promises improvement. In the absence of a truly rule-based business environment, local authorities have come to enjoy effective autonomy from the centre. This has allowed local governments to wield power disproportionate to their status and to protect inefficiencies within local economies. In general, officials are answerable only to their local chapter of the CCP, rules governing business are weak or not properly enforced, and corruption is endemic.

Provincial and municipal bureaucracies have over the years built up a web of tariff and non-tariff barriers that are designed either to protect businesses on their turf and/or to line the pockets of local officials. Some provinces, for example, have exacted hefty "licence fees" to keep out products, such as automobiles, manufactured in other parts of the country.

The hope is that the introduction of defined market-access rules enforceable (indirectly) by foreign adjudicators will erode this power base. Bureaucrats will have less control over how people conduct their businesses, and indeed their lives. Regional monopolies will be dismantled, while inefficient state-owned enterprises so far reliant on preferential treatment will have to compete with foreign and domestic private firms — or fail.

The test

The undoing of local protectionism will be perhaps the most important yardstick by which China's participation in the WTO is measured. Few doubt that local officials will wage rear-guard actions to protect their interests. But the central government appears equally intent on enforcing the new regime, giving blanket coverage in state media to WTO issues, introducing a steady stream of WTO-compliant laws and regulations, and establishing a corps of bureaucrats and government departments responsible for overseeing the implementation of WTO obligations.

Though impossible to determine when Beijing will be able to bring provincial power bases to heel, central-government victory is likely — it can not afford to fail. The liberalisation programmeme initiated over 20 years ago has set in motion economic development that requires continual advancement. Without it, rising unemployment and social discontent could lead to widespread unrest, which could potentially threaten the government.

That is not to suggest that liberalisation under the WTO will be enough to complete smoothly China's transition from feudal state to industrial powerhouse. Indeed, the prospects of China converting its illiterate farmers into the skilled service sector workers it will need seems even more remote than sustaining economic growth at a fast enough clip (over 10% a year) to create sufficient new jobs. But while success under the WTO may not be guaranteed, social upheaval and political oblivion seem far more certain consequences if reform is not carried to the next logical step.

2. ON WHY THE US SUPPORT WTO MEMBERSHIP FOR CHINA

(*This section is extracted from "The Impact of WTO/PNTR On Chinese Politics" by Joseph Fewsmith*[1], *NBR Publications: NBR Analysis: Vol. 11, No. 2: Essay 2 The National Bureau of Asian Research 2000. The original footnotes are left out in this reprint.*)

In examining the political impact of Sino-U.S. relations on Chinese domestic politics, it is useful to distinguish the perspectives of three groups in Chinese society: elite policymakers, intellectual "opinion makers," and the broader, mostly urban, public. The impact of PNTR on all three levels would be positive, while its denial would be negative.

Impact on Intellectuals

Starting with China's intellectuals, the single most surprising change in the nation's trajectory over the last decade is the dramatic change in perceptions of the United States. In the 1980s intellectuals overwhelmingly viewed the United States positively. Pictures of students and intellectuals in Tiananmen Square calling for democracy and raising a statue of the "goddess of democracy" remain deeply engraved in our memories. China has changed a great deal over the past decade, and the very positive image of the United States that prevailed at the time has faded and been replaced by a much darker image. It is now widely believed that the

[1]Joseph Fewsmith is associate professor of international relations at Boston University and a specialist on the political economy of China. His publications include *Dilemmas of Reforms in China: Political Conflict and Economic Debate* (1994) and *Party, State, and Local Elites in Republican China* (1985).

United States does not care for human rights or oppose abuses by the Chinese government, but rather that it is simply opposed to China and to the Chinese people. As some have said, regardless of what China does—whether it improves its human rights record, listens to the United States in trade and international relations, follows or rejects socialism—the United States will still oppose China; the United States simply will not let China join the world.1 Needless to say, such expressions of nationalistic emotion do not promote China's integration into the international system.

The rise of China's "new nationalism" is a complex phenomenon reflecting both domestic and international factors. Domestically, the 1990s brought rapid socio-economic change as income gaps, both intra-regional and inter-regional, grew dramatically, millions of rural residents streamed into cities looking for new opportunities to make a living, and crime and problems of social order increased. At the same time, ideology evaporated and a new search for values and identity began. This search has taken remarkably varied forms, from the Mao cult of the early 1990s, to New Confucianism, post-modernism, and religion—including everything from Buddhism and Christianity, to shamanism and Falungong (the banned spiritual movement). If there is any thread that connects these various responses to the loss of ideology, it is a revival of nativism. And it is this nativist impulse that so clearly distinguishes the 1990s from the cosmopolitanism of the 1980s.

Internationally, this turn toward nativism has been reinforced by the collapse of socialism in Eastern Europe and the Soviet Union and the break-up of the latter. For Chinese of very different intellectual orientations, the experience of the Soviet Union stands as a powerful negative example. The loss of territory, the decline in economic well-being and living standards, and the decline in international influence all stand as reminders of what China does not want. Many people attribute the break-up of the Soviet Union to its overzealous pursuit of the Western model and Western advice: "shock therapy" to privatize the economy and rapid change to democratize the political system. Some go further and attribute the fate of the Soviet Union to the successful efforts of the United States to undermine socialism and bring about "peaceful evolution."

At the same time, many Chinese—including some who are quite liberal and open-minded in their thinking—are convinced that the United States fears the emergence of a prosperous and stable China and will do anything in its power to "hold China down." This negative view of the United States contrasts dramatically with the positive image that prevailed in the 1980s and marks a remarkable failure in the battle for public opinion. Unfortunately, many actions by the United States have contributed to that failure.

When did public opinion in China begin to change? The single most important turning point came in 1993 when the United States, through a resolution of Congress and through the U.S. Olympic Committee, opposed China's bid to host the summer Olympics in the year 2000. One can argue that the Chinese propaganda apparatus played this issue brilliantly. It used the campaign to build up Chinese pride, something that was sorely lacking in the period immediately following Tiananmen, and then set up the United States as the bogey man if that bid were to fail, which it did. The propaganda campaign may have been brilliant, but it could not have succeeded without U.S. help. This exercise of "leverage," more than any other single event, convinced students, intellectuals, and ordinary Chinese alike that the United States opposed China, not the Chinese government. As if to drive the message home, that summer the U.S. navy forcibly inspected a Chinese ship, the Yin He (Milky Way), which was believed to be carrying precursor chemicals for the making of chemical weapons to Iran. When none were found, the United States was widely viewed as a bully.

Impact on Popular Opinion

These and other incidents have largely faded in the memory of Americans, but they remain touchstones for public opinion in China. Moreover, such incidents set the background for the first major wave of anti-American public opinion, showing that such sentiment had moved beyond the realm of China's intellectual elite to a larger public. In 1994 a young author named Wang Shan published a book called *Looking at China Through a Third Eye*. The book was largely a critique of Deng Xiaoping's reforms, but the title of its first chapter stated its nationalist premise clearly: "Don't interfere in China." Wang's book became the surprise best-seller of 1994 and clearly indicated a new trend in popular opinion.

The next wave of nationalist opinion came in 1995 after Lee Teng-hui, then-president of Taiwan, was granted a visa to conduct a "private" visit to his alma mater, Cornell University. Perhaps Lee's visit could have passed quietly had it indeed been handled as a private visit, but it was not, and the reaction in China—at all levels of society and in the government— was intense. The developing crisis in the Taiwan Strait dramatically influenced popular opinion [in China] of the United States. A public opinion poll conducted at the time found that 87.1 percent of respondents believed that the United States was the country "least friendly" to China. Reflecting cynicism about American motives, 85.4 percent responded that they believed that the United States engaged in the Gulf War "out of its own interests."

It is no surprise that *China Can Say No* was published that year, selling perhaps two million copies. One aspect of this highly emotional, nationalistic book that rang true with many readers was the authors' claim to have been strongly influenced by the United States in the 1980s, only to have become disillusioned in the 1990s. They had come to realize, they claimed, that the United States was not the bastion of idealism they had previously thought it was; "human rights" was merely a facade behind which Washington pursued its national interests. In fact, far from championing ideals in the world, the United States was an arrogant, narcissistic, hegemonic power that acted as a world policeman; now it was doing everything in its power to keep China from emerging as a powerful and wealthy country. *China Can Say No* was not the only such book published; indeed, at least a dozen imitators sprang up, expressing their emotions and tapping the market. Anti-Americanism was a seller.

Impact on Elite Politics

If the change in public perception of the United States over recent years is clearly toward the negative, is there any evidence that better relations will engender better public opinion and better public policy? In fact there is, and the difference that a more positive approach can make is quite clear if one contrasts the 1997-1998 period, during which both sides worked to improve relations, with 1999, when a serious downturn in relations took place.

The improvement in relations in 1997-1998 resulted from leaders in both Washington and Beijing moving away from the very confrontational approach that emerged during the crisis in the Taiwan Strait. China wanted respect, and the United States wanted to defuse the threat of conflict in the Taiwan Strait and elsewhere. The process of improving relations was not easy. The United States rightly demanded the release of political prisoners such as Wei Jingsheng and Wang Dan and an improvement in China's human rights behavior, while China wanted new assurances that the United States would not support independence for Taiwan. Long and difficult negotiations resulted in the exchange of summits, as President Jiang Zemin traveled to the United States in October 1997 and President Clinton visited China in June 1998. Such summit diplomacy is necessarily limited. A better atmosphere can be created, but unless differences over everything from security issues to trade and human rights are tackled, results are temporary at best. This is what ultimately set back relations, starting in late 1998. Nevertheless, it is quite revealing that the improvement in Sino-U.S. relations in this period contributed to the greatest relaxation of China's political atmosphere since Tiananmen.

As relations warmed, Jiang Zemin worked to link domestic reforms to the improvement in Sino-U.S. relations. By the summer of 1997, prior to Jiang's visit to the United States, there was already a visible relaxation of the political atmosphere. In the fall, just prior to his departure for the United States, Jiang presided over the Fifteenth Party Congress, perhaps the most reform-oriented in Chinese Communist Party history. Jiang emphasized economic reform through the further adoption of the shareholding system and political reform through "rule by law." At the time, Jiang also highly praised the elections that had been carried out at the village level since the late 1980s and endorsed raising them to the township level in the future. If carried out, this would be the most important change in China's political system since 1949.

The intellectual atmosphere also loosened visibly as writers began to publish controversial new works during the so-called "Beijing spring." These works, such as *Crossed Swords*, called for new reforms, and the government self-consciously worked to cool nationalist emotions. To justify the change in foreign policy, semi-official books began to argue the case for better Sino-U.S. relations. The most important of these was *China Will Not Be "Mr. No"* by senior researcher Shen Jiru. Shen argued that the Soviet Union brought about its own demise by refusing to interact normally with the United States; excessive nationalism, the implicit argument went, was self-destructive. There is little question that Jiang Zemin's efforts to promote domestic reform in this period were supported by the improvement in Sino-U.S. relations.

Unfortunately these trends were sharply reversed in 1999, and the impact on Chinese domestic politics has been apparent. Among the many reasons for this downturn in relations were illegal campaign contributions, the crackdown on democracy advocates, allegations of nuclear spying, the failure of Premier Zhu Rongji to secure a WTO agreement during his trip to the United States in April 1999, and the military campaign in Yugoslavia. The single largest cause was accidental: the tragic bombing of the Chinese embassy in Belgrade.

The impact of these events—particularly the circumvention of the United Nations to take military action in Yugoslavia, the failure of Zhu's trip, and the bombing of the Chinese embassy—had an immediate and negative impact on Chinese politics. Zhu was mercilessly abused, both in the corridors of power and in the court of public opinion. His position in government suffered visibly over the summer and fall, and rumors were rife that he would resign or be forced to resign. Less well known is the criticism that Jiang Zemin faced. It was widely held that his policies toward the United States had been too "soft" and that he should do something to "stand up" to the Americans.8

The impact, as one might imagine from the outpouring of emotion in the days following the bombing, was not limited to criticism of the top leadership. On one hand, many intellectuals favorably inclined toward the United States were so outraged that they could not but express their anger and concern for the future. Even Shen Jiru, the author of *China Will Not Be "Mr. No"* worried openly about the course of events. On the other hand, a new wave of nationalism, one that dwarfed all previous waves, swept over China. For instance, a new book called *China under the Shadow of Globalization* was soon published and self-consciously depicted itself as standing in the tradition of *China Can Say No*. In the best populist tradition, the primary author heaped contempt on the intellectual elite of China, especially so-called "liberals" who favored better relations with the United States. He depicted them as lapdogs, saying they "support the U.S., support everything about the U.S." It should be noted that these "liberals," so denounced by the nationalists, are precisely the people and organizations who have gone out on a limb to support an improvement in Sino-U.S. relations and back China's entry into the WTO. If PNTR were to fail in the Congress, these are the people who would be hurt. Just after the bombing of the Chinese embassy, a senior Chinese analyst of Sino-American relations commented to me [Joseph Fewsmith] poignantly that U.S. actions "have dealt a severe blow to liberals in China." Failure to support PNTR would grievously compound the damage to those in China working to reform the country.

PNTR and Furthering Reform in China

The preceding outline of the interaction between the state of Sino-U.S. relations and Chinese domestic politics suggests the magnitude of the impact the United States has on China. This effect is something Americans often do not notice, in part because the positive changes made by China in response to the United States are incremental. For instance, it is difficult to capture in words or pictures the impact that working in U.S.-owned joint ventures has had on thousands of Chinese. Nor is it easy to convey the power of popular images on Chinese thinking—such as the realization from watching American TV shows that citizens have rights when faced by arrest. This is real leverage.

To argue that better relations promote reform in China is not to argue that the United States can or should compromise its principles but rather that the right tools must be adopted in order to exert positive leverage. Indeed, the negotiation of the WTO agreement itself is a very good example of how the United States can exert leverage to move China in directions that are compatible both with its own long-term interests and with integrating China into the global order as a normal nation. Indeed, it took many years to reach an acceptable agreement, and those within China who argued for the agreement recognized that joining the world is the way to promote China's own reforms. These are the people the United States should support through its actions, and rejecting PNTR would severely undercut them and the reforms they have been working to expand.

This understanding of the issues was confirmed by a recent trip to Beijing, during which I [Joseph Fewsmith] asked many specialists what the impact would have been if the House of Representatives had not supported PNTR. The thought that PNTR would not be supported by the U.S. Congress was simply staggering. All agreed that the impact would be far-reaching and negative. The rejection of PNTR would require a comprehensive reassessment of China's policy toward the United States; the possibility of cooperation on many issues of concern to both nations, including arms proliferation, human rights, and regional security concerns, would be setback severely. Fortunately, the House supported PNTR, and it is hoped that the Senate will do so as well.

Some historical perspective is necessary when thinking about PNTR. When President Nixon traveled to China in 1972, China was still in the throes of the Cultural Revolution. Mao Zedong was still in command, there were no private markets, intellectuals were still raising pigs on so-called "May 7 cadre schools," and labor camps were filled with political prisoners. Nixon was treated to a performance of "The Red Detachment of Women," one of only eight model operas that were permitted to be performed. Nearly three decades later—not a long period in historical terms—China has changed dramatically. Communes are gone, the planned economy has shrunk to a shadow of its former self, and incomes have increased dramatically. Personal freedoms, while by no means perfect, are greater than at any other time in Chinese history. China's opening to the United States is a major reason for these changes, a dramatic demonstration of the impact of international influence.

The decision on PNTR is a moment when Congress can decide to move history forward or set it back. It is not a routine decision that can be changed or revised next year [2001] or the year after. It is a decision to incorporate China into or to isolate it from the global order. For the United States, it is an opportunity to gain, rather than to give up, leverage.

c h a p t e r   8

Agriculture

A. CHINA'S COMMITMENTS

(This section on China's commitments is drawn from data provided in the US White House Factsheets on China WTO Accession, last updated on 17 February 2000, available on the website of US-China Business Council at http://www.uschina.org/public/wto/factsheets. Certain adjustments were made according to China accession documents, marked in square bracket.)

1. General

a. Tariff Bindings

By joining the WTO, China is committing to establish a "tariff-only" import regime; all non-tariff barriers will be eliminated. Any other measure, such as inspection, testing, and domestic taxes must be applied in a manner that is consistent with WTO rules requiring a transparent and non-discriminatory system and all health measures must be based on sound science.

The tariff on agricultural products will decline from an overall average of 22% to 17.5% [15%[1]], while the average duty on agricultural products of U.S. priority interest will fall from 31% to 14%. Specific commitments to lower tariffs, to be phased-in by the year 2004 in equal annual installments, are listed below.

b. Tariff-Rate Quota Administration

China, like many WTO Members, including the United States, will use a tariff-rate quota (TRQ) system and state trading for certain sensitive commodities (including wheat, corn, rice, cotton, and soybean oil). Under this system, a specific quantity of imports will be allowed in at a low duty [10 percent or less, except for sugar 15% by 2004] while imports above that

---

[1]Figure obtained from *"Embracing the Opportunities, Meeting the Challenges—Special Supplement on China's Accession to the WTO"*, November 2001 available at the web address of Trade and Industry Department of HKSAR government at *http://www.info.gov.hk/tid/wto_accesion/content.htm#Other%20Services*; according to Report No. GAO-03-4 of the United States General Accounting Office, this tariff rate will be achieved by 2010, p. 72 of the Report, *"Analysis of China's Commitments to Other Members"*, October, 2002.

level will face a higher duty. China made specific commitments to administer these TRQs based on economic rather than political criteria. These commitments are designed to ensure a transparent and consistent system for allocating shares of the TRQ to end users and creating provisions to ensure that quota-holders are not impeded in utilizing their quotas. If TRQs are not utilized they are redistributed to other end users who have an interest in importing. Moreover, a specific share of the TRQ will be reserved for importation through state trading enterprises and a specific share will be reserved for importation by non-state trading entities. Finally, if a TRQ share that was reserved to be imported by a state trader is not contracted for by October for any given year, it will be reallocated to non-state trading entities.

China will eliminate its existing TRQ system on imports of certain products and subject them only to tariffs: barley, soybeans, rape seed, peanut oil, sunflower oil, corn oil and cottonseed oil.[2]

c. Trading Rights and Distribution

Before WTO accession, foreign companies' ability to do business in China was strictly limited because the right to engage in trade (importing and exporting) was restricted to a small number of companies that received specific authorization or who imported goods to be used in production. This limited exports of foreign countries.

China agreed that any entity would be able to import most products into any part of China. This commitment is phased in over the three-year period with all entities being permitted to import and export at the end of the period. A select list of products will be partially exempt from this rule and some trade will continue to be channeled through China's state trading enterprises (including wheat, corn, rice, and cotton; state trading will be phased out for soybean oil). However, specific commitments to end monopoly import status have also been established. Trading rights for these products will be phased in, gradually increasing the number of entities allowed to import.

China — which generally prohibits companies from distributing imported products or providing related distribution services — will permit foreign enterprises to engage in the full range of distribution services. These rights will be phased in over a three-year period for almost all products, including grains.

d. Export Subsidies

China has committed not to use export subsidies for agricultural products when it joins the WTO. This commitment is particularly useful for addressing potential exports of corn, rice, and cotton, which in the past have displaced U.S. product from third-country markets.

e. Domestic Support

China has committed to cap and reduce trade-distorting domestic subsidies. The specific level will be determined through multilateral negotiations in Geneva on the protocol and working party report. China also committed to provide greater transparency to make its domestic support measures more predictable.

---

[2]ibid.

f. Sanitary and Phytosanitary Measures

China has committed to fully abide by the terms of the *WTO Agreement on Sanitary and Phytosanitary Measures*, which requires that all animal, plant, and human health import requirements be based on sound science, not political agendas or protectionist concerns. Additionally, China and the United States agreed bilaterally the terms for the removal of scientifically unjustified restrictions on importation of U.S. wheat, citrus, and meat.

g. Anti-dumping

The *US–China Bilateral* Agreement explicitly permits the United States to continue to use its current non-market economy methodology for 15 years after China's accession to the WTO.

h. Safeguards

China has committed to a strong product-specific safeguard that allows the United States to address import surges. Specifically, the safeguard allows the United States to restrain increasing imports from China that cause or threaten to cause market disruption for 12 years after accession. After that, current U.S. safeguard provisions — Section 201 — remain available to address increasing imports.

2. Commitment to the US: US–China Agricultural Cooperation Agreement

Apart from the general commitments outlined above, China also made some other commitments to the US during their bilateral negotiation. The main points of the *US–China Agricultural Cooperation Agreement* are summarized below.

a. Removal of Sanitary/Phytosanitary Barriers to key US goods

On April 10, 1999 the U.S. and China signed an agreement on U.S. – China Agricultural Cooperation, which resolved sanitary and phytosanitary trade disputes on citrus, meat, Pacific-northwest wheat, and other grains.

b. Resolution of Trade Disputes

China agreed to the immediate removal of longstanding barriers to U.S. citrus, meat, and wheat and other grains. In addition, China agreed to accelerate the removal of all other non-tariff measures restricting trade in agricultural products that cannot be justified under WTO rules.

c. Citrus

Under the Agreement, China will lift bans on imports of U.S. citrus. For the first two harvest seasons Arizona, Texas and approved counties in Florida and California will be permitted to export citrus produced in areas free of fruit flies and from areas outside of a 20-kilometer zone around fruit fly outbreaks.

During the interim period, the U.S. and China also agreed to study the size of the quarantine zone. If agreement cannot be reached, then the 20-kilometer zone will be eliminated (i.e., the much less restrictive U.S. standard will apply).

On January 28, Chinese officials completed the pre-program initiation inspection tour of U.S. citrus producing regions, as stipulated in the Agreement. Based on this visit, the officials indicated that they anticipated being able to approve U.S. citrus exports to China soon.

d. Wheat and other Grains

Under the Agreement, China will lift the ban on imports of wheat from 7 states in the Pacific Northwest (the ban was due to the presence of TCK spores in shipments).

China will import all types of U.S. wheat from all regions of the United States to all ports in China provided it is at or below a tolerance level of 30,000 TCK spores per 50 gram sample.

Equivalent tolerance levels will be applied to other grains possibly contaminated with TCK.

For one year, the U.S. and China will undertake a joint project on the TCK tolerance level for exports to China. If agreement cannot be reached, 30,000 TCK spores per 50-gram sample will continue to be applied.

China agreed not to apply any other restrictions, including measures that would require a change of destination for any shipment.

China also agrees that there is no other outstanding phytosanitary issue to prohibit exports of U.S. wheat.

e. Meat

Under the Agreement, China will lift the ban on U.S. exports of all meat and poultry accompanied by a USDA/FSIS certificate of wholesomeness.

China will still have the right to randomly audit the U.S. certification system through plant inspections and through inspection of imported U.S. product at the Chinese port of entry.

f. Technical Cooperation and Scientific Exchanges

The U.S. and China agreed to increase mutual cooperation in the field of high technology and encourage research institutes and agricultural enterprises to collaborate in high-tech research and development. The specific project areas include:

— field and horticultural products;
— biotechnology;
— meat, poultry, and livestock;
— aquaculture;
— natural resources and the environment.

B. IMPACT ON CHINA

Many people in China fear that the commitments China made to the WTO and especially to the US would create serious problems for its agrarian sector.

1. Expanded market for US agricultural export

(The following information is obtained from "China's WTO accession to significantly boost U.S. agricultural exports" dated 13 June 2001, archives of "Briefing Rooms", Economic Research Centre, US Department of Agriculture, http://www.ers.usda.gov/ briefing/wto/china.htm, which briefed on an article "China's WTO Accession Would Boost U.S. Ag Exports and Farm Income", March 2000 of Agricultural Outlook Magazine.)

From the US point of view, the terms it exacted from China would significantly boost US agricultural export to China.

According to the United States Agriculture Department (USDA) baseline projections, published in USDA Agricultural Baseline Projections to 2010, released on February 22, 2000, the U.S. gains from China's WTO accession would come in two forms: increased volume of exports to China and stronger world prices.

China's participation in the World Trade Organization will result in at least US$2 billion per year in additional U.S. agricultural exports by 2005.

The total value of U.S. exports of wheat, rice, corn, cotton, soybeans and soybean products would increase by US$1.6 billion dollars in 2005 when the [US–China bilateral] agreement is fully implemented. The average annual value of U.S. exports from 2000 through 2009 would increase by US$1.5 billion dollars.

By 2005, the largest increases in the annual value of China's net agricultural imports are likely to be for corn (US$587 million), wheat (US$543 million), and cotton (US$359 million).

Tariffs would also be reduced significantly for other products, such as poultry, pork, beef, citrus, other fruits, vegetables, tree nuts, and forest and fish products. This could result in an additional US$350-450 million in U.S. export growth, bringing the total gain to about US$2 billion annually by 2005.

Agricultural exports to China could be even higher in 2005 than this nearly US$2 billion annual estimate, because China's projected 7-percent annual GDP growth will likely increase demand for many other products not included in the estimate, including dairy products such as cheese, snack foods, grocery items, wine, beef, distilled spirits and tobacco.

Although higher feed costs and reduced government payments (loan deficiency payments) would offset part of the increase in cash receipts, net farm income would be higher by US$1.7 billion in 2005, and higher by an annual average US$1.1 billion per year over the 2000-09 period.

2. Pressure on the Chinese rural sector

The estimates on WTO accession on China's agricultural sector, especially on the rural labour that is going to be displaced, had been most controversial.

Yu and Zheng (2000) in their CASS Report[3] find that the rural sector will be worse off at least in the first ten years (2001-2010). The findings on main agricultural products are summarized in Table 8.1.

From Table 8.1 it is clear that the main food crop sectors, rice and wheat, will suffer from substantial shrinkage in output, thanks to increased imports. Raw materials for the

Table 8.1 Impact of WTO membership on China's Agricultural Production 2001-5

| | Impact of WTO on China's Agriculture | | | | | | | |
| | Output | | Employment | | Import | | Export | |
Products	Billion RMB	%	10,000	%	Billion RMB	%	Billion RMB	%
Rice	−4.6	−1.4	−246.1	−2.8	5.6	300	0	12
wheat	−17.2	−9	−540.3	−14.2	26.8	206	0	73.3
other cereals	0.3	0.1	1.6	0	10.4	226	0	0.2
cotton	−11.7	−12.6	−498.2	−22.6	45	427	0	209.4
other non-food crops	11.3	1.8	151.1	1.9	0.7	10.9	0.1	1.1
forestry	1.3	1.1	5.4	1.4	1.1	10.7	0	−2.2
fleece	−3	−37	−10	−38	5.1	86.6	0	−15.4
other animal products	73.7	5.7	104.1	5	1	77.1	2.8	13
all other agr products	7.8	5.2	57.2	5.1	0.1	19.4	0	4.6
Total	57.9		−975.2		95.8		2.9	

Source: Extracted from Table 1–11, *The CASS Report by Yu and Zheng, 2000*

---

[3]See beginning of Chapter 6 for CASS Report by Yu and Zheng 2000.

textile & clothing industries, cotton and fleece, will bear the full brunt of WTO accession. Total loss in output in these two sectors amount to RMB21.8 billion and RMB15 billion respectively when the commitments are fully implemented by 2005.

The impact on rural employment would be even severe. Since China's rural work force is heavily engaged in the production of food crops and raw materials for industry, the reduction in output in these two main areas means that substantial number of workers would be displaced. It is estimated by CASS Report by Yu and Zheng 2000 that by 2005, nearly 9.6 million rural workers would lost their jobs.

Trade in agricultural products would be heavily in China's disadvantage upon entry into the WTO. CASS finding shows that imports of agricultural products would increase by RMB 96 billion against a meager 3 billion in export.

Since the agricultural sector is the worst hit one, it is expected that rural income will actually decline by 2005. Yu and Zheng estimated that rural income will decline by 2.1 percent while factor price for agricultural land will decline by 18.4 percent.

Both Yu and Zheng are slightly on the optimistic side on the unemployment created by WTO membership. According to Ma Xiaohe, chief of the Agriculture Sector of the State Economic Development and Planning Commission, the total size of the rural labour displaced double the estimate made by Yu and Zheng.[4]

Thanks to a much higher domestic price for most agricultural products, as is clear from Table 8.2, the size of rural labour being displaced from their land will reach 25 million, almost 150% higher than the estimate made by the CASS Report by Yu and Zheng (2000), see Table 8.3.

Table 8.2 Differentials between Chinese and world agricultural prices

Crops	Unit	Price domestic	World	excess %
Wheat	RMB/ton	1140	911	25.10%
Rice	RMB/ton	1707	1451	17.60%
Corn	RMB/ton	855	625	36.80%
Soyabean	RMB/ton	2100	1513	38.80%
Oil	RMB/ton	4400	2731	61.10%
Sugar	RMB/ton	3825	2247	70.20%
Cotton	RMB/ton	11756	11110	5.80%
Pork	RMB/ton	8930	59431	−85%
Beef	RMB/ton	11360	31419	63.80%

Note: Prices are normalized and standardized. All prices were based on the August 2000 figures. Domestic sugar price was based on the price in September 2000.

Source: Ma, Xiaohe. "An analysis on the impact of WTO accession on China's agriculture", State Economic Development and Planning Commission, 2001

[4]Ma, Xiaohe "An analysis on the impact of WTO Accession on China's agriculture", State Economic Development and Planning Commission, 2001, appeared on 14 August 2001 at the Chinese version of China Macroeconomic Information Network at http://www.macrochina.com.cn.

Table 8.3 Rural unemployment by sectors: 2000–2005

Sector	2001–2005 (in 10,000)
wheat	146
oil-bean	235
corn	115
rice	106
cotton	1948
Total	2550

Source: Ma, Xiaohe, ibid.

Chinese Premier Zhu Rongji had admitted that the most seriously hit sector upon of China's WTO accession would be the agricultural sector.

CHINA'S RURAL UNEMPLOYMENT

The impact of WTO accession on rural unemployment is difficult to quantify. Different research institutes yielded grossly different results, ranging from 9.6 million in the most optimistic study to 176 million in the most pessimistic one. This could due to different criteria used, and whether direct or indirect impacts are included. The political attitudes of the forecasting institutes towards WTO membership could also be a significant factor affecting the results of the studies. To give readers an overall view, the various estimates quoted in Chapters 6, 7 and 8 are recapitulated in Table 8.4 below.

Table 8.4 Different Estimates on Job Loss due to WTO membership

Different Estimates on Rural Unemployment On WTO Accession		
Forcasting Institute	Job Loss In Million	Source & Notes
Chinese Academy of Social Sciences	9.6	CASS Report, 2000
Centre for Development Research		China Times, 20 Nov, 1999
– job loss in 3 key sectors of rice,		
wheat, cotton sectors	12.8	
– total job loss	176.0	
Ministry of Agriculture	20.0	People's Daily 28 Feb 2002
State Economic Development &		Ma Xiaohe, 2001
Planning Commission		
– job loss in 5 key sectors (rice,		
wheat, cotton plus oilseeds and corn)	25.5	

chapter 9

Impact on China's industrial
Enterprises: A Snapshot

The Hong Kong Trade Development Council (TDC) developed a handy scheme of analyzing the impact of WTO on China's industrial enterprises. Basically it identified four channels of positive influences and four channels of negative ones, from China's perspective, in the following manner:[1]

1. THE CHANNELS OF IMPACT

A. Channels of Negative Impacts

Channel N1: Tariff reductions on imports of industrial products.
Channel N2: Elimination of non-tariff barriers, that is, of licenses, quotas and tendering requirements as well as registration requirements, over selected import products.
Channel N3: The opening-up of trade rights and distribution markets.
Channel N4: Relaxation of the conditions on foreign investment.
Channel N1-N2 is set to lead to an increase in imports, while Channel N4 to a rise in foreign-funded enterprises' (FFE) market shares. Meanwhile Channel N3 is expected to help both, with a better sales prospect for both imported and FFEs-produced products. Such a situation will undoubtedly pose a threat to existing industrial enterprises on their market shares.

B. Channels of Positive Impacts

Channel P1: Reduction in tariff & non-tariff barriers on China's exports in overseas markets.
Channel P2: Tariff reductions on imports of raw and semi-finished materials.
Channel P3: Improvement in the economy and market institution expected from WTO entry.
Channel P4: Better access to foreign investment with the Channel P3 as well as N4.
Channel P1 is expected to improve export prospect, while Channel P2 to cut import costs, for many enterprises.

All the enterprises would benefit, with varying degrees, from Channel P3, that is, from the expected expansion of trade, consumption and investment activities and improvement in corporate and banking structures and law system. Meanwhile Channel P4 means that further

---

[1]Source: "*A General Assessment of the Impact of WTO Entry on China's Industrial Enterprises*", archives of "WTO Accession Monitor", July 2000, HKTDC web site, *http://www.tdctrade.com*

market opening would benefit the enterprises by offering them better access to updated technology and management as well as funds, on the other hand.

2. NEGATIVE (N) IMPACT BY SECTOR WITH IMPACT CHANNELS

A. From Channel N1

a) Seriously affected: cars, and daily-use chemicals
b) Pronouncedly affected: buses & trucks, auto components, telecom equipment, synthetic petrochemicals, pharmaceuticals, air-conditioners, precision machinery, textiles and garments, computer products, and high-end steel products.

B. From Channel N2

a) Seriously affected: cars, refined oils, and high-end steel products.
b) Pronouncedly affected: synthetic petrochemicals, farm-use chemicals, complete sets of equipment, precision machinery, mainframes & mini-computers, garments, and mid-class steel products.

C. From Channel N3

a) Seriously affected: auto components, telecom equipment, refined oils, synthetic petrochemicals, daily-use products, pharmaceuticals, PCs, peripheral computer equipment, and high-end steel products.
b) Pronouncedly affected: cars, buses & trucks, farm-use chemicals, TVs, air-conditioners, washing machines, machinery products, textiles & garments, food products, and low-end & mid-class steel products.

D. From Channel N4

a) Seriously affected: telecom services, and pharmaceuticals.
b) Pronouncedly affected: auto components, petrochemicals, farm-use chemicals, JVs, washing machines, complete sets of equipment, precision machinery, power generation & equipment, garments, computers, steel products, toll roads, and international shipping.

3. POSITIVE (P) IMPACT BY SECTOR WITH IMPACT CHANNELS

A. From Channel P1

a) Remarkably benefited: textiles & garments, electrical appliances, food products, and international shipping.
b) Pronouncedly benefited: buses & trucks, chemicals, low-end machinery products, PCs, irons & steels, low-end steel products, toll roads, and railways.

B. From Channel P2

a) Pronouncedly benefited: cars, buses & trucks, telecom equipment, daily-use chemicals, electrical appliances, garments, PCs, and peripheral computer equipment.

C. From Channel P3

a) Remarkably benefited: TVs, air-conditioners, textiles & garments, food products, toll roads, and international shipping.
b) Pronouncedly benefited: cars, buses & trucks, auto components, crude oils, refined oils, chemicals, refrigerators, washing machines, low-end machinery products, power generation and equipment, computers, steel products, and railways.

D. From Channel P4

a) Remarkably benefited: auto components, refined oils, garments, high-end steel products, and international shipping.
b) Pronouncedly benefited: cars, buses & trucks, telecom services & equipment, crude oils, synthetic petrochemicals, pharmaceuticals, TVs, air-conditioners, complete sets of equipment, precision machinery, power generation & equipment, textiles, computer products, food products and mid-class steel products.

4. OVERALL IMPACT BY SECTOR

Using this scheme, it identified the sectors that is likely to be affected by WTO membership either for good or bad.

A. Those Negatively affected included:

a) Seriously: cars, telecom services, refined oils, synthetic petrochemicals, pharmaceuticals, high-end steel products.
b) Pronouncedly: daily-use chemicals, farm-use chemicals, complete sets of machinery equipment, precision machinery, peripheral computer equipment, and mid-class steel products.
c) Moderately: auto components, telecom equipment, mainframe & mini-computers, PCs, and low-end steel products.

B. Those Positively affected included:

a) Remarkably: textiles & garments, electrical appliances, toll roads, and international shipping.
b) Pronouncedly: buses & trucks, power generation, food products, and railways.
c) Moderately: crude oils, low-end machinery products, power equipment, and irons & steels.

Appendix A The Impact of WTO on China's Industrial Enterprises (1a)-[Pre-WTO & Post-WTO Trade Regime]

Industry	Current International Competitiveness				Current Tariff & Non-tariff Barriers		Post-WTO Tariffs and Market Liberalization					
	In price	In quality	Net exports over output (%)	FFEs* market share	Non-tariff controls**	Average tariff (%)	Average tariff (%) 2001	2005	Eliminating non-tariff controls	Newly allowed JV ownership 2001	2006	Full opening of trade & distribution
Auto												
Cars	weak	weak	-3.4	over 90%	tight	90	72	25 (2006)	2005	n.a.	n.a.	2003
Buses & Trucks	strong	reasonable	-0.8	small	tight***	50	42	25 (2006)	2004	n.a.	n.a.	2003
Components	strong	weak	-0.4	40%	loose	23	16	10 (2006)	2003	n.a.	n.a.	2003
Telecom												
Basic services	weak	weak	n.a.	none	n.a	n.a	n.a	n.a	n.a	0%	49%	n.a
Non-basic services	weak	weak	n.a.	none	n.a	n.a	n.a	n.a	n.a	30%	50%	n.a.
Equipment-manufacturing	strong	reasonable	9.5	45%	loose	13	9	0	2001	n.a.		2003
Petrochemicals												
Crude oils	strong	reasonable	-30.0	small	loose	2	1	0	2004	n.a		2005
Refineries	reasonable	weak	-20.0	small	tight	7	6	6	2004	n.a		2005
Synthetic petrochemicals	reasonable	weak	-80.0	fair	loose	14	12	5	2004	n.a		2003
Chemicals												
Daily used products	strong	reasonable	20.0	50%	negligible	30	20	6	2001	n.a.		2003
Farm used products	reasonable	weak	-25.0	small	tight	5	3	2	2002	n.a		2005
Pharmaceuticals	strong	weak	-35.0	1/3	loose	13	10	5	2002	n.a		2003
Electrical appliances												
Color TVs	strong	strong	11.0	below 15%	tight***	37	34	30	2002	n.a.		2003
Refrigerators	strong	strong	3.0	below 5%	tight***	30	26	20	2001	n.a.		2003
Washing machines	strong	reasonable	6.0	below 10%	tight***	30	26	20	2001	n.a.		2003
Air-conditioners	strong	strong	4.5	below 15%	tight***	25	21	15	2002	n.a.		2003
Machinery												
Complete sets of equipments	reasonable	weak	-40.0	small	tight	15	13	10	2002	n.a.		2003
Precision machinery	weak	weak	-70.0	small	tight	16	12	4	2004	n.a.		2003
Low-end products	strong	reasonable	10.0	small	loose	12	10	9	2001	n.a.		2003

The Impact of WTO on China's Industrial Enterprises (1b)–[Pre-WTO & Post-WTO Trade Regime]

Industry	Current International Competitiveness				Current Tariff & Non-tariff Barriers		Post-WTO Tariffs and Market Liberalization					
	In price	In quality	Net exports over output (%)	FFEs* market share	Non-tariff controls**	Average tariff (%)	Average tariff (%) 2001	2005	Eliminating non-tariff controls	Newly allowed JV ownership 2001	2006	Full opening of trade & distribution
Power												
Generation	reasonable	reasonable	negligible	small	n.a.	n.a.	n.a.	n.a.	n.a.	n.a.	n.a.	n.a.
Equipment-manufacturing	reasonable	weak	–25.0	small	loose	17	14	11	2002	n.a.	n.a.	2003
Textile & garments												
Textiles	strong	strong	18.0	small	loose	23	18	8	2001	n.a	n.a	2003
Garments	strong	strong	65.0	pronounced	loose	32	25	15	2002	n.a	n.a	2003
Computer-manufacturing												
Mainframes & mini-computers	strong	reasonable	–200.0	small	loose	9	6	0	2001	n.a.	n.a.	2003
PCs	strong	strong	25.0	25%	loose	15	10	0	2001	n.a.	n.a.	2003
Peripheral equipment	strong	strong	55.0	70%	loose	9	6	0	2001	n.a.	n.a.	2003
Food	strong	reasonable	7.0	pronounced	negligible	35	33	30	2001	n.a.	n.a.	2003
Steel												
Irons & steels	strong	reasonable	–20.0	negligible	loose	3	2	2	2005	n.a	n.a	2003
Low-end steel products	strong	reasonable	–5.0	small	loose	10	8	5	2005	n.a.	n.a.	2003
Mid-class steel products	reasonable	weak	–25.0	small	tight	8	6	5	2005	n.a.	n.a.	2003
High-end steel materials	reasoanble	weak	–110.0	fair	tight	12	10	6	2005	n.a.	n.a.	2003
Transportation												
Toll roads	strong	reasonable	n.a.	small	n.a.	n.a.	n.a.	n.a.	n.a.	49%	100%	n.a.
International shipping	strong	weak	n.a.	fair	n.a.	n.a.	n.a.	n.a.	n.a.	49%	49%	n.a.
Railways	strong	reasonable	n.a.	negligible	n.a.	n.a.	n.a.	n.a.	n.a.	49%	100%	n.a.

Note: All the percentage numbers are estimates
*: Foreign-funded enterprises, including both the joint ventures (JVs) and the wholly foreign funded enterprises
**: Including licenses, quotas, tendering requirements and registration requirements, over selected import products
***: Nominally tight

Appendix B The Impact of WTO on China's Industrial Enterprises (2a) - [Negative and Positive Impacts]

Industry	WTO Impact on Existing Enterprises								Overall Impact	
	Negative Impact				Positive Impact					
	From tariff reductions on products	From eliminating non-tariff controls	From opening trade & distribution system	From relaxing conditions on FDI	From reduction in tariff & non-tariff barriers overseas	From tariff reductions on input materials	From improvement in economy & institution	From better access to foreign investment	Negative	Positive
Auto										
Cars	S	S	P	M	N	P	P	P	S	
Buses & Trucks	P	M	P	M	P	P	P	P		P
Components	P	M	S	P	M	M	P	R	M	
Telecom										
Basic services	n.a.	n.a.	n.a.	S.	n.a.	n.a.	P	P	S	
Non-basic services	n.a	n.a.	n.a.	S	n.a.	n.a.	P	P	S	
Equipment manufacturing	P	M	S	M	M	P	P	P	M	
Petrochemicals										
Crude oils	M	M	M	P	N	N	P	P		M
Refineries	M	S	S	P	M	M	P	R	S	
Synthetic petrochemicals	P	P	S	P	M	M	M	P	S	
Chemicals										
Daily-use products	S	M	S	M	P	P	P	M	P	
Farm-use products	M	P	P	P	P	M	P	M	P	
Pharmaceuticals	P	M	S	S	P	M	P	P	S	
Electrical appliances										
TVs	M	M	P	P	P	P	R	P		R
Refrigerators	M	M	M	M	R	P	P	M		R
Washing machines	M	M	P	P	R	P	P	M		R
Air-conditioners	P	M	P	M	R	P	R	P		R
Machinery										
Complete sets of equipment	M	P	P	P	M	M	M	P	P	
Precision machinery	P	P	P	P	M	M	M	P	P	
Low-end products	M	M	P	M	P	M	P	M		M

The Impact of WTO on China's Industrial Enterprises (2b) - [Negative and Positive Impacts]

Industry	WTO Impact on Existing Enterprises								Overall Impact	
	Negative Impact				Positive Impact					
	From tariff reductions on products	From eliminating non-tariff controls	From opening trade & distribution system	From relaxing conditions on FDI	From reduction in tariff & non-tariff barriers overseas	From tariff reductions on input materials	From improvement in economy & institution	From better access to foreign investment	Negative	Positive
Power										
Generation	n.a.	n.a.	n.a.	P	n.a.	n.a.	P	P		P
Equipment manufacturing	M	M	M	P	M	M	P	P		M
Textiles & Garments										
Textiles	P	M	P	M	R	M	R	P		R
Garments	P	P	P	P	R	P	R	R		R
Computer-manufacturing										
Mainframes & mini-computers	P	P	M	P	N	M	P	P	M	
PCs	P	M	S	P	P	P	P	P	M	
Peripheral equipment	P	M	S	M	M	P	M	P	P	
Food	M	M	P	P	R	M	R	P		P
Steel										
Irons & steels	N	M	M	M	P	N	P	M	M	
Low-end steel products	M	M	P	P	P	M	P	M		M
Mid-class steel products	M	P	P	P	M	M	P	P		
High-end materials	P	S	S	P	N	M	P	R	S	
Transportation										
Toll roads	n.a.	n.a.	n.a.	P	P	n.a.	R	M		R
International shipping	n.a.	n.a.	n.a.	P	R	n.a.	R	R		R
Railways	n.a.	n.a.	n.a.	M	P	n.a.	P	M		P

Note: Se: serious, P: pronounced, R: remarkable, M: moderate, N: negligible

Appendix A summarizes the findings of the TDC study. 1a and 1b in the appendix sets out the pre-WTO level of competitiveness and protection of various industries in China, as well as the post-WTO scenario and China's commitment to open up the sector concerned. Against this background, 2a and 2b in the appendix list all the positive and negative factors for any specific industrial sectors, and the overall impact of WTO accession on the sector is listed. The appendix therefore provides a quick glimpse on the differential impacts of WTO on China's industrial sectors.

chapter 10

Light Industries

A. CHINA'S COMMITMENTS ON MAIN LIGHT INDUSTRIAL PRODUCTS

(*This section on China's commitments is drawn from data provided in the US White House Factsheets on China WTO Accession, last updated on 17 February 2000, available on the web site of US–China Business Council, available at http://www.uschina.org/public/wto/factsheets. Certain adjustments were made according to China accession documents, marked in square bracket.*)

1. Tariff

a. Textiles and Apparel

China will reduce its tariffs on textiles and apparel products from its current average tariff of 25.4% to [12%]. Reductions will commence upon accession and will be completed by January 1, 2005.

Tariff rates agreed to in the 1997 *U.S-China Bilateral Textile Agreement* will be implemented and bound in the WTO by 2001. Further tariff reductions will be implemented by 2005.

b. Toys

China will eliminate its tariffs — as high as 35% before WTO accession — on products in the Uruguay Round sectoral initiative of toys. This sector includes video games, billiard tables, and bowling equipment as wells as traditional toys. Reductions will commence upon accession and will be fully implemented by January 1, 2005.

c. Paper

China will reduce its tariffs on paper and paper products from its average pre-WTO tariff of 14.2% to 5.5%. Reductions will commence upon accession and will be fully implemented by January 1, 2005 [newsprint by 2006]. Tariffs on U.S. priority paper products will reach 2% or 5% by year 2004.

d. Medical Equipment

China will reduce its tariffs on medical equipment from its average pre-WTO tariff of 9.9% to about [4%]. Reductions will begin on accession and will be completed by January 1, 2003.

e. Distilled Spirits, Beer and Wine

Tariffs on beer, at 70% before WTO accession, will be eliminated by [2004].

Tariffs on U.S. priority exports of distilled spirits (whiskies, rum, vodka, and liqueurs), at 65% before WTO accession, will be reduced to 10% by 2005.

Tariffs on most wine, at 65% before WTO accession, will be reduced to [14-20%] by 2004.

f. Furniture

China will reduce its average pre-WTO tariff rate of 22% to 0% on all furniture items covered by the Uruguay Round sectoral initiative. Reductions will commence upon accession and will be fully implemented by January 1, 2005.

g. Cosmetics

China will reduce its tariffs from levels as high as 45% before WTO accession to 10% or 15% by 2004 or 2005. Tariffs on US priority exports will reach 6.5% by 2008.

h. Scientific Equipment

China will reduce its tariffs on scientific equipment from its average pre-WTO tariff of 12.3% to 6.5%. Reductions will commence upon accession and will be completed by January 1, 2003.

2. Trading Rights and Distribution

Before WTO accession, in China, the right to engage in trade (importing and exporting) was strictly limited; only companies that received specific authorization or who imported goods to be used in production had such rights. This limited the ability of foreign companies to do business in China. China agreed that companies in China and foreign companies would be able to import most products, including textile and apparel products, into any part of China three years after accession. This commitment is phased in over the three-year period.

China also generally prohibited companies from distributing imported products or providing related distribution services such as repair and maintenance services. China will permit foreign enterprises to engage in the full range of distribution services over a three-year phase-in period for almost all products, including textile and apparel products.

3. Quotas

a. on Textile

Most Chinese quotas on priority U.S. exports will be eliminated upon accession, except that quotas on thirty yarn, synthetic filament tow, and fiber products will be eliminated after one year.

The United States will apply the WTO *Agreement on Textiles and Clothing* to China with a phase-out of US quotas under that Agreement.

b. on other goods

Quota on most of other light industrial products will be eliminated upon accession.

4. Safeguards

a. on Textile

China has committed to two strong provisions to address concerns regarding import surges of textile and apparel products:

A textile safeguard provides a mechanism to address market disruption in this sector based on provisions in 1997 *U.S.-China Bilateral Textiles Agreement*. The mechanism allows the imposition of quotas [by US] if market disruption occurs. This provision covers all products under the WTO *Agreement on Textiles and Clothing* as of 1 January 1995. The mechanism remains in effect until 31 December 2008.

China has also agreed to a product-specific safeguard that addresses rapidly increasing imports from China that cause or threaten to cause market disruption on a product-specific basis. This provision remains in effect for 12 years after accession.

There is no Safeguards provision on other light industrial products.

5. Anti-dumping

The U.S. and China agreed that the former would be able to maintain its current anti-dumping methodology, which treats China as a non-market economy. This provision will remain in effect for 15 years.

6. Subsidies

China has agreed to certain subsidy rules, including rules applicable to state-owned enterprises. Specifically, where government benefits are provided to an industry sector and state-owned enterprises are the predominant recipients or receive a disproportionate share of those benefits, the United States could take action under its unfair trade laws.

In addition, the [bilateral] agreement establishes that the United States can determine whether government benefits, such as equity infus ions or soft loans, have been provided to an industry using market-based criteria rather than Chinese government benchmarks.

7. Tendering

For a number of light industrial products, like medical and scientific equipment, China also committed that tendering requirements for non-government purchases will be eliminated within four years of accession.

8. Other Commitments

To alleviate the uncertainty associated with China's inconsistent application, refund, and waivers of its 17% VAT tax, China has agreed to apply all taxes and tariffs uniformly to both domestic and foreign businesses.

For paper products, China has agreed to provide treatment to the United States on par with China's preferential programs. For example, if China grants a lower tariff rate to Malaysia than is applied in China's tariff schedule due to a WTO-consistent preferential program, that rate must also be provided to the United States for paper products.

For such products as paper, medical and scientific equipment products, cosmetics, distilled spirits, beer and wine, China has agreed not to apply or enforce export performance, local content, and similar requirements as a condition on importation or investment approval.

B. IMPACT ON CHINA: TEXTILES

China is the world's largest textile producer and exporter and therefore this sector stands to gain most from a more liberalized trading system upon accession to the WTO.

Since 1974 international trade in textiles had been put under the framework of *Multifibre Arrangement* (MFA) which deviated from the free trade principle enshrined by the GATT. Under MFA developed countries had always imposed quantitative restrictions of a discriminatory nature on developing countries that export textile goods.

This situation was not corrected until 1995 when the *Agreement on Textile and Clothing* (ATC) was signed at the end of a long negotiation known as the Uruguay Round of talks that started in 1986. Since then international trade in textile was brought within the WTO framework. This will greatly benefit textile exporters.

According to the CASS Report by Yu and Zheng 2000[1], upon WTO membership, export restrictions imposed on China will be removed. This will greatly enhance Chinese export of

---

[1] See beginning of Chapter 6 for CASS Report by Yu and Zheng 2000

Table 10.1   Impact of WTO membership on China's textile industry

Year	Impact on Textile Export of WTO Membership							
	Non-member			Member			Difference	
	Quantity million ton	Value US$ billion	% growth in value	Quantity million ton	Value US$ billion	% growth in value	Quantity %	Value %
2000 actual	3.32	52	–	–	–	–	–	–
2005 forecast	3.71	63	21.2	4.4	80	53.8	18.6	27.0
2010 forecast	4.11	82	30.2	5.1	108	71.4	24.1	31.7

Source: Table 3–12, the CASS Report by Yu and Zheng 2000

textile goods. It estimated that by 2010, total output of textile goods will reach 12.5 to 13.5 million tons with roughly half of it exported. Total export earnings from textile goods will reach US$ 90 to 100 billion.

The CASS Report finds that WTO membership will make a significant difference on China's textile exports, as shown in Table 10.1. Without membership, textile export will grow modestly at an average annual rate of 8 percent during 2001-2010 to reach US$ 82 billion from its 2000 actual earnings. With WTO membership, however, it will accelerate to 11 percent to break the US$ 100 billion mark. In other words the difference in export earnings would be as high as US$ 32 billion.

C. IMPACT ON CHINA: OTHER LIGHT INDUSTRIES

(*This section is retrieved from "Why China's Light Industry Does Not Fear WTO Membership", dated 5 January 2000, "WTO" archives of Chinaonline web site.*)

Light industry is perhaps the only sector in China that does not fear WTO membership, thanks to the low cost of production in China.

The 29 December [2000] Zhongguo Jingji Shibao (China Economic Times) offered an in-depth analysis of the expected impact of WTO membership on China's light industry, and concluded that the industry as a whole is well-equipped to compete and has little to fear. The impact will vary for specific industries depending on the degree to which they are already open, the extent to which current production is efficient, low cost, and relatively high-tech, and whether or not they are already major exporters.

The paper said that according to an investigation by the State Light Industry Bureau, there are three reasons why light industry will not suffer unduly from the opening of the market:

1. The proportion of state-owned enterprises in China's light industry sector has dropped to 63% while the proportion of private enterprises has risen to 37%. This indicates the industry's ability to adapt to the market-oriented ownership systems and mechanisms appropriate for WTO membership.

2. China's light industry has long since begun to open up to the outside world. In 1998, light industry exports totaled US$54.96 billion, which accounted for 36% of total light industry output.

In the 20 years since the opening up policy was introduced, light industry has absorbed US$40 billion in foreign investment, and the number of foreign-funded enterprises has reached 20,000.

Meanwhile, many light industry enterprises, such as Qingdao Hai'er, Jinan Qingqi and Wuxi Little Swan, have been investing abroad to establish competitive multinational enterprises.

3. China's light industry boasts considerable industrial scale and competitive capacity. Some Chinese enterprises are now leading world producers of bicycles, household ceramics, leather shoes, refrigerators, washing machines, electric fans, electric irons, electric cooking utensils and plastic film.

China is the world's second largest producer of synthetic detergents, beer and salt, and the third largest producer of machine-finished paper, table sugar, home air-conditioners and watches.

Advantages And Disadvantages Of WTO Entry

While the impact of WTO entry on China's light industry will not be negligible, the advantages are expected to outweigh the disadvantages.

On the plus side, WTO entry will expand exports and transnational business, thus boosting China's economic growth.

Secondly, increased foreign investment resulting from WTO entry will help adjust China's industrial structure.

Thirdly, WTO entry will accelerate technological upgrading in light industry enterprises.

Fourthly, WTO entry will lower the costs of imported raw materials and thus make finished products more competitive in terms of price.

On the minus side, China's technology-intensive industries may suffer from foreign competition.

Secondly, many light industry products that are made from agricultural raw materials, that meet domestic needs, and that have long been protected by tariffs will suffer from China's WTO entry.

Thirdly, some state-owned enterprises will suffer.

The report [by State Light Industry Bureau] groups light industries into four categories in accordance with their ability to withstand competition.

Group A: Industries Long Since Open To Foreign Competition Could Benefit

After WTO entry, industries that are already open and have absorbed much foreign investment such as home electrical appliances, home chemical products and beer will benefit from China's WTO membership and will not require government protection.

1. Home Electrical Appliances

In 1998, home electrical appliance exports totaled US$3.51 billion, an increase of 9.3% year-on-year. The products were exported to 183 countries and regions. World-famous multinational companies and groups producing home electrical appliances have established joint ventures in China that openly compete with domestic enterprises. The output of 60 such joint ventures accounted for 10% of total output in 1998.

Famous domestic enterprise groups have seen a rapid growth in competition. Production and market shares are becoming more concentrated. Domestic brands of home electrical appliances now enjoy 80% of the domestic market. Domestic products generally enjoy a price advantage.

After WTO entry, the influx of products with high-tech components such as vortex compressors and top-loading washing machines will hurt this industry somewhat since the home electrical appliance industry in China is weak in the manufacture of high-tech products at present.

2. Home Chemical Products

The home chemical products industry was one of the first to open to the outside world. Since reform and opening-up policies were introduced, the industry has absorbed about US$1 billion in foreign investment.

Famous multinational companies such as Unilever of Holland, P&G from the United States, Hankel from Germany and the Kao Corporation of Japan have all established joint ventures in China. Before WTO accession, the total output of all the joint ventures accounted for 20% of total output in this industry. Thus, generally speaking, the industry will not be much affected by WTO entry.

3. Cosmetics

There are altogether 570 joint ventures producing cosmetics in China, many established by world-famous companies. Their annual sales volume accounts for over 40% of the total national sales volume in this industry. The production and sale of cosmetics has been globalized.

Although tariffs on cosmetics will drop dramatically after China's WTO entry, the prices of these imports will remain high. For a long time to come, only the wealthy will be able to buy these imported products, so domestic enterprises will not be seriously hurt.

4. Detergent

Many joint ventures in this industry have been established by world-famous multinational corporations. The domestic market has been gradually globalized. The toilet soap produced by joint ventures accounts for 50% of total output. In 1998, the output of washing machine detergent approached 2 million tons, and of that, the amount produced by wholly foreign-owned companies and joint ventures accounted for 30%. China has long exported about 40,000 tons of such detergent.

Most of the oils used in making toilet soap, such as palm-kernel oil and beef/mutton fat, were imported under high tariffs. Thus, lowering the tariffs will benefit the detergent industry.

5. Batteries

China is a major producer as well as exporter of batteries. Of the 14 billion batteries produced in 1998, 9 billion were exported, earning US$359 million in foreign exchange. WTO entry will not benefit foreign battery producers even the tariff is lowered. On the contrary, WTO membership will eliminate the tariff barriers that China faces and make her eligible for the Generalized System of Preferences, which will expand China's exports of middle and low-grade batteries.

6. Beer

China's beer output in 1998 amounted to 19.88 million tons, ranking second to that of the United States. Eighty percent of domestic brewers, which produce more than 50,000 tons annually, have established joint ventures with world-famous brewers. Before WTO accession, the output of these joint ventures accounted for 31% of the total output. Thus the beer industry was already quite open.

That industry has long enjoyed a favorable balance of trade, with exports greatly surpassing imports. With the further lowering of tariffs on beer, imports will increase, but due to problems in preserving freshness and transporting over long distances, the increase will be small. WTO membership will cause a sharp drop in tariffs on agricultural products such as barley, which will greatly benefit China's beer production by reducing production costs and thus increasing competitiveness.

Group B: Export-Oriented Industries Will Not Be Adversely Affected

WTO entry will bring more benefit than harm to industries such as electric lighting, glassware for daily use and light industrial machinery that produce much output for export and for which the high prices of imports will minimize importation even after tariffs are reduced.

1. Electric Lighting

Electric light fixture exports in 1998 amounted to US$2 billion, accounting for one-third of the total sales volume of this industry. Meanwhile, imports totaled only US$200 million. WTO entry will increase imports of high quality lamps and lanterns, but their high prices will limit the increase, so in general the industry will not be adversely affected.

2. Glassware For Daily Use

The annual output of glassware for daily use was about 7.2 million tons before WTO accession. Even if tariffs decrease after WTO entry, imports will not increase; thus domestic producers of pots and bottles will not be much affected. But from a long-term perspective, WTO entry will be unfavorable to the upgrading of China's domestic glassware.

3. Pen-Making

China's pen and pencil-making industry leads the world in production and exports. The output of ballpoint pens and mechanical pencils ranks third. WTO entry, by decreasing the tariffs that China faces, will increase exports still further, especially for middle and low-grade pens. However, imports of high-grade pens will increase and will eventually dominate the market for such pens.

Group C: Industries Based On Agricultural Products Could Suffer

WTO entry will hurt some industries based on agricultural products, such as dairy products, wine, and glutamate. The industry producing white wine will be least affected. The impact on the beverage industry will be mixed.

1. Dairy products

The output of dairy products in 1998 amounted to 565,000 tons. The powdered milk industry will be the most affected by WTO entry. The import tariff rate on powdered milk [in 2000] was 25%, resulting in a price of RMB 21,000 (US$2,539) per ton. Without the tariff, the price is RMB 16,000 (US$1,935) per ton. Since the price of domestic milk powder was RMB 18,500 (US$2,237) per ton, the elimination of the tariff will harm the domestic industry.

The output of butter and cheese is small in China, so the reduction of tariffs on these imported products will not have much impact on domestic producers. On the contrary, increased imports will foster domestic demand, thus enabling the development of the domestic industry.

2. Hard Liquor, Millet Wine And Wine

Before accession, wine/liquor imports were curtailed by high tariffs to protect domestic producers. With WTO entry, tariffs will drop sharply, thus hurting newly established enterprises with small production capacities.

3. Glutamate

China is a major producer and consumer of glutamate. Before accession, the output of glutamate was 1.2 million tons. In 1998 China produced 650,000 tons of commercial glutamate, but exported less than 10,000 tons. Since domestic enterprises have higher production costs than foreign enterprises, WTO entry will bring great harm to the domestic enterprises.

4. Soda And Orange Juice

WTO entry, by reducing tariffs, will increase imports of concentrated orange juice. Meanwhile, domestic production of carbonated beverages will be harmed. In 1997, Pepsi and Coca-Cola produced 2.425 million tons of soda in China, accounting for 23% of China's total beverage output and 49% of soda output. WTO entry is likely to lift restrictions on the total output and investment of Pepsi and Coca-Cola, which will harm domestic enterprises.

Group D: Uncompetitive Industries Will Suffer

WTO entry will hurt industries that have high production costs, lack competitive capacity, produce new products, and that generally lag behind technologically-advanced foreign enterprises that enjoy economies of scale. Such industries include the pulping and papermaking, sugaring, and MDI-producing enterprises.

1. Pulping And Papermaking

Papermaking is a pillar industry of China's national economy. Of its output, 90% becomes the means of production for other industries. Only 10% is for daily consumption. The annual output of machine-made paper and paperboard in 1998 amounted to 28 million tons, ranking third in the world but still having a long way to go compared with the standards of developed countries.

For instance, China has only about 600 varieties of paper, and 50% of output is comprised of middle- and low-grade products. By comparison, advanced nations boast over 1,000 varieties of high- or middle-grade paper. In China, 200 tons of water are used to produce each ton of newsprint, while advanced nations use only 20 tons of water.

The prospects for China's papermaking industry after WTO entry are not good since it is hard to compete with foreign counterparts. Of the 60% of papermaking enterprises that could be affected by WTO entry, many will go bankrupt and 700,000 people could lose their jobs.

So far as supply is concerned, China's WTO entry will greatly harm the papermaking industry since it relies heavily on imports. In the past, China was largely self-sufficient in paper, and imports merely played a complementary role. By 1998, however, imports had increased to 5.77 million tons, accounting for 20% of total demand.

Of those 1998 imports, 236,400 tons were newsprint; 346,400 tons were paper for printing and writing; 984,800 tons were art paper; 1.2636 million tons were kraft paper and paperboard; 341,400 tons were white paperboard; 542,400 tons were coated paperboard and white cardboard; and 990,800 tons were corrugated paper. Between 2000 and 2005, perhaps 25% of China's paper needs will be met by imports.

Tariffs on the above seven types of paper range from 12% to 15%. Increasing imports have already been hurting the domestic papermaking industry. With WTO entry and consequent reductions of tariffs, imports will grow still more and further damage domestic industries.

Of these seven types of paper, high value-added products (such as art paper and coated white cardboard) will be affected the most. Low value-added products (such as Kraft paperboard and corrugated paper) will also be affected, but less so.

The impact of WTO entry will vary by types of paper:

Newsprint: This is a special product in that China has successfully implemented anti-dumping measures for it. Thus, China's WTO membership will not affect it much.

Art paper: Imports now dominate the domestic market and market demand keeps increasing. The annual domestic output once reached as high as 500,000 to 600,000 tons. In recent years, for various reasons, many manufacturers have halted production, depressing annual output to 150,000 tons. There are now several joint ventures producing art paper. Thus, the tariff decrease will have little effect on domestic enterprises.

High-grade packing paperboard: Most of the raw materials for middle- and high-grade kraft paperboard, white paperboard and cloth-coated white paperboard, such as waste paper and commercial wood pulp, are imported, and there is not much difference between Chinese and foreign products. Since the import tariffs for these products are already zero, across-the-board tariff decreases will not affect the industry.

2. Sugar Industry

China's 1998-99 sugar output reached 8.862 million tons, slightly exceeding market demand. The total estimated loss of the industry is RMB 3 billion (US$362.8 million). After WTO entry and consequent adjustments in quotas and tariffs, the imported sugar allowance in the first year will be 850,000 tons [1.68 million tons] and the tariff [in–quota rate would be 20% on accession whereupon the 15% tariff will take effect in 2004.][2]

For example, the average price of raw sugar [in 2000] in the international market was 6.8 cents/pound. The comprehensive price of raw sugar (CIF plus tariff, i.e., cost, insurance, freight and tariff) was about RMB 2,047 (US$247.5)/ton. The price of imported, refined white granulated sugar was about RMB 2,547 (US$308)/ton, which was RMB 303 (US$36.6) lower (tax included) than China's production cost of RMB 2,850 (US$344.6)/ton.

Once the cheaper sugar enters the domestic market, the domestic sugar price will fall to the same level. Thus RMB 300 (US$36.3) will be lost per ton. To avoid loss, sugar manufacturers will probably decrease the purchase price of raw sugar. Thus, those most hurt by WTO entry will be sugar farmers.

All nations protect their sugar industries. Such government intervention results in domestic sugar prices higher than the international market price and a relatively stable sugar market. The import quota management system will continue to protect China's sugar industry.

3. MDI

MDI is the raw material for polyurethane in the plastics industry. MDI production being small scale and expensive, China's product cannot compete with cheaper foreign products. The tariff rate on MDI [in 2000] was 28.7% (including a customs tariff of 10%, a value-added tax of 17% and other miscellaneous tax). Once the tariff is cut to 5%, MDI manufacturers will suffer greatly.

After China's WTO entry, manufacturers of labor-intensive, light industry products such as bicycles, sewing machines, toys, clocks and watches, furniture, hardware, enamelware, ceramics, canned foods, leather shoes, fur products, drawn work, tungsten and molybdenum products may explore international markets and increase exports.

---

[2]Figures in square bracket are obtained from China accession documents.

chapter 11

Heavy Industries

A. CHINA'S COMMITMENT: AUTOMOBILE

(The section on China's commitments is drawn from data provided in the US White House Factsheets on China WTO Accession, last updated on 17 February 2000, available on the web site of US-China Business Council, available at : http://www.uschina.org/public/wto/factsheets. Certain adjustments were made according to China accession documents, marked in square bracket.)

1. Tariff on Autos

Tariffs on autos (100% and 80% [before WTO accession]) will decrease as follows:

Rate	2000	2001	2002	2003	2004	2005	1/2006	7/2006
100%	77.5%	61.7%	50.7%	43.0%	37.6%	30.0%	28.0%	25.0%
80%	63.5%	51.9%	43.8%	38.2%	34.2%	30.0%	28.0%	25.0%

This reflects an acceleration of tariff cuts in the first years after accession as compared with China's previous offer set out below.

Rate	2000	2001	2002	2003	2004	2005
100%	87.5%	75.0%	62.5%	50.0%	37.5%	25%
80%	70.83%	61.66%	52.5%	43.33%	34.16%	25%

2. Tariff on Auto Parts

Tariffs will be phased down from an average of 23.4% to an average of 10%. For any auto parts tariff with a differential between the base rate and the final rate of less than 20 percentage points, the original schedule prevails resulting in fully phased-in tariffs cuts in 2000, 2001, 2002, 2003, and 2004 depending on the product. For products with differentials of 20–30 percentage points, the final duties will be phased in by January 1, 2006, with a 30% initial cut and remaining reductions made in equal annual installments thereafter. For products with differentials above 30 percentage points, final rates will be phased in July 1, 2006, with a 25% initial cut and remaining reductions made in equal annual installments thereafter.

3. Quotas

Quotas on autos will be phased out by 2005 with an initial level of $6.0 billion, which exceeds the actual level of trade prior to implementation of the 1994 Auto Industrial Policy. Quotas will grow 15% annually until eliminated.

4. Distribution and Trading Rights

In China, received the right to engage in trade (importing and exporting) was strictly limited; only companies that received specific authorization or who imported goods to be used in production have such rights. This limited the ability of U.S. and foreign companies to do business in China, and had limited US and foreign exports. China agreed that companies in China and foreign companies would be able to distribute most products, including autos and auto parts, into any part of China three years after accession. This commitment is phased in over the three-year period.

China also generally prohibited companies from distributing imported products or providing related distribution services such as repair and maintenance services. China will permit foreign enterprises to engage in the full range of distribution services over a three-year phase-in period for almost all products, including autos and auto parts.

5. Auto-Financing

[Before WTO accession,] only certain Chinese banks were authorized to conduct auto financing and only for certain vehicle models. Upon accession non-bank financial institutions will be permitted to provide auto financing without any market access or national treatment limitations.

6. Safeguards

China has committed to strong provisions to address import surges. This safeguard takes the form of a special mechanism that addresses rapidly increasing imports from China that cause or threaten to cause market disruption on a product-specific basis for 12 years after accession.

7. Anti-Dumping

China has agreed to include a provision in its protocol that explicitly permits continued use of non-market economy methodology. The provision in China's protocol will remain in effect for 15 years from China's accession.

8. Subsidies

China has agreed to certain subsidy rules, including rules applicable to state-owned enterprises. Specifically, where government benefits are provided to an industry sector and state-owned enterprises are the predominant recipients or receive a disproportionate share of those benefits, the United States could take action under its unfair trade laws.

9. Local Content

China has agreed to eliminate local content requirements immediately after it accedes to the World Trade Organization and not to enforce provisions in existing contracts that impose this requirement.

These commitments combined with the other market-opening steps that China will take, such as cutting tariffs, eliminating quotas and permitting US companies to distribute products in China, will result in better access for foreign exports and eliminate false incentives or requirements to use domestic goods.

10. Technology Transfer

China has agreed that it will not condition import or investment approvals on technology transfer or on conducting research and development in China.

China will also have to provide better intellectual property protection for technology that is transferred and eliminate requirements mandating that the Chinese partner in a joint venture gains ownership of trade secrets after a certain number of years.

11. Offsets

China has agreed that importation and investment will not be conditioned on providing offsets.

12. Other Commitments

To alleviate the uncertainty associated with China's inconsistent application, refund, and waivers of its 17% VAT tax, China has agreed to apply all taxes and tariffs uniformly to both domestic and foreign businesses.

China has agreed not to apply or enforce export-performance requirements and similar requirements as a condition on importation or investment approval.

B. CHINA'S COMMITMENT: OTHER HEAVY INDUSTRIAL PRODUCTS

1. Tariffs

a. Iron & Steel

China will reduce its tariffs on steel and steel products from its average pre-WTO tariff of 10.3% to 6.1%. Reductions will commence upon accession and will be completed by [2004].

b. Chemicals

China will reduce average chemical tariffs by more than 50% by January 1, 2005. Specifically, the average rate of 14.74% will be reduced to a final average rate of [7%].

These reductions include reductions on all priority U.S. chemical exports and involve full implementation of more than two-thirds of the 1,100-plus products in the *Chemical Tariff Harmonization Agreement* (CTHMA) of the Uruguay Round. China will also significantly reduce tariffs on the remaining items.

c. Machinery

For most machinery items, like construction equipment, China will reduce its average pre-WTO tariff rate of 13.6% by over 50 percent to [5-10%]. Reductions will commence upon accession and will be fully implemented by January 1, 2004.

d. Civil Aircraft

Tariffs will be bound and reduced from the average pre-WTO rate of 14.7% to a final average rate of 8% [4%] starting upon China's accession and with most reductions completed by January 1, 2002 [2003]. China actually applies lower or no tariffs for most products in this sector.

2. Trading Rights and Distribution

Before WTO accession, US and foreign companies' ability to do business in China was strictly limited because the right to engage in trade (importing and exporting) was restricted to a small number of companies that received specific authorization or who imported goods to be used in production. This limited US and foreign exports. China agreed that any entity would be able to import most products, including steel, into any part of China. This commitment is phased in over the three-year period with all entities being permitted to import and export at the end of the period.

China — which generally prohibited companies from distributing imported products or providing related distribution services — will permit foreign enterprises to engage in the full range of distribution services. These rights will be phased in over a three-year period for almost all products, including steel.

3. Safeguards

China has committed to a strong product-specific safeguard that allows the United States to address import surges. Specifically, the safeguard allows the United States to restrain increasing imports from China that cause or threaten to cause market disruption for 12 years after accession. After that, current U.S. safeguard provisions — Section 201 — remain available to address increasing imports.

4. Anti-dumping

The [US-China Bilateral] Agreement explicitly permits the United States to continue to use its current non-market economy methodology for 15 years after China's accession to the WTO.

5. Subsidies

China has agreed to certain subsidy rules, including rules applicable to state-owned enterprises. Specifically, where government benefits are provided to an industry sector and state-owned enterprises are the predominant recipients or receive a disproportionate share of those benefits, the United States could take action under its unfair trade laws.

In addition, the [bilateral] agreement establishes that the United States can determine whether government benefits, such as equity infusions or soft loans, have been provided to an industry using market-based criteria rather than Chinese government benchmarks.

6. Quotas

Quotas will be eliminated on virtually all chemicals upon accession. Similarly quotas will be eliminated upon accession for all items in the *Agreement on Trade in Civil Aircraft*.

7. Tendering Requirements

Tendering requirements for non-government purchases will be eliminated within two years of accession.

8. Local Content

On civil aircraft trade, China has agreed to eliminate local content requirements immediately after it accedes to the World Trade Organization and not to enforce provisions in existing contracts that impose this requirement.

These commitments combined with the other market-opening steps that China will take, such as cutting tariffs, eliminating quotas and permitting US companies to distribute products in China, will result in better access for US exports and eliminate false incentives or requirements to use domestic goods.

9. Technology Transfer

China has agreed that it will not condition import or investment approvals on technology transfer or on conducting research and development in China.

China will also have to provide better intellectual property protection for technology that is transferred and eliminate requirements mandating that the Chinese partner in a joint venture gains ownership of trade secrets after a certain number of years.

10. Offsets

On civil aircraft trade, China has agreed that importation and investment will not be conditioned on providing offsets.

11. Other Commitments

China has agreed not to apply or enforce export performance, local content, and similar requirements as a condition on importation or investment approval.

To alleviate the uncertainty associated with China's inconsistent application, refund, and waivers of its 17% VAT tax, China has agreed to apply all taxes and tariffs uniformly to both domestic and foreign businesses.

C. IMPACT ON CHINA'S AUTOMOBILE INDUSTRY

1. The Pressure

China's auto industry is another worse-hit sector with accession to the WTO. In terms of output loss, it is the largest sufferer of all sectors. In terms of job loss it is second only to agriculture. According to the CASS Report by Yu and Zheng 2000[1], the industry will lose RMB 80 billion in output and 0.5 million jobs by 2005. This is due mainly to the surge of import of foreign cars which is expected to increase by 105 percent to top RMB 40 billion by 2005.

2. Infancy of the Chinese Automobile Industry

(This section is extracted from "Impact of WTO Membership on China's Passenger Car Industry", dated 17 May 1999, the WTO News archives of Chinaonline web site, quoting an article of Jinrong Shibao (Financial Times) dated 4 May 1999. Sub-titles are inserted by editor.)

---

[1]See beginning of Chapter 6 for CASS Report by Yu and Zheng 2000.

Although the country's auto industry dated back to the 1950s, China's passenger car industry did not emerge until the 1980s, and therefore is a typical infant industry characterized by the following features:

a. Low Efficiency

In 1998, annual production of domestic cars reached 520,000 vehicles. With the exception of the Santana, most Chinese firms lack sufficient manufacturing volume. A 1998 ranking of the world's top ten auto manufacturers showed the annual output of top-ranked General Motors of the United States reached 7.5 million vehicles, and tenth-ranked Citroen of France had output of 2.27 million, representing 14 times and 4 times China's annual output respectively.

[Before WTO accession], there were about 120 auto manufacturers in China with a total annual output of 1.6 million automobiles, compared to 18 in the rest of the world, with an average annual output of over one million each. This gives an indication of the inefficiency of the Chinese industry.

b. Low Labor Productivity

China has eight major passenger car producers, with several dozen models on the market. Among them, only two are brands of purely domestic manufacturers. The rest offer imported models. In Chinese passenger car companies, the average annual output per worker is less than 10 vehicles, only half the level of foreign firms.

c. Low Product Quality and a Gap in Pricing

The vast majority of China's current models still only have comparable quality levels of foreign makes in the 1980s. And prices for domestically produced cars are far off the track of international standards.

According to projections, import duties on passenger cars will decline as China joins the WTO, falling from the current levels of 60–80% in 2000 to around 30% in 2005 and finally to 25% in 2006. This lack of protection will create serious problems for the industry.

3. Challenges

First, the large-scale entry into the China market of high quality, low priced foreign brands will force China's domestic auto industry to adjust the structures of the industry and of its products. A group of domestic auto enterprises that have low technology and a small scale of production will be eliminated by the increasingly fierce market competition.

Second, China's passenger car enterprises will be forced to further strengthen cooperation with internationally famous automobile manufacturers, learning and drawing from their experience to enhance the competitiveness of domestically produced autos.

Table 11.1 Expected Growth of the Chinese Automobile Industry: 2000–2005

	WTO and China's Auto-Industry			
	Market Demand for Cars (in 10,000)			
Car Types	1998	2000	2000	2005
	actual	actual	estimate	estimate
private cars	51	61.27	75–77	128–139
passenger cars	46	70.09	50–55	55–68
trucks	66	77.49	66–76	106–121
Total	163	208.86	188–208	289–328

Note: the '2000 actual' refers to the actual sales of that year. (The Actual Sales 2000 is taken from "*China Transportation Yearbook 2001*", compiled by Ministry of Transportation. It is included to facilitate comparison and provide a gauge of the accuracy of the estimate for 2005.

Source: Extracted from Table 7-17, the CASS Report by Yu and Zheng 2000 quoting "*The 10th Five Year Plan for China's Automobile Industry*" compiled by the Ministry of Machinery.

4. Opportunities

The expected fall in passenger car prices after accession to the WTO will help stimulate demand for cars, thereby encouraging the government to adopt policies that are conducive to car purchases and to car use.

According to the Ministry of Machinery, WTO membership will almost double for all types of cars, and for private cars, to more than double, in five years' time. The ministry estimated that small private cars will grow at an annual rate of 33 percent for the next five years so that by 2005 the share of private cars in total car demand will increase from 22 percent in 2000 to 60 percent in 2005, thus presenting a huge opportunity for car makers in China and from abroad.[2]

D. IMPACT ON CHINA'S MACHINERY INDUSTRY

Chinese machinery industry is quite advanced in terms of the utilization of foreign funds, technological innovation and import and export trade. It is currently the largest export industry and foreign currency earner.

However most of the top ten exported machines and electrical equipment are labor-intensive and raw material-intensive products with relatively low technology and added value. Hence the industry also face severe competition from abroad.

---

[2] Quoted from *CASS Report by Yu and Zheng, 2000*, Group Report VII "WTO and China's Automotive Industry", Section IV, "Prediction of China's Automobile Market in Five Years to Come".

Effect of WTO On China's Machinery Industry

(This section is extracted from "China Seeks Ways to Protect Infant Machinery Industry", dated 10 February 2000, the "Machinery Industry" archives of Chinaonline web site. According to Chinaonline, the extract is excerpted from the CASS Report by Yu and Zheng 2000.[3] Sub-titles are inserted by the editor.)

a. Eliminating Trade Barriers will have Limited Impact as a Whole

Import tariff reductions on China's machinery products had already begun [before WTO accession], and some tariffs were close to the standards stipulated by WTO. Further reductions will be limited. China's machinery product exports have developed rapidly. The rate of dependence on the global market is 27%. Sector competitiveness has improved continually.

Some products have enjoyed somewhat of a competitive advantage, such as metalworking equipment, complete sets of equipment, instruments and meters as well as electrical wire and cable. In general, further tariff reductions and elimination of non-tariff barriers will have limited impact on the machinery industry.

b. Many Uncompetitive Enterprises will Suffer

Industries that will be most adversely affected fall into three categories: (1) new industries involving high technology, high value-added products, and intensive processing; (2) industries that are redundant, low-level, that have not yet achieved economies of scale, and whose prices are higher than international levels; (3) industries whose enterprises are scattered and not standardized and have not achieved economies of scale.

c. Opportunities

China's machinery industry is facing favorable opportunities for getting ahead in the international market, for attracting international capital and for gaining a good place in the international division of production.

The implementation of the "Investment Measures Regarding Trade" put forward by the WTO will strengthen foreigners' confidence and accelerate their investments in China's technology-intensive and capital-intensive machinery industry. This will promote optimization of the product structure and improvement of enterprise organizational structure.

---

[3]According to Chinaonline.com, the excerpt was extracted from "China After WTO Entry", published in January 2000 by the Social Sciences Archive Publishing House, and edited by Yu Yongding, Zheng Bingwen. The volume was a joint effort of the Research Institute of Economics and Politics and the Graduate School of the Chinese Academy of Social Sciences ("CASS").

China's machinery products will benefit automatically from most-favored-nation treatment and other preferential treatment offered by import countries. This will improve the export environment for machinery products. China can also utilize the WTO's consultation and reconcilement measures to settle trade disputes so that the machinery industry will face less friction in international competition.

E. IMPACT ON CHINA'S METALLURGICAL INDUSTRY

1. Iron & Steel

(This section is extracted from "China's Mining Industry And the WTO", dated 3 August 1999, the "Metal Industry" archives of Chinaonline web site. Sub-titles are inserted by the editor.)

a. WTO Benefits Import of Iron Ore

China has insufficient iron rich ore resources and relies on foreign iron ore resources to develop its steel industry. Hence it encourages the import of iron ore by implementing zero customs duty on imports (actually, a 1% provisional tax rate has been in effect).

China imported 31.2 million tons of iron ore in 1998, accounting for approximately 20% of iron ore consumption. Low customs duties of 1% to 3% have been in effect for steel products, while higher duties of 6% to 40% have been applied to steel materials.

After China joins the WTO, import duties on most steel materials will drop sharply, although special individual steel materials may continue to be protected by high rates. For the majority of steel materials, if domestic production firms are unable to raise quality and reduce costs in the next two or three years, they will be threatened by high quality, low priced imports.

b. Inefficient Firms to Suffer

According to forecasts, close to 1,000 medium and small sized steel enterprises with small production and poor performance will be threatened. And certain downstream processing industries, such as stainless steel cold rolling and silicon-steel sheet, will experience even more difficulties if the state does not adopt protective measures. These industries started up relatively late, have developed slowly and have relatively out-of-date equipment.

2. Aluminum Oxide

a. Tariff Cut

Upon accession to the WTO, the tariff rate of aluminum oxide will drop to [8] percent from 18 percent before WTO accession. High quality but cheaper sand-mould aluminum oxide will create stiff competition in the domestic market.

b. Uncompetitive Nature of China's Producer

There are altogether 68 big aluminum oxide manufacturers out of 29 countries in the world, whose total output in 1998 was 48.62 million tons, Only one belongs to China, the Shanxi Aluminum Oxide Works. Elsewhere plants in China are small. The combined output in 1998 was only 3.33 million tons.

F. IMPACT ON CHINA'S PETROCHEMICAL INDUSTRY

(This section is retrieved from "The Impact of WTO Admission on China's Fertilizer Industry", dated 13 July 1999, the "Chemical Industry" archives of Chinaonline web site. Sub-titles are inserted by the editors.)

1. Chemical Fertilizers

China's chemical fertilizer industry can expect some good opportunities but it can also find more than a few problems, according to a long analytical article in the Zhongguo Huagong Bao (China Chemical News) of 29 June 1999.

China will face several types of problems. Some arise from the scale of production and its relevance to regional and social conditions. Others are systemic, relating to both management efficiency and policies and the present state of technology. Still others deal with an imbalance of resources and raw materials and thus relative production cost. Finally, there are those relating to tariff policies and government policies regarding imports, exchange rates, investment, production and distribution.

Inefficiency in Production Scale and Technology

It is important to bear in mind that the great majority of manufacturers of chemical fertilizers in China who account for over 50% of total production, are small producers. Over many decades of planned economy, these small and largely inefficient producers obtained support both from the central government and from local governments, which practice their own kinds of protectionism, often involving restrictions on the distribution system.

With an enormous population and heavy pressure to give everyone a job, these small-scale enterprises "maintain social stability". This comes at a significant price, though. The government has granted them a strong degree of support in tax policies and water and electricity charges.

Related to this are the problems of competitiveness of older state-owned enterprises. In effect many of both sorts (and they are not mutually exclusive) lose money. Fear of the "heavy social burden", that is, of large-scale closing downs and layoffs have kept these plants operating beyond the prime of their efficiency.

The systemic problems can relate to management efficiency and policies and the state of technology. Overall, China's chemical fertilizer industry has not realized the transition from a planned economy to a market economy. There is a very noticeable lack of practical and management experience in the international chemical fertilizer trade. At the same time there is not really a well-established production, distribution, and servicing network. There exists a conflict of interest between different departments, various regions and problems involved in the transportation infrastructure, such as in the railway system.

Overall technology and equipment in China's chemical fertilizer industry is relatively backward. The more advanced countries in the field have developed towards lower energy consumption and environmentally friendly technology and equipment. China's technological development has not been uniform.

Some large-scale nitrogen fertilizer installations that China imported and domestically produced in the 1970s have been brought up to 1980s standards. A few new factories have even reached the standards of the 1990s. Certain mid- to large-scale phosphorous compound fertilizer projects that were established since the 1980s have, through upgrades, reached 1990's standards.

If we compare the larger Chinese chemical fertilizer plants to more advanced, foreign ones, though, there are still gaps in equipment load, turnover rate, and consecutive operating cycle. In terms of both energy consumption and environmental protection, there is still a big gap between those Chinese enterprises that still use anthracite coal and [those that use] foreign advanced technologies.

Resource Bottleneck

Another problem in China is an imbalance between resources and raw materials energy sources. In the area of nitrogen fertilizers, while foreign producers often use natural gas, an inexpensive and clean fuel, most nitrogen fertilizer production in China uses anthracite coal—expensive, not environmentally friendly, and costly to transport. In China natural gas is neither plentiful nor cheap; only 20% of nitrogen fertilizer producers use it.

As to phosphorus fertilizers, major exporters like the USA and countries in North Africa have abundant phosphorus and sulfur and can buy inexpensive ammonium compounds in the world market. China has phosphorus but not in great quantity, so only a small portion can be used directly for fertilizer. The process used in China is expensive and there are few sources of sulfur and ammonium compounds in China. Thus China is forced to use low quality phosphorus concentrates, such as ordinary calcium and calcium-magnesium compounds. To supplement this low-quality phosphorus fertilizer, greater quantities must be imported.

The sulfuric acid used in phosphorus fertilizers represents a problem. More than 80% of the world's sulfuric acid production is from sulfur itself. Even with an oversupply of sulfur in the world's market and resulting current low prices, China still uses iron sulfide in more than 70% of its own sulfuric acid production. There is an urgent need to transfer to imported sulfur for this purpose.

Government Policies Causing Extra Difficulties

Another set of problems involve government policies at present, whether they relate to tariffs, exchange rates, imports, investments, or production and distribution. At present China's import policy is low tariff, no value added tax, but with import quotas. As China joins the WTO and competition from abroad stiffens, some problems may arise from these policies.

The development of China's tariff policy on fertilizer imports harkens back to the days when domestically produced chemical fertilizers were really quite inadequate to cope with the demand. The Chinese government instituted subsidies and tax benefits to offset the high cost of imported chemical fertilizer. When domestic nitrogen fertilizers were able to step in and fulfill the demand, the government withdrew the subsidy, but continued to have no value-added tax on chemical fertilizer imports. While the original objective of the tax-free policy was to alleviate the hardships on the farmers, it actually served as a boon to foreign companies and made China's domestic industry even less competitive.

Then there is the problem of RMB exchange rate. Since the Southeast Asian financial crisis first began in 1997, the Chinese government has been following a highly responsible policy of maintaining a stable RMB exchange rate. This cost China dearly, making many of their commodities, including chemical fertilizers, much less competitive with Southeast Asian production. China needs to set a rate of exchange that will reflect the actual competitive situation of China's chemical fertilizers.

China's import policies towards foreign fertilizers reflect global issues. China imported nitrogen fertilizer from Eastern Europe and the countries of the former Soviet Union, potassium fertilizer mostly from the same region and Canada, and phosphorus fertilizer mostly from the United States. After China stopped the import of urea indefinitely in 1997, both phosphorus and potassium fertilizer imports maintained very heavy volume.

Investment is another area that demands close scrutiny. Because of a shortage of domestic investment in construction for the chemical fertilizer industry, it has been forced to rely too much on foreign capital or imported technology. In some cases foreign capital was not used wisely and lead to duplication of large quantities of unnecessary technology and equipment. This forced up investment costs and lowered their efficiency.

In the case of phosphorus, these imports, especially from the USA, were high mainly because China's government wanted to decrease the embarrassingly large trade surplus with America.

This was a more important factor than China's small shortage of domestic supply. Perhaps with this surplus in mind the Chinese government purchased a huge quantity of di-ammonium phosphate (DAP) from the USA as well, with negative repercussions to China's own fledgling phosphorus compound fertilizer industry.

Production and distribution of chemical fertilizers have to be looked at globally nowadays. When China makes huge chemical fertilizer purchases in the world market, this represents a rather large proportion of the total international trade volume, thus influencing the whole world's prices. Yet the survival and development of China's own chemical fertilizer industry also depends on world prices.

When there is a shortage of fertilizer in China, the massive demand triggers a rise in the world's prices but when China's domestic situation improves, imported prices are lower, creating the appearance of low international prices. In effect, China's very size works against itself in the international market.

Expected Impacts of WTO

After China joins the WTO, China will eliminate its tax-free policy on foreign fertilizers, assuring a level playing field for the domestic producers. Within China, mid- and large size producers will compete with the smaller ones, bereft of their privileges. This may cause mergers and alternative production, along with some diversions to other industries at least.

Some chemical fertilizers produced by China would seem to be competitive on world markets. The USA's production cost for di-ammonium phosphate (DAP), for example, is about 200 to 300 RMB a ton (US$24-$36.25) less than that of China's domestic product. Ocean freight and handling charges may add US$20-$30 a ton, though, bringing Chinese prices in some markets lower than American ones.

Overall, the total cost of China's fertilizer is much higher than that of foreign products. This is because of rampant bad asset and financial charges within the industry. In the cases of the Guiqi Chemical Fertilizer Factory in Jiangxi and Yunfeng Chemical industries in Yunnan, for example, bad assets, depreciation, and finance charges represent 15% to 20% of total production costs. If the industry could break away from this it could become far more competitive.

Looking at DAP, for example, we find that the C & F price in 1998 was about RMB 1,950 (US$233) a ton. Without the 13% value added tax, the actual domestic market price was about RMB 2,100 (US$254) a ton. As for domestic DAP, the selling price is around RMB 2,000 (US$241) ex-factory, including the VAT. According to the present C & F price, if imported DAP needed to pay the VAT, it would sell for RMB 2,350 to 2,400 a ton (US$284-290). Under these conditions, Chinese DAP should be even more competitive.

When China goes into the WTO there will be an introduction of market competition that will be a force for reform and adjustment across the whole industry. The industry will finally have a chance to shake off the planned economy model which emphasizes total volume growth over everything else. Efficiency will increase. After all, reform and openness are fundamental policies for the country, whether it joins the WTO or not.

Coping with the WTO Pressure

Strategies have been suggested for the problems we have observed. For one thing, restructuring of the chemical fertilizer industry needs to take place. A few of the small-scale enterprises that are in good condition should undergo either consolidation or expansion. Mid-size enterprises should improve their technology. Larger enterprises should be constructed in appropriate locations. Production goals should be set higher for those enterprises that are in better shape.

The issue of excessive debt has to be addressed. The government needs to use a variety of means — such as injecting capital, transferring debt to equity, and obtaining investments from large conglomerates, mergers, and bankruptcies. Investment stimuli should be keyed to increases in productivity. The best and the strongest should be the firms that warrant government support.

Development of China's concentrated phosphorus compound fertilizer industry should be speeded up. Nitrogen and phosphorus fertilizer production should be better balanced and high concentration products favored over low-concentration ones. Better utilization methods should be studied for natural gas in the production of nitrogen fertilizer. Imports of sulfur might help develop the phosphorus compound fertilizer industry. Raw materials used in the fertilizer industry should be adjusted for greater efficiency.

A huge, densely populated agricultural country like China cannot develop its agriculture based on foreign imports. A certain measure of self-sufficiency in the production of chemical fertilizers is necessary, not only in quantity but also in variety. After China joins the WTO non-competitive enterprises may need to shut down, stop production, merge, or change products. A policy of seeking to maximize profit regardless of long-term goals would be risky and foolhardy.

Brand names need to be given more serious consideration. At present foreign chemical fertilizers often sell for about a hundred to two hundred RMB (US$12-24) more per ton than comparable domestic products. The foreign products may not really be of higher quality. It is just because the domestic product lacks name recognition among farmers.

Finally, greater attention needs to be paid to exports. In 1998, China exported over a million tons of chemical fertilizers. The export of heavy calcium fertilizer represented over half of domestic production and there was a net export of urea. More can be done.

2. Oil & Gas

(This section is retrieved from "Oil Slick: China's WTO entry may hurt petrochemical industry", dated 6 June 2000, the "Chemical industry" archieves of Chinaonline web site.)

While crude oil prices are expected to remain stable, China's petrochemical industry as a whole will likely experience a severe setback as a result of China's entry into the WTO.

Zhou Fengqi, vice-chairman of the China Energy Research Society, recently asserted that China's entry into the WTO will benefit its energy prospecting and development and impose little impact on the country's crude oil market. The production and sale of domestic refined oil, however, will face severe challenges from overseas competitors, according to the June 1 2000 edition of Zhongguo Shiyou Bao (China Petroleum News).

China's prospecting and development markets have long been open to Chinese-foreign cooperation. According to WTO rules, licensing mineral exploitation is not considered one of the non-tariff barriers. After China's entry into WTO, it will continue control the market as more overseas capital and advanced technologies are introduced, generally in China's interests.

According to Zhou, the domestic crude oil market already has initial links with the international market. Since the tariff on crude oil is already quite low (about 1 percent), its reduction to zero after WTO entry is predicted to have negligible impact on the Chinese market. Impact on China's crude oil market will mainly depend on crude oil prices in the international market. If the world oil price remains at US$22-28 per barrel, impact on China's crude oil production will be of trifling insignificance.

However, the petrochemical market as a whole will experience a level of competition unprecedented in its intensity. Zhou pointed out that the domestic petrochemical industry has not yet developed an economy of scale, so the technical and economic indicators of refineries and chemical plants are at a low level and product costs are far higher than overseas. The cost of China refined oil is usually 50 percent higher per ton than that of large overseas companies. As a result, the domestic price of refined oil is about two times the international price. With increased foreign competition, China's oil and petrochemical industries will face shrinking market shares at home. At present, foreign petroleum and petrochemical products already control nearly 50 percent of the Chinese market.

Following China's entry into the WTO, the market share of domestic petrochemical products will further decrease, leading to higher investment risks. If Chinese enterprises are unable to compete in the international market, excess domestic production capacity coupled with increased inflow of foreign products will lead to an oversupply that will ultimately mar the petroleum and petrochemical markets. Investment in petrochemicals will bring about few returns and the marketing system will be bogged down in an awkward situation.

Only 20 percent of China's approximately 90,000 gas stations is owned by the China National Petroleum Corp. (CNPC) and the China Petrochemical Corp. (SINOPEC). Both are state-owned. Due to lax management, many gas stations have become sales outlets for smuggled oil products. Oil multinationals are planning takeovers of these gas stations and their marketing networks at high prices so as to assert final control over China's terminal marketing network, a national network of gas retailers, such as gas stations.

China will be required to lift three major tariff barriers after it joins the WTO. First, China will have to eliminate major non-tariff barriers to trade, which include product import and quota licensing—such as the requirement for approval in the import of refined oil—and authorization of business operations—such as in the case of chemical fertilizer. In accordance with WTO regulations, China would gradually lift its import quotas over the five years following its joining the WTO. During the five-year transitional period, the quota shall increase 15 percent annually over the initial amount agreed to by the Chinese government.

Secondly, China will have to cut its tariffs. Currently, China implements a fixed tariff for crude oil of RMB 16 (US$1.93) per ton. The tariff rates for major petrochemical products are: 9 percent for gasoline, 9 percent for kerosene, 6 percent for diesel oil and naphtha, 12 percent for heavy oil, 18 percent for polyethylene, 16 percent for other synthesized resin, and 15 percent for urea. According to an agreement signed between China and the United States, if China joins the WTO, the tariff on crude oil shall be reduced to zero; gasoline, 5 percent; other refined oil, unchanged; and synthesized resin, 6.5 percent. Tariffs on petroleum and petrochemical products will decrease substantially.

Thirdly, China will have to open its markets. According to WTO rules, China should gradually open its trade and distribution services for refined oil, chemical fertilizer and other petrochemical products. China will be scheduled to open its chemical fertilizer and refined oil markets in three years and its wholesale chemical fertilizer and refined oil markets in five years. China has struggled to retain the exclusive right to import petrochemicals and will keep this right for a considerable period of time, but eventually this right will be revoked.

HEAVY INDUSTRIES

G. ESTIMATE OF LOSS IN PRODUCTION AND JOB

The CASS Report by Yu and Zheng 2000 shows that the heavy industrial sector as a whole is also a net loser upon China's WTO accession. By 2005, the whole sector will experience a net loss in terms of output and employment. While imports of foreign goods will increase, export will remain unchanged or slightly decrease. The details are presented in Table 11.2

Table 11.2   Impact of WTO Membership on China's Heavy Industries

Impact of WTO on China's Heavy Industries								
Heavy Industries	Output		Employment		Import		Export	
	Billion RMB	% (over 1998)	10,000	% (over 1998)	Billion RMB	% (over 1998)	Billion RMB	% (over 1998)
petroleum refinery	−16.7	−3.5	−3.1	−2.6	11.1	35.1	−1.6	−6.8
coal & natural gas	−1.5	−1.6	−0.3	−1.2	0	1.7	−0.6	−4.3
chemical	95	3.8	58.9	4.2	92.5	26.8	32.7	14.4
construction materials	−11.3	−0.8	5.7	0.3	0.8	2.8	−4	−4.2
metallurgy	−28.9	−1.7	−4.2	−0.5	3.1	1.6	−5.2	−5.7
metal goods	−3.4	−0.4	4.9	0.9	2.9	8	−3.5	−3.8
machinery	−51	−3.1	−29.8	−2.2	49.3	10.2	−8.6	−4.4
automobile	−81.2	−15.1	−49.8	−14.5	41.8	105.1	−0.9	−7.8
other transport vehicle	−0.6	-0.2	2.5	0.8	2.3	4.8	−1.6	−4.0
electrical machinery	−28.6	−3.2	−9.7	−1.8	11.1	12	−5.6	−4.9
telecom & electronic goods	−43.8	−4.7	−10.9	−3.3	12.9	5.2	−13.4	−5.2
meters & instruments	−4.5	−5.8	−7.8	−5	3.1	9.7	−0.7	−6.4
machinery repair	1	0.9	2.4	1.5	0	0		
Total	−175.5		−41.2		230.9		−13	

Source: Extracted from Table 1–11, CASS Report by Yu and Zheng 2000

chapter 12

Information Technology Products and Telecom Services[1]

Telecom and "information technology" (IT) are frequently linked together since modern IT technology relies heavily on telecommunication as a medium for the transmission of data, so much so that the two are virtually inseparable. Yet in fact we are talking about two separate things: the tangible products as well as the intangible services made possible by using the products.

In WTO terms, the tangible products belong to trade in goods and it is mainly concerned with tariffs and quotas while intangible services belong to trade in services and it is mainly a problem of market access for foreign suppliers.

This chapter will be divided into two parts. Part I deals mainly with the "product" aspect of the industry and Part II the "service" aspect.

PART I — IT PRODUCTS

A. China's Commitments

1. Scope of Products in China's commitment

China's commitment includes products covered by the *WTO Information Technology Agreement* (ITA), which are:

a. computer and accessories
b. telecom facilities
c. semi-conductor
d. manufacturing facilities for semi-conductors
e. software
f. scientific instruments & office automation equipment

(This section on China's commitments is drawn from data provided in the US White House Factsheets on China WTO Accession, last updated on 17 February 2000, available on the web site of US-China Business Council, available at : http://www.uschina.org/ public/wto/factsheets. Certain adjustments were made according to China accession documents, marked in square bracket.)

---

[1]Please refer to Appendix 3 of this book which details the commitments China made regarding opening up its service sectors.

2. Tariffs

China will sign on to the *Information Technology Agreement* (ITA) on accession, thereby committing to eliminate tariffs on all products covered by the ITA. Tariff reductions from the pre-WTO applied average of 13% will commence upon accession. Tariffs on two-thirds of the ITA products will be eliminated by January 1, 2003, and tariffs on all the remaining products will be eliminated by January 1, 2005.

The basic principles of the ITA is that it is solely a tariff cutting mechanism. There are three basic principles that one must abide by to become an ITA participant: 1) all products included in the agreement must be covered, 2) all must be reduced to a zero tariff level, and 3) all other duties and charges must be bound at zero. There are no exceptions to product coverage, however for sensitive items, it is possible to have an extended implementation period. The commitments undertaken under the ITA in the WTO are on an MFN basis, and therefore benefits accrue to all other WTO Members.

3. Quotas

Quotas will be eliminated upon accession.

4. Trading Rights and Distribution

Before WTO accession foreign companies'ability to do business in China was strictly limited because the right to engage in trade (importing and exporting) was restricted to a small number of companies that received specific authorization or who imported goods to be used in production. This limited foreign exports. China agreed that any entity would be able to import most products, including ITA products, into any part of China. This commitment is phased in over the three-year period with all entities being permitted to import and export at the end of the period.

China — which generally prohibited companies from distributing imported products or providing related distribution services — will permit foreign enterprises to engage in the full range of distribution services. These rights will be phased in over a three-year period for almost all products, including ITA products.

5. Other Commitments

China has agreed not to apply or enforce export performance, local content, and similar requirements as a condition on importation or investment approval.

To alleviate the uncertainty associated with China's inconsistent application, refund, and waivers of its 17% VAT tax, China has agreed to apply all taxes and tariffs uniformly to both domestic and foreign businesses.

6. Computer and Related Services

Foreign service suppliers who are certified engineers or who hold a bachelor's degree and have had three years experience in computer services will be able to provide services in China.

For consultancy services related to hardware installation, data processing and tabulation services, and time-sharing services, foreign-service suppliers will be able to operate in China without limitations upon accession. These services can also be provided through cross-border delivery.

For software implementation services, systems and software consulting services, systems analysis services, systems design services, programming services, systems maintenance services, data processing services, input preparation services, foreign service suppliers will be able to operate in China upon accession through joint ventures [with foreign majority ownership permitted]. These services can also be provided through cross-border delivery.

B. Impact on China

1. Rapid Growth of the IT Sector

(The following two sections are extracted from "Liberalisation of Software Industry", archives of "Business Alert-China", Issue 03, 15 March 2001, HKTDC web site, sections head are inserted by the editor.)

a. Past Record

IT is one of China's fastest growing industries. The increasing computerisation in both the private and public sectors makes China a market with huge potential. According to the Centre of Computer and Microelectronics Industry Development (CCID) under the Ministry of Information Industry (MII), China's IT market, the largest in Asia after Japan, was valued at US$20.7 billion in 1999. CCID estimates put the growth rate of China's IT market in 2000 at 20%, to the tune of US$25 billion. As a key component of the IT sector, the software industry accounted for US$2.2 billion of the total market value in 1999. The software market is the fastest growing segment and was expected to grow to around US$ 2.4 billion in 2000.

Table 12.1 Growth of China's IT industry

	GROWTH OF CHINA'S IT MARKET					
	1997		1998		1999	
	Sales		Sales		Sales	
	US$ (billion)	Growth %	US$ (billion)	Growth %	US$ (billion)	Growth %
Hardware	12.5	45.5	13.9	11.2	15.7	12.9
Software	1.3	21.7	1.7	30.8	2.2	29.4
Information Services	1.8	31.1	2.3	27.8	2.8	21.7
Total	15.6	41.3	17.9	14.7	20.7	15.6

Source: Centre of Computer and Microelectronics Industry Development (CCID) under the Ministry of Information Industry (MII), quoted by Business Alert-China, Issue 03, 15 March 2001, HKTDC web site

According to Internet Data Centre (IDC), about 14.8 million personal computers (PCs) were installed in China as at 1999 and 7.2 million PCs were sold in 2000. The number of PCs in China is expected to increase to 35.1 million by 2003. The financial sector accounts for around 30% of China's IT spending, followed by the telecommunications sector (20%) and transport sector (10%). The number of independent software firms increased from 2,000 in 1999 to 5,000 in 2000, employing more than 150,000 software engineers. Around 30,000 students majoring in software engineering graduate annually.

The industry is supervised by MII, which is responsible for drafting laws and regulations and setting technology standards. The Ministry of Science and Technology (MST) and MII have set up 15 software industry parks in China to encourage investment and R&D. Major parks include the Beijing Software Industry Base, Shanghai Pudong Software Park, Tuopu International Software Park, Shenyang Northern University Software Park, Dalian Software Park, Chengdu Western Software Park, Hefei Software Park and Zhuhai Southern Software Park. MST and MII offer favourable policies including tax concessions and loan facilities to software firms. Some privileges are also extended to foreign entities engaged in product development in the parks. According to IDC, most of the IT product sales are concentrated in Guangdong (16%), Shanghai (25%) and Beijing (38%). The government tries to raise the IT industry's output from the current 2% to 3–4% of GDP.

In light of China's WTO accession, its manufacturing and services sectors need more IT application to enhance their competitiveness against foreign competition. According to forecasts by IDC, by 2004 China would spend over US$5 billion on buying software, with products and related services accounting for 25% of the country's total IT spending.

b. The Software Sector

China's software market can be divided into three segments: systems, tools, and application software. System software includes operating systems for PCs, minicomputers, main frames, workstation, networks and Chinese language platforms. Around 90% of this market is dominated by foreign firms. Software tools include database management, language and development tools, anti-virus software, and translation software. More than 70% of this market is dominated by foreign companies. Application software includes word processing, game software, education software, CAD/CAM software, multimedia software, and communications software. Around 60% of this market is dominated by foreign players. Before WTO accession, China's software industry was actively seeking to upgrade its R&D capacity and technological competency in a bid to compete with foreign products. Major Chinese software developers include Founder, North East University Software Group, China Computer Software Technology & Service Corporation, Star, Hope, and Great Wall Software.

In the system software segment, operating systems for PCs account for around 90% of the market. The financial/insurance sector (25%) and government departments (22%) are the major users of operating systems for mini/main frame computers and workstations. The telecommunications sector (28%) and academic institutions are the main users of operating systems for network. Date base management and communications software accounts for around 70% of the software tools segment. The telecommunication sector (30%), financial/ insurance sector (26%), and transportation and energy sector (21%) are the major users. MIS software and document management software accounts for around 60% of the application software segment. The financial/accounting sector (25%) and manufacturing sector (7.5%) are the major user of MIS software. The document management software market is dominated by publishing software (62%) and word-processing software (15%).

Table 12.2 Growth of China's Software Industry

A. Composition of China's Software Industry					
Types	1999 RMB 100 million	share %	2000 RMB 100 million	share %	Growth %
products	182	41.2	238	40.1	30.8
services	238.5	54.0	322	54.3	35.0
export	21.0	4.8	33	5.6	57.1
Total	441.5		593		
compared with:					
computer industry	1720	25.7	2150	27.6	
GDP	82000	0.54	89000	0.67	

B. Types of Software						
Types	1995	1996	1997	1998	1999	2000
			RMB 100 million			
system	6.5	8.5	13.7	17.4	21.0	33.2
support	15.0	20.0	27.5	35.9	44.8	49.6
application	46.5	63.5	70.8	84.7	116.2	155.0
Total	68.0	92.0	112.0	138.0	182.0	238.0
Growth	39%	35.3	21.7	23.2	31.9	30.7

Source: Xu Shun-cheng, "*On the present and future situation of China's software industry*", New and High Technology Industries, No. 1, 2002

c. Future Growth upon WTO Accession

(Information in this section is drawn from two articles, "Information industry's added value will comprise 5% of China's gross domestic product by 2005", dated 24 October 2000 of "Telecom" archives , and "Information industry accomplishes 2001 target", dated 10 January 2002 of "InfoTech" archives, Chinaonline web site.)

According to the Ministry on Information Industry, the information industry will continue its rapid growth during the 10th Five-Year Plan (2001 to 2005) such that by 2005 the sector's added value will comprise 5 percent of China's gross domestic product by 2005 when a comprehensive and reasonably structured information industry system is formed mandated by membership in the WTO.

By 2005, the total business volume of China's information sector will exceed RMB 3 trillion (US$362.4 billion), according to the Oct. 19 Zhongguo Jingji Shibao, (China Economic Times).

In terms of China's national economic growth, information is quickly becoming the strategic pillar industry. Zhang Guobao, deputy-director of the State Development Planning Commission (SDPC), said at the opening ceremony of the China-Japan Information Cooperation and Technology Exhibit on Oct. 19, 2001 that:

— The information industry grew at an average annual rate of 30 percent during the Ninth Five-Year Plan (1996 to 2000).

— In 2001 the business volume of the country's telecommunications operations totaled RMB 366.9 billion (US$44.31 billion), up 24 percent over 2000.

The total value of the electronic information product-manufacturing sector amounted to RMB 1.35 trillion (US$163.04 billion), up 27 percent over 2000. Of that amount, RMB 750 billion (US$90.58 billion) consisted of revenue from sales, rising 24 percent over 2000.

The sector achieved RMB 65 billion (US$7.85 billion) in taxes on profits.

The communications business scored RMB 362.4 billion (US$43.77 billion) in revenues in the first 11 months of 2001, growing 13.8 percent compared with the same period in 2000.

2. Impact of WTO Accession on China's IT Industry

a. General Picture

(The following section is extracted from a report by Steve Rasin titled "MII Official: Domestic Telecom Equipment Makers To Boost China Market Share Despite WTO Entry", dated 17 May 2000, "Telecom" archives of Chinaonline web site.)

Steve Rasin of Chinaonline reported on 17 May 2000 that local market share for domestic producers of telecom equipment will increase over the next three years after China enters the World Trade Organization (WTO).

According to the report, Mr. Lei Zhenzhou, of the Ministry of Information Industry's China Academy of Telecommunications Research, said the market share for local manufacturers of mobile switching equipment would be 40 percent in 2001, rising to 70 percent by 2003; for base stations, 25 percent in 2001, rising to 50 percent by 2003; for handsets, 10 percent to 15 percent in 2001, rising to 30 percent by 2003. Lei disclosed this forecast at the May 16 China Telecom 2000: "China at a Crossroads" conference.

Lei summed up the Chinese attitude toward the dangers and advantages of WTO accession.

"On the positive side, WTO accession will bring more investment, technology and improved management to China. On the negative side, local producers will be forced to cut prices and margins while more revenues and profits will go into (foreign) pockets," he said.

"By the end of 2000, China already becomes the world's second largest market for mobile phones, second only to the U.S. By 2010 there will be 250 million wireless subscribers," said Christine keck, Director, Asia Pacific Programs at the Technology Industry Association or TIA.

Paul Kullman, Commercial Attache at the U.S. Embassy in Beijing, said that China is creating a "transparent telecom licensing system and interconnection regulations," and is in the process of drafting a Telecommunications Act, he said.

To strengthen local producers during the phase-in period under WTO, Beijing will continue to promote the "buy local" policy, increase financial support to key companies, stop cut-throat competition and end local protectionism, said Kullman, who follows the telecommunications industry at the embassy.

"In the next three years China's telecommunications transmission, access and hardware investments will amount to $24 billion and focus primarily on improving consumer access," he predicted.

b. For Equipment Manufacturers, Opportunity to Grow

(The text here and that under sub-section "c" are extracted from "WTO and China's Telecom Industry: Problems For Services, Good News For Manufacturers" dated 2 June 1999, "WTO" archives of Chinaonline web site, quoting the 3 April [1999] Zhongguo Zhengquan Bao (China Securities.)

The telecommunications equipment market in China is already open to foreign companies. The impact of joining WTO on the telecom equipment industry would be much less than on telecom service, as little competition will be added to the market. The 8 giants in world telecom equipment have already entered the China market and have received national treatment. After China joins WTO, there won't be any new or stronger competitors.

The telecom equipment industry in China has in fact penetrated the international market, and joining WTO will provide more opportunity. In competing with the "8 giants," 5 local companies (Julong, Datang, Jinpeng, Zhongxin and Huawei) stand out, and the digital SPC telephone exchanger they have developed is at an advanced global standard. The telephone exchangers developed independently by local companies have taken 60% of the China market. Foreign products will not gain much competitive advantage in terms of price, even if free of customs duty after joining WTO, so there won't be much impact on the telecom equipment industry of China.

For these enterprises, joining WTO would mean removing some obstacles for penetrating the international market and bring more opportunities for development.

The manufacturing costs for telecom equipment will be sharply lowered. Both joint ventures and wholly domestic telecom equipment manufactures rely on import sources for large proportions of their components and parts, which are charged 12% customs duties. After joining WTO, the import tariff rate will be reduced to around 3%, or even free of duty; this will bring greater competitive advantages in price for made-in-China products.

c. But Domestic Manufacturers Still Have Problems

It has to be admitted that domestic telecom enterprises are still far behind multinational giants like Motorola, Nokia and Ericsson in competitive strength. After joining the WTO, a certain degree of shock can be expected, though not a big shock.

In the first place, domestic enterprises are weak in R&D; enterprises and products with low technology content will be eliminated. Due to poor supervision, domestic companies in cooperation with foreign parties have not acquired the high tech, or have only received the manufacturing process, while the development and design techniques have not been transferred. Many joint ventures have not even established any R&D center, and for lack of ability to digest new technologies and make innovations, development of new products is impossible. These types of enterprises will be at substantial risk of elimination after joining the WTO.

A second issue that should be addressed as soon as possible is that of efficient economic scale. Of telecom equipment that embodies independent intellectual property, only SPC exchanging equipment has obtained a certain economy of scale. Most products such as mobile phones are just in an early stage of manufacture. Some have just emerged from the development process, and their performance is still far below that of internationally recognized brands. These products have not achieved economics of scale. If this problem is not solved before joining the WTO, the potential for growth in market share will be restricted post-accession.

Market share is a third problem: Share for some products may fall to some extent after government protection is removed. The rapid growth of domestic telecom enterprises depends on the support of government. Among the advantages of the telecommunication service industry, local purchase policies are of great importance. After entering the WTO, these favorable policies will be eliminated sooner or later. Learning to grow without government protection is a major issue that local telecom enterprises must start managing now.

PART II TELECOMMUNICATION SERVICES

A. China's Commitments

(The section on China's commitments is drqwn from data provided in the US White House Factsheets on China WTO Accession, last updated on 17 February 2000, available on the web site of US-China Business Council available at: http://www.uschina.org/ public/wto/factsheets. Certain adjustments were made according to China accession documents, marked in square bracket.)

Foreign service suppliers are currently prohibited from providing telecom services in China. After China's accession, foreign suppliers will be permitted to provide a broad range of services as described below:

1. Value-Added and Paging Services

Foreign service suppliers will be able to provide the following services: electronic mail, voice mail, on-line information and data base retrieval, electronic data interchange, enhanced/value-added facsimile services (including store and forward, store and retrieve), code and protocol conversion, on-line information and data processing (including transaction processing), and paging services.

Foreign service suppliers may hold [no more than] 30 percent foreign equity share upon accession, 49 percent after one year, 50 percent after two years.

Foreign service suppliers may provide services to Beijing, Shanghai, and Guangzhou upon accession, to Chengdu, Chongqing, Dalian, Fuzhou, Hangzhou, Nanjing, Ningbo, Qingdao, Shenyang, Shenzen, Xiamen, Xian, Taiyuan and Wuhan [after one year], and nationwide [after two years].

2. Mobile Voice and Data Services

Foreign service suppliers will be able to provide all analogue/digital/cellular services and personal communications services.

Foreign services suppliers may hold [no more than] 25 percent foreign equity share [upon accession], 35 percent [after one year], and 49 percent [after three years].

Foreign service suppliers may provide services [in and between] Beijing, Shanghai, and Guangzhou [upon accession, in and between] Chengdu, Chongqing, Dalian, Fuzhou, Hangzhou, Nanjing, Ningbo, Qingdao, Shenyang, Shenzen, Xiamen, Xian, Taiyuan and Wuhan [after one year], and nationwide after five years.

3. Domestic and International Services

Foreign service suppliers will be able to provide domestic and inernational voice, packet-switched data transmission services, circuit-switched data transmission services, facsimile services. International closed user groups voice and data services are also included. [Use of private leased circuit is permitted.]

Foreign service suppliers may hold a 25 percent foreign equity share three years after accession, 35 percent after five years, and 49 percent after six years.

Foreign service suppliers may provide services in Beijing, Shanghai, and Guangzhou after three years, Chengdu, Chongqing, Dalian, Fuzhou, Hangzhou, Nanjing, Ningbo, Qingdao, Shenyang, Shenzen, Xiamen, Xian, Taiyuan and Wuhan after five years, and nationwide after six years.

4. Internet and Satellite Services

Internet and satellite services are included, but not explicitly scheduled, following the scheduling convention of most WTO members, including the United States.

Internet Services are Subsumed Under Value-Added Services

For satellite services, China has attached to its services schedule and signed the "Notes for Scheduling Basic Telecom Services" (S/GBT/W/2/REV. 1). This means unless explicitly excluded in China's sectoral column, any basic service may be provided through any means of technology (e.g., cable, wireless, satellites).

5. Access to International Services

All international telecommunications services suppliers shall be licensed by China's telecommunications authorities, which will act as an independent regulatory authority. The decisions and procedures used by regulators shall be impartial with respect to all market participants.

6. Other Commitments

China has agreed to undertake all the obligations contained in the WTO Reference Paper on pro-competitive regulatory principles. China also made commitments in accordance with the Notes for Scheduling Basic Telecom Services (S/GBT/W/2/REV. 1) and Market Access Limitations on Spectrum Availability (S/GBT/W/3).

B. Impacts on Telecommunication Services

1. General Picture

(This piece is retrieved from "Telecom Industry could see Bankruptcies after WTO, official says", dated 9 April 2001, archives of "Telecom Industry", Chinaonline web site, quoting a report by the April 2, 2001 Hexun Caijing (Homeway Financial News.))

According to Mr. Shi Fenghai, deputy director of the State Development Planning Commission High-Tech Industry Department, China's telecom industry could be impacted by incoming foreign investment after China has joined the WTO. While the telecom industry's overall performance should be quite good, he predicted, the first bankruptcy in the industry could soon occur.

Shi said China's telecom industry should be able to maintain its roughly 25 percent growth during the 10th Five-year Plan (2001 to 2005) without too many obstacles. He added that both the scale and capacity of China's telecom network would be the world's largest.

Initially, he said, foreign investment would most likely concentrate in the highly profitable arenas, such as international long-distance, domestic long-distance and Internet protocol (IP) telephony services, as well as eastern regions and cities such as Beijing, Shanghai and Guangzhou.

But because China's telecom service industry has great growth potential, Shi predicted, some foreign companies would be willing to increase their Chinese market share in the long run even though they may suffer from short-term financial losses.

As a result of more operators in the market, some of China's telecom companies would probably encounter various levels of business difficulties. They might even become victims of the first bankruptcies in China telecom industry, Shi warned.

2. China To Buffer Telecom Industry From Shock Of WTO Entry

(Extracted from an article bearing the same title, dated 6 December 1999, "WTO" archives of Chinaonline web site, quoting a report on 25 November 1999 by Hong Kong Ta Kung Pao.)

Quoting government sources, the Hong Kong Ta Kung Pao, a paper related to the Chinese government, said that WTO membership will have two impacts on China's telecom industry. The relative weakness of China's telecom industry will cause problems in the short run, but WTO entry will benefit the industry in the long run and solve certain bottlenecks.

Short Term Harm

1. WTO Entry will Threaten The Position of China's Telecom Companies

Propelled by the globalization of the telecom industry, leading foreign telecom companies are vying to establish strategic international alliances. Due to local protectionism, the competitiveness of China's telecom companies has yet to be tested.

It is expected that once China opens its telecom market, these international tycoons will race to stake claims in this biggest, most promising market. This could threaten the leading position of China telecom companies in the domestic market.

2. Domestic Enterprises will not be well Protected due to Inadequate Telecom Policies

The ending of such practices as separating postal from telecom service and separating government administration from private enterprise has meant that existing regulations administering the telecom industry no longer suit present needs.

Given the time constraints, it is unlikely that the Ministry of Information Industry will have a complete system of telecom administration regulations in place at the time of formal WTO entry, nor will laws and criteria concerning service facilities, equipment and telecom service be published soon. Under such circumstances, China telecom industry cannot be adequately protected from foreign competition.

3. Foreign Funds will Challenge Domestic Information Security

Many developing countries did not sign the *Service & Trade General Agreement* and the February 1997 *Basic Telecommunications Agreement* (BTA) of the WTO because of the national security issue. The access of foreign funds to China telecom industry is expected to undermine domestic information security.

Given that Americans have "spied" on other countries in the name of the United Nations, the Chinese believe that it is unlikely that the United States will be better behaved in China.

4. Competition will Hinder Expansion of Basic Telecom Services to Remote Areas

Many developing countries are concerned that foreign telecom giants will provide services only to those areas offering high returns, and ignore public needs. Furthermore, it is feared that competition between foreign and local telecom companies will reduce the revenue of the latter.

As this will undermine progress toward providing services to outlying districts and therefore affect the expansion of basic domestic services as a whole, it will hinder economic development and the improvement of living standards.

Developed countries, particularly the United States, have implemented highly detailed regulations and rules protecting basic telecom services. With such protection guaranteed, the United States can safely relax restrictions on the access of foreign telecom companies to local markets. In view of this, China must lay down its own policies and rules for protecting basic services before opening its telecom market.

Long Term Benefits

1. China's Telecom Industry will become more Competitive

China has experimented with opening her telecom market for the last five years. Competition in the areas of paging, group telephones and Internet business is heating up, but competition with respect to mobile phones, landline phones and digital communication is lackluster.

WTO entry will force China to perfect current telecom supervision rules and regulations to create a fairer market environment. Meanwhile, the access of foreign companies to China's telecom markets will boost competition in the domestic telecom market.

2. WTO Entry will Provoke Improvements in Quality and Efficiency of Telecom Service

Having made rapid progress in the 1990s, China now boasts a sizeable telecom infrastructure, which can basically meet the demands of the socialist market economy and the Chinese people. Difficulties in telephone installation and handling telecom business have been solved, and improvement in service quality is the current goal.

As long as China Telecom enjoys a monopoly in the domestic telecom market, it will be hard to improve service quality and cut service prices. Based on the experiences of other countries and basic market economic principles, Chinese experts have determined that the most efficient method for improving service quality is to open the market, thus introducing competition.

Foreign competition is expected to solve various problems such as inefficient operation and poor quality service resulting from the long-term monopoly of state-owned telecom enterprises.

This will enable China's telecom industry to progress from the initial focus on scale and quantity to the more intense focus on profit and efficiency, helping it keep up with the international pace.

3. WTO Entry will Accelerate the Transformation of State-Owned Telecom Companies

The introduction of foreign funds into China state-owned telecom enterprises will quicken the latter private enterprise evolution and improve their operational efficiency. Although to some degree the corporate evolution of China Telecom is complete, its management personnel, who are used to working under a planned economy, are not well versed in the operation laws of corporate enterprises under a market economy.

Introducing foreign funds and adding new shareholders to the board of China Telecom, especially foreign shareholders, will improve the company operating efficiency since the latter are familiar with operating private enterprises.

4. WTO Entry will Enable China's Telecom Industry to Compete Internationally

China's telecom industry, because it is responsible for meeting the demands of the national economy, needs to take its place in the international market in order to foster the nation's economic development.

The development of many internationally renowned telecom companies has been closely tied to the expansion of their domestic business. With further progress made in China's reform and opening to the outside world, more and more Chinese companies are vying for places in the international market.

Due to long-term business relations and the language factor, these international telecom companies will continue to rely on the services of China Telecom. This is a golden opportunity for China Telecom to access the international market.

Entry into the WTO helps China telecom enterprises win a just international competitive environment. With the globalization of the telecom market and with every country's business expansion, international friction in the telecom market is increasing, and each side tries to dominate telecom trade negotiations.

After entry into the WTO, China may resort to the arbitration mechanisms of the WTO to resolve international telecom disputes. Therefore such entry helps China protect her interests in international telecom competition.

Suggested Measures for Coping with Problems of WTO Entry

1. Set Restrictions on the Influx of Foreign Funds

Since the telecom industry concerns the nation sovereignty and security and affects every aspect of life, it is imperative to maintain the leading position of domestic enterprises. The extent of the participation of foreign funds in domestic enterprises must therefore be rigorously controlled so long as investment enthusiasm is not hurt.

The major reasons are as follow. First, the security and stability of the State is an essential condition for economic development. The telecom system is key for maintaining the political stability and security of a nation.

Secondly, it is clear from the [*Basic Telecommunications*] *Agreement* that many countries, including the United States, have set restrictions on the influx of foreign funds. In addition, according to market economic principles, the most common, reasonable and most efficient method to control an enterprise is to be its shareholder. Therefore, domestic enterprises must hold 51% of the shares of telecom enterprises, or at least be leading shareholders.

2. Strengthen the Competitiveness of Domestic Enterprises

Many countries have fostered internal domestic competition before opening their markets to the outside world with an aim of strengthening the competitiveness of domestic enterprises and accumulating relevant experience. China should therefore allow domestic telecom enterprises to compete to enable them to prepare to excel in international competition.

3. Lay Down Complete, Transparent Telecom Policies

The formulation of complete, stable and transparent telecom administration policies is the first WTO prerequisite for member countries to open their telecom markets. The BTA stipulates that definite regulations should be formulated concerning the prevention of activities that thwart competition, concerning connection networks, universal service, public issuance of permits, independent administrative organizations, and the fair distribution of communication resources.

Secondly, only complete, transparent telecom administration policies can ensure the confidence of foreign-funded enterprises in the China telecom market and their active participation. Only in this way can China achieve the final aim of introducing advanced foreign technology and management experience and thus promote the rapid progress of China's telecom industry.

C. The Potential Growth

1. General Picture

(This section is extracted from "China to speed up drafting of telecom law, Wu Jichuan says" dated 12 February 2001, archives of "Telecom Industry" of Chinaonline web site, quoting the 10 February 2001 Hong Kong Ming Pao.)

Mr. Wu Jichuan, minister of the Ministry of Information Industry (MII) disclosed that there are seven companies currently dominate the basic operations of the telecom business in China. There are, however, more than 3,000 different enterprises engaged in Internet-related and other value-added businesses. Furthermore, new telecom companies are constantly enlarging their market share.

Wu predicted that the size of China's information market will quadruple in the next 10 years. Presently, telephone use has reached 20.1 percent nationwide and the length of optical cable now extends to 1.25 million kilometers (776,714 miles). There are now 230 million subscribers of fixed telephones and mobile phones. Computers with Internet access number 8.9 million, the number of Chinese-language Web sites has reached 260,000, and there are approximately 22.5 million Internet users (though the certainty of this figure has been fiercely debated). He had even higher hopes for the future, the story said.

By his predictions, the 2005 growth rate of the information industry will be more than 20 percent, and the industry will account for more than 8 percent of the country's gross domestic product.

By 2010, Wu said there would be 500 million subscribers of fixed and mobile telephones, and the national telephone-use rate will reach 40 percent.

2. China's Telecom Revenue to Reach 1 Trillion Yuan (RMB) in 2005

(Wu's statement was reported by Huang Ying, the English People's Daily, 18 December 2001)

In a separate occasion, Wu disclosed that China's telecom industry is scheduled to reap a revenue of RMB 1 trillion in communication services by 2005 and complete a reliable information network by 2010.

Strategy for Next Ten Years

The strategy of China's telecommunication industry for next ten years is given as follows:

1. To reach a revenue of one trillion yuan in communication business by 2005, of which some 80 billion yuan from the post sector, 920 billion yuan from the telecom sector, with an average increase of 23 percent in the coming five years;
2. To have the world biggest scale and capacity of fixed and mobile phone nets, with the number of phone users to reach 500 million and realize the village — village phone communication;
3. To raise the number of data-, multimedia- and Internet-users to some 200 million persons, with the Internet surfer population to reach some 15 percent of all.

Further Goals

By 2010, China will establish an information-resourceful communication network that can transfer gigantic data at a high speed by narrow-band or broadband, wire or wireless ways at any time in most regions throughout the country, Wu added.

D. Forbidden Ground: Radio & TV

(This section is extracted from an article "China to keep radio, TV closed to foreign investment, says SARFT official", dated 30 November 2000, archives of "Media and entertainment", Chinaonline web site, quoting the 29 November 2000 Zhongguo Zhengquan Bao (China Securities.))

According to an official at the Film and TV Information Network Center of the State Administration of Radio, Film & Television (SARFT), radio and TV networks, as a special sector under government control, are not open to foreign capital. The provincial and local companies that have involved foreign capital in their cable operators will be cleaned up in the future.

The official also stated that China would only open the telecom sector after joining the World Trade Organization, but not the radio and TV sector.

Previous reports said that the cable network would be divided into two platforms, with an A platform for TV programming and a B platform for value-added telecom services. The reports had suggested that foreign investors might be allowed to take part in the operations of the B platform, the story said.

However, the SARFT official said that foreign investment is denied access to both platforms. The radio and TV networks are forbidden zones to foreign investment, and SARFT officials have repeatedly stressed that they will not go against state regulations.

The official also said that the China Radio and TV Network Cable Group would be established before the end of the year [2000], according to the article.

chapter 13

Financial Services[1]

China's commitments on financial services include the insurance, banking and securities sectors. Each of these will be dealt with separately in this chapter.

A. INSURANCE

1. China's Commitments to Open Insurance Business

(The summary below is extracted from an article "China Commitment to Open Insurance Business" by Shi Liu, dated 21 January 2002, "Industrial Profile" archives of WTO Accession Monitor, web site of Hong Kong Trade Development Council ("HKTDC".))

China will open its insurance business to the outside world on a full scale after its accession to the World Trade Organization (WTO). The main commitments of the Chinese government in opening the insurance business are as follows:

a. Form of the Businesses

Immediately after China's entry to the WTO, non-life insurers from abroad will be allowed to set up branches or joint ventures in China. Foreign firms will be allowed to hold as much as 51% of the stake in the joint ventures. Two years after the entry, non-life insurance firms from abroad will be allowed to set up solely funded sub-firms in China, i.e. there will be no restriction on the form of enterprise establishment. Immediately after the entry, foreign life insurers will be allowed to set up joint ventures in China, and hold no more than 50% stake in the joint ventures. They will also be allowed to choose their partners independently. Investors of the joint ventures are allowed to make joint venture clauses independently within the scope committed. Immediately after China's WTO accession, the foreign stake in Sino-foreign joint venture insurance brokerage companies may reach 50%, and the proportion may not exceed 51% within three years after the accession. Five years after the WTO entry, foreign insurance brokerage companies will be permitted to set up solely funded sub-firms. With gradual cancellation of geographical limitations, foreign insurance companies will, after approval, be

---

[1]Please refer to Appendix 3 of this book which details the commitments China made regarding opening up its service sectors.

permitted to set up branches. The qualification conditions for initial establishment do not apply to the establishment of internal branches.

b. Geographical Limitations

Immediately after the WTO entry, foreign life and non-life insurance firms [and brokers] will be allowed to offer services in Shanghai, Guangzhou, Dalian, Shenzhen and Foshan. Two years after the entry, their business could be extended to Beijing, Chengdu, Chongqing, Fuzhou, Suzhou, Xiamen, Ningbo, Shenyang, Wuhan and Tianjin. All geographical restrictions will be lifted three years after the entry.

c. Business Scope

Immediately after the entry, non-life insurers from abroad will be permitted to engage in "general insurance policies" and large-scale commercial insurance without any geographical limitation, and offer non-life services to overseas enterprises, property insurance to foreign-funded enterprises in China, and related liability insurance and credit insurance services. Two years after the entry, non-life insurers from abroad will be able to offer all kinds of non-life insurance services to Chinese and foreign customers. Immediately after the entry, foreign life insurance companies will be permitted to provide individual (non-group) life insurance services to foreign citizens and Chinese citizens. [Three] years after the entry, they will be permitted to provide health insurance, group insurance, pension insurance and annual pay insurance services to Chinese and foreign citizens. Immediately after the entry, foreign reinsurance companies will be permitted to provide life and non-life reinsurance services in the form of branch company, joint venture company or solely funded sub-firm. There are no geographical restrictions or quantity limits in license granting.

d. Business License

Immediately after the WTO entry, China is committed to abolishing the restrictions on the number of licenses issued to foreign insurers. Foreign insurers must satisfy the following conditions before applying for licenses in China: a business history of more than 30 years in a WTO member, operating a representative office in China for two consecutive years and holding no less than US$5 billion in total assets as of the end of the year prior to the application.

e. On Large Scale Commercial Insurance

Large scale commercial insurance refers to insurance provided to large industrial and commercial enterprises. Its standards are: the annual premium paid by such an enterprise at the time when China enters the WTO exceeds RMB 800 thousand, and its investment tops RMB 200 million; one year after the WTO entry, the annual premium paid by the enterprise should exceed RMB 600 thousand and its investment should exceed RMB 180 million; two years after the WTO entry, the annual premium paid by the enterprise should exceed RMB 400 thousand and its investment should exceed RMB 150 million.

f. On Legal Insurance Scope

China has committed that the 20% proportion for reinsurance provided by Sino-foreign direct insurance companies to Chinese reinsurance companies will not be changed immediately after the WTO entry and will be lowered to 15% one year after the entry, 10% two years after the entry, 5% three years after the entry, and cancelled four years after the entry. However, foreign capital insurance companies will not be permitted to engage in third party liability insurance of motor vehicles, liability insurance for public transport vehicles, commercial vehicle drivers and carriers, and other legal insurance services.

g. On General Insurance Policy Brokerage Service

National treatment will be granted. However, the geographical scope for opening to foreign capital insurance brokerage companies will follow that to foreign insurance companies, i.e., they will be allowed to do business in Shanghai, Guangzhou, Dalian, Shenzhen and Foshan immediately after the WTO entry, in ten more cities two years after the entry, and in all cities three years after the entry.

h. On Application Qualification of Insurance Brokerage Companies

Aside from the above conditions of a 30-year operating history and running representative office for two consecutive years, there are also conditions in the aspect of asset scale: in excess of US$500 million at the time of entry, in excess of US$400 million one year after the entry, in excess of RMB 300 million two years after the entry, and in excess of RMB 200 million four years after the entry.

i. On Trans-Territory Delivery in Insurance Services

Besides, the Chinese government has, in accordance with the *General Agreement on Service Trade*, made commitments with regard to the trans-territory delivery and other methods in insurance services:

Except for a) international marine shipping, aviation and freight transport insurance, b) reinsurance and large scale commercial insurance and c) brokerage services relative to these insurances, the Chinese government has not made any commitment with regard to trans-territory delivery; with regard to consumption outside the territory, no limits were set on other services except for insurance brokerage on which no commitment was made; with regard to natural personnel flow, except for trans-industrial level commitment (i.e. general commitment covering insurance industry), no commitment was made on others.

2. Size of the Market

(Extracted from "Insurance Industries will grow 12% a year, experts say", dated 18 January 2001, "Economic News" archives of Chinaonline web site quoting 16 January 2001 Zhongguo Jinji Shibao (China Economic Times.))

In the next five years following WTO accession, the annual growth rate of the Chinese insurance industry would be sustained at about 12 percent, according to the estimate made by Ma Yongwei, chairman of the China Insurance Regulatory Commission (CIRC)[2] and reported by the 16 January [2001] Zhongguo Jingji Shibao (China Economic Times).

By the year 2005, the total value of insurance premiums will reach RMB 280 billion (US$33.82 billion), constituting 2.3 percent of the total gross domestic product value. The average premium per person will be RMB 230 (US$27.78).

Ma Yongwei announced that from now until an unspecified time, the CIRC would concentrate on opening the industry domestically before opening to foreign entities. He promised that the Commission will gather research to craft transitional articles and will support the growth of the domestic insurance industry to its utmost.

3. Impact of WTO Accession on China's Insurance Market

(Extracted from the article "China Commitment to Open Insurance Business" by Shi Liu, dated 21 January 2002, "Industrial Profile" archives of WTO Accession Monitor, web site of HKTDC.)

As a matter of fact, China's insurance market has been opened to the outside world at a fast speed and high starting point. So far, 26 foreign insurance companies have been approved to operate insurance business in China. Among them, quite a few are international banking and insurance integrated financial groups in the ranking of Fortune Top 500. Ma Yongwei, chairman of the CIRC [January, 2002], said that there are now 40 domestic and foreign capital insurance companies in China, including 5 solely state-owned companies, nine shareholding companies, 13 Sino-foreign joint ventures and 13 branches of foreign insurance companies. At present, foreign insurance companies have about 1% share in the Chinese insurance market, and the development space is great.

Compared with foreign rivals, China's insurance industry is obviously less competitive. According to a document released by Beijing branch of the CIRC, the results of a recent survey of 5,000 residents on the Beijing insurance market show that among the residents having bought life insurance, only 17% show satisfaction of the after-sale service, 64.5% say "it is so-so and needs improvement" and 18.5% show dissatisfaction. Besides, the insurees know little about their rights. Only 25.65% say they are very clear about the insurance clauses, 19.2% say they have not even read the clauses, 47.7% say they have read but do not fully understand the clauses, and 7.9% say they have tried to read but can not understand. Also, a survey of 1,600 residents who have not bought insurance shows the respondents are reluctant to buy insurance on the grounds that "it is easy to buy insurance but difficult to claim for indemnity", "insurance is unnecessary for the moment" and "no suitable insurance products have been found". Poor service quality has become an important reason restraining the development of the insurance market in China.

---

[2]Mr. Wu Dingfu was appointed new chairman of CIRC in October, 2002.

After the WTO entry, as the WTO stresses the principles of MFN and national treatment, the domestic insurance industry will adopt new rules of game. Meanwhile, foreign insurers, Sino-foreign joint venture insurance companies and Chinese insurers will undertake full competition to create a new pattern in which foreign insurers and Sino-foreign joint venture insurers will have obvious advantages in quantity. The domestic insurance will thus face a severe challenge.

B. BANKING SERVICES

1. China's Commitments to Open Banking Services

(The commitments given below are taken from the archives of "Economic Forum", web site of HKTDC", 2001 and can be checked against China's Services Schedule in Appendix 3.)

a. Types of services included

China commits to open the following banking services:

— Acceptance of deposits and other repayable funds from the public;
— Lending of all types, including consumer credit, mortgage credit, factoring and financing of commercial transaction;
— Financial leasing
— All payment and money transmission services, including credit, charge and debit cards, travelers cheques and bankers drafts (including import and export settlement);
— Guarantees and commitments
— Trading for own account or for account of customers: foreign exchange

b. Geographic Restrictions

— For foreign currency business, there will be no geographic restriction upon accession.
— For local currency business, the geographic restriction will be phased out as follows:
— Upon accession (wto), Shanghai, Shenzhen, Tianjin and Dalian;
— Within one year after accession (wto+1), Guangzhou, Zhuhai, Qingdao, Nanjing and Wuhan;
— Within two years after accession (wto+2), Jinan, Fuzhou, Chengdu and Chongqing;
— Within three years after accession (wto+3), Kunming, Beijing and Xiamen;
— Within four years after accession (wto+4), Shantou, Ningbo, Shenyang and Xi'an.
— Within five years after accession (wto+5), all geographic restrictions will be removed.

c. Clients

For foreign currency business, foreign financial institutions will be permitted to provide services in China without restriction as to clients upon accession.

For local currency business:

— wto+2 (within two years after accession): foreign financial institutions will be permitted to provide services to Chinese enterprises.
— wto+5 (Within five years after accession): foreign financial institutions will be permitted to provide services to all Chinese clients. Foreign financial institutions licensed for local currency business in one region of China may service clients in any other region that has been opened for such business.

d. Licensing

Criteria for authorization to deal in China's financial services sector are solely prudential (i.e., contain no economic needs test or quantitative limits on licenses). Within five years after accession, any existing non-prudential measures restricting ownership, operation, and juridical form of foreign financial institutions, including on internal branching and licenses, shall be eliminated.

e. Minimum Capital Requirements and Other Qualification Criteria:

— subsidiary of a foreign bank or a foreign finance company in China: total assets of more than US$10 billion at the end of the year prior to filing the application.
— a branch of a foreign bank in China: total assets of more than US$20 billion at the end of the year prior to filing the application.
— A Chinese-foreign joint bank or a Chinese-foreign joint finance company in China: total assets of more than US$10 billion at the end of the year prior to filing the application.
— Qualifications for foreign financial institutions to engage in local currency business are as follows: three years business operation in China and being profitable for two consecutive years prior to the application.

f. Other Commitments

— Except for geographic restrictions and client limitations on local currency business (listed in the market access column), foreign financial institution may do business, without restrictions or need for case-by-case approval, with foreign invested enterprises, non-Chinese natural persons, Chinese natural persons and Chinese enterprises.

— For financial leasing services, foreign financial leasing corporations will be permitted to provide financial leasing service at the same time as domestic corporations.

g. Other Financial Services

In addition to the scope of activities listed above, China also agrees to include the following fields in the WTO list of commitments.

— Motor vehicle financing by non-bank financial institutions.
— Provision and transfer of financial information, and financial data processing and related software by supplier of other financial services;

Table 13.1 China's commitments to open up the banking business

	BANKING BUSINESS IN CHINA	
TYPES OF BUSINESS	TARGET	CUSTOMERS
A. Corporation Banking	FIEs	Chinese Corporations
1. Deposits		
a. RMB	ok	wto+2
b. foreign currency	ok	ok (requires PBOC approval)
2. Lending		
a. RMB	ok	wto+2
b. foreign currency	ok	ok
3. Settlements & remittances	ok	wto+2
4. Foreign Exchange transaction	ok	wto+2
5. Guarantee	ok	wto+2
B. Consumer Banking	Overseas citizens	Chinese citizens
1. Deposit	ok	wto+5
2. Credit card	ok	wto+5
3. Mortgage	ok	wto+5
4. Other consumer credits	ok	wto+5
C. Interbank Transactions	FIEs	Chinese corporations
1. Deposit	ok	wto+2
2. Lending	ok	wto+2
3. Discounting	ok	ok

Note:

FIEs: foreign-invested enterprises

ok: business that is allowed before WTO accession

wto+2 or 5: two or five years after accession to WTO

Source: Extracted from "*China's Banking Reform and WTO*", December 1999, archives of "Economic Forum" of HKTDC web site

— Advisory, intermediation and other auxiliary financial services including credit reference and analysis, investment and portfolio research and advice, advice on acquisitions and on corporate restructuring and strategy.

Some of China's commitments are listed in Table 13.1.

2. Impacts on China's Banking Sector

(Much of this section is retrieved from "Foreign And Chinese Banks To Compete Over Intermediary Transactions", dated 17 December 1999, "WTO" archives of Chinaonline web site, quoting the 14 December 1999 Zhongguo Gongshang Shibao (China Business Times.))

The 14 December 1999 Zhongguo Gongshang Shibao (China Business Times) evaluated the advantages and disadvantages of WTO accession for China's financial sector and focused on the negative implications for domestic banks, including increased instability and intensified competition in areas such as intermediary business.

Advantages of WTO Entry

1. Financial reforms will be prompted, such as the reform of interest rates and internal management mechanisms.
2. New market mechanisms will be imported, competition in the finance sector will be better enforced, and the variety of financial services and the quality of service will improve.
3. Financial technologies and advanced financial products will be imported along with advanced management mechanisms and policies, causing the efficiency of resource allocation and capital utilization to improve.

Disadvantages of WTO Entry

1. Competition in the domestic banking industry will intensify.
2. The operating risk for domestic commercial banks will increase.
3. Financial supervision and safeguarding the stability of the financial system will become more difficult.

Major Areas Of Expansion For Foreign Banks

Foreign banks will expand their business primarily in the following areas:

1. Foreign exchange. The rapid expansion of foreign banks in this type of business will threaten that of local banks.
2. RMB business. Here the growth of foreign banks is expected to be speedy, but local banks will retain major marketing shares while foreign banks target intermediary transaction, in which business their market share is likely to increase rapidly.
3. Settlement business. At present, foreign banks handle about 30% of the international settlement business; within 10 years from the date of China's formal opening of the finance sector, they may capture half of the market.
4. Derivatives. In this field, foreign banks have huge advantages over local banks. It is an area that involves much risk and is difficult to supervise.

5. Wholesale/retail business. Foreign banks will make much progress in wholesale banking, while in retail banking, they will threaten domestic banks only in major cities.

Analysis of the Implications

According to experts, China's foreign exchange and RMB savings business will be transformed after WTO accession. If the number of foreign bank branches increases by 100 to a total of 279 within 3 years after WTO entry, the volume of their foreign currency business will double.

In 1998, 179 foreign banks acquired foreign currency deposits totaling US$4.55 billion. Based on a growth of 50%, the balance of foreign currency deposits of 279 foreign banks will reach US$10.46 billion, which is equivalent to transferring 10% of the current foreign reserve of US$60 billion.

Given this, some experts recommend that a ceiling be set on the amount of RMB currency available to foreign banks. There are currently 25 foreign banks with RMB business licenses, and they have acquired total RMB deposits of RMB 3.7 billion (US$447 million), with an average balance of RMB 148 million (US$18 million) each.

Should the figure be increased 10 fold, i.e., each of the 279 foreign banks acquires RMB 1.48 billion (US$179 million) in deposits, the balance will reach RMB 412.92 billion (US$50 billion), an estimated 5% of China's total deposits.

In addition, foreign banks will seek to compete in international business relating to remittance, collection and settlement under L/Cs. At present, the gap between foreign banks and local banks in the import/export settlement business is much smaller than that in the deposit business because it is the easiest area for foreign banks to enter. If domestic banks do not improve service, their market share will gradually diminish.

In the meantime, WTO accession will lead to much instability and a more volatile environment for domestic banks. External instability could be brought into China through the domestic subsidiaries [of foreign financial institutions.]

Additionally, the risks of multinational financial business are generally higher than that of local business. Fluctuations in international financial markets will also swiftly reach China, causing instability in bank management.

Furthermore, these trends will make financial supervision more difficult. As foreign banks enter the market, illegal activities may increase. Certain foreign banks might, through legal or illegal means, transfer the risks of investment banking to commercial banking. All of this will challenge financial supervision.

According to a Bank of China study, in five years' time after China's WTO accession, foreign banks will gain a substantial market share of China's financial sector. Its findings is listed in Table 13.2.

Table 13.2 The market share of foreign banks in China's financial sector

	The market share of foreign banks in China's financial sector 5 years after WTO accession
MARKET SHARE OF FOREIGN BANKS	(%)
TYPES OF BUSINESS	
Deposits	
a. Foreign currency (rate of increase in market share)	15
b. Renminbi Loans (rate of increase in market share)	10
Loans	
a. Foreign currency (market share)	Can be > 33
b. Renminbi (market share)	15
Financial intermediary	> 50
Transaction in financial derivatives	Substantial
Investment bank business	Substantial
Market share of foreign banks 10 Years after WTO Accession	1/3

Source :"*Cost and Benefits Analysis of China's Banking Sector on WTO Accession*" by Dr. Wang Yuan-lung, Institute of International Finance, Bank of China, quoted by Shi Wei in *"Time Table for Market-Opening and Strategies For Various Industries on China WTO Accession"*, Table 5-7, Yangcheng Evening News Publications, 2001.

3. China's Banking Reform and WTO Accession

(This section is extracted from "China's Banking Reform and WTO", December 1999, "Economic Forum" of HKTDC web site.)

Banking reform, together with the state-owned enterprises (SOE) reform, are the two most important while unaccomplished reforms for China. China's commitment to further reform and to join the WTO are set to step up the pace of these two reforms by bringing in international competition.

China's Inefficient Banking System

China's rapid economic progress in the past two decades has made banking reform an increasingly urgent job for the country. As the economy becomes more and more market oriented, the banking system's inadequacies have become increasingly acute. The inability of the banking system to allocate the country's capital efficiently is arguably one of the most serious problems of the country's economic infrastructure. A lot of the country's savings is channeled by the banking system to many inefficient and loss-making enterprises. On the other hand, many promising and credit-worthy firms and individuals are deprived of the credit and financial services they need, and hence their development has been constrained. In many instances, firms have to run unnecessary risk as banks could not provide the financial services they need. Longer term, if this inefficient allocation process persists, the country's financial stability would also be compromised, as bad debts in the banking system, which are already rather high, continue to build up.

Banking reform has been going on since the mid-1980s. More rapid progress has been made in recent years.

In spite of the progress in the past decade, China's banking reform has still a long way to go. The four state-owned commercial banks, which account for about 70% of the banking sector's deposits and loans, are still wholly state-owned. While they are told to become commercial banks and they have become more selective in their lending, they are still obliged to do some mandatory policy loans and are still guided by the government's industrial policy and macroeconomic management initiatives. Even the 13 shareholding commercial banks are neither genuine shareholding nor real commercial banks. Except for the only one private bank, the absolute majority of shareholders of these banks are other state-owned institutions. They are free of policy loans, but are not completely immune from government's industrial policy. As to the large number of city commercial banks, they are very small, and even less commercial given the inevitable interference from local governments.

Domestic banks, especially the state banks, remain inefficient. In 1998, for example, all the four state banks had their return-on-assets (ROA) and return-on-equity (ROE) below 0.1% and 1.5%, based on reported figures. Many problems inherited from the past have yet to be sorted out. These include poor management, lax internal control, backward technology, lack of a credit culture, and too many staff (over 1.5 million employees). The shareholding commercial banks are in general better than the state banks. But on the whole, they are still relatively weak when compared with international standard.

One main problem for the banking sector is the high ratio of bad and doubtful assets. The estimated ratio of NPLs [non-performing loans] to assets vary between 20% and 50% for China's banking sector as a whole, and 25%–55% for the 4 state banks. If banks have to make provisions for these NPLs in accordance with international standards, many domestic banks are probably actually making losses, instead of their reported profits.

Foreign Banks as a Whole Still Play a Relatively Modest Role in China

The opening up of the banking market to foreign banks started in the mid-1980s, initially in the Special Economic Zones and subsequently expanded to other cities. But the scale of operations of foreign banks in China, taken as a whole, is still relatively modest. Total assets, liabilities, and outstanding loans of all foreign banks were USD31.4 billion, USD28.6 billion and

USD22.6 billion at September 99, equivalent to only 2.3%, 2.4% and 1.7% of the respective totals of domestic banks. Their main business is foreign currency business with foreign-invested enterprises (FIEs), with only limited services for the SOEs. In particular, businesses denominated in the RMB are strictly restricted to the FIEs in selected locations. Consumer banking with Chinese citizens is totally prohibited.

China's WTO entry is expected to lead to an overall opening-up of the country's banking sector in 5 years, providing long-awaited business opportunities for foreign banks.

The agreement reached between China and the US on China's WTO accession includes a phased opening up programme of China's banking market to foreign banks.

The biggest breakthrough in this deal is the opening of the consumer banking business. The potential of this business is enormous given the huge size of China's population and the high growth rate in the country's economy.

More importantly, the opening-up will come at a time when a range of consumer banking business will be fast growing. Credit card, mortgage credit and other consumer credit for education, cars, durable goods, traveling, etc. have only started to develop in recent years in China. Since then, these consumer loans have grown very strongly. But they accounted for less than 1% of total outstanding loans of the banking system at the end of 1998. Such loans are set to grow rapidly in the coming decade and beyond.

The implications for foreign banks' corporate and investment banking business will also be revolutionary.

All these come at a time when reform of the SOEs in China will be given a bigger push, generating a lot of new corporate finance, debt restructuring and other advisory services businesses for investment bankers. And as companies in China become more sophisticated in organizing their finances, good corporate banking services will have much more room to grow.

Along with the above, other banking businesses such as the transactions amongst financial institutions and treasury activities should also grow in line with the growth in the banking market. Another possible development is the increase in mergers and acquisitions amongst banks. This could be amongst domestic financial institutions, or cross-border, as some foreign banks may be interested in building up partnership with selected Chinese banks, taking advantage of their domestic network and market intelligence.

Overall, assuming that China's total lending of the banking system grows by 13% a year between 2002 and 2010, it would not be unreasonable to expect a compound growth rate of 40% per annum for foreign banks' lending in China, if the liberalization process goes ahead as expected. If foreign banks' lending grow at this rate, foreign banks would have an 8% market share in China's total loans by 2010.

The Opening-up will Undoubtedly Bring in Intense Competition for Domestic Banks

Given the relatively weak performance of many domestic banks, the opening up of the banking market is set to make life more difficult for most of them. Their market shares are set to fall and many of their good customers may be attracted to the foreign banks.

Most affected are likely to be the four state banks. Some of their good corporate customers will be the main future target of foreign banks. They are also too big and hence are less flexible, and they will take more time to reform themselves.

Similarly, the shareholding commercial banks would also feel the pressure. But the weakening of the dominant position of the state banks would provide the shareholding commercial banks with opportunities to grab market shares.

The competition to the city commercial banks will be modest, as their customers are mostly the small and medium-sized enterprises and low-income individuals that are less likely to be the targets of foreign banks.

But overall, China will benefit from further banking reform.

More competition will certainly undermine the market position of existing banks. But to the extent that the existing players have to reform and step up their efforts to better service their customers in order to survive the competition, customers will benefit from more competition. Banks will not only have to be more responsive to meet their customers' needs, they will also have to be more innovative in developing new products and more efficient in delivering their services.

An example of this is the likely development of electronic banking in China. Opening up the country's banking market to foreign banks is set to accelerate the modernization process of banking in China. To help overcome the competitive disadvantage caused by the lack of adequate bank branches, foreign banks will have to invest and rely more on various electronic means to attract and service their corporate and retail customers. As domestic banks respond to the challenge, China's banking market will mature much more rapidly than before.

The advertising industry in China is also likely to be another major beneficiary as foreign banks enter the retail market. Branding is the name of the game in retail banking. Foreign banks will have to invest a lot to enhance the image of their brand name in China.

Ultimately, the very purpose of having more efficient financial services is to enhance the competitive edge of the corporate sector, and to provide better services to the consumers. Some foreign banks could also help China's firms to compete more effectively as and when the latter expand into overseas markets.

Longer term, healthy competition will not only result in better customer service and more services innovation, but also a banking system that will be more vigilant in its risk assessment capabilities. When competition builds up, banks will have to be more precise in their risk-reward assessment of various types of business in the market. A more efficient banking system will therefore help China to allocate the country's scarce capital resources to firms and sectors which could use these resources most efficiently.

International competition is also an external catalyst to the banking reform and the integration of the country's banking system into the international framework.

Opening up the country's banking market to more international competition will not only give the domestic banking reform process more discipline, but also encourage the development of a banking environment which is more in line with international standards. As more and more foreign banks are involved and as their scale of operation grow, China's banking system, including the legal framework, as well as supervisory standards and practices, will move towards international norms and practices faster.

But changes will only come gradually and instability of the banking system due to excessive competition is unlikely.

Some people are worried that domestic banks would collapse due to the aggressive expansion of foreign banks. But it is unrealistic to expect changes to come overnight. Firstly there are many ways for the Chinese government to control the pace of foreign banks' expansion without breaching the WTO agreements. For example, when and how far the "one city-one branch" restriction will be relaxed is entirely at the discretion of the authorities. Secondly there are various institutional hurdles to resist changes for domestic banks if these were to happen too rapidly and stability is compromised. Thirdly, one should not underestimate the competitive advantage of domestic banks over foreign banks, such as their relationship with enterprises and the governments, and their large number of branches.

There is also concern that the high level of NPLs for the domestic banks would trigger a collapse of confidence on domestic banks once depositors are given a choice between domestic and multinational banks. Again this is an exaggeration as China's fiscal position is strong enough to contain the problems related to the current level of NPLs in the banking system.

The liberalization programme under the WTO deal is likely to prove a watershed change in China's banking scene.

C. SECURITIES AND ASSET MANAGEMENT

1. China's Commitments

a. foreign companies can deal directly in "B shares" (without Chinese intermediary) upon accession, including cross border trading in B shares, upon accession.
b. foreign firms can conduct domestic securities investment funds management business through a joint venture with foreign minority equity share (up to 33% equity share capital upon accession, 49 percent by three years after accession).

c. foreign firms can establish securities operation as a joint venture with a minority (up to 1/3) equity share for foreign investors to underwrite A, B, and H shares, and corporate and government debt and trade all these securities except A shares by 3 years after accession.

d. foreign firms are eligible for "special" membership in all exchanges upon accession.

e. criteria for authorization to deal in China's financial industry are solely prudental (i.e. contain no economic needs test or quantitative limits on licences.)

2. Further Elaboration by Chinese Officials: Difference Between Securities Sector and Securities Market

(This section is extracted from "CSRC releases WTO pledges regarding securities industry" dated 13 December 2001, "WTO" archives of Chinaonline web site, quoting a report by Xinhua News Agency.)

The China Securities Regulatory Commission (CSRC) has released on 11 Dec 2001 a statement explaining its commitments to open the securities sector after entering the World Trade Organization.

A CSRC spokesperson said that opening the securities sector and opening the securities market are two different concepts, and that the latter is part of the capital market and not included in the WTO agreement China signed, according to a report in the Dec. 11 [2001] Xinhua News Agency.

According to the spokesperson, opening the securities sector means allowing foreign securities service providers to participate in the securities business in China, and is a form of service trade as defined by WTO.

To be specific, it means that foreign securities services providers may enter the China market and provide intermediary services to Chinese residents who invest yuan in the domestic securities market. It does not involve the flow of capital across country borders.

On the other hand, opening the securities market means allowing foreign investors to freely buy and sell Chinese securities and it results in capital flow across country borders. The securities market is part of the capital market, or the capital account, and is not included in China's WTO agreements.

The spokesperson said that the stock exchanges would accept applications from foreign companies or their representative offices for B-share trading or special membership in Chinese stock exchanges.

China does not restrict the number of geographical locations of these joint ventures [securities operations], the spokesperson said.

Foreign capital flows into Chinese securities will be restricted.

Zhou Xiaochuan, chairman of the CSRC, said at a recent forum [end of 2001] that China's WTO entry does not mean foreign investments will be allowed into the A-share market.

Zhou reiterated what the CSRC spokesperson said above, that service trade and capital flows are two different concepts.

The rules of international service trade are made by the WTO, but opening the capital market is related to functions of the International Monetary Fund, he said. Therefore, the impact of China's WTO entry on the country's capital market is reflected more on the service sector, he said.

Zhou said that the time frame regarding allowing foreign capital into the A share market depends on the progress in making the yuan convertible on the capital account.

3. Impact on China's Securities Market

(This section is extracted from the research by Standard Chartered Bank entitled "Emerging and Transforming Securities Industry in China — Markets, Institutions and Legal System", August 2001, archives of "Economic Forum", HKTDC web site.)

a. Positive Impacts

— On local securities houses, positive impact will be a long term one, that is, foreign investors' penetration in JV securities houses and JV fund management companies will undoubtedly accelerate the pace of their reforms by bringing in international competition. It would also enable the reforms to target on international practices by forcing and also facilitating a learning process of the practices.

— On stock market, the A-share market opening will provide a new way of attracting foreign investment, which should help sustain the expansion of the stock market with large capital inflows to the country. This is important, not only because the SOEs reform requires more capital, especially quality capital, to facilitate the listing of more SOEs, but also because foreign investors would be a more effective supervisor over the performance of listed companies and market irregularities.

b. Negative Impacts

— On securities houses, given poor competitiveness of Chinese securities houses as compared to international securities houses as shown above, the emergence of JV securities firms is set to have an adverse impact on local securities houses. Given the nature of the securities business, which is basically a business of personal relationships, the impact would be that the JV houses take away both customers and talent staff from the local houses.

— On stock market, the negative impact would be an increased volatility of the market as a result of foreign investors' speculations with the help of JV securities houses. This is also set to bring about difficulties for the country's FX control.

c. Overall Impacts

Overall, the impact should be negative in short term, and positive in long term.

— The severity of short-term pain depends on the pace of opening-up. A too fast pace would be destructive leading to a collapse of domestic securities houses as well as the stock market. This will very much hinge on the approach and strategies as well as skills the government adopt to deal with the reforms and opening-up.

— How much of the positive long-term effect can be gleaned will also count on how the reforms and opening-up are carried out. Well-managed reforms and opening-up would enable China to maximize the long-term benefits, which will be incomparably more significant than the short-term pain.

d. A Balancing Act for the CSRC

Given the above, the CSRC is set to play a balancing act, to press ahead with the reforms and opening-up on the one hand, and to carefully control the pace of the reforms and opening-up in order to keep the risks under check and ensure the reforms and opening-up will not go in a destructive way on the other.

This means that, while bolder moves of reforms and opening-up are set to be forthcoming, basic reform approach would continue to be gradualist, with market restrictions being relaxed gradually. Meanwhile crackdown efforts on market irregularities will be constantly hanging on, and the "Groping in the river as you touch stones" will remain one of the strategies, so that over-killing of the reforms and opening-up would always happen while would be corrected immediately.

4. Expected Further Market Opening-up with WTO Accession

(This section is extracted from a research by the Standard Chartered Bank entitled "Emerging and Transforming Securities Industry in China – Markets, Institutions and Legal System", August 2001, archives of "Economic Forum", HKTDC web site.)

According to the research by the Bank, China was very cautious about the concessions regarding the opening-up of its securities markets, although the specific commitments are not that much; however, not committed does not necessarily mean will not happen. The bank is optimistic that the further opening will take place in the following areas:

a. A higher degree of foreign ownership in JV securities firms and the participation of the JV securities firms in A-share trading and B-share cross trading, are expected to follow if the committed opening-up goes well.

b. The key step for stock market opening-up relates to the opening of A-share market to foreign investors. While not mentioned in WTO agreement and hence not committed, it is believed that the opening is only a matter of time, as it is in China's own interest in terms of modernization and sustainable development of its stock market.

c. While the question is the timing and the institutional arrangements for the opening, major concern is the RMB's full convertibility. RMB's convertibility on capital account is not a requirement of WTO. Hence it is totally up to the Chinese government when to make this move. A sensible way for the government regarding the timing is likely to be that the move will be made only when it is judged not to disrupt the economy, society and markets. Given that RMB's non-convertibility would be the last defending line for market and economic stability after WTO entry, the RMB is not likely to become fully convertible in next 5 years. Hence a full opening-up of China's stock market is not anticipated until 2005.

d. However, a variant of QFII (Qualified Financial Institutional Investors) system is expected to be introduced to deal with the issue. Hence the opening is likely to be made possible 2–3 years after WTO entry when overall market opening-up and reforms in the context of WTO accelerate while the full RMB convertibility issue being put on the government's reform agenda. It is likely that the full convertibility will start with the stock market opening-up.

e. The merge of A-shares and B-shares are also something that will happen sooner or later, while it is also related to the RMB convertibility. The B-shares' opening to local residents last February indicates that the merger is already under the consideration of the government. It is likely to take place together with or just following the introduction of the variant of the QFII system. And this is likely be followed by a merge of A-shares and H-shares some time later.

f. Before these happen, an initiative to allow H-shares and red chips listed in Hong Kong to issue CDRs (Chinese Depositary Receipts) in domestic market, is currently under consideration. The benefits expected from the initiative would be three folds: to enable Chinese investors to invest in good Chinese names, to enable these good names to raise funds in domestic stock markets, and to raise the standards and quality of listed companies in China's stock market.

Expected Growth of China's Securities Market upon WTO Accession

[The Standard Chartered Bank made a rosy picture of China's stock market upon WTO accession. According to its estimate, China's stock market will witness a more rapid and exciting development over the next decade, driven by both demand and supply.]

It is expected that, over the next 10 years,

a) Market capitalization will nearly quadruple,
b) number of listed companies will double,
c) stock market prices will nearly triple,
d) number of investment accounts, as well as number of investors, will triple,
e) securities investment funds rise by 5 times, and
f) number of securities houses increase by 1.2 times.

The bank's forecast is summarized in Table 13.3.

Table 13.3 China's stock market development: Outlook for 2001–2010

CHINA'S STOCK MARKET DEVELOPMENT OUTLOOK FOR 2001–2010				
	2000	2005	2010	2010/2000 growth %
No. of listed companies	1088	1665	2170	99.4
Stock Market price index				
Shanghai A shares	2074	3680	5800	179.7
Shenzhen A shares	636	1080	1700	167.3
Market capitalization (RMB billion)	4809	10000	19000	295.1
No. of securities investment accounts (million)	58	107	174	200.0
No. of investors (million)	20	41	70	250.0
Valuation of Securities investment funds (RMB billion)	85	230	510	500.0
No. of securities houses	90	140	200	122.2

Source: Exhibit 57, *"Emerging and Transforming Securities Industry in China — Markets, Institutions and Legal System"*, August 2001, archives of "Economic Forum", HKTDC web site

chapter 14

Distribution, Transportation & Logistics and Tourism[1]

This chapter deals with China's commitments concerning the provision by foreign operators of services related to the cross-border movements of goods and persons. It covers wholesale and retail, movements of freight by different modes of transportation, and logistics, as well as the hotel and tourism industry.

DISTRIBUTION

A. China's Commitments

(The section on China's commitments is drawn from data provided in the US White House Factsheets on China WTO Accession, last updated on 17 February 2000, available on the web site of US-China Business Council, available at : http://www.uschina.org/ public/wto/factsheets. Certain adjustments were made according to China accession documents, marked in square bracket.)

1. Distribution Services

Prior to WTO accession, China generally prohibited companies from distributing imported products or providing related distribution services such as repair and maintenance services.

China agreed to liberalize its distribution system, one of the primary commitments sought by U.S. manufacturers and agricultural exporters.

China's distribution commitment is comprehensive, covering commission agents services, wholesaling, retailing, franchising, sales away from a fixed location, as well as related subordinated activities, such as inventory management or repair and maintenance services.

China also made specific commitments related to distribution, such as rental and leasing services, air courier services, freight forwarding, and packing services. These commitments are found elsewhere in China's schedule under the relevant services categories.

---

[1]Please refer to Appendix 3 of this book which details the commitments China made regarding opening up its service sectors.

Current restrictions for all products are phased-out within three years from the date of accession, unless specifically noted below. This tracks with China's commitment to phase in trading rights within three years.

2. Wholesale and Commission Agents Services

Within one year of accession, foreign service suppliers will be permitted to establish joint ventures.

Within two years from the date of accession, foreign majority equity share is allowed and all geographic and quantitative restrictions are eliminated.

Within three years from the date of accession, foreign service suppliers may establish wholly owned subsidiaries, [except for chemical fertilizers, processed oil and crude oil, see below for exceptions].

3. Retailing Services

Upon accession, foreign service suppliers will be permitted to establish no more than two joint ventures in the five Special Economic Zones (Shenzhen, Zhuhai Shantou, Xiamen, and Hainan) and four cities (Tianjin, Guangzhou, Dalian and Qingdao). Four joint ventures are permitted in Beijing and Shanghai. Two among the four joint ventures established in Beijing may set up branches in Beijing. Upon accession, foreign service suppliers will be permitted to establish as a joint venture in Zhengzhou and Wuhan.

Within two years from the date of accession, foreign majority equity share is allowed in these joint ventures, and geographic restrictions will be further liberalized to include all provincial capitals and Chongqing and Ningbo.

Within three years from the date of accession, there will be no restrictions on equity, geographic areas, or on the number of service suppliers. [see below for exceptions]

4. Franchising and Sales Away from a Fixed Location

Franchising, sales away from a fixed location (both wholesale and retail) and related subordinated activities are permitted without restrictions in three years.

5. Exceptions

For chain stores with more than 30 outlets that distribute different brands/types of motor vehicles and products subject to state trading from multiple suppliers, China will only permit minority equity participation within five years. Restriction will be lifted in five years.

Excluded from China's commitments are wholesaling [and agent commissioning] for salt, and wholesaling and retailing for tobacco.

China specified different end-points for liberalization for the product categories identified below. China is still obligated to provide market access and national treatment without restrictions, but there are no interim "benchmark" commitments as provided for other products.

— For chemical fertilizers, China will allow foreigners to provide wholesale and retail services within five years from the date of accession.
— For books, magazines and newspapers, China will allow foreigners to provide wholesale services within three years from the date of accession, and retail services within five years [retail not specified in China's Schedule].
— For pharmaceutical products and pesticides, China will allow foreigners to provide wholesale and retail services within three years from the date of accession.
— For mulching film, China will allow foreigners to provide wholesale services within three years from the date of accession, and retail services within [three] year.
— For crude oil and processed petroleum products, China will allow foreigners to provide wholesale services within five years from the date of accession. For processed petroleum products, retail services will be permitted within three years from the date of accession. (Note: Crude oil is not excepted from China's retail commitment, so it will be treated as any other product.)

6. Other Commitments

Upon accession, foreign companies may distribute all products manufactured in China, including those excepted products noted above. They may also provide the related subordinate services, as defined in Annex [2] of China's Services Schedule. Within one year from the date of accession, foreign-invested companies may distribute both products made in China as well as imported products.

This means companies can establish as either an equity joint venture of no more than fifty percent [upon accession], or as a contractual joint venture, in which the terms of the agreement are decided upon by the parties to the agreement, in accordance with Chinese law.

7. Services Related to Distribution

a. Maintenance and Repair Services

Foreign service suppliers will be able to provide repair and maintenance services for household consumer goods, motorcycle, auto, and office machinery, including computers.

Foreign service suppliers may establish as joint ventures upon accession, hold a majority equity share in one year, and be free of restrictions within three years.

b. Technical Testing and Analysis, Freight Inspection Services

Foreign service suppliers which have been engaged in inspection services in their home countries for more than three years and hold [US$350,000] in registered capital are permitted to establish joint ventures upon accession, [and] hold majority equity share within two years, and be free of restrictions within four years.

"Statutory inspection" services are excluded from freight inspection services commitments.

c. Rental and Leasing

China's commitments cover rental and leasing services for machinery and equipment without operators, and personal and household goods, except for videotapes.

Foreign service suppliers may establish as joint ventures upon accession, hold a majority equity share in one year, and be free of restrictions within three years.

Foreign service suppliers will have global assets of US$5 million.

d. Packaging Services

Foreign service suppliers may establish as joint ventures upon accession, hold a majority equity share within one year, and be free of restrictions within three years.

e. Courier Services

China's commitments cover land-based international courier services and all services related to an international shipment handled by an express carrier.

Foreign service suppliers are permitted to establish as a joint venture upon accession [with no more than 49% of equity share], hold a majority equity share within one year, and be free of restrictions within four years.

f. Storage and Warehousing Services

Foreign service suppliers are permitted to establish as joint ventures upon accession [with no more than 49% of equity share], hold a majority equity share within one year, and will be free of restrictions within three years.

g. Freight Forwarding Agency Services

In order to establish in China, foreign service suppliers should have at least three consecutive years experience. The minimum registered capital of a joint venture shall be no less than US $1 million.

Foreign service suppliers are permitted to establish a joint venture upon accession, and hold a majority equity share within one year. The length of operation shall not exceed 20 years.

After one year of operation in China, a joint venture may set up a branch if it adds US$120,000 to the original registered capital for each branch established.

All restrictions are eliminated within four years.

h. Advertising Services

[see Chapter 15]

i. Freight Transportation by Rail, and by Road in Trucks or Cars

[See section on "Transportation & Logistics" below].

B. Significance of China's Commitment

(The following article by Eric Wenberg[2] titled "Trading and Distribution in China under the WTO", originally appeared in the May 2001 edition of AgExporter Magazine and is extracted from the "Commentary" archives of Chinaonline.com dated 4 June 2001, with slight modifications effected by the editors.)

According to Eric Wenberg, senior analyst with Foreign Agriculture Service commodity and marketing programs in Washington, D.C., China's commitments on opening up the wholesale and retail markets mean great potential for foreign producers of goods and is as significant as the lowering of tariff and elimination of quotas. "Distribution rights are critical," he said.)

China's commitments on distribution extend the right to import and distribute products beyond China's state trading enterprises and a few privileged private companies. These are vital to the interests of U.S. agricultural exporters.

China's trade policy differs from the international norm in that foreign companies are generally prohibited from importing, warehousing and selling foreign products. Reduced tariffs are of little benefit if U.S. companies lack flexibility in managing their supply chain.

China heavily regulates distribution of imported products. Foreign companies, including U.S. exporters, are generally prohibited from distributing products that are imported into China. When a foreign company formally registers to conduct business, this limitation is printed on a business license.

These restrictions, which have the effect of creating inefficiencies, tend to fragment the import market. This, in turn, constrains the number of companies that import, complicating supply chain management and reducing foreign investments in distribution infrastructure. They also interrupt clear transmission of market information from consumers to company executives.

Regulation has also meant importers and distributors able to buy abroad and sell products into China's domestic economy are few, while competition to find these companies is fierce.

Before WTO accession, a foreign company could easily transfer assets to, or control, a subsidiary company. This limited the willingness of some companies to expand their distribution network. China's regulations have created a scarcity of reliable distributors and importers.

---

[2]Eric Wenberg is a senior analyst with Foreign Agriculture Service commodity and marketing programs in Washington, D.C.

Moreover, with more intermediaries needed, corruption abounds. Competition to find reliable partners is fierce.

Trouble with Trading Rights

The other side of the distribution bind is the right to import. Before WTO accession this right was confined to Chinese companies or foreign-invested enterprises (FIEs). But these firms were limited in what they could do.

Joint venture companies might market products they produce in China, but they were unable to import and market products from the United States, even if they are identical to the joint venture product.

Meanwhile, Chinese companies could get authority to import, but most were legally blocked from having foreign currency. Before accession, the only way Chinese importers could effectively operate was to find a partner with access to a foreign currency bank account and form a joint venture.

Foreign representative offices were closely monitored and legally constrained. For example, a foreign company without the proper licensing or corporate structure could either sell a product or warehouse it, but not both.

This policy made the simple practice of clearing and warehousing goods for sale an enormous headache for exporters. The U.S.-China Business Council ranked this as one of U.S. companies' top-three concerns in doing business in China.

Successful companies have strategies for distribution. They can register in special free-trade zones where regional officials have authority to supersede some restrictions. They can create a Chinese company. They can also develop a business partnership with an importer with rights to process documents.

How WTO will Help

U.S. trade negotiators used the WTO accession process to address these concerns. The resulting agreement included provisions that address the issue of trading and distribution rights—a subject rarely seen in multilateral negotiations.

Once these reforms are in place, Chinese companies will be forced to compete more directly against each other and foreign firms. This ultimately will give Chinese consumers greater access to a diversity of goods.

Generally, restrictions on distribution of products are to be phased out within three years of the date of China's WTO accession.

There are certain trade areas where China's regulations will still apply, such as tobacco and salt. Still, the benefits of WTO are getting good reviews from companies in China now.

TRANSPORTATION & LOGISTICS

A. China's Commitments[3]

1. Maritime Transport

China commits to open up maritime transport service including international transport (freight & passengers), auxiliary services, such as maritime cargo handling services, customs clearance services, container & depot services and maritime agency services.

Foreign companies operating a fleet under the national flag of the People's Republic of China will be allowed, under the following conditions:

— Foreign service suppliers are permitted to establish joint venture shipping companies.
— Foreign investment shall not exceed 49 per cent of the total registered capital of the joint venture.
— The chairman of board of directors and the general manager of the joint venture shall be appointed by the Chinese side.

2. Land Transport

China has committed to open up freight transportation both by rail and by road in trucks or cars, under the following conditions:

— only in the form of joint ventures, with foreign investment not to exceed 49 per cent.
— for rail transport, within three years after China's accession, foreign majority ownership will be permitted and within six years after China's accession, wholly foreign-owned subsidiaries will be permitted.
— for road transport, within one year after China's accession, foreign majority ownership will be permitted, within three years after China's accession, wholly foreign-owned subsidiaries will be permitted.

3. Air Transport

In air transport, China currently allows only two types of services: aircraft repair and maintenance services, as well as computer Reservation System (CRS) services.

a. Aircraft Repair and Maintenance

Foreign service suppliers are permitted to establish joint venture aircraft repair and maintenance enterprises in China with Chinese holding controlling shares. Licenses for the establishments of joint ventures are subject to economic needs test.

China also requires that the joint ventures thus formed have the obligation to undertake business in the international market.

---

[3]This section on China's commitment is derived from the China's Services Schedule, see Appendix 3 in this book.

b. Computer Reservation System (CRS) Services

Foreign Computer Reservation System, when having agreements with Chinese aviation enterprises and Chinese Computer Reservation System, may provide services to Chinese aviation enterprises and Chinese aviation agents by connecting with Chinese Computer Reservation System.

Foreign Computer Reservation System may provide services to representative offices and sales offices established in the destination cities in China by foreign aviation enterprises which have the right to engage in business according to the bilateral aviation agreements.

Direct access to and use of foreign Computer Reservation System by Chinese aviation enterprises and agents of foreign aviation enterprises are subject to approval of the General Administration of Civil Aviation of China (CAAC).

4. Inland Waterway

China will allow international shipping in ports open to foreign vessels to operate in its inland waterway.

5. Elaboration by Chinese Officials

(This piece is translated by Chinaonline.com, appeared in news archive of "transportation industry" on 18 December, 2001, titled "China lifts foreign-investment restrictions on freight-transport sector".)

The 7 December 2001 Zhongguo Shang Bao (Business Daily) reported that the Ministry of Communications and Ministry of Foreign Trade and Economic Cooperation jointly issued new rules regarding foreign investment in the sector that handles the road transportation of freight.

According to the new rules, foreign investors are permitted to form joint ventures or wholly owned companies engaged in road-cargo transportation, storage, loading and unloading; vehicle maintenance and repair; and other supplementary services related to road transportation.

China promised to open these services to foreign participation as part of the country's agreements for entrance into the WTO.

Stipulations contained in the new rules include investment forms, ownership changes, business scope and scale expansion and operational-period extensions for foreign-invested road-transportation companies.

The new rules require the Chinese partner of a joint venture road-transportation company to apply for the establishment of the company with transportation authorities in the city where the joint venture will be located.

Provincial and municipal transportation authorities should review an application within 15 business days, and the Ministry of Communications should decide within 30 business days whether to approve the joint venture.

The government review and approval should not exceed 60 days.

According to the new rules, the previous restrictions on foreign ownership have been lifted.

Although the restrictions on foreign ownership have been lifted, the rules stipulate that a foreign investor may still voluntarily agree to own less than 49 percent of the joint venture and have this included as part of the contract.

China did not promise to lift restrictions on foreign investment in its road-passenger transportation sector, and thus, current restrictions apply.

B. Impact on China's Logistics Market

1. Expected Size of China's Logistics Market

(The following section is retrieved from the archives of "Industrial Profile" of WTO Accession Monitor, Hong Kong Trade Development Council ("HKTDC") web site, an article titled "China's Logistics Market", by Si Ping dated 15 October 2001.)

The modern logistics marker, known as the third profit source, is heating up following network fever. Perhaps because Chinese modern logistics enterprises have not grown up, foreign giants have shown keen interest in China's logistics market. Federal Express, DHL Worldwide Express and American President Lines Co. Ltd. all expressed their intention to find a niche in China's logistics market.

According to World Bank estimates, the logistics cost makes up 16.7% of the GDP. Suppose China's GDP in 2000 is RMB 8,900 billion, the goods flow cost would be RMB 1,335 billion, if the cost is taken as 15% of the GDP and would be RMB 1,780 billion if the cost is taken as 20% of the GDP. The total spending on logistics by a third party is about 10% according to the 1999 survey by the China Warehousing Association.

The survey shows that 45% of the enterprises would choose new goods distributors within one or two years and 75% will opt for new types of goods distributors instead of the original warehousing and transportation enterprises and 60% of the enterprises would contract out integrated goods flow to new types of goods distributors. This indicates the considerable size of the logistics market.

According to executive vice-president of the China Goods Flow and Procurement Federation Ding Junfa, China's logistics industry will enter a period of rapid development because it is impossible for the national economy to realise a shift from extensive operation to intensive operation without development of the logistics market.

With WTO entry moving closer, the challenges by foreign logistics giants are being increasingly felt. China has already made the following commitments when reaching agreements with the United States and EU concerning goods flow:

— China will lift restrictions and give foreign companies the right to undertake goods distribution, whereby foreign companies may distribute both imported products and products made in China. This will be executed in wholesale, transportation and service trades in which there are the most stringent restrictions with regard to distribution.

— China will lift all the restrictions on foreign service providers and allow them to enter the current market, without any restrictions with regard to market access or market activities. Similar commitment has also been made in auxiliary distribution service, such as leasing, express delivery, warehousing, goods cabin, technical testing and analysis and packaging service. Restrictions in these areas will be lifted in 3–4 years. During the period, foreign service providers may build wholly-owned subsidiaries or operational organisations.

The future challenge will come not only from foreign countries but also the domestic buyer's market. It is, therefore, the most practical for Chinese enterprises to lower logistics cost, to improve their competitiveness.

The challenges will also bring about development opportunities for Chinese logistics enterprises. It will help boost the awareness of improving competitiveness and motivate the development of the logistics industry and also accelerate the pace of building a number of modern goods distribution enterprises capable of competing on the international market.

The challenges will make Chinese ports become modern logistics centres. With the development of the modern logistics industry, the ports will have to increase transit goods centres and transportation and warehousing facilities to replace the traditional loading and unloading and stockpiling practices.

WTO entry will also stimulate the influx of foreign capital and the development of imports and exports and that will stimulate the demand for logistics.

China has made gratifying achievements in the goods distribution industry. The Shanghai Customhouse has already built an international express mail regulation centre at the Pudong international airport, which handles 7,500 pieces of express mail an hour. China's EMS has also offered a series of new services. There is, however, still a long way to go before Chinese logistics enterprises are able to compete equally with foreign giants.

2. Tapping China's Logistics Market

(This section is extracted from a report "China's Freight Forwarding and Logistics", July 2000, "Economic Forum/Service Industry" of HKTDC's web site. This report was written for Hong Kong-based freight forwarding and logistics services companies, particularly small and medium-sized enterprises (SMEs), and others interested in the industry.)

China's accession to the WTO is widely expected to boost China's trading activities with other countries. There will also be a gradual phase-out of restrictions on distribution and retailing.

All these imply that the demand for quality freight forwarding and logistics services (FFLS) will escalate in the coming years.

There is already substantial foreign involvement in China's freight forwarding market, although most foreign companies are only authorised to conduct business in international freight forwarding. Moreover, the logistics industry is still evolving, and the potential for growth is huge. China's entry into the WTO will result in a significant liberalisation in distribution-related services for foreign participation.

Freight Forwarding and Logistics Services in China

There is little integration in the provision of FFLS in China. Most companies participate in one or a few of the sub-sectors, rather than providing a total service for the whole logistics flow.

There are over 1,500 licensed international freight forwarding operators in China. Of these around 450 are Sino-foreign joint ventures. They are mainly responsible for the international aspect of the freight management. The inland transportation within China from and to the seaports/airports is currently handled by the domestic freight forwarders who usually are sub-contracted by the international freight forwarders. This picture will change in the future when foreign-invested freight forwarders are allowed to conduct domestic business.

Current Policy and Regulations on Foreign Participation

The provision of integrated logistics services is a new concept in China. The sector is generally viewed as a set of individual industries, such as trucking and freight forwarding. The regulatory environment for FFLS within which foreign firms must operate reflects this understanding of the sector.

Currently, foreign freight forwarders can only set up minority-owned joint ventures in China, although wholly-owned operations have been allowed on exceptional cases. They may also appoint a Chinese forwarder and set up a local representative office.

China's WTO Accession Will Lead to Substantial Liberalisation

The demand for both international and domestic FFLS will escalate after China becomes a member of the WTO. Exports are expected to rise by an additional 2.4% per year over the first five years of accession, while the effect on imports could be higher. On the domestic front, restrictions on distribution of most products will be phased out over the next few years. Foreign firms will be able to distribute imported products as well as those made in China.

China has made significant market access commitments in services related to distribution including maintenance and repair, rental and leasing, packaging, courier, freight transportation, storage and warehousing and freight forwarding. Most restrictions are to be phased out by the middle of this decade, at which time foreign service suppliers would be allowed to set up wholly-owned subsidiaries in most sectors.

While the market size of FFLS will increase substantially, so will be the intensity of competition. China's WTO accession will therefore bring both opportunities and challenges for foreign companies.

TOURISM, TOUR OPERATORS AND THE HOTEL INDUSTRY

A. China's Commitments[4]

1. Hotels (including apartment buildings and restaurants)

a. Foreign services suppliers may construct, renovate and operate hotel and restaurant establishments in China in the form of joint ventures with foreign majority ownership permitted and within four years after accession, wholly foreign-owned subsidiaries will be permitted.
b. Foreign managers, specialists including chefs and senior executives who have signed contracts with joint venture hotels and restaurants in China shall be permitted to provide services in China.

2. Travel Agency & Tour Operator

a. Foreign services suppliers who meet the following conditions are permitted to provide services in the form of joint venture travel agencies and tour operators in the holiday resorts designated by the Chinese government and in the cities of Beijing, Shanghai, Guangzhou and Xi'an upon accession:

— a travel agency and tour operator mainly engaged in travel business;
— Annual world-wide turnover exceeds US$ 40 million.

b. Capital Requirements

The registered capital of joint venture agency/tour operator shall be no less than RMB 4 million. Within three years after China's accession, the registered capital shall be no less than RMB 2.5 million. Within three years after accession foreign majority ownership will be permitted.

Within six years after accession, wholly foreign-owned subsidiaries will be permitted and geographic restrictions will be removed.

c. Business Scope Allowed

The business scope of the travel agency/tour operator is as follows:

i.   travel and hotel accommodation services for foreign travellers which can be made directly with transportation and hotel operators in China covering such operations;
ii.   travel services and hotel accommodation services for domestic travellers which can be made directly with transportation and hotel operators in China covering such operations;

---

[4]This section on China's commitment is derived from China's Services Schedule, see Appendix 3 in this book.

iii. conducting of tours within China for both domestic and foreign travellers, and

iv. travellers check cashing services within China

d. Business Scope Disallowed

Joint venture or wholly-owned travel agencies and tour operators are not permitted to engage in the activities of Chinese traveling abroad and to Hond Kong China, Macao China and Chinese Taipei

B. Impact on the Chinese Tourism Industry

1. Size & Prospect of China's Tourism Industry

(*Extracted from archives of "tourism", Chinaonline.com, an article titled "China's tourism industry earns US$54.58B in '00", 17 January 2001, also quoting a report by Renmin Ribao (People's Daily) dated 11 January 2001.*)

In 2000 the number of foreign visitors broke the 10 million mark for the first time to reach 10.19 million, an increase of 20 percent over 1999. Meanwhile, the number of domestic tourists reached 744 million.

China's tourism industry revenue totaled RMB 451.9 billion (US$54.58 billion) in 2000, an increase of nearly 13 percent over 1999, He Guangwei, director of the China National Tourism Administration, announced on 11 January at the National Tourism Work Conference.

Of the total, foreign currency revenue amounted to US$16.2 billion, up 15 percent, and domestic tourism income reached RMB 317.55 billion (US$38.35 billion), an increase of 12 percent.

According to He, the tourism industry in 2001 expects to handle 90 million people crossing China's borders, including 11 million foreign tourists, and plans to bring in US$18 billion in foreign currency revenue.

In addition, the industry will serve 760 million domestic tourists who will generate revenues of RMB 350 billion (US$42.27 billion). Total tourist revenue in 2001 is expected to reach RMB 500 billion (US$60.39 billion), an increase of 11 percent over 2000.

(*The following paragraphs are retrieved from "Have plan, will travel: China unveils tourism strategy", archives of "Tourism", Chinaonline.com dated 11 January 2001, quoting 9 January issue of Renmin Ribao Haiwaiban (People's Daily Overseas Edition).*)

The China National Tourism Administration's development goals for the 10th Five-Year Plan (2001 to 2005) were published in the 9 January issue of Renmin Ribao Haiwaiban (People's Daily Overseas Edition.)

By 2005, China hopes to receive 85 million tourists and to take in RMB 18.3 million (US$ 2.2 million) in foreign exchange income from tourism. In addition, it aims to bring in RMB

500 billion (US$60.39 billion) from 1.1 billion domestic tourists and to receive 16.36 million overseas Chinese tourists on the mainland. If all goes as planned, by 2005 tourism will make up 5.8 percent of China's gross domestic product, of RMB 750 billion (US$90.58 billion).

If the goals of the 10th Five-Year Plan are reached, tourism will bring in more than US$90 billion in foreign exchange income, boost the GDP by RMB 3 trillion (US$362.32 billion) and create jobs for more than 8 million people.

At the end of 1999, China had 237,000 hotels and guesthouses, of which 7,035 hotels and 889,400 guesthouses served foreign guests. Of China's 292 transportation companies and 7,326 travel agencies, 1,256 are international, the story added.

Tourism makes up 10.7 percent of the world's combined GDP and accounts for 11.3 percent of global consumption. Currently, China's figures stand at less than half of this figure, the story added.

At the same time the World Tourism Organization predicted that China will attract 130 million tourists annually by the year 2020, making it the world's top tourist destination.

(*The following is retrieved from "China To Be World's Top Tourist Draw By 2020", archives of "Tourism", Chinaonline.com, 15 October 1999*)

The latest report by the organization also predicted that Chinese tourists traveling abroad will also become a formidable group by that time as well, rising to nearly 100 million a year.

Currently, China attracts 24 million foreign tourists annually, while the number of Chinese travelers going abroad has quietly grown to 8.4 million.

By 2002, tourism in Asia will increase to 405 million, up from 84.4 million in 1995, and one quarter of these tourists will head to China, the group forecasts.

2. Impact on China's Hotel Industry

(*The following section is an article retrieved from the "Tourism" archives of Chinaonline.com dated 26 July 2000, original title "Hotel Sector may have reservations about WTO entry"*)

A slew of Chinese industries are bracing for the onrush of competition triggered by entry into the World Trade Organization. The hotel industry is not exception.

A recent report in the July 19 edition of Zhongguo Luyou Bao (China Tourism News) delineates eight major challenges faced by China's hotel sector after WTO entry. Here they are:

Small- and Medium-size Hotels to be Adversely Affected

It is explicitly stipulated in the China-U.S. WTO Agreement that within three years, China shall permit operators who are capable of building 100 percent foreign-owned hotels to enter into the Chinese market without limitation; these operators shall be allowed to hold the majority equity upon the entry.

The all-round entry of foreign capital will produce far-reaching influence over the development of the hotel sector. On the one hand, foreign direct investment will increase substantially. As an important component of the supporting system of social services, the hotel sector has been of great appeal to foreign investors because of its high profit margin and stable value-added capacity.

On the other hand, foreign investments in hotels will cover a wider range of size and scope. Subjects of investment will extend from large multinationals to smaller companies. Target localities will extend from large- and medium-size cities and tourist attractions in the central and western regions. Objects of investment will be more diversified from business hotels to convention hotels, apartment hotels and student hotels.

The direct competition on a larger basis will impose significant impact upon the traditional market currently held by most Chinese hotels. Many small- and medium-size hotels with stable customer sources will bear the brunt. Next will be hotels with comprehensive functions such as convention, exhibition and apartment.

State-Owned Hotels to Restructure

With regard to the ownership structure, the influx of foreign capital may result in major adjustments of existing Chinese hotels. Solely foreign-owned hotels, joint ventures and Chinese-foreign cooperative hotels will increase, constituting a threat to hotels of other types of ownership, especially state ownership. The aggregate number of foreign-funded hotels will swell further to increase the dependence of the hotel sector on foreign capital.

Currently, state-owned hotels are evidently disadvantaged in the market competition with foreign-invested hotels either in terms of the construction of customer network, human resources or managerial expertise. The pattern of competition following the WTO entry will directly form a strong impact on these enterprises, which will eventually lead to the division of this camp. Some of them, primarily the 12 listed hotels such as the Shanghai New Jingjiang, the Guangzhou East and the Hunan Huatian will continue building a modern corporate system through direct dialogues so as to enhance their core competitiveness. The others will go bankrupt or be taken over and reorganized. In short, the new round of competition will enable hotel enterprises to become more independent market subjects.

Overseas Hotels to Launch Massive Attack

According to provisions of related WTO agreements, China shall further reduce barriers of market entry and widen the service trade market. It can be predicated that foreign operators will become more enthusiastic about the development of the immense China market. The frequency and intensity of business communication will undergo a qualitative leap. That will produce adequate customer sources for a new takeoff of tourist hotels. The number of overseas tourists and their duration of stay in China will leap to a new high level.

However, in the new round of competition for customer sources, Chinese hotels will feel the group attack of overseas hotels. Overseas hotels can enlarge their market share of customer sources and form a flow of customers within their own brands by taking advantages of information collection, hotel reservation, marketing promotion, management and training. For instance, the Holiday Inn Group managed 23 hotels in China in 1998. Shangri-La and New World have considered China as their first choice of overseas business expansion.

The influx of overseas hotel groups will also promote the diversion of traditional customer sources. Special hotels characterized by more definite functions and more specialized services, such as apartment hotels and convention/exhibition hotels, will play a leading role in the diversion by taking advantage of their mature service modes and rich experiences. In the meantime, consumption concepts of customers will become mature.

Industry Management to Feature Equal Treatment

Changes in the composition of a trade will inevitably lead to the reform of management bodies of the trade. According the WTO regulations, China shall gradually open its sector of service trade. That means administrative interference will be changed fundamentally. China will have to rely on market orientation and legal construction as the main means of trade management so as to realize real national treatment towards foreign-funded hotels. In the mediation of conflicts between Chinese-funded hotels and foreign-funded hotels, biased and discriminative measures will have to be abandoned. Instead, strict law enforcement and rational inducement shall be employed to create a fair and reasonable atmosphere for competition.

Specifically, China needs to do the following preparatory work for the future open market:

1) Accelerate the adjustment of policies relating to the utilization of foreign capital so that related policies can jibe with international practices and the utilization of foreign capital can scale up in tourism;
2) Continue to give the government a leading role in the development of the trade; and
3) Speed up the drafting and completion of laws and regulations on the trade management.

Some Hotels to Merge or go Bankrupt

Foreign capital permitted for entry will enter China's hotel sector in two forms. One is direct investment from specialized hotel groups with solid financial strength. The other is capital operation though purchase, merger and trust by mainly smaller hotel companies and investors. The latter is different from the former in the choice of profit source. They pay more attention to the value-added capacity of the hotel and hope to obtain considerable interests during a relatively short construction cycle.

Due to the drastic difference between state-owned hotels and foreign-invested hotels in general competitiveness, it is predicted that a number of Chinese hotels will become the target of foreign mergers or acquisitions. Meanwhile, the upgrading competition will accelerate the concentration of profits. Hotels that lack well defined market strategies and clear-cut market positioning will go bankrupt and become new market subjects after debt reorganization, bankruptcy liquidation and further assets operation. During the reorganizations and adjustments, foreign capital will play a more active and important role than before.

It is noteworthy that quite a number of Chinese hotels are currently in a state of insolvency. Two reasons account for their still staying out of the bankruptcy proceedings.

First, as a downstream industry in the chain of national economy, hotels lack operational exit following the bankruptcy liquidation and can hardly shift to other purposes.

Second, owing to the ambiguous definition of investment subject characterized by such as the fusion of government functions and enterprise management, there exist many abnormal phenomena against the inherent law of market. Hotel enterprises do not want to or are not willing to go bankrupt. That explains why the entire industry has maintained operation despite the low efficiency. Once a sizable capital is injected, this last bubble will burst, which will eventually force the enterprises back to the rational operation according to the market law.

Trained Personnel to Become the Rage at the Market

The quality of the human resources is the decisive factor in hotel competition. Immediately after the WTO entry, foreign hotel groups, out of the strategic consideration of swiftly occupying the Chinese market, may collect trained personnel globally. The aggregate of foreign national managers and technicians will thus drastically increase. But from a long-term point of view, foreign enterprises will boldly employ local personnel to avoid blunders such as excessive export of management, rash preparatory work and improper personnel allocation.

The management mode and corporate ideal of foreign-invested hotels demand a large number of useful trained personnel. Foreign-invested hotels will solve this problem through mature training modes. Currently, most foreign hotel groups have established a complete training system. For instance, the Holiday Inn Group has established multiple Holiday Inn colleges around the world to train general managers and chief food and beverage supervisors for member hotels.

Hilton Group has established the Hilton Hotel Management College jointly with Houston University. Besides centralized training, foreign hotels have developed a complete system for in-house on-the-job training. As to the selection of trained personnel, they will ensure a wide and timely selection through a dynamic talent tracking system, large-capacity talent bank and highly reputable international headhunting companies.

The seizing and re-molding of skilled personnel by foreign enterprises will produce a significant impact on state-owned hotels regarding talent stock and talent appraisal. In this battle for seizing talents, it is impossible to build any non-technical barriers by raising salaries, imposing personnel restriction and employing other means against the law of talent cultivation. The realistic alternative is to adopt market techniques such as the incentive of options and creation of an environment for fair competition.

Development of New Technologies Most Pressing

Although China's tourist hotel sector has made impressive progress, it is an undeniable fact that many advanced practical technologies and managerial expertise are still abroad. China's hotel sector still remains at the stage of imitation and borrowing, and few Chinese hotels have set up their own R&D center. After the WTO entry, more and deeper direct dialogues will make the Chinese rapidly realize their slowness in technical and managerial innovation and force them to start their own R&D in the ruthless market competition.

Large hotel groups should set up technical development center as early as possible to conduct proprietary research and development on operation means such as information network system management, e-commerce and individualistic service technology under the condition of modern materials and technologies.

Such research and development should become the buttress of the technical innovation of small- and medium-size hotels. They should develop multiple forms of industry-academy-research integration and establish open and stable cooperation relations with colleges and universities and scientific research institutes. In addition, they should enhance international cooperation to track and absorb the world most advanced scientific and technological achievements to form their own technological advantages.

Hotels to Become More Affordable

The elimination of tariff barriers will enable hotels to install higher-grade hardware facilities at relatively low cost. They will also be benefited regarding equipment, articles, food and raw materials. All the benefits will eventually pass on to customers through the allocation by market mechanism. People may enjoy facilities and services at lower price not by sacrificing the service quality. Hotels will be truly in a popular style. Investment that concentrates in star-level hotels at the enticement of profit will turn to projects that are closer to popular consumption.

chapter 15

The Professional Services and Summary of All Services Sectors[1]

China's WTO accession commitments also include a variety of professional services, yet space limitation does not permit us to detail the commitments on each of these services. Therefore in this chapter we are going to outline the impacts only of some of the more common professional services. Concerned readers are advised to go direct to the schedules for specific details. We shall wind up discussion on services with a chart provided jointly by the Hong Kong Trade Development Council and the Trade and Industry Department of the Hong Kong Government comparing pre- and post-WTO arrangements in all different services sectors.

1. ARCHITECTURE/CONSTRUCTION/ENGINEERING/INFRASTRUCTURE/PROPERTY

(*This piece is retrieved from archives of the web site of Hong Kong Trade Development Council ("HKTDC") entitled "China's WTO Accession: Bricking Up the future - Infrastructure and Real Estate Opportunities for Hong Kong on the Chinese Mainland", 13 December 2001. Although it targets at Hong Kong companies, its principles can be applied, with due modifications, to foreign companies outside Hong Kong.*)

China's WTO accession opens up opportunities in four main areas, namely, road infrastructure, real estate development, property services, and architectural and engineering services.

Road infrastructure: The mainland government plans to substantially upgrade the domestic road network to cater for the needs of the transportation, distribution and logistics industries and aid the development of inland provinces. Hong Kong investors are strong in providing a total solution to the financial and technical requirements of a road project. As the leading foreign investor/developer, Hong Kong is expected to continue to play an important role in constructing highways to link up the nation. To build and manage a modern highway network, expertise in technical services such as feasibility studies, urban planning, public transportation management, environmental impact assessment, etc is needed, providing opportunities for Hong Kong companies. It is

---

[1]Please refer to Appendix 3 of this book which details the commitments China made regarding professional services.

expected that with China's accession to the WTO, project tendering procedures will be more in line with international practices, giving a more level playing field for Hong Kong players.

Real estate: With a strong rise in urban residents' interest in buying their own homes, the government's ambitious housing reform policy will enter a critical phase over the next few years. In the coming five years, China will build a total of 5.7 billion square metres of houses, of which urban houses will be 2.7 billion square metres, up 15% from that of the past five years. Hong Kong companies are very experienced in developing community housing projects in China. They have strong supporting linkage services to offer a total solution for a real estate project. These services include property services, architectural and engineering services, financial services, marketing and professional services. Generally speaking, Hong Kong real estate development companies are ahead of their mainland counterparts in the management of construction projects, and Hong Kong companies have a comparative advantage when it comes to quality of construction. In addition to the high-end market, they are also expected to seek opportunities in the potentially huge market for the increasingly affluent middle class in major cities.

Property services: Property services cover three major sectors, namely property agency, property management and surveying (valuation, building surveying and land surveying). It is expected that Hong Kong companies will continue to be the dominant foreign players after China's WTO accession, because Hong Kong companies have accumulated substantial experience and market knowledge and are more creative in marketing strategy and flexible in corporate management. As the quality of property services has become an important element in determining the success of a real estate proejct, the target customers of Hong Kong's property services companies will in the future no longer be restricted to foreign/Hong Kong developers, but mainland local developers as well.

Architectural and engineering services: Hong Kong architectural firms now occupy a position of strength in the mainland market. Many Hong Kong engineering companies have already established a presence on the mainland. China's entry to the WTO would stimulate demand for architectural and engineering services in construction-related projects such as hotels, high-rise buildings, infrastructure development and housing. In the housing sector, large-scale projects in major urban cities would provide opportunities for Hong Kong architectural firms as mainland home buyers are increasingly concerned about design and quality standards. Although Hong Kong engineering services have successfully expanded in the general building, hotel and luxury housing market, they will face competitive challenges in the middle price range commodity housing market in China.

Hong Kong's overall expertise and experience in road construction, real estate development, town planning, urban facilitates management and construction related services should make Hong Kong companies a major force in capturing the opportunities offered by China's urbanisation process. They are particularly suited to play the role of catalyst in this transformation process by providing management skills, professional knowledge and funding sources. With substantial China market know-how, Hong Kong companies are also ideal partners for other foreign players who are trying to break into the mainland market.

2. ADVERTISING

(This piece is extracted from an article entitled "China's Advertising Market Holds Great Promise", 15 May 2001, archives of "Service Industries", WTO Accession Monitor of HKTDC web site. Similar to the previous section, this is also written for Hong Kong audience, but the principles also apply to foreign firms.)

China is Asia's second largest advertising market after Japan. According to a survey by ACNielsen, China's advertising market led the region with a staggering 57% growth in 2000, with total expenditure amounting to US$9.7 billion.

The consumer market has become very competitive in China in recent years. In the past, only foreign brands would spend huge amounts on advertising, but now domestic companies have emerged as major advertisers. According to the ACNielsen report, last year's top 10 advertising accounts were all domestic brands.

China's huge advertising market can be divided into three tiers according to advertising expenditure. The first tier includes cities like Shanghai, Beijing and Guangzhou, which together account for half to total advertising expenditure in the country. The second tier covers the four provinces of Zhejiang, Jiangsu, Sichuan and Liaoning; while the third tier covers the remaining 23 provinces. Competition is intense in China's advertising market, especially in Shanghai, Beijing and Guangzhou.

Market Regulations

With a few exceptions, foreign advertising agencies were not allowed to set up branches or invest in domestic advertising agencies before 1992. Even today [just upon WTO accession], foreign advertising agencies can only set up equity or contractual joint ventures and cannot operate as sole proprietors in China. Foreign firms have to obtain approval from the central government for participation in advertising business and must apply to MOFTEC and State Administration of Industry and Commerce (SAIC) for permission to establish joint ventures (JVs). Foreign equity in these JVs may not exceed 49%, and the registered capital must not be less than US$300,000. The content of advertising is also subject to strict supervision according to law.

Foreign advertising agencies first entered the China market in 1993. Most of them chose to set up branches with local partners in Beijing, Shanghai and Guangzhou.

The majority of these, such as O&M, Leo Burnett, Saatchi & Saatchi, McCann-Erikson, Euro RSCG and DDB, are multinational companies. Many of them are members of the Association of Accredited Advertising Agents of Hong Kong. In addition, there are some smaller JV advertising agencies that specialise in design, production, photography and other aspects.

According to China's WTO commitments, foreign firms will be permitted to hold controlling shares in advertising agencies in China after its WTO accession. With the lowering of import tariffs on consumer goods, the gradual lifting of restrictions on the distribution of foreign products and the growing interest of foreign companies in the China market upon WTO entry, competition is expected to intensify.

Upon accession, Hong Kong-based advertising agencies mainly operated in the first-tier cities of Shanghai, Beijing and Guangzhou. With the gradual maturity of the first-tier market, growth of the second-tier market is expected to accelerate with the help of local governments.

Taking advantage of the current market development, small- and medium-sized Hong Kong advertising agencies can consider venturing into the mainland market. Hong Kong advertising agents are well-known for their advanced production and printing technologies as well as their experience in international competition and sensitivity to market changes. Their small scale of operation also enables them to offer more flexible services.

Hong Kong's advertising professionals will also benefit from China's WTO accession. Due to the lack of professional expertise in the mainland, many international advertising agencies operating in China have to rely on Hong Kong for support. Hong Kong boasts a well-developed advertising industry with an established core of professionals providing a wide range of services including creative advertising, graphic design and production. In many cases, advertising agencies would conduct research and design of the promotion concept in Hong Kong. Sometimes the actual production would take place in the mainland, while the production crews are often recruited in Hong Kong.

3. CONSULTANCY

(*This piece, entitled "Consulting Service Braces Itself for WTO Entry", written by Lan Dai, 18 December, 2000, is retrieved from the archives of "Industrial Profile", WTO Accession Monitor of HKTDC web site, sub-headings are inserted by the Editor*)

Before Accession to WTO

With the reform policy strengthened and reform target defined, consulting service has become an important part of China's tertiary industry in the national industrial policy.

Statistics show that China has more than 40,000 registered consulting enterprises and organisations, employing more than two million people. According to a recent survey [2000] on the tertiary industry in Beijing, the city's consulting service sector registered an increase of 32.8% employees, 56.6% in added value, 50.7% in original value of fixed assets, and 59.7% in pre-tax profit as compared with 1985, much higher than that of the tertiary industry. There are now 7,761 consulting service enterprises in Beijing, employing 126,000 people, and RMB 5.5 billion in registered capital, according to the Beijing Municipal Bureau of Industry and Commerce. The average contractual value of technical consulting is RMB 1.004 billion.

Statistics from Shanghai show that there are 597 independent consulting agencies registered with the Municipal Commission of Science and Technology, including 262 for science and technology, 89 for engineering, 108 for economy, and others for community, management, policy decision, and legal and foreign affairs.

The total number of consulting organisations has reached more than 6,800 in Shanghai, boasting over 117,000 employees. They have completed more than 120,000 consulting services, generating an annual income of more than RMB 1.16 billion.

China's consulting industry is now focusing on five areas, namely, engineering, management, comprehensive consulting (on policy making), technology and specific industries. However, the industry is still in the development stage according to an analysis report made by the China International Economic Consulting Company. The report listed the following factors:

First, the state-owned enterprises are still the main clients, with enterprises of different ownerships on a par, averaging over 20%.

Second, only a small part of consulting enterprises business is overseas business. Less than 10% of China's consulting enterprises have targeted foreign companies. The proportion of consulting enterprises with service focusing on foreign clients, (including those of private-owned firms, Sino-foreign joint venture and cooperation companies) is 28% for state-owned, 33% for collective, and 37% for private companies. The proportion is 47% for Sino-foreign consulting companies. Owing to the huge foreign-related consulting service market which has a high return, the utilisation of foreign funds by Chinese consulting enterprises is not as good as expected. In contrast, foreign-funded companies have demonstrated a strong edge of competition on the market.

Thirdly, township enterprises have been forgotten by the consulting service. Only a few consulting enterprises have set their eyes on township enterprises. Foreign-funded consulting companies pay less attention to township enterprises. State-owned consulting enterprises, most of which were formerly designing and research institutes, are large, overstaffed, and technologically strong. In a market economy they are, however, weak.

Collective and private consulting enterprises are market orientated, active and good in specific areas. They are, however, changeable and face operating difficulties.

Foreign-funded enterprises have presented a strong pep of development. Their business has focused on foreigners, by using international operation methods. Their service quotes are high and they gain a high economic return. The rising number of foreign-funded enterprises has exerted pressure on China's consulting industry.

Owing to the impact of policy, degree of specialisation and market mechanism, China's consulting sector is now far behind India in the utilisation of the World Bank loans worth several billion US dollars. Chinese consulting companies have not been able to take the initiative, thus influencing domestic facilities. Chinese companies have their own advantages, but foreign counterparts still have snatched 80–90% of the expenses on project consulting services.

After Accession to WTO

With the entry of WTO, foreign companies would become more active on the China market, which will create huge pressure and challenges for China's consulting industry. Foreign consulting companies are ready to enter China and compete for a share of the market. Their advantages include: First, large scale, reputation, rich experience, ability, and name. Second, flexibility, featured by dual operation function of convenient service and high-grade ideology. They can serve the needs of government, big companies and enterprises, or families, and small enterprises. Third is their scientific management and advanced facilities, boasting high-profile experts, and computer control systems.

At the same time, competition on the consulting market, following globalisation of the economy, will become fiercer. Consulting service enterprises in the developed countries will expand their operation to China and compete to serve enterprises and government organisations. They will undoubtedly snatch a share of the market.

Local enterprise culture will face new challenges. The utilisation of modern IT technology such as internet, can break the limits of boundary to provide consulting services abroad. When expanding international exchange, the Chinese culture will be influenced by foreign culture, causing crisis of survival.

The WTO membership will create competition amongst personnel. Experts with innovation and creativeness will be the main target of foreign-funded companies which will promise high pay. The outflow of expertise will cause great losses, which would not be replaceable immediately.

4. ACCOUNTANCY

(Extracted from "2001 White Paper" The American Chamber of Commerce, People's Republic of China, available at http://www.amcham-china.org.cn/publications/white/2001/en-33_2.htm.)

Pre-WTO efforts

Over the past year, China has made significant progress in strengthening its accounting profession. Specifically, the Chinese Institute of Certified Public Accountants (CICPA), a government body under the Ministry of Finance, has acted to:

— delink Chinese accounting firms from government agencies
— clean-up and reform licensed activities (tax agents, valuation agents, etc.)
— reorganize functions and personnel at the CICPA
— create a website and launch a professional publication
— arrange a visit by senior CICPA officials to the United States and Canada to learn more about professional examination systems and to build international ties with professional organizations
— establish two national accounting institutes for continued professional education of accountants
— plan the launch of a special training program under which the CICPA would place about 20 young Chinese CPAs, selected by the CICPA on the basis of their professional skills and language ability, in the United States, Canada, and Europe for a year or 18 months

each, to learn about international business and management of international accounting firms, eventually to become the leaders of a modernized profession
— commit overall to improve the transparency of regulatory rules and rule making
— promise to establish an advisory committee to the CICPA, with participation by international accounting firms, and consult with them on major policy initiatives
— acknowledge the desirability of the CICPA functioning more like a professional organization than a government agency.

Harmonization of Standards

While much progress has been made, some pervasive problems still remain. There is still an overriding need for harmonization of China's accounting and reporting standards with international accounting standards (IAS). Furthermore, one of the practical difficulties encountered in analyzing the financial statements of Chinese enterprises is that there are different accounting standards for state-owned enterprises, publicly listed companies, and foreign-invested enterprises. In addition, misstatements in financial statements are not uncommon, and the reliability of audited financial statements varies. Thus it is very difficult to interpret and compare the financial statements of Chinese enterprises with those in other countries, and even within China quickly, to speed foreign investment brought by reliable financial reporting, and to help in China's drive against corruption, international accounting firms need greater flexibility to establish and operate practices in China. China now allows foreign accounting firms to affiliate with domestic firms and include them as "member firms" of the international organizations.

However, such member firms are not allowed income tax deductions for salaries exceeding low prescribed amounts, and they are not permitted to maintain foreign currency bank accounts. Therefore, while some international firms might wish to operate in China through member firms, as they do in other countries, these significant tax and foreign exchange disadvantages make it impractical. Consequently, they are forced to operate in China as joint ventures with domestic firms, which may compromise quality and management standards.

Foreign nationals may take Chinese CPA qualifying examinations and if successful may obtain licenses to practice public accounting. However, Chinese authorities do not yet permit qualified foreign individuals to become partners in domestic CPA firms or Chinese member firms of international organizations. This limits the flexibility of foreign firms to manage their China operations and also may limit the development of domestic firms.

WTO Impact

China's entry into the WTO will allow existing operations to continue under current arrangements, while broadening possibilities for new participation by foreign nationals and foreign equity. Grandfather clauses protect existing joint ventures, member firms, business consulting firms, and other offices from future regulatory changes that might interfere with operations. The partners in any future member firms that may be established must be Chinese licensed CPAs (similar to requirements in most other countries), but there are no limitations on the participation of foreign nationals and foreign equity.

China's WTO accession agreements explicitly exclude accounting, tax, management consulting, and legal services from the general restriction that representative offices are not permitted to be engaged in profit-making activities. In the past, the representative offices of accounting firms were excluded from profit-making activities. Therefore, this is a further liberalization. For new entities providing taxation, management consulting, computer-related and software implementation services, operations are required to be conducted through joint ventures; however, majority foreign ownership is permitted. Wholly foreign-owned operations will be permitted in these service areas five years after accession.

5. LEGAL SERVICES

(Extracted from an article by Hongming XIAO, "The Internationalization of China's Legal Services Market", in "Perspective", Volume 1, No. 6, 30 June 2000, published by the Overseas Young Chinese Forum, available at http://www.oycf.org/Perspectives/ 6_063000 internationalization_of_ china.htm)

WTO and the Opening-Up of China's Legal Services Market

In the bilateral negotiations for China's entry into the WTO, both the United States and the European Union pressed China to open the legal services market. Their major demands included:

(1) Permitting foreigners to take China's Lawyer's Qualification Exam and be licensed to practice Chinese law;
(2) Permitting foreign law offices in China to hire Chinese lawyers;
(3) Eliminating limitations on the number and location of foreign law offices in China;
(4) Permitting foreign law firms to open offices in more than one Chinese city.

The Prospect of China's Opening of Legal Services Market

The development of legal services market is determined by the level of economic development. The advanced legal services industry in the United States and the European Union countries results from their long histories of developed legal professions and globalized economies. As a developing country, China is still on the learning curve of know-how and management, and has a long way to go before it is integrated into the world economy. Because of their traditional connections and language skills, foreign lawyers will continue to play an important role in foreign investment in China. For a period of time, Chinese lawyers will remain at a disadvantage.

(1) Chinese lawyers are inexperienced in international practice. Good legal service depends on experience through long-time practice in transactions under certain regulatory regime.

For Chinese lawyers, many practices such as finance and securities have only recently come into China as a result of the open-door policy and economic reform, while many international transactions are totally new to them.

(2) Management of law firms needs to be improved. In the past twenty years, Chinese law firms have evolved from the absolute dominance of state-sponsored firms to the current state of a mixture of partnerships, cooperatives and state-supported firms. As a well-accepted institution, partnership has contributed a great deal to the Chinese legal profession's development. However, many problems in internal operation and management remain unresolved. It remains a challenge for Chinese legal profession to build, on a contractual basis, professionalism-oriented law firms on a larger scale.

(3) The Chinese regulation of foreign law firms relies on the administrative system. In other words, judicial and administrative agencies exercise the authority to license and regulate. This situation has entangled these agencies in routine matters and made them short on policy-oriented research. By contrast, the internationally accepted regulatory practice is for the legal profession to be self-governed by its professional association.

WTO Accession Spells Opportunities

(The following comments are extracted from two sources, an article entitled "Legal Sector to Open Wider", 15 September 2001, archives of "Services Industry", WTO Accession Monitor, HKTDC web site, and the "2001 White Paper", American Chamber of Commerce, People's Republic of China, available at http://www.amcham-china.org.cn/ publications/white/2001/en-33_2.htm)

Foreign law firms have been waiting for the opening of China's legal sector for a long time. With its rapid economic development, China is an important target for multinational companies seeking investment opportunities. Following China's WTO entry, foreign trade and investment will increase, fueling greater demand for legal services.

China has promised to lift all geographical and quantitative restrictions on foreign law firms one year after its entry into the WTO. Since foreign law firms are already allowed to set up offices in 15 major cities, the lifting of geographical limitations will have but a small impact. However, the removal of quantitative restrictions will be of big help to their business expansion in China. Before WTO accession, they have to be very careful choosing their location because they can only set up one office in China. That explains why most foreign law firms have their offices in Beijing (the political centre) and Shanghai (the financial centre). Foreign law firms prefer Guangzhou where most of their clients are based.

China's accession to the WTO will bring a measure of relief on market access issues for foreign law firms. China's bilateral accords with the United States and the European Union lift the quantitative and geographical restrictions on the establishment of representative offices by foreign law firms effective within one year after China's accession to WTO. China's accord with the EU, which applies to U.S. and other foreign law firms as well as their EU counterparts under WTO rules, also allows foreign law firm representative offices to provide information on the impact of the Chinese legal environment. This provision acknowledges the role of foreign law firms in providing their understanding of the Chinese legal system with respect to foreign investment and trade (duiwai jingji fa or foreign-related economic law) without disturbing the prohibitions on the issuance of legal opinions on Chinese law or representing clients in Chinese courts.

The WTO accords will not alleviate other fundamental barriers to the operation of foreign law firms in China. Law firms are prohibited from stationing members of the Chinese bar in their China offices unless such attorneys relinquish their local bar memberships. This exacts hardship on such attorneys and reduces the incentives for foreign law firms to hire and train Chinese lawyers.

The WTO accession agreements have actually caused tightening of restrictions on foreign law firms in some areas. China's bilateral accords with the United States and European Union provide that the chief representative of a foreign law firm representative office must be a partner or equivalent which is more stringent than under [pre-WTO] requirements. All attorneys or representatives under the EU accord must be members of the bar of a WTO member and also have practiced for no less than two years (which need not be consecutive). These conditions limit the ability of foreign law firms to assign junior attorneys to their offices in China which increases their cost of operations and reduces their competitiveness relative to Chinese law firms.

6. SUMMARY OF CHINA'S MARKET ACCESS COMMITMENTS FOR THE SERVICE SECTOR[2]

Pre- and Post-WTO Market Access Conditions

Distribution

Pre-WTO Barriers/Regulations	Post-WTO Market Access Conditions
Commission agents' services *Wholesale trade services* • Except for the pilot JV trading companies, JV retailing companies JV wholesaling companies, and	*Commission agents' services* *Wholesale trade services** • Majority ownership in JVs allowed within 2 years, with no geographic or quantitative restriction by then. There will also be no

[2]This is a joint publication of Trade and Industry Department, Hong Kong Government and the Hong Kong Trade Development Council (TDC), "*China's Accession to the WTO, Embracing the Opportunities, Meeting the Challenges*", November 2001, available at Hong Kong government's web site at http://www.info.gov.hk/tid/wto_accession/content.htm#Other%20Services, and the archives of "Economic Forum" at HKTDC web site. Column heading is revised by the editors. Readers may check the post-WTO conditions against China's Services Schedule in Appendix 3.

foreign R&D centres, foreign companies are not allowed to distribute products produced by other enterprises or overseas.

- Except for dealing in the wholesale distribution of their own products produced in China, foreign manufacturing enterprises are prohibited from being involved in wholesaling of other products.
- Except for JV wholesaling companies, foreign firms are prohibited from being involved in wholesale businesses.
- JV wholesaling companies are only allowed in the centrally administered municipalities (Beijing, Chongqing, Shanghai and Tianjin), and foreign investors can only have minority ownership.

Retail services
- JVs are only allowed in the capital cities of provinces and autonomous regions, centrally administered municipalities, independent planning cities with provincial status and Special Economic Zones.
- For JV retail enterprises with less than 3 outlets, the foreign partner can own up to 65% of the share. Except specifically exempted by the State Council, those with more than 3 outlets should be majority owned by the Chinese partner.

Approved JV retail enterprises may expand into the wholesale business.

restriction on equity/form of establishment within 3 years.
- JVs can distribute all imported and domestically produced products within 1 year except that distribution of books, newspapers, magazines, pharmaceuticals, pesticides & mulching film to be allowed in 3 years; and chemical fertilizers, processed oil & crude oil to be allowed in 5 years.
- Foreign-invested enterprises can distribute their products manufactured in China and to provide full range of related subordinate services, including after sales services, for the products they distribute.

*The market access conditions above do not apply to the distribution of salt and tobacco.

*Retail services**
- JVs are allowed in 5 Special Economic Zones and Beijing, Shanghai, Tianjin, Guangzhou, Dalian, Qingdao, Zhengzhou & Wuhan upon accession, with majority foreign ownership permitted in 2 years.
- In Beijing and Shanghai, no more than 4 JVs are allowed. 2 JVs in Beijing can set up branches within Beijing. No more than 2 JVs are allowed in other localities.
- All provincial capitals, Chongqing and Ningbo will also be open to JVs in 2 years.
- No geographic quantitative restriction, equity/form of establishment restriction within 3 years.

	• However, chain stores with more than 30 outlets selling different types and brands of motor vehicles and products subject to state trading from multiple suppliers will be limited to minority-owned JVs only, with the limitation for motor vehicles to be eliminated in 5 years. • Retailing of all products (excluding books, newspapers and magazines) within 1 year after accession except that retailing of pharmaceuticals, pesticides, mulching films and processed petroleum to be allowed in 3 years while retailing of chemical fertilizers to be allowed in 5 years. **The market access conditions above do not apply to the retailing of tobacco.
Franchising *Wholesale/retail away from a fixed location* • Independent legal entities with registered trademarks, company names, products and patents, as well as no less than one year good operation performance are allowed to act as franchisors. • Foreign retail chain stores are not allowed to expand their networks by franchising. • There has been a ban on all direct sales activities since Apr 1998. All direct sales enterprises funded by both foreign and domestic capital were shut down or transformed into in-shop sales.	*Franchising* *Wholesale/retail away from a fixed location* • No restriction on establishment in 3 years. China will consult with WTO members when developing regulations on sales away from a fixed location.

Transport/Distribution-Related Services

Pre-WTO Barriers/Regulations	Post-WTO Market Access Conditions
Freight transport by rail and road (in trucks or cars) • Only Chinese nationals and Chinese-owned companies are permitted to conduct surface transportation. • Foreign participation for cross-boundary operations with Foreign requires JV partnership.	*Freight transport by rail and road (in trucks or cars)* • Operate only as minority ownership JVs upon accession. • For road transport, majority ownership JVs and wholly-owned subsidiaries will be allowed in 1 year and 3 years respectively. • For rail transport, majority ownership JVs and wholly-owned subsidiaries will be allowed in 3 years and 6 years respectively.
Storage & warehousing • Foreign firms are permitted to own warehouses only in foreign trade zones (FTZs), provided that such warehouses are used to store materials necessary to their own production and service activities in china. • Outside the FTZs, foreign firms are not permitted to own or manage warehouses.	*Storage & warehousing* • Operate only as minority ownership JVs upon accession. • Majority ownership JVs and whooly-owned subsidiaries will be allowed in 1 year and 3 years respectively.
Freight forwarding • Foreign companies may operate only as minority ownership JVs. • Wholly foreign-owned freight forwarders exist but are exceptions. • The business of JVs is limited to certain geographical areas. • Very few JVs are allowed to handle domestic freight forwarding.	*Freight forwarding* • Majority ownership JVs and wholly-owned subsidiaries will be allowed in 1 year and 4 years respectively. • JV can set up branches after 1 year of operation (requiring US$120,000 in additional registered capital per branch). • A foreign freight forwarder can set up another JV after its

first JV has been in operation for 5 years

Within two years after accession, the requirement will be reduced to 2 years.

Aircraft repair and maintenance

- Foreign companies can invest, through minority share in JVs, in aircraft maintenance.

Aircraft repair and maintenance

- The Chinese side in a JV must hold controlling shares or be in a dominant position.
- Granting of licenses is subject to economic needs tests.

Unlike domestic firms, JVs have the obligation to undertake business in the international market.

Maritime transport

- Operation of international shipping of freight and passengers (e.g. liner, bulk and tramp) is allowed. JVs with minority ownership is also permitted to register for operation under Chinese flag.

Courier services

- Foreign express operators are allowed to set up JVs in China and required to invest no less than US$ 1 million in an entity whose term may not exceed 20 years. The Chinese partner should hold at least a 50% stake in the JV. JVs are generally not allowed to do domestic express business.
- A waiting period of 1 year for establishing branches and 5 years for forming a second JV.

Courier services

- Covers courier services using one or more transport modes except services reserved to the postal authorities.
- Majority ownership JVs and wholly-owned subsidiaries will be allowed in 1 year and 4 years respectively.

Telecommunications and Internet

Pre-WTO Barriers/Regulations	Post-WTO Market Access Conditions
Overall • Foreign investment (ownership and/or management) in any form of telecommunications services is not allowed.	*Overall* • China undertakes the obligations contained in the WTO Reference Paper on pro-competitive regulatory principles. *Value-added services (such as Internet services) and Paging services* • Minority-owned (upto 30%) JVs allowed upon accession in/and between Shanghai, Guangzhou and Beijing. • Expand to Chengdu, Chongqing, Dalian, Fuzhou, Hangzhou, Nanjing, Ningbo, Qingdao, Shenyang, Shenzhen, Xiamen, Xian, Taiyuan and Wuhan (referred to as "other cities" thereafter) within 1 year after accession. Ownership can rise to 49%. • No geographic restriction within 2 year after accession. Ownership can rise to 50%. • (Internet services are subsumed under value-added services) *Mobile voice & data services* • Minority-owned (up to 25%) JVs allowed upon accession to provide service in and between Shanghai, Guangzhou and Beijing. • Expand to "other cities" 1 year after accession. Ownership can rise to 35%. • 3 years after accession, ownership can rise to 49%.

	• No geographic restriction 5 years after accession.
	Domestic and international services
	• Minority-owned (up to 25%) JVs allowed within 3 years after accession to provide service in and between Shanghai, Guangzhou and Beijing.
	• Expand to "other cities" within 5 years after accession. Ownership can rise to 35%.
	• No geographic restriction within 6 years after accession. Ownership can rise to 49%.
	Satellite services
	• China has attached and signed "Notes for Scheduling Basic Telecom Services" which provides that unless explicitly excluded, any basic services may be provided through any means of technology, incl. satellites.

Banking

Pre-WTO Barriers/Regulations	Post-WTO Market Access Conditions
Overall	*Overall*
• Wholly foreign-owned banks and joint-ventures are allowed.	• All geographic and client restrictions will be removed within 5 years after accession.
• Foreign banks are allowed to open one branch in each of all major cities.	• Licensing to be based on prudential criteria only. Within 5 years after accession, any existing non-prudential measures restricting ownership, operation and juridical form of foreign banks, including on internal branching and licenses, shall be eliminated.
• Local firms and individuals are off-limits to foreign banks. Domestic banks are thus effectively shielded from foreign competition.	

	• Financial leasing will be allowed for foreign banks when allowed for domestic banks. • Non-bank financial institutions can give credit facilities for the purchase of motor vehicles upon accession. • To establish a subsidiary in China, a foreign bank needs to have total assets of over US\$10 billion. • To establish a branch in China, a foreign bank needs to have total assets of over US\$20 billion.
Foreign currency business • Most foreign banks can only conduct business in foreign currencies with foreign firms and individuals.	*Foreign currency business* • No geographical and client restriction on foreign currency business upon accession.
RMB business • 32 foreign banks have been licensed to conduct limited RMB business in Shanghai (24) and Shenzhen (8) with foreign firms and individuals. • Those in Shanghai can also serve clients in Jiangsu and Zhejiang, while those in Shenzhen can also serve Guangdong, Guangxi and Hunan.	*RMB business* • Renminbi (RMB) business will be restricted to Shanghai, Shenzhen, Dalian, Tianjin upon accession; expand to Guangzhou, Zhuhai, Qingdao, Nanjing and Wuhan within 1 year; to Jinan, Fuzhou, Chengdu and Chongqing within 2 years; to Kunming, Beijing and Xiamen within 3 years; to Shantou, Ningbo, Shenyang and Xian within 4 years. No geographic restriction within 5 years after accession. • Foreign banks can conduct RMB business with local firms within 2 years after accession. • Foreign banks can conduct RMB business with local individuals within 5 years after accession.

316

	• Foreign banks licensed for RMB business in one region may service clients in other regions that have been opened for such business. • To qualify for RMB business, a foreign bank needs to have at least 3 years business operation in China and has been profit-making for the previous 2 years.

Insurance

Pre-WTO Barriers/Regulations	Post-WTO Market Access Conditions
Overall • Less than 20 foreign insurers have been allowed to operate in China. Strict geographic and scope of business restrictions. • Foreign insurance companies are allowed to operate only in Shanghai and Guangzhou, though AIG has branches in Shenzhen and Foshan. • One branch is allowed in each city.	*Overall* • Prudential criteria for licensing. Foreign insurers are qualified for a license if they have more than 30 years of experience in a WTO member country; a representative office established in China for 2 consecutive years; and global assets of over US$5 billion. Asset requirements for brokers will be set at US$500 million upon accession and be gradually reduced to US$200 million in 4 years. • Upon accession, foreign insurers and insurance brokers can provide services in Shanghai, Guangzhou, Dalian, Shenzhen and Foshan. Within 2 years, areas will be expanded to Beijing, Chengdu, Chongqing, Fuzhou, Suzhou, Xiamen, Ningbo, Shenyang, Wuhan and Tianjin. All geographic restrictions will be eliminated within 3 years.

Non-life insurance	• Internal branching will be permitted consistent with the phase out of geographic restrictions.
• Foreign non-life insurers are allowed to establish branches, but their clients are restricted to organisations involving foreign investment. Moreover, foreign insurers cannot underwrite vehicle insurance.	*Non-life insurance* • Branch or JVs with 51% foreign ownership will be allowed upon accession. Wholly-owned subsidiaries will be allowed in 2 years. • Upon accession, foreign insurers can provide master policy and/or large scale commercial risk insurance, which has no geographic restriction. They can also provide insurance of enterprises abroad, property insurance, related liability insurance and credit insurance of foreign-invested companies consistent with geographical restrictions as outlined in the *Overall* section. • Consistent with the geographical restrictions as outlined in the *Overall* section, foreign insurers can provide the full range of non-life insurance services to both foreign and local clients in 2 years.
Life insurance • Wholly foreign-owned insurance companies exist but are the exceptions for life insurers. Since 1997, only JVs have been approved for life insurers. Foreign life insurers are restricted to write individual life products.	*Life insurance* • JVs with 50% foreign ownership will be allowed upon accession. • Consistent with geographical restrictions as outlined in the *Overall* section, foreign insurers can provide individual insurance to foreign and Chinese citizens upon accession and provide health, group and pension/annuities insurance in 3 years.

Reinsurance	*Reinsurance*
• Overseas reinsurers are not allowed to write local currency business. • Property/casualty insurers are obliged to have 20% of their business reinsured by China Reinsurance Company.	• Upon accession, foreign insurers will be permitted to provide reinsurance services for life and non-life insurance as a branch, JV or wholly foreign-owned subsidiary without geographic or quantitative restrictions. • The 20% obligatory reinsurance cession to China Reinsurance Company to be phased out four years after accession.

Securities/Asset Management

Pre-WTO Barriers/Regulations	Post-WTO Market Access Conditions
	Overall • Prudential criteria for authorization.
Securities • Foreign securities firms can only trade B-shares (issues that can only be bought and sold by foreign investors) via shared commission. • Foreign securities firms can access the B-share market for underwriting business. • Foreign securities firms may underwrite international offerings of debt and equity.	*Securities* • Foreign securities firms can establish JVs (with ownership of up to 1/3) to engage (without Chinese intermediary) in underwriting A-shares and in underwriting and trading B- and H-shares as well as government and corporate debt, launching of funds within 3 years after accession. • Foreign securities institutions can also engage in direct cross-border trading in B shares (without Chinese intermediary) upon accession.

Asset management	*Asset management*
• No foreign access for asset management. • Foreign fund management companies can act as advisors for domestic fund companies.	• Minority ownership (33%) in JVs will be allowed to engage in domestic securities investment fund management business upon accession; ownership ceiling to rise to 49% within 3 years after accession.

Professional Services

Pre-WTO Barriers/Regulations	Post-WTO Market Access Conditions
Legal	*Legal*
• Foreign law firms cannot engage in Chinese law practice. • Foreign law firms can set up profit-making representative offices in Beijing, Shanghai, Guangzhou, Shenzhen, Haikou, Dalian, Qingdao, Ningbo, Yantai, Tianjin, Suzhou, Fuzhou Wuhan, Xiamen, Zhuai, Hangzhou, Chengdu, Shenyang and Kunming. • A foreign law firm can have only 1 office in China.	• Representative office, while can neither practice Chinese law nor employ Chinese national registered lawyers, can enter into long-term "entrustment" contracts providing for close working relationships with firms practicing Chinese law. • Geographic and quantitative restrictions to be eliminated within 1 year after accession. • The representative shall be practitioner lawyers in a WTO member and have practiced for no less than 2 years outside China. The chief representative shall be a partner or equivalent and have practiced for at least 3 years outside China. • All representatives shall be resident in China no less than 6 months each year.

Accounting

- JVs exist, but approvals for new JVs unlikely in the future. Foreign accounting firms can accept Chinese accounting firms as member firms.
- Foreign accounting firms can provide consulting services to foreign companies, Chinese firms listed overseas and on B-share market.
- Foreigners are allowed to sit for Chinese CPA examination. Qualified foreign accountants can only provide consulting services.

Accounting

- Partnership or incorporated accounting firms are limited to CPAs licensed by Chinese authorities.
- Foreign accounting firms can affiliate with Chinese firms and enter into contractual agreement with their affiliated firms in other WTO members.
- Foreigners who have passed the Chinese CPA examination will receive national treatment upon accession (i.e. they can form partnership or incorporated accounting firms).
- Existing JVs are not limited only to CPAs licensed by Chinese authorities.
- Accounting firms providing taxation and management consulting services will not be subject to JV restriction.
- No mandatory localization requirement.

Medical and dental services

- JV hospitals or clinics allowed. Such JVs must operate as a "profit-marking" entity. No religious activities are allowed.
- Foreign doctors can provide medical services in China only after obtaining approval from Ministry of Health.

Medical and dental services

- JV hospitals or clinics with foreign majority ownership permitted.
- Quantitative limitations in line with China's needs.
- The majority of doctors and medical personnel shall be of Chinese nationality.
- Foreign doctors can provide short-term medical services in China after they obtain licenses from Ministry of Health.

Business Services

Pre-WTO Barriers/Regulations	Post-WTO Market Access Conditions
Management consulting *Taxation services* • JVs allowed.	*Management consulting* *Taxation services* • Majority ownership in JVs will continue to be allowed upon accession. Wholly-owned subsidiaries allowed within 6 years.
Advertising • Foreign companies may operate only as minority ownership JVs.	*Advertising* Only in the form of JV. Majority ownership and wholly-owned subsidiary permitted in 2 and 4 years respectively. *Computer services* • Foreign service suppliers who are certified engineers or who hold a bachelor's degree and have had 3 years experience can provide services in China. For software implementation and data processing services, commercial presence is limited to JV only. *Technical testing & analysis services and freight inspection* • Exclude statutory inspection services for freight inspection services.

	Foreign partner in a JV should have over 3 years operating history. Registered capital of the JV should be no less than US$350,000. Majority ownership and wholly owned subsidiary permitted in 2 and 4 years respectively.
	Others
	• JV with foreign majority ownership is also allowed for other business services such as photographing, convention, translation and interpretation.

Construction & Related Engineering Services

Pre-WTO Barriers/Regulations	Post-WTO Market Access Conditions
Architecture services	*Architectural services*
• Although minority-owned JV is allowed, foreign architectural firms are unlikely to obtain an architect business license and establish a wholly-owned presence in China.	*Engineering services*
	Integrated engineering services
	Urban planning
	• Majority-owned JVs allowed.
• The government has strict requirements on qualified employees for different categories of design institutes.	For cross-border supply of services, can only take place through cooperation with Chinese professional organizations except scheme design.
• Most foreign architectural firms are operating under license of individual projects in China. Such license only allows the architectural firm to work on a single project.	
Engineering services	
• Wholly or majority foreign-owned engineering firms are only allowed in Shanghai. Otherwise, minority-owned JV is the norm for foreign participation.	

Construction & related engineering services

- JVs with majority foreign ownership allowed upon accession. Wholly foreign-owned enterprises permitted within 3 years for undertaking foreign-funded projects as well as certain Chinese invested projects.
- Registered capital requirements for domestic and JV construction enterprises are slightly different.
- JV construction enterprises have the obligation to undertake foreign-invested construction projects.

Real estate services

- It is difficult for a wholly or majority foreign-owned real estate services provider to obtain a business licence in China. Most of them have to form joint venture with a Chinese partner in order to enter the market.
- Various practitioner licences are required to provide different kinds of property services. Foreigners are not eligible to obtain those licences issued by the municipal construction commission.

Real estate services

- Wholly owned firms are permitted for own or leased properties except for high standard real estate projects.
  For services on a fee/contract basis, JVs with foreign majority ownership permitted.

Maintenance & repair services
Rental & leasing services

- Only in the form of JV. Majority ownership and wholly owned subsidiary permitted in 1 year and 3 years respectively.

Audiovisual

Pre-WTO Barriers/Regulations	Post-WTO Market Access Conditions
Films Imports of 10 foreign films per year on a revenue-sharing basis.	*Films* Imports of 20 foreign films per year on a revenue-sharing basis.
Audio-visual products • Foreign participation in distribution is prohibited.	*Audio-visual products* • Distribution of audio-visual products (excl. films) in the form of contractual JV permitted.
Cinema Theatre • Foreign investors are allowed to build cinemas in China in the form of minority-owned JV.	*Cinema Theatre* • JV with foreign ownership up to 49% will continue to be allowed.

Tourism and Travel

Pre-WTO Barriers/Regulations	Post-WTO Market Access Conditions
Hotel JVs allowed.	*Hotel* • Allow unrestricted access and wholly owned hotels within 4 years after accession, with majority ownership allowed upon accession. Foreign managers and specialists with contracts with JV hotels and restaurants in China shall be permitted to provide services in China.
Travel agency and tour operator • Minority ownership in JV travel agencies.	*Travel agency and tour operator* • Allowed to operate in government designated holiday resorts as well

• Foreign partner in a JV should have annual turnover of over US$ 50 million. Registered capital of the JV should be no less than RMB 5 million.	as Beijing, Shanghai, Guangzhou and Xian. • Majority ownership allowed within 3 years after accession. Wholly owned enterprises within 6 years after accession with geographic restriction removed. • Eliminate restriction on branching within 6 years after accession.

Other Services

Pre-WTO Barriers/Regulations	Post-WTO Market Access Conditions
Environmental • JVs allowed. *Education* • JVs allowed in non-profit-making educational activities, but restricted to those areas that do not compete with China's compulsory education.	*Environmental* • JVs with majority foreign ownership will continue to be allowed upon accession. *Education* • Joint schools with majority ownership permitted for delivering primary, secondary, higher, adult and other education services. • Individuals with Bachelor's degree or above and appropriate professional titles/certificate with two years professional experiences can also be employed to provide service.

THE FIRST U.S. CONGRESSIONAL REVIEW
OF CHINA'S COMMITMENTS, OCTOBER, 2002

Preface
(Part III)

The following pages contain selected tables and figures from a report prepared and released in October 2002 by United States General Accounting Office ("the GAO Report"), which give analyses and/or examples of China's commitments.

GAO was instructed to monitor China's compliance with its WTO commitments. The GAO Report, an "Analysis of China's Commitments to Other Members [of WTO]", is the first of such work prepared for submission to the Congressional Committees of U.S.

GAO had conducted a detailed analysis of China's accession agreement. It systematically analyzed (1) the scope and types of China's WTO commitments; and (2) the interrelationships among commitments set forth in China's accession agreement. GAO identified nearly 700 individual commitments in China's accession documents including multiple pledges contained in various paragraphs of the Protocol, Report of the Working Party [on China' Accession to WTO], yet to count the number of market access commitments in goods and services schedules, such as tariffs, and product-specific commitments in additional annexes.[1]

The full report is available at the website: www.gao.gov/cgi-bin/getrpt?GAO-03-4.

---

[1]*See* Appendix 1 of the GAO Report for methodology adopted in counting the number of commitments

330

THE FIRST U.S. CONGRESSIONAL REVIEW OF CHINA'S COMMITMENTS

Table 1 Eight General Areas and Number of China's Trade Regime Commitments* in Each Area

Area	Number of commitments	Description of area
Trade framework	82	Includes uniform application of trade measures, transparency, judicial review, nondiscrimination, and revisions to related laws and regulations.
Import regulation	227	Includes border measures affecting imports, such as customs duties, other taxes, and charges; nontariff measures, such as quantitative restrictions (quotas); regulatory measures, such as standards for determining the value of imports (customs valuation); and technical barriers to trade, such as packaging, marketing, or labeling requirements.
Export regulation	9	Includes border measures affecting exports, including licensing requirements, export duties, and other taxes and charges.
Trading rights and industrial policies	117	Includes China's restrictions on the right to import or export products (trading rights), limitations on trading to certain entities (state trading), and industrial policies such as price controls, subsidies, regulations on state-owned enterprises, investment requirements, and restrictions affecting foreign exchange.
Agriculture	101	Includes border measures and other policies that affect the agricultural sector such as customs duties, tariff-rate quotas, export subsidies, domestic support, and measures restricting imports for health and environmental reasons (sanitary and phytosanitary measures).
Services	45	Includes regulations and restrictions affecting trade in services and operations of foreign services suppliers in China, including commitments on nondiscrimination and market access for particular service sectors.
Intellectual property rights	34	Includes laws and regulations providing for the protection and enforcement of intellectual property rights such as copyrights, trademarks, and patents.
Safeguards and trade remedies	70	Includes additional protection of products faced with market disruption caused by surges in imports from China, the ability to use alternate methodology in antidumping and countervailing duty cases, and review of China's trade practices through a special WTO review mechanism.
Total	**685**	

*[Exclude market access commitments]

Source: GAO analysis of China's Commitments to other Members [of WTO], p. 7, Table 1, footnotes omitted.

Table 2 Commitment Types in China's Protocol and Working Party Report

Commitment type	Commitments of this type require China to:	Example of commitment type
Definitional	Use a certain type of term or meaning in its commitments and regulations. These commitments can also be an elaboration or clarification of an existing practice, law, or process.	Services: In the insurance sector, China committed to defining a "master policy" as a policy that provides blanket coverage for the same legal person's property and liabilities located in different places.
Reporting	Report some type of information to the WTO.	Agriculture: China committed to notifying the WTO about all sanitary and phytosanitary regulations and measures within 30 days after accession.
Transparency	Improve the openness of China's trade regime by, for example, publishing information, designating an enquiry point, or providing clarifying information on rules, laws, or processes.	Trade framework: China committed to making available to WTO members, upon request, regulations and other measures pertaining to or affecting trade in goods, services, TRIPS, or the control of foreign exchange before such measures are implemented or enforced.
Laws and regulations	Create, modify, or repeal an existing law or regulation in order to comply with a WTO requirement.	Intellectual property rights: China committed to amending its trademark law in compliance with the TRIPS agreement.
Guidance	Implement a commitment by following a specific procedure. These commitments can also describe the process China will follow, the responsible authorities (for example, ministry or level of government), and the principles that describe the procedure.	Import regulation: China committed to accepting that the approving organization for a quota application will issue an import license within 3 working days, and within 10 days in exceptional cases.
Adhere to WTO	Confirm or reiterate adherence to a separate WTO commitment or agreement such as the General Agreement on Services or the agreement on Trade-Related Aspects of Intellectual Property Rights.	Trading rights and industrial policies: China committed to eliminating subsidies provided in connection with special economic zones and other special economic areas that were inconsistent with the WTO Agreement on Subsidies and Countervailing Measures.
Non-discrimination	Confirm or reiterate adherence to WTO principles of national treatment and most favored nation	Trade framework: China committed to treating foreign individuals and enterprises no less favorably than their domestic counterparts with regard to the procurement of inputs and goods necessary for production.

Source: GAO analysis of China's Commitments to other Members [of WTO], p. 9, Table 2, footnote omitted.

Table 3 Products Most Protected By China's Tariff Measures Allowable Under WTO Regime

Product description: certain types of	Tariffs 2001 (percent)	Tariffs 2010 (percent)	U.S. Exports to China, 2001 (in thousands)
Wheat (subject to TRQs)	74%	65%	$21,736
Corn (subject to TRQs)	74	65	1,225
Rice (subject to TRQs)	74	65	184
Barley	65	65	0
Vermouth	65	65	70
Manufactured tobacco and substitutes	65	65	23
Cane or beet sugar (subject to TRQs)	55 to 71.6	50	354
NPK chemical fertilizer (covered by TRQ)	50	50	n.a.
Diammonium chemical fertilizer (covered by TRQ)	50	50	n.a.
Urea (covered by TRQ)	50	50	n.a.
Photographic film	55.7	47	94
Motorcycles	52.3 to 53.8	45	24
Corn and rice flours (subject to TRQs)	64	40	345
Cotton (subject to TRQs)	61.6	40	42,981
Fermented beverages (cider, perry, mead)	60.5	40	18
Photographic film	53.3	40	667
Motorcycles	51.7	40	0
Ethyl alcohol	40	40	507
Wool (subject to TRQs)	38	38	2,238*
Beverage bases and flavored waters	44 to 50	35	10,550*
Photographic paper	45	35	71*
Jewelry and imitation jewelry	36.7 to 42.5	35	2,126
Gas water heaters	35	35	4,773
Electric heaters, hair dryers, toasters, coffee makers	35	35	732
Television cameras and video cameras	35	35	467*

Legend

n.a.: not available.

TRQ: tariff-rate quota

*U.S. export values for these products are approximations.

Source: GAO analysis of China's Commitments to other Members [of WTO], p. 19, Table 4, original title "Products for which China's Bound Tariff Rates will be 35 percent or Higher in 2010", footnotes simplified.

Table 4 Selected Products and Service Sectors Most Protected By China's Non-tariff Measures Allowable Under WTO Regime

Products and services sectors	Restrictions and trade-distorting measures, with the phaseout schedule
Automobiles and parts	• Wide range of rates, but tariffs on certain automobiles falling from over 50 percent (2001) to 25 percent (2006); lower on parts • Quotas and licenses (removed by 2005) • Restrictions on distribution (gradual removal of restrictions by 2006; most removed by 2004) • Restrictions on third-party auto liability insurance and driver and operator liability for buses and other commercial vehicles (not removed)
Chemical fertilizers	• Tariff-rate quota (increased quotas through 2006, but not removed) • In-quota tariff rate of 4 percent; out-of-quota rates of 50 percent • State trading (imports; not removed) • Government guidance pricing on urea (not removed) • Foreign distribution excluded (removed by 2006)
Corn, cotton, rice	• In-quota tariff rates between 1 and 10 percent; out-of-quota rates between 10 and 65 percent • Tariff-rate quota (increased quotas through 2004, but not removed) • State trading (both imports and exports; not removed) • Government guidance pricing (not removed)
Legal services	• Restrictions on the scope of business, form of establishment, and national treatment–nationality/residency and qualifications requirements (not removed) • Government guidance pricing (not removed)
Life insurance services	• Restrictions on scope of business, form of establishment, participation of foreign capital, cross-border trade, and national treatment–licensing requirements (not removed)
Natural rubber	• 20 percent tariff rate • Quotas and licenses (removed by 2004) • Designated trading (removed by 2004)
Processed oils (gasoline, kerosene, diesel)	• Tariffs between 6 and 9 percent upon accession • Quotas and licenses (removed by 2004) • State trading (both imports and exports; not removed) • Government guidance pricing (not removed) • Foreign distribution excluded (removed in 2004 for retailing services and 2006 for wholesale and commission agents' services)
Sugar	• Tariff-rate quota (increased quotas through 2004, but not removed) • In-quota tariff rate falling from 20 percent to 15 percent by 2004; out-of-quota rate of 50 percent • State trading (imports)

(Continued)

Telecommunications services (value added)	• Restrictions on form of establishment, participation of foreign capital, and cross-border trade (not removed) • Government pricing (not removed)
Tobacco	• Final tariff rates range from 65 to 10 percent on a variety of tobacco products. Most tariff reductions phased in by 2004 • State trading (imports; not removed) • Price controls (not removed) • Foreign distribution excluded (not removed)
Vegetable oils (soy bean, palm, rape seed)	• Tariff-rate quota (increased quotas until removed in 2006) • In-quota tariff rate of 9 percent; out-of-quota rate of 63.3 percent, falling to 9 percent in 2006 • State trading (imports; not removed) • Government guidance pricing on soy bean and rapeseed oil (not removed)
Wheat	• Tariff-rate quota (increased quotas through 2004, but not removed) • In-quota tariff rates between 1 and 10 percent; final out-of-quota rates of 65 percent • State trading (imports; not removed) • Government guidance pricing on certain wheat products (not removed)
Wool and wool tops	• Tariff-rate quota (increased quotas through 2004, but not removed) • In-quota tariff rates of 1 percent (wool) and 3 percent (wool tops); out-of-quota rates of 38 percent • Designated trading (removed by 2004)

Source: GAO Analysis of China's Commitments to other Members [of WTO], 34–35, Table 9, original title "Selected Products and Services Sectors Subject to Multiple Restrictions and Trade-Distorting Measures".

Table 5 Types of Trade-Distorting Measures Addressed by China's WTO Accession Agreement

Type of trade-distorting measure	Products affected by measure: certain types of	Approximate share of U.S. exports to China (2001) of products subject to the measure[a] (percent)	Phaseout schedule
Designated trading	Natural rubber, timber, plywood, wool, acrylic, and steel	1%	Removed by 2004
Export duties	Fish products, base metals (lead, zinc, aluminum, tungsten, etc.), mineral products	Not applicable (should affect Chinese exports of products)	Not removed
Export subsidies	None (China committed to eliminating all export subsidies upon accession)	Not applicable (should affect Chinese exports of products)	Eliminated upon accession

Government guidance pricing	Grains (wheat, corn, rice, and soybeans), vegetable oils (soybean, rape, colza, and mustard), processed oil, fertilizer (urea), silkworm cocoons, and cotton	6–7	Not removed
Licensing	Automobiles, motorcycles, parts, and a variety of other products	1	Removed by 2005
Price controls	Tobacco, edible salt, natural gas, pharmaceuticals	Less than 1	Not removed
Quotas	Automobiles, motorcycles, parts, and a variety of other products	1	Removed by 2005
State trading (imports)	Grains (wheat, corn, and rice), vegetable oils (soybean, palm, rape, colza, and mustard oils), sugar, tobacco, crude oil, processed oil, chemical fertilizers, and cotton	About 1	Not removed
State trading (exports)	Tea, rice, corn, soybeans, tungsten ore, ammonium paratungstates, tungstate products, coal, crude oil, processed oil, silk, cotton, woven fabrics, antimony products, and silver	Not applicable (should affect Chinese exports of products)	Not removed
Tariff-rate quotas	Wheat, corn, rice, soybean oil, palm oil, rapeseed oil, sugar, wool, cotton, fertilizer, wool tops	Less than 1	Quota amount and private trading share increase over some period but tariff-rate quota removed only on vegetable oils
Tendering	Transport equipment and high-tech apparatus	1–6	Removed by 2004

[a]These percentages are based on GAO's analysis of U.S. exports to China in 2001 of products subject to these measures. U.S. exports to China of all types of fertilizer, including types not covered by tariff-rate quotas, account for about 2 percent of U.S. exports to China.

Source: GAO analysis of China's Commitments to other Members [of WTO], p. 21, Table 5, footnotes simplified.

Table 6 Number of WTO Services Sectors where China Made Commitments

General WTO services sector	Number of subsectors included in WTO general sector	Number of subsectors included in China's commitments
Business	46	26
Communication	24	17
Construction	5	5
Distribution	5	5
Education	5	5
Environmental	4	4
Financial	17	13
Health-related and social	4	0
Tourism and travel-related	4	2
Recreation, cultural, and sporting	5	0
Transport	35	11
Other	Number of subsectors not specified	No commitments in this sector
Total	154	88

Source: GAO analysis of China's Commitments to other Members [of WTO], p. 25, Table 6, footnote omitted.

Table 7 Eight Types of Limitations in China's WTO Services Schedule

Limitation type	Description	Example of limitation type
Cross-border	Limitation on providing a service across national borders. In some cases, services may be provided only by establishing a commercial presence in China.	Wholesale distribution services are not permitted to be provided across borders.
Form	Limitation on the legal form of establishment, such as those requiring that services be provided through a joint venture with a Chinese partner.	Foreign providers of software implementation services may establish in China only in the form of a joint venture.
Equity	Limitation on the amount or share of foreign equity in a service operation.	Within 2 years following accession, foreign investment in certain types of telecommunications services shall be no more than 50 percent.
Geographic	Limitation on the specific geographic locations in which service providers are allowed to operate.	Certain foreign banking services are restricted to designated cities. These restrictions are phased out over time.

(Continued)

Nationality	Limitation on national treatment based on the residency or nationality of a service provider.	Legal service representatives shall be resident in China for no less than 6 months each year.
Number	Limitation on the number of foreign service providers or quantity of output or operations.	Number of foreign-invested medical and dental service operations subject to quantitative limits based on China's needs.
Scope	Limitation on the scope of business that may restrict certain types of services within a sector or restrict the type of client to whom services may be provided.	Commitments on courier services exclude services specifically reserved for Chinese postal authorities by law.
Qualifications	Limitation on national treatment through qualifications, standards, or licensing requirements.	Licensing requirements for foreign insurance providers require more than 30 years' establishment experience in a WTO member country.

Source: GAO analysis of China's commitments to other Members [of WTO], p. 26, Table 7, footnote omitted.

Table 8: Example's of China's WTO Commitments Relating to China's Import Regulation

Topic	China committed to
Tariffs, taxes, and charges	• Binding (not to raise tariffs beyond a certain level) all tariff lines and bind at zero other duties and charges. • Eliminating tariffs and other duties and charges on information technology products. • Conforming customs fees and charges to WTO rules, such as limiting duties to the approximate cost of services rendered. • Providing nondiscriminatory treatment to imports with respect to tariffs, charges, and border tax adjustments.
Nontariff measures (licensing, quotas, tendering)	• Gradually eliminating licensing, quota, and tendering requirements for certain products. • Refraining from instituting new, nontariff measures beyond those listed in China's scheduled commitments. • Ensuring that China's quota and licensing system conforms to WTO rules, including that they be administered in a transparent, nondiscriminatory manner. • Ensuring that entities holding quota allocations also receive necessary import licenses. • Abiding by specific time frames for allocating quotas and a minimum validity period for issued licenses. • Publishing key information on licensing and quota allocation rules and procedures, including lists of products subject to licensing and tendering requirements or other trade restrictions, criteria for obtaining licenses or quotas, and amount of quota available.

(Continued)

	• Reallocating unused quota by a specific date to encourage full quota utilization.
Industrial tariff-rate quotas (TRQ)	• Establishing annual TRQs for certain fertilizer and wool top products and gradually increase quota levels during a phasein period. (See table 9.)
	• Abiding by specific time frames for allocating initial quota and reallocating unused quota to encourage full TRQ utilization.
	• Publishing information on amount of quota allocations available and respond to inquiries within 10 days to increase transparency about what entities received quota allocations.
	• Reserving a portion of all TRQs for private traders, and allocate quotas directly to endusers to increase private competition and reduce state intervention.
	• Allocating at least 10 percent of TRQ to new quota-holders in the first year.
Regulatory border measures (rules of origin, customs valuation, preshipment inspection)	• Ensuring that laws and regulations conform to the WTO agreements for rules of origin, customs valuation, and preshipment upon accession.
	• Refraining from using minimum or reference prices, such as an artificial market price, for customs valuation purposes.
	• Adopting two WTO decisions that affect how certain products are treated for customs valuation purposes within 2 years of accession.
Technical barriers to trade	• Bringing all technical regulations, standards, and conformity assessment procedures into conformity with WTO rules, including the nondiscriminatory application of and opportunity to comment on proposed rules.
	• Ensuring that imported products are not subject to multiple or duplicative conformity assessment requirements.
	• Unifying China's conformity assessment procedures and inspection certificates marks for both imported and domestic products, and shorten the time frames for obtaining the unified certification mark.
	• Increasing the use of international standards and recommendations as the basis of technical regulations, standards, and conformity assessment rules.
	• Publishing information on adopted and proposed technical regulations, standards, and conformity assessment procedures, including criteria used and regulatory bodies having responsibilities for administering such rules.
	• Adopting the WTO *Code of Good Practice* within 4 months of accession (includes provisions for nondiscriminatory treatment, the avoidance of using standards as barriers to trade, the use of international standards in standards setting, and measures to increase transparency).

Source: GAO analysis of China's Commitments to other Members [of WTO], pp. 50–51, Table 13, footnotes omitted.

Table 9 Timetable for Selected Chinese WTO Commitments Relating to Import Regulation

Date	Commitment
April 2002	Technical barriers to trade: Notify acceptance of the WTO's Code of Good Practice, contained in annex 3 of the WTO Agreement on Technical Barriers to Trade.
December 2002	Technical barriers to trade: Ensure that all conformity assessment bodies can undertake assessments for both imported and domestic products.
June 2003	Technical barriers to trade: Assign respective responsibilities to conformity assessment bodies solely on the basis of scope of work and type of product, without giving consideration to product origin.
December 2003	Customs valuation: Within 2 years adopt two WTO customs valuation decisions concerning the treatment of interest charges and the valuation of carrier media-bearing software for data-processing equipment.
January 2005	Nontariff barriers: Complete the elimination of all licensing and quotas for products listed in China's schedule of commitments.
January 2010	Tariffs, taxes, and charges: Tariff reductions are completed.

Source: GAO analysis of China's Commitments to other Members [of WTO], p. 58, Table 15.

Table 10: Examples of China's WTO Commitments Relating to Agriculture

Topic	China committed to
Agriculture tariffs	• Binding its tariff rates upon accession. • Reducing its tariff rates through 2010.
Tariff-rate quotas	• Applying tariff-rate quotas to wheat, corn, rice, soybean oil, palm oil, rapeseed oil, sugar, wool, and cotton. • Reserving a portion of TRQs for importation through non–state-trading enterprises, and progressively increasing the portion for edible oils and corn. • Administering TRQs on a transparent, predictable, uniform, fair, and nondiscriminatory basis using clearly specified time frames, administrative procedures, and requirements. • Designating a single, central authority to make the decisions regarding all allocations and reallocations to end-users.
Subsidies	• Eliminating export subsidies on agricultural products. • Including investment input subsidies (such as fertilizer) in the WTO calculation of domestic support. • Limiting the level of allowable domestic support for specific products to 8.5% of the product production value, and limiting the aggregate level of support to 8.5% of the total agricultural output value.
SPS measures	• Complying with the WTO Agreement on Sanitary and Phytosanitary Measures, and ensuring that all of China's laws, regulations, decrees, requirements, and procedures relating to SPS measures conform to WTO SPS rules upon accession. • Notifying the WTO of laws, regulations, and other measures relating to China's SPS, including products and relevant international standards, guidelines, and recommendations.

Source: GAO analysis of China's Commitments to other Members [of WTO]. p. 71, Table 19.

Table 11 Examples of China's WTO Commitments Relating to Safeguards and Other Trade Remedies

Topic	China committed to
Product-specific safeguard	• Allowing WTO members to withdraw concessions or limit imports when Chinese products are imported to WTO members and cause or threaten to cause market disruption. • Allowing WTO members to withdraw concessions or limit imports only for such time as is necessary to prevent or remedy market disruption. • Allowing China to suspend application of substantially equivalent concessions when a WTO member adopts a measure in response to (1) a relative increase in Chinese imports, and when the measure remains in effect for more than 2 years, or (2) an absolute increase in imports, when the measure remains in effect more than 3 years. • Allowing WTO members to withdraw concessions or otherwise limit Chinese imports if the application of the product-specific safeguard by another WTO member against China threatens to cause significant diversions of trade into the market of the other importing WTO member. • Terminating the product-specific safeguard on December 11, 2013, 12 years after China's accession to the WTO. • Requiring WTO members to follow various procedural requirements when invoking the product-specific safeguard against China. • Requiring WTO members to apply objective criteria in assessing whether actions taken against China to prevent or remedy market disruption cause or threaten to cause significant diversion of trade.
Textile safeguard	• Allowing WTO members to invoke the textile safeguard against China when imports of Chinese textiles or apparel products cause market disruption that threatens to impede the orderly development of trade. • Holding shipment of textiles and apparel to certain levels, upon request for consultations to ease market disruption. • Permitting WTO members to use the textile safeguard until December 31, 2008, 4 years after expiration of the WTO Agreement on Textiles and Clothing. • Allowing WTO members to apply safeguard measures under the textile safeguard only for 1 year, without reapplication, unless otherwise agreed. • Prohibiting the textile safeguard and product-specific safeguard from being applied to the same product at the same time.

Price comparability in determining Chinese dumping	• Allowing importing WTO members to use a methodology not based on strict comparison with Chinese domestic prices or costs in determining price comparability for antidumping, when producers under investigation cannot clearly show that market economy conditions prevail in industry involved. • Requiring importing WTO members to use Chinese prices or costs in determining price comparability for antidumping, when producers show market economy conditions prevail. • Allowing use of alternate methodology for antidumping actions for 15 years after China's accession. • Requiring WTO members to follow certain procedures when using alternate methodology in antidumping cases. • Revising its antidumping regulations and procedures prior to WTO accession, to fully implement antidumping agreement.
Price comparability in determining Chinese subsidies	• Allowing WTO members to use methodologies for identifying Chinese subsidies that are not based on prevailing terms and conditions in China. • Allowing use of alternate methodologies for determining subsidies without including a termination date. • Revising its countervailing duty regulations and procedures prior to accession, to fully implement China's obligations under the WTO Agreement on Subsidies and Countervailing Measures.
Product-specific safeguard	• Allowing WTO members to withdraw concessions or limit imports when Chinese products are imported to WTO members and cause or threaten to cause market disruption. • Allowing WTO members to withdraw concessions or limit imports only for such time as is necessary to prevent or remedy market disruption. • Allowing China to suspend application of substantially equivalent concessions when a WTO member adopts a measure in response to (1) a relative increase in Chinese imports, and when the measure remains in effect for more than 2 years, or (2) an absolute increase in imports, when the measure remains in effect more than 3 years. • Allowing WTO members to withdraw concessions or otherwise limit Chinese imports if the application of the product-specific safeguard by another WTO member against China threatens to cause significant diversions of trade into the market of the other importing WTO member. • Terminating the product-specific safeguard on December 11, 2013, 12 years after China's accession to the WTO. • Requiring WTO members to follow various procedural requirements when invoking the product-specific safeguard against China.

	• Requiring WTO members to apply objective criteria in assessing whether actions taken against China to prevent or remedy market disruption cause or threaten to cause significant diversion of trade.
Transitional review mechanism	• Authorizing relevant WTO subsidiary bodies and General Council, within 1 year after China's WTO accession, and annually for 8 years, to review China's implementation of its WTO commitments. • Providing relevant information to each subsidiary body in conjunction with WTO subsidiary body review. • Allowing final review in the tenth year after China's accession or at an earlier date decided by General Council.

Source: GAO analysis of China's commitments To Other Members [of WTO], pp. 88–89, Table 23, footnote omitted.

Table 12 Timetable for Selected Chinese WTO Commitments Relating to Safeguards and Other Trade Remedies

Date	Commitment
December 11, 2002	Requires review of China's implementation of its WTO commitments by WTO subsidiary bodies and General Council, under transitional review mechanism, within 1 year of China's accession to the WTO.
December 31, 2008	Phases out textile safeguard a little more than 7 years after China's accession and 4 years after termination of the WTO Agreement on Textiles and Clothing on January 1, 2005.
December 11, 2011	Requires annual reviews of China's implementation of its WTO commitments for 8 years, under transitional review mechanism, with a final review in the 10th year or at an earlier date decided by the General Council.
December 11, 2013	Phases out product-specific safeguard 12 years after China's accession.
December 11, 2016	Phases out use of alternate methodology for antidumping cases 15 years after China's accession.

Source: GAO analysis of China's Commitments to other Members [of WTO], p. 93, Table 24.

Figure 1: Average Chinese Tariff Rates by Industry Category, 2001 and 2010

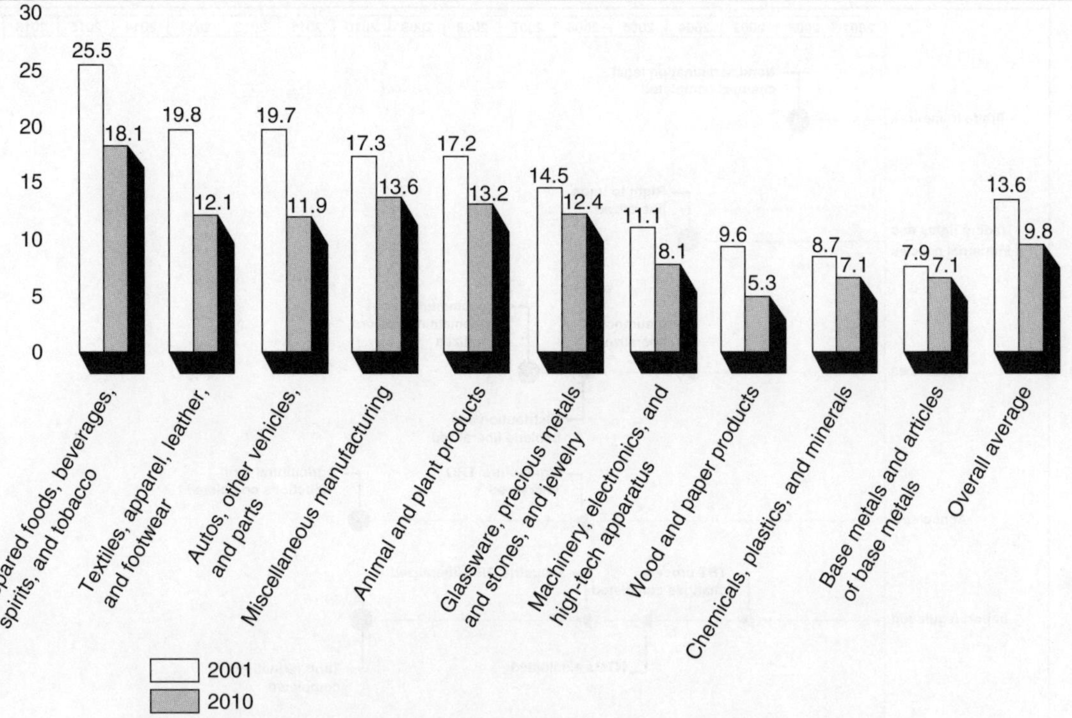

Note: Categories are based on aggregated groupings of the international harmonized system (HS) nomenclature, a World Customs Organization classification system for traded products.

Source: GAO analysis of China's Commitments to other Members [of WTO], p. 16, Figure 1.

344

Figure 2: Summary of Key Phasein Dates for China's WTO Commitments, 2001–2016

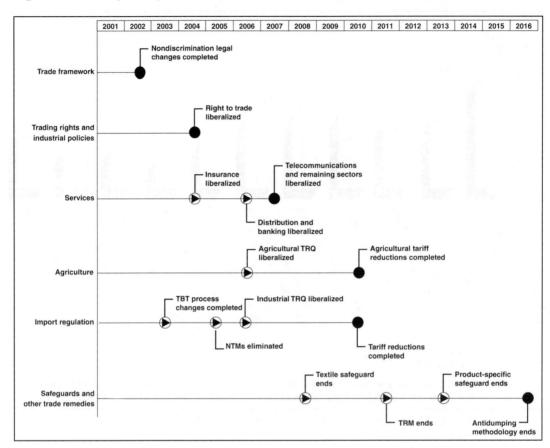

Legend

NTM: nontariff measure

TBT: technical barriers to trade

TRQ: tariff-rate quota

TRM: transitional review mechanism

Note 1: No commitments in the areas of export regulation and IPR have phase in periods.

Note 2: Commitments to liberalize agricultural TRQs and various services sectors are scheduled to be phased in by the dates shown. but other restrictions on these sectors that China did not commit to removing may remain in place.

Source: GAO analysis of China's Commitments to other Members [of WTO], pp. 30–31, Figure 3.

Bibliography

BOOKS OR OFFICIAL DOCUMENTS

International Chamber of Commerce, *Intellectual Property & International Trade - A Guide to the Uruguay Round TRIPS Agreement*, ICC Publishing S.A. (Paris), ICC Publication No. 522, 1996.

Shi Wei, *Time Table for Market-Opening and Strategies For Various Industries on China WTO Accession*, Yangcheng Evening News Publications, 2001.

Trade Development Council, Hong Kong, *A General Assessment of the Impact of WTO Entry on China's Industrial Enterprises*, July 2000.

UN Statistical Division, *Manual on Statistics of International Trade in Services,* final draft 6 September, 2001.

White House, *Fact Sheets on US-China Bilateral Agreement*, 1999

WTO publications

Yu Yongding and Zheng Binwen, *The Research Report on China's Entry into WTO – The Analysis of China's industries*, a Chinese Academy of Social Sciences Study (also abbreviated as the CASS Report by Yu and Zheng 2000), Social Sciences Documentation Publishing House, 2001.

Journal articles and web articles

Details as acknowledged or annotated in each chapter.

Appendix 1

LIST OF LEGAL TEXTS: THE WTO AGREEMENTS

The WTO framework takes a single undertaking approach in that the Agreement establishing the WTO encompasses the *GATT*, as modified by the Uruguay Round, and all agreements and arrangements concluded under its auspices and the complete results of the Uruguay Round. It was signed in Marrakesh on 15 April, 1994. The WTO's agreements are often called the Final Act of the 1986–1994 Uruguay Round of trade negotiations. Accession to WTO entails the acceptance of all the covered agreements without exception.

(A). The Uruguay Round Agreements

Final Act embodying the results of the Uruguay Round of Multilateral Trade Negotiations

AGREEMENT ESTABLISHING THE WORLD TRADE ORGANIZATION

Its Annexes:

ANNEX 1

ANNEX 1A: MULTILATERAL AGREEMENTS ON TRADE IN GOODS

General Agreement on Tariffs and Trade 1994

General Agreement on Tariffs and Trade 1947

Marrakesh Protocol to the General Agreement on Tariffs and Trade 1994

Understanding on the Interpretation of Article II:1(b) of the General Agreement on Tariffs and Trade 1994 ("other duties and charges")

Understanding on the Interpretation of Article XVII of the General Agreement on Tariffs and Trade 1994 (on state trading enterprises)

Understanding on Balance-of Payments Provisions of the General Agreement on Tariffs and Trade 1994

Understanding on the Interpretation of Article XXIV of the General Agreement on Tariffs and Trade 1994 (on regional trade agreements)

Understanding in Respect of Waivers of Obligations under the General Agreement on Tariffs and Trade 1994

Understanding on the Interpretation of Article XXVIII of the General Agreement on Tariffs and Trade 1994 (on concession withdrawal)

Agreement on Agriculture

Agreement on the Application of Sanitary and Phytosanitary Measures

Agreement on Textiles and Clothing

Agreement on Technical Barriers to Trade

Agreement on Trade-Related Investment Measures

Agreement on Implementation of Article VI of the General Agreement on Tariffs and Trade 1994 (antidumping)

Agreement on Implementation of Article VII of the General Agreement on Tariffs and Trade 1994 (customs valuation)

Agreement on Preshipment Inspection

Agreement on Rules of Origin

Agreement on Import Licensing Procedures

Agreement on Subsidies and Countervailing Measures

Agreement on Safeguards

ANNEX 1B: GENERAL AGREEMENT ON TRADE IN SERVICES

ANNEX 1C: AGREEMENT ON TRADE-RELATED ASPECTS OF INTELLECTUAL PROPERTY RIGHTS INCLUDING TRADE IN COUNTERFEIT GOODS

ANNEX 2: UNDERSTANDING ON RULES AND PROCEDURES GOVERNING THE SETTLEMENT OF DISPUTES

ANNEX 3: TRADE POLICY REVIEW MECHANISM

ANNEX 4: PLURILATERAL TRADE AGREEMENTS
ANNEX 4(a) AGREEMENT ON TRADE IN CIVIL AIRCRAFT
ANNEX 4(b) AGREEMENT ON GOVERNMENT PROCUREMENT
ANNEX 4(c) INTERNATIONAL DAIRY AGREEMENT [terminated end of 1997]
ANNEX 4(d) INTERNATIONAL BOVINE MEAT AGREEMENT [terminated end of 1997]

(B). Uruguay Round Ministerial Decisions and Declarations

Decision on Measures in Favour of Least-Developed Countries

Declaration on the Contribution of the World Trade Organization to Achieving Greater Coherence in Global Economic Policymaking

Decision on Notification Procedures

Declaration on the Relationship of the World Trade Organizations with the International Monetary Fund

Decision on Measures Concerning the Possible Negative Effects of the Reform Programme on Least-Developed and Net Food-Importing Developing Countries

Decision on Notification of First Integration under Article 2.6 of the Agreement on Textiles and Clothing

Decision on Proposed Understanding on WTO-ISO Standards Information System

Decision on Review of the ISO/IEC Information Centre Publication

Decision on Anti-Circumvention

Decision on Review of Article 17.6 of the Agreement on Implementation of Article VI of the General Agreement on Tariffs and Trade 1994 [anti-dumping]

Declaration on Dispute Settlement Pursuant to the Agreement on Implementation of Article VI of the General Agreement on Tariffs and Trade 1994 or Part V of the Agreement on Subsidies and Countervailing Measures

Decision Regarding Cases where Customs Administrations have Reasons to Doubt the Truth or Accuracy of the Declared Value

Decision on Texts Relating to Minimum Values and Imports by Sole Agents, Sole Distributors and Sole Concessionaires

Decision on Institutional Arrangements for the General Agreement on Trade in Services

Decision on Certain Dispute Settlement Procedures for the General Agreement on Trade in Services

Decision on Trade in Services and the Environment

Decision on Negotiations on Movement of Natural Persons

Decision on Financial Services

Decision on Negotiations on Maritime Transport Services

Decision on Negotiations on Basic Telecommunications

Decision on Professional Services

Decision on Accession to the Agreement on Government Procurement

Decision on the Application and Review of the Understanding on Rules and Procedures Governing the Settlement of Disputes

Decision on the Acceptance of and Accession to the Agreement Establishing the World Trade Organization

Decision on Trade and Environment

Organizational and Financial Consequences Flowing from Implementation of the Agreement Establishing the World Trade Organization

Decision on the Establishment of the Preparatory Committee for the World Trade Organization

UNDERSTANDING ON COMMITMENTS IN FINANCIAL SERVICES

(C). Post 1994 achievements

Post-1994 goods agreement (Information Technology Agreement)

Post-1994 GATS Protocols:

-Second Protocol: financial services (adopted 21 July 1995)
-Third Protocol: movement of natural persons (adopted 21 July 1995)

-Fourth Protocol: basic telecommunications (adopted 30 April 1997)

-Fifth Protocol: financial services (adopted 14 November, 1997)

Post-1994 accession protocols (include new member's schedules of commitments in goods and services)

Other major legal documents:

Preferential treatment for least-developed countries—Decision on Waiver, (adopted 15 June 1999)

Source: www.wto.org (Sighted as at January and August, 2002).

Report of the Working Party on the Accession of China

Appendix 2(a)

LEGAL INSTRUMENTS ON CHINA'S ACCESSION TO THE WORLD TRADE ORGANIZATION

Decision: Accession of the People's Republic of China

Protocol on the Accession of the People's Republic of China (*attached as Appendix 2(b) of this book*)

— Annex 1A: Information to be Provided by China in the Context of the Transitional Review Mechanism
— Annex 1B: Issues to be Addressed by the General Council in Accordance with Section 18.2 of China's Protocol of Accession
— Annex 2A1: Products Subjects to State Trading (Import)
— Annex 2A2: Products Subjects to State Trading (Export)
— Annex 2B: Products Subjects to Designated Trading
— Annex 3: Non-Tariff Measures Subject to Phased Elimination
— Annex 4: Products and Services Subject to Price Controls
— Annex 5A: Notification Pursuant to Article XXV of the Agreement on Subsidies and Countervailing Measures
— Annex 5B: Subsidies to be Phased Out
— Annex 6: Products Subject to Export Duty
— Annex 7: Reservations by WTO Members
— Annex 8: Schedule CLII-People's Republic of China
Part I: Most-Favored-Nation Tariff
      Section I: Agricultural Products
      Section I-A: Tariffs
      Section I-B: Tariff Quotas
      Section II: Other Products
Part II: Preferential Tariff (if applicable)
Part III: Non-Tariff Concessions
      Section A: Tariff-rate Quotas on Fertilizer and Wool Tops
      Section B: Other Non-tariff Concessions

Sources: www.wto.org/www.chinawto.gov.cn

Appendix 2(b)

PROTOCOL ON THE ACCESSION OF THE PEOPLE'S REPUBLIC OF CHINA

Preamble

The World Trade organizations ("WTO"), pursuant to the approval of the Ministerial Conference of the WTO accorded under Article XII of the Marrakesh Agreement Establishing the World Trade Organization ("WTO Agreement"), and the People's Republic of China ("China"),

Recalling that China was an original contracting party to the General Agreement on Tariffs and Trade 1947,

Taking note that China is a signatory to the Final Act Embodying the Results of the Uruguay Round of Multilateral Trade Negotiations,

Taking note of the Report of the Working Party on the Accession of China in document WT/ACC/CHN/49 ("Working Party Report"),

Having regard to the results of the negotiations concerning China's membership in the WTO,

Agree as follows:

Part I—General Provisions

1. General

1. Upon accession, China accedes to the WTO Agreement pursuant to Article XII of that Agreement and thereby becomes a Member of the WTO.

2. The WTO Agreement to which China accedes shall be the WTO Agreement as rectified, amended or otherwise modified by such legal instruments as may have entered into force before the date of accession. This Protocol, which shall include the commitments referred to in paragraph 342 of the Working party Report, shall be an integral part of the WTO Agreement.

3. Except as otherwise provided for in this Protocol, those obligations in the Multilateral Trade Agreements annexed to the WTO Agreement that are to be implemented over a

period of time starting with entry into force of that Agreement shall be implemented by China as if it had accepted that Agreement on the date of its entry into force.

4. China may maintain a measure inconsistent with paragraph 1 of Article II of the General Agreement on Trade in Services ("GATS") provided that such a measure is recorded in the List of Article II Exemptions annexed to this Protocol and meets the conditions of the Annex to the GATS on Article II Exemptions.

2. Administration of the Trade Regime

(A) Uniform Administration

1. The provisions of the WTO Agreement and this Protocol shall apply to the entire customs territory of China, including border trade regions and minority autonomous areas, Special Economic Zones, open coastal cities, economic and technical development zones and other areas where special regimes for tariffs, taxes and regulations are established (collectively referred to as "special economic areas").

2. China shall apply and administer in a uniform, impartial and reasonable manner all its laws, regulations and other measures of the central government as well as local regulations, rules and other measures issued or applied at the sub-national level (collectively referred to as "laws, regulations and other measures") pertaining to or affecting trade in goods, services, trade-related aspects of intellectual property rights ("TRIPS") or the control of foreign exchange.

3. China's local regulations, rules and other measures of local governments at the sub-national level shall conform to the obligations undertaken in the WTO Agreement and this Protocol.

4. China shall establish a mechanism under which individuals and enterprises can bring to the attention of the national authorities cases of non-uniform application of the trade regime.

(B) Special Economic Areas

1. China shall notify to the WTO all the relevant laws, regulations and other measures relating to its special economic areas, listing these areas by name and indicating the geographic boundaries that define them. China shall notify the WTO promptly, but in any case within 60 days, of any additions or modifications to its special economic areas, including notification of the laws, regulations and other measures relating thereto.

2. China shall apply to imported products, including physically incorporated components, introduced into the other parts of China's customs territory from the special economic areas, all taxes, charges and measures affecting imports, including import restrictions and customs and tariff charges, that are normally applied to imports into the other parts of China's customs territory.

3. Except as otherwise provided for in this Protocol, in providing preferential arrangements for enterprises within such special economic areas, WTO provisions on non-discrimination and national treatment shall be fully observed.

(C) Transparency

1. China undertakes that only those laws, regulations and other measures pertaining to or affecting trade in goods, services, TRIPS or the control of foreign exchange that are published and readily available to other WTO Members, individuals and enterprises, shall be enforced. In addition, China shall make available to WTO Members, upon request, all laws, regulations and other measures pertaining to or affecting trade in goods, services, TRIPS or the control of foreign exchange before such measures are implemented or enforced. In emergency situations, laws, regulations and other measures shall be made available at the latest when they are implemented or enforced.

2. China shall establish or designate an official journal dedicated to the publication of all laws, regulations and other measures pertaining to or affecting trade in goods, services, TRIPS or the control of foreign exchange and, after publication of its laws, regulations or other measures in such journal, shall provide a reasonable period for comment to the appropriate authorities before such measures are implemented, except for those laws, regulations and other measures involving national security, specific measures setting foreign exchange rates or monetary policy and other measures the publication of which would impede law enforcement. China shall publish this journal on a regular basis and make copies of all issues of this journal readily available to individuals and enterprises.

3. China shall establish or designate an enquiry point where, upon request of any individual, enterprises or WTO Member all information relating to the measures required to be published under paragraph 2(C)1 of this Protocol may be obtained. Replies to request for information shall generally be provided within 30 days after receipt of a request. In exceptional cases, replies may be provided within 45 days after receipt of a request. Notice of the delay and the reasons therefor shall be provided in writing to the interested party. Replies to WTO Members shall be complete and shall represent the authoritative view of the Chinese government. Accurate and reliable information shall be provided to individuals and enterprises.

(D) Judicial Review

1. China shall establish, or designate, and maintain tribunals, contact points and procedures for the prompt review of all administrative actions relating to the implementation of laws, regulations, judicial decisions and administrative rulings of general application referred to in Article X:1 of the GATT 1994, Article VI of the GATS and the relevant provisions of the TRIPS Agreement. Such tribunals shall be impartial and independent of the agency entrusted with administrative enforcement and shall not have any substantial interest in the outcome of the matter.

2. Review procedures shall include the opportunity for appeal, without penalty, by individuals or enterprises affected by any administrative action subject to review. If the initial right of appeal is to an administrative body, there shall in all cases be the opportunity to choose to appeal the decision to a judicial body. Notice of the decision on appeal shall be given

to the appellant and the reasons for such decision shall be provided in writing. The appellant shall also be informed of any right to further appeal.

3. Non-discrimination

Except as otherwise provided for in this Protocol, foreign individuals and enterprises and foreign-funded enterprises shall be accorded treatment no less favourable than that accorded to other individuals and enterprises in respect of:

(a) the procurement of inputs and goods and services necessary for production and the conditions under which their goods are produced, marketed or sold, in the domestic market and for export; and

(b) the prices and availability of goods and services supplied by national and sub-national authorities and public or state enterprises, in areas including transportation, energy, basic telecommunications, other utilities and factors of production.

4. Special Trade Arrangements

Upon accession, China shall eliminate or bring into conformity with the WTO Agreement all special trade arrangements, including barter trade arrangements, with third countries and separate customs territories, which are not in conformity with the WTO Agreement.

5. Right to Trade

1. Without prejudice to China's right to regulate trade in a manner consistent with the WTO Agreement, China shall progressively liberalize the availability and scope of the right to trade, so that, within three years after accession, all enterprises in China shall have the right to trade in all goods throughout the customs territory of China, except for those goods listed in Annex 2A which continue to be subject to state trading in accordance with this Protocol. Such right to trade shall be the right to import and export goods. All such goods shall be accorded national treatment under Article III of the GATT 1994, especially paragraph 4 thereof, in respect of their internal sale, offering for sale, purchase, transportation, distribution or use, including their direct access to end-users. For those goods listed in Annex 2B, China shall phase out limitation on the grant of trading rights pursuant to the schedule in that Annex. China shall complete all necessary legislative procedures to implement these provisions during the transition period.

2. Except as otherwise provided for in this Protocol, all foreign individuals and enterprises, including those not invested or registered in China, shall be accorded treatment no less favourable than that accorded to enterprises in China with respect to the right to trade.

6. State Trading

1. China shall ensure that import purchasing procedures of state trading enterprises are fully transparent, and in compliance with the WTO Agreement, and shall refrain from taking any

measure to influence or direct state trading enterprises as to the quantity, value, or country of origin of goods purchased or sold, except in accordance with the WTO Agreement.

2. As part of China's notification under the GATT 1994 and the Understanding on the Interpretation of Article XVII of the GATT 1994, China shall also provide full information on the pricing mechanisms of its state trading enterprises for exported goods.

7. Non-Tariff Measures

1. China shall implement the schedule for phased elimination of the measures contained in Annex 3. During the periods specified in Annex 3, the protection afforded by the measures listed in that Annex shall not be increased or expanded in size, scope or duration, nor shall any new measures be applied, unless in conformity with the provisions of the WTO Agreement.

2. In implementing the provisions of Article III and XI of the GATT 1994 and the Agreement on Agriculture, China shall eliminate and shall not introduce, re-introduce or apply non-tariff measures that cannot be justified under the provisions of the WTO Agreement. For all non-tariff measures, whether or not referred to in Annex 3, that are applied after the date of accession, consistent with the WTO Agreement or this Protocol, China shall allocate and otherwise administer such measures in strict conformity with the provisions of the WTO Agreement, including GATT 1994 and Article XIII thereof, and the Agreement on Import Licensing Procedures, including notification requirements.

3. China shall, upon accession, comply with the TRIMs Agreement, without recourse to the provisions of Article 5 of the TRIMs Agreement. China shall eliminate and cease to enforce trade and foreign exchange balancing requirements, local content and export or performance requirements made effective through laws, regulations or other measures. Moreover, China will not enforce provisions of contracts imposing such requirements. Without prejudice to the relevant provisions of this Protocol, China shall ensure that the distribution of import licenses, quotas, tariff-rate quotas, or any other means of approval for importation, the right of importation or investment by national and sub-national authorities, is not conditioned on: whether competing domestic suppliers of such products exist; or performance requirements of any kind, such as local content, offsets, the transfer of technology, export performance or the conduct of research and development in China.

4. Import and export prohibitions and restrictions, and licensing requirements affecting imports and exports shall only be imposed and enforced by the national authorities or by sub-national authorities with authorization from the national authorities. Such measures which are not imposed by the national authorities or by sub-national authorities with authorization from the national authorities, shall not be implemented or enforced.

8. Import and Export Licensing

1. In implementing the WTO Agreement and provisions of the Agreement on Import Licensing Procedures, China shall undertake the following measures to facilitate compliance with these agreements:

(a) China shall publish on a regular basis the following in the official journal referred to in paragraph 2(C) 2 of this Protocol:

— by product, the list of all organizations, including those organizations delegated such authority by the national authorities, that are responsible for authorizing or approving imports or exports, whether through grant of licence or other approval;

— procedures and criteria for obtaining such import or export licences or other approvals, and the conditions for deciding whether they should be granted;

— a list of all products, by tariff number, that are subject to tendering requirements, including information on products subject to such tendering requirements and any changes, pursuant to the Agreement on Import Licensing Procedures;

— a list of all goods and technologies whose import or export are restricted or prohibited; these goods shall also be notified to the Committee on Import Licensing;

— any changes to the list of goods and technologies whose import and export are restricted or prohibited.

Copies of these submissions in one or more official languages of the WTO shall be forwarded to the WTO for circulation to WTO Members and for submission to the Committee on Import Licensing within 75 days of each publication.

(b) China shall notify the WTO of all licensing and quota requirements remaining in effect after accession, listed separately by HS tariff line and with the quantities associated with the restriction, if any, and the justification for maintaining the restriction or its scheduled date of termination.

(c) China shall submit the notification of its licensing procedures to the Committee on Import Licensing. China shall report annually to the Committee on Import Licensing on its automatic import licensing procedures, explaining the circumstances which give rise to these requirements and justifying the need for their continuation. This report shall also provide the information listed in Article 3 of the Agreement on Import Licensing Procedures.

(d) China shall issue import licences for a minimum duration of validity of six months, except where exceptional circumstances make this impossible. In such cases, China shall promptly notify the Committee on Import Licensing of the exceptional circumstances requiring the shorter period of licence validity.

2. Except as otherwise provided for in this Protocol, foreign individuals and enterprises and foreign-funded enterprises shall be accorded treatment no less favourable than that accorded to other individuals and enterprises in respect of the distribution of import and export licences and quotas.

9. Price Controls

1. China shall, subject to paragraph 2 below, allow prices for traded goods and services in every sector to be determined by market forces, and multi-tier pricing practices for such goods and services shall be eliminated.

2. The goods and services listed in Annex 4 may be subject to price controls, consistent with the WTO Agreement, in particular Article III of the GATT 1994 and Annex 2, paragraphs 3 and 4 of the Agreement on Agriculture. Except in exceptional circumstances, and subject to notification to the WTO, price controls shall not be extended to goods or services beyond those listed in Annex 4, and China shall make best efforts to reduce and eliminate these controls.

3. China shall publish in the official journal the list of goods and services subject to state pricing and changes thereto.

10. Subsidies

1. China shall notify the WTO of any subsidy within the meaning of Article 1 of the Agreement on Subsidies and Countervailing Measures ("SCM Agreement"), granted or maintained in its territory, organized by specific product, including those subsidies defined in Article 3 of the SCM Agreement. The information provided should be as specific as possible, following the requirements of the questionnaire on subsidies as noted in Article 25 of the SCM Agreement.

2. For purpose of applying Articles 1.2 and 2 of the SCM Agreement, subsidies provided to state-owned enterprises will be viewed as specific if, inter alia, state-owned enterprises are the predominant recipients of such subsidies or state-owned enterprises receive disproportionately large amounts of such subsidies.

3. China shall eliminate all subsidy programmes falling within the scope of Article 3 of the SCM Agreement upon accession.

11. Taxes and Charges Levied on Import and Exports

1. China shall ensure that customs fees or charges applied or administered by national or sub-national authorities, shall be in conformity with the GATT 1994.

2. China shall ensure that internal taxes and charges, including value-added taxes, applied or administered by national or sub-national authorities shall be in conformity with the GATT 1994.

3. China shall eliminate all taxes and charges applied to exports unless specifically provided for in Annex 6 of this Protocol or applied in conformity with the provisions of Article VIII of the GATT 1994.

4. Foreign individuals and enterprises and foreign-funded enterprises shall, upon accession, be accorded treatment no less favourable than that accorded to other individuals and enterprises in respect of the provision of border tax adjustments.

12. Agriculture

1. China shall implement the provision contained in China's Schedule of Concessions and Commitments on Goods and, as specifically provided in this Protocol, those of the Agreement on Agriculture. In this context, China shall not maintain or introduce any export subsidies on agricultural products.

2. China shall, under the Transitional Review Mechanism, notify fiscal and other transfers between or among state-owned enterprises in the agricultural sector (whether national or sub-national) and other enterprises that operate as state trading enterprises in the agricultural sector.

13. Technical Barriers to Trade

1. China shall publish in the official journal all criteria, whether formal or informal, that are the basis for a technical regulation, standard or conformity assessment procedure.

2. China shall, upon accession, bring into conformity with the TBT Agreement all technical regulations, standards and conformity assessment procedures.

3. China shall apply conformity assessment procedures to imported products only to determine compliance with technical regulations and standards that are consistent with the provisions of this Protocol and the WTO Agreement. Conformity assessment bodies will determine the conformity of imported products with commercial terms of contracts only if authorized by the parties to such contract. China shall ensure that such inspection of products for compliance with the commercial terms of contracts does not affect customs clearance or the granting of import licences for such products.

4. (a) Upon accession, China shall ensure that the same technical regulations, standards and conformity assessment procedures are applied to both imported and domestic products. In order to ensure a smooth transition from the current system, China shall ensure that, upon accession, all certification, safety licensing, and quality licensing bodies and agencies are authorized to undertake these activities for both imported and domestic products, and that, one year after accession, all conformity assessment bodies and agencies are authorized to undertake conformity assessment for both imported and domestic products. The choice of body or agency shall be at the discretion of the applicant. For imported and domestic products, all bodies and agencies shall issue the same mark and charge the same fee. They shall also provide the same processing periods and complaint procedures. Imported products shall not be subject to more than one conformity assessment. China shall publish and make readily available to other WTO Members, individuals, and enterprises full information on the respective responsibilities of its conformity assessment bodies and agencies.

    (b) No later than 18 months after accession, China shall assign the respective responsibilities of its conformity assessment bodies solely on the basis of the scope of work and type of product without any consideration of the origin of a product. The respective responsibilities that will be assigned to China's conformity assessment bodies will be notified to the TBT Committee 12 months after accession.

14. Sanitary and Phytosanitary Measures

China shall notify to the WTO all laws, regulations and other measures relating to its sanitary and phytosanitary measures, including product coverage and relevant international standards, guidelines and recommendations, within 30 days after accession.

15. Price Comparability in Determining Subsidies and Dumping

Article VI of the GATT 1994, the Agreement on Implementation of Article VI of the General Agreement on Tariffs and Trade 1994 ("Anti-Dumping Agreement") and the SCM Agreement shall apply in proceedings involving imports of Chinese origin into a WTO Member consistent with the following:

(a) In determining price comparability under Article VI of the GATT 1994 and the Anti-Dumping Agreement, the importing WTO Members shall use either Chinese prices or costs for the industry under investigation or a methodology that is not based on a strict comparison with domestic prices or costs in China based on the following rules:

    (i) If the producers under investigations can clearly show that market economy conditions prevail in the industry producing the like product with regard to the manufacture, production and sale of that product, the importing WTO Member shall use Chinese prices or costs for the industry under investigation in determining price comparability;

    (ii) The importing WTO Member may use a methodology that is not based on a strict comparison with domestic prices or costs in China if the producers under investigation cannot clearly show that market economy conditions prevail in the industry producing the like product with regard to manufacture, production and sale of that product.

(b) In proceeding under Parts II, III and V of the SCM Agreement, when addressing subsidies described in Articles 14(a), 14(b), 14(c) and 14(d), relevant provisions of the SCM Agreement shall apply; however, if there are special difficulties in that application, the importing WTO Member may then use methodologies for identifying and measuring the subsidy benefit which take into account the possibility that prevailing terms and conditions in China may not always be available as appropriate benchmarks. In applying such methodologies, where practicable, the importing WTO Member should adjust such prevailing terms and conditions before considering the use of terms and conditions prevailing outside China.

(c) The importing WTO Member shall notify methodologies used in accordance with subparagraph (a) to the Committee on Anti-Dumping Practices and shall notify methodologies used in accordance with subparagraph (b) to the Committee on Subsidies and Countervailing Measures.

(d) Once China has established, under the national law of the importing WTO Member, that it is a market economy, the provisions of subparagraph (a) shall be terminated provided that the importing Member's national law contains market economy criteria as of the date of accession. In any event, the provisions of subparagraph (a)(ii) shall expire 15 years after the date of accession. In addition, should China establish, pursuant to the national law of the importing WTO Member, that market economy conditions prevail in a particular industry or sector, the non-market economy provisions of subparagraph (a) shall no longer apply to that industry or sector.

16. Transitional Product-Specific Safeguard Mechanism

1. In cases where products of Chinese origin are being imported into the territory of any WTO Members in such increased quantities or under such conditions as to cause or threaten to cause market disruption to the domestic producers of like or directly competitive products, the WTO Member so affected may request consultations with China with a view to seeking a mutually satisfactory solution, including whether the affected WTO Member should pursue application of a measure under the Agreement on Safeguards. Any such request shall be notified immediately to the Committee on Safeguards.

2. If, in the course of these bilateral consultations, it is agreed that imports of Chinese origin are such a cause and that action is necessary, China shall take such action as to prevent or remedy the market disruption. Any such action shall be notified immediately to the Committee on Safeguards.

3. If consultations do not lead to an agreement between China and the WTO Member concerned within 60 days of the receipt of a request for consultations, the WTO Member affected shall be free, in respect of such products, to withdraw concessions or otherwise to limit imports only to the extent necessary to prevent or remedy such market disruption. Any such action shall be notified immediately to the Committee on Safeguards.

4. Market disruption shall exist whenever imports of an article, like or directly competitive with an article produced by the domestic industry, are increasing rapidly, either absolutely or relatively, so as to be a significant cause of material injury, or threat of material injury to the domestic industry. In determining if market disruption exists, the affected WTO Member shall consider objective factors, including the volume of imports, the effects of imports on prices for like or directly competitive articles, and the effect of such imports on the domestic industry producing like or directly competitive products.

5. Prior to application of a measure pursuant to paragraph 3, the WTO Member taking such action shall provide reasonable public notice to all interested parties and provide adequate opportunity for importers, exporters and other interested parties to submit their views and evidence on the appropriateness of the proposed measure and whether it would be in the public interest. The WTO Member shall provide written notice of the decision to apply a measure, including the reasons for such measure and its scope and duration.

6. A WTO Member shall apply a measure pursuant to this Section only for such period of time as may be necessary to prevent or remedy the market disruption. If a measure is taken as a result of a relative increase in the level of imports, China has the right to suspend the application of substantially equivalent concessions or obligations under the GATT 1994 to the trade of the WTO Member applying the measure, if such measure remains in effect more than two years. However, if a measure is taken as a result of an absolute increase in imports, China has a right to suspend the application of substantially equivalent concessions or obligations under the GATT 1994 to the trade of the WTO Member applying the measure, if such measure remains in effect more than three years. Any such action by China shall be notified immediately to the Committee on Safeguards.

7. In critical circumstances, where delay would cause damage which it would be difficult to repair, the WTO Member so affected may take a provisional safeguard measure pursuant to a preliminary determination that imports have caused or threatened to cause market disruption. In this case, notification of the measures taken to the Committee on Safeguards and a request for bilateral consultations shall be effected immediately thereafter. The duration of the provisional measure shall not exceed 200 days during which the pertinent requirements of paragraphs 1, 2 and 5 shall be met. The duration of any provisional measure shall be counted toward the period provided for under paragraph 6.

8. If a WTO Member considers that an action taken under paragraphs 2, 3 or 7 causes or threatens to cause significant diversions of trade into its market, it may request consultations with China and / or the WTO Member concerned. Such consultations shall be held within 30 days after the request is notified to the Committee on Safeguards. If such consultations fail to lead to an agreement between China and the WTO Member or Members concerned within 60 days after the notification, the requesting WTO Member shall be free, in respect of such product, to withdraw concessions accorded to or otherwise limit imports from China, to the extent necessary to prevent or remedy such diversions. Such action shall be notified immediately to the Committee on Safeguards.

9. Application of this Section shall be terminated 12 years after the date of accession.

17. Reservations by WTO Members

All prohibitions, quantitative restrictions and other measures maintained by WTO Members against imports from China in a manner inconsistent with the WTO Agreement are listed in Annex 7. All such prohibitions, quantitative restrictions and other measures shall be phased out or dealt with in accordance with mutually agreed terms and timetables as specified in the said Annex.

18. Transitional Review Mechanism

1. Those subsidiary bodies[1] of the WTO which have a mandate covering China's commitments under the WTO Agreement or this Protocol shall, within one year after accession and in accordance with paragraph 4 below, review, as appropriate to their mandate, the implementation by China of the WTO Agreement and of the related provisions of this Protocol. China shall provide relevant information, including information specified in Annex 1A, to each subsidiary body in advance of the review. China can also raise issues relating to any reservations under Section 17 or to any other specific commitments made by other Members in this Protocol, in those subsidiary bodies which have a relevant mandate. Each subsidiary body shall report the results of such review promptly to the relevant Council established by paragraph 5 of Article IV of the WTO Agreement, if applicable, which shall in turn report promptly to the General Council.

---

[1]Council for Trade in Goods, Council for Trade-Related Aspects Intellectual Property Rights, Council for Trade in Services, Committees on Balance-of-Payments Restrictions, Market Access (covering also ITA), Agriculture, Sanitary and Phytosanitary Measures, Technical Barriers to Trade, Subsidies and Countervailing Measures, Anti-Dumping Measures, Customs Valuation, Rules of Origin, Import Licensing, Trade-Related Investment Measures, Safeguards, Trade in Financial Services.

2. The General Council shall, within one year after accession, and in accordance with paragraph 4 below, review the implementation by China of the WTO Agreement and the provisions of this Protocol. The General Council shall conduct such review in accordance with the framework set out in Annex 1B and in the light of the results of any reviews held pursuant to paragraph 1. China also can raise issues relating to any reservations under Section 17 or to any other specific commitments made by other Members in this Protocol. The General Council may make recommendations to China and to other Members in these respects.

3. Consideration of issues pursuant to this Section shall be without prejudice to the rights and obligations of any Member, including China, under the WTO Agreement or any Plurilateral Trade Agreement, and shall not preclude or be a precondition to recourse to consultation or other provisions of the WTO Agreement or this Protocol.

4. The review provided for in paragraphs 1 and 2 will take place after accession in each year for eight years. Thereafter there will be a final review in year 10 or at an earlier date decided by the General Council.

PART II—SCHEDULES

1. The Schedules annexed to this Protocol shall become the Schedule of Concessions and Commitments annexed to the GATT 1994 and the Schedule of Specific Commitments annexed to the GATS relating to China. The staging of concessions and commitments listed in the Schedules shall be implemented as specified in the relevant parts of the relevant Schedules.

2. For the purpose of the reference in paragraph 6(a) of Article II of the GATT 1994 to the date of that Agreement, the applicable date in respect of the Schedules of Concessions and Commitments annexed to this Protocol shall be the date of accession.

PART III—FINAL PROVISIONS

1. This Protocol shall be open for acceptance, by signature or otherwise, by China until 1 January 2002.

2. This Protocol shall enter into force on the thirtieth day following the day of its acceptance.

3. This Protocol shall be deposited with the Director-General of the WTO. The Director General shall promptly furnish a certified copy of this Protocol and a notification of acceptance by China thereof, pursuant to paragraph 1 of Part III of this Protocol, to each WTO Member and to China.

4. This Protocol shall be registered in accordance with the provisions of Article 102 of the Charter of the United Nations.

Done at Doha this tenth day of November two thousand and one, in a single copy, in the English, French and Spanish languages, each text being authentic, except that a Schedule annexed hereto may specify that it is authentic in only one or more of these languages.

Sources: www.chinawto.gov.cn/www.wto.org

Appendix 3

CHINA'S SCHEDULE OF SPECIFIC COMMITMENTS IN SERVICES
(*see* Chapter 3)

Notes for reading the China's schedule

1. Attempt has been made by the editor to ensure that the re-arranged format of China's Schedule in the following pages has not altered or affected the contents and meanings of any of the commitments as displayed in the original Schedule. Footnotes denoted with [Ed.] are inserted by the editor, they are not included in the original schedule.

2. The Schedule consists of two parts. Part 1 "Horizontal Commitments" stipulates limitations that apply to all sectors of service; these often refer to a particular mode of supply notably *commercial presence* and *presence of natural persons* (*see* below for definition).

    As with the commitments made by other WTO Members in their respective national schedules, in identifying the sectors to which the *GATS* principles of market access[1] and national treatment[2] would apply, China expressed its specific commitments in two different approaches, *either*:

    2.1 a negative listing approach by describing the nature of the limitation, the exceptions to *GATS*' obligations of market access or national treatment that it wished to maintain, or

    2.2 an affirmative listing approach by describing what China is offering in the respective service sector and mode of supply rather than the limitations they are maintaining.

3. As with other national schedules, the following terminology was used and was taken to mean:

    3.1 **"None"** — Where there are no limitations on market access or national treatment in a given sector and mode of supply in Part II of the Schedule, the entry reads **NONE**. However, it should be *noted* that even when the term NONE is used in this

---

[1]Article XVI:2 of the *GATS* lists six categories of restrictions which may not be adopted or maintained unless they are specified in the Schedule, these include four types of quantitative restriction plus limitations on types of legal entity and on foreign equity participation.

[2]Article XVII of the *GATS* is to accord to the services and services suppliers of any other Member treatment no less favourable than is accorded to domestic services and service suppliers.

part, it must be borne in mind that, as noted in Chapter 3, there *may be relevant horizontal limitations* in Part I of the Schedule.

3.2 **"Unbound"** — All commitments made by China in the Schedule are binding on China *unless* otherwise specified as **"*unbound*"** which means China has undertaken no commitment and wishes to remain free to act as it may desire in a given sector *and* mode of supply. That is, China is free to introduce or maintain measures inconsistent with obligations of "market access" or "national treatment" under *GATS*.

3.3 **"Unbound*"** — In some situations, a particular mode of supply — such as the cross-border supply of bridge-building services — may not be technically possible or feasible. In such cases the term UNBOUND* has been used, usually in conjunction with an explanatory footnote stating "Unbound due to lack of technical feasibility".

4. The sectors in the China's Schedule are listed in an order that corresponds to the GATT Secretariat Classification (*see* Appendix 4), also used for *GATS*. There are certain sectors of services in which China did *not* make commitments,[3] or where commitments had been made in one particular sector of service, they concern certain sub-sectors only. Hence, the Schedule contained only those sectors/sub-sectors in which China had made its commitments, the alphanumerical sequential order of sectors/sub-sectors as listed in the Schedule appear incomplete.

5. In most cases, the sectoral entries are accompanied by numerical references to the Central Product Classification System (provisional version) of the United Nations, which gives a detailed explanation of the services activities covered by each listed sector or sub-sector. It is based on this classification system that the GATT Secretariat classification mentioned in paragraph 4 above was drafted.

6. All commitments in a Schedule are bound unless otherwise specified.

7. There are three annexes to this Schedule and two "Notes" by Chairman of the Group on Basic Telecommunication, appended at the end of this Schedule.

8. Definition of **"Services"**.

A country's market access commitments with respect to a particular service sector may vary depending upon how the service is delivered. *GATS* does not give an all-embracing definition for trade in services. However, *GATS* distinguishes between four modes of supplying services[4]: cross-border trade, consumption abroad, commercial presence, and presence of natural persons.

i. Cross-border supply" is defined to cover services flows from the territory of one Member into the territory of another Member (e.g. banking or architectural services transmitted via telecommunications or mail);

---

[3]China did not make commitments in respect of *health-related and social services* (sector 8); *recreational, cultural and sporting services* (sector 10); *other services not included elsewhere* (sector 12) and in respect of some services activities under individual service sectors of which it had made commitments. *Compare* China Schedule with "*GATS* Services Sectoral Classification" in Appendix 4 to identify the sectors/sub-sectors of services in which China had not made commitments.

[4]Article 1 of the *GATS*.

ii.   *"Consumption abroad"* refers to situations where a service consumer (e.g. tourist or patient) moves into another Member's territory to obtain a service;

iii. *"Commercial presence"* implies that a service supplier of one Member establishes a territorial presence, including through ownership or lease of premises, in another Member's territory to provide a service (e.g. foreign banks setting up operations in a country); and

iv.   *"Presence of natural persons"* consists of persons of one Member entering the territory of another Member to supply a service (e.g. accountants, doctors or teachers). The Annex on Movement of Natural Persons specifies, however, that Members remain free to operate measures regarding citizenship, residence or access to the employment market on a permanent basis, *GATS* shall not govern these measures.

THE SCHEDULE
(WTO Document No. WT/ACC/CHN/49/Add.2)

PART I. HORIZONTAL COMMITMENTS

Application to sector: All sectors included in this Schedule

China commitments on "Limitations on Market Access"

Commercial Presence

In China, foreign invested enterprises include foreign capital enterprises (also referred to as wholly foreign-owned enterprises) and joint venture enterprises and there are two types of joint venture enterprises: equity joint ventures and contractual joint ventures.[5]

The proportion of foreign investment in an equity joint venture shall be no less than 25 per cent of the registered capital of the joint venture.

The establishment of branches by foreign enterprises is unbound, unless otherwise indicated in specific sub-sectors, as the laws and regulations on branches of foreign enterprises are under formulation.

Representative offices of foreign enterprises are permitted to be established in China, but they shall not engage in any profit-making activities except for the representative offices under CPC 861, 862, 863, 865 in the sectoral specific commitments [respectively legal services; auditing, accounting and bookkeeping services; taxation services; and management consulting services].

The conditions of ownership, operation and scope of activities, as set out in the respective contractual or shareholder agreement or in a licence establishing or authorizing the operation or supply of services by an existing foreign service supplier, will not be made more restrictive than they exist as of the date of China's accession to the WTO.

The land in the People's Republic of China is State-owned. Use of land by enterprises and individuals is subject to the following maximum term limitations:

(a) 70 years for residential purposes;
(b) 50 years for industrial purposes;
(c) 50 years for the purpose of education, science, culture, public health and physical education;
(d) 40 years for commercial, tourist and recreational purposes;
(e) 50 years for comprehensive utilization or other purposes.

---

[5]The terms of the contract, concluded in accordance with China's laws, regulations and other measures, establishing a "contractual joint venture" govern matters such as the manner of operation and management of the joint venture as well as the investment or other contributions of the joint venture parties. Equity participation by all parties to the contractual joint venture is not required, but is determined pursuant to the joint venture contract.

Presence of Natural Persons —

Unbound except for measures concerning the entry and temporary stay of natural persons who fall into one of the following categories:

(a) Managers, executives and specialists defined as senior employees of a corporation of a WTO Member that has established a representative office, branch or subsidiary in the territory of the People's Republic of China, temporarily moving as intra-corporate transferees, shall be permitted entry for an initial stay of three years;

(b) Managers, executives and specialists defined as senior employees of a corporation of WTO Members, being engaged in the foreign invested enterprises in the territory of the People's Republic of China for conducting business, shall be granted a long-term stay permit as stipulated in the terms of contracts concerned or an initial stay of three years, whichever is shorter;

(c) Service salespersons — persons not based in the territory of the People's Republic of China and receiving no remuneration from a source located within China, and who are engaged in activities related to representing a service supplier for the purpose of negotiation for the sale of services of that supplier where:

    (a) such sales are not directly made to the general public and

    (b) the salesperson is not engaged in supplying the service: entry for salespersons is limited to a 90-day period.

China commitments on "Limitation on National Treatment"

Commercial presence—

Unbound for all the existing subsidies to domestic services suppliers in the sectors of audio-visual, aviation and medical services.

Presence of natural persons—

Unbound except for the measures concerning the entry and temporary stay of natural persons who fall into the categories referred to in the market access column.

PART II. SECTOR-SPECIFIC COMMITMENTS

1. SECTOR — BUSINESS

A. Sub-sector: Professional Services
a. Legal Services (CPC 861, excluding Chinese law practice)

China commitments (any limitations/requirements or offers for services supplied in different modes)
Limitations of market access: **Cross-border supply** – None **Consumption abroad** – None **Commercial presence** – Foreign law firms can provide legal services only in the form of representative offices in Beijing, Shanghai, Guangzhou, Shenzhen, Haikou, Dalian, Qingdao, Ningbo, Yantai, Tianjin, Suzhou, Xiamen, Zhuhai, Hangzhou, Fuzhou, Wuhan, Chengdu, Shenyang and Kunming only. Representative offices can engage in profit-making activities. Representative offices in China shall be no less than the number established upon the date of accession. A foreign law firm can only establish one representative office in China. The above-mentioned geographic and quantitative limitations will be eliminated within one year after China's accession to the WTO. Business scope of foreign representative offices is only as follows: (a)   to provide clients with consultancy on the legislation of the country/region where the lawyers of the law firm are permitted to engage in lawyer's professional work, and on international conventions and practices; (b)   to handle, when entrusted by clients or Chinese law firms, legal affairs of the country/region where the lawyers of the law firm are permitted to engage in lawyer's professional work; (c)   to entrust, on behalf of foreign clients, Chinese law firms to deal with the Chinese legal affairs; (d)   to enter into contracts to maintain long-term entrustment relations with Chinese law firms for legal affairs; (e)   to provide information on the impact of the Chinese legal environment. Entrustment allows the foreign representative office to directly instruct lawyers in the entrusted Chinese law firm, as agreed between both parties. The representatives of a foreign law firm shall be practitioner lawyers who are members of the bar or law society in a WTO member and have practiced for no less than two years outside of China. The Chief representative shall be a partner or equivalent (e.g., member of a law firm of a limited liability corporation) of a law firm of a WTO member and have practiced for no less than three years.

Presence of natural persons – Unbound except as indicated in Horizontal Commitments.

| Limitation on National Treatment |

Cross-border supply – None

Consumption abroad – None

Commercial presence – All representatives shall be resident in China no less than six months each year. The representative office shall not employ Chinese national registered lawyers outside of China.

Presence of natural persons – Unbound except as indicated in Horizontal Commitments.

b. Accounting, auditing and bookkeeping services (CPC 862)

China commitments
(any limitations/requirements or offers for services supplied in different modes)

| Limitations on market access |

Cross-border supply – None

Consumption abroad – None

Commercial presence – Partnerships or incorporated accounting firms are limited to Certified Public Accountants (CPAs) licensed by the Chinese authorities.

Presence of natural persons – Unbound except as indicated in Horizontal Commitments.

| Limitation on national treatment |

Cross-border supply – None

Consumption abroad – None

Commercial presence – None

Presence of natural persons – Unbound except as indicated in Horizontal Commitments.

Additional Commitments

– Foreign accounting firms are permitted to affiliate with Chinese firms and enter into contractual agreements with their affiliated firms in other WTO members.
– Upon accession to the WTO, issuance of licenses to those foreigners who have passed the Chinese national CPA examination shall be accorded national treatment.

- – Applicants will be informed of results in writing no later than 30 days after submission of their applications.
- – Existing contractual joint venture accounting firms are not limited only to CPAs licensed by Chinese authorities.
- – Accounting firms providing services in CPC 862 can engage in taxation and management consulting services. They will not be subject to requirements on form of establishment in CPC 865 and 8630.

c. Taxation services (CPC 8630)

China commitments
(any limitations/requirements or offers for services supplied in different modes)

Limitations on market access

Cross-border supply – None

Consumption abroad – None

Commercial presence – Only in the form of joint ventures, with foreign majority ownership permitted. None, within six years of China's accession, foreign firms will be permitted to establish wholly foreign-owned subsidiaries.

Presence of natural persons – Unbound except as indicated in Horizontal Commitments.

Limitation on national treatment

Cross-border supply – None

Consumption abroad – None

Commercial presence – None

Presence of natural persons – Unbound except as indicated in Horizontal Commitments.

d. Architectural services (CPC 8671);
e. Engineering services (CPC 8672);
f. Integrated engineering services (CPC 8673);
g. Urban planning services (except general urban planning) (CPC 8674)

China commitments
(any limitations/requirements or offers for services supplied in different modes)

Limitations on market access

Cross-border supply – None for scheme design. Co-operation with Chinese professional organisations is required except scheme design

Consumption abroad – None

Commercial presence – Only in the form of joint ventures, with foreign majority ownership permitted.

Within five years after China's accession to the WTO, wholly foreign-owned enterprises will be permitted

Presence of natural persons – Unbound, except as indicated in Horizontal Commitments

Limitation on national treatment

Cross-border supply – None

Consumption abroad – None

Commercial presence – Foreign service suppliers shall be registered architects/engineers, or enterprises engaged in architectural/engineering/urban planning services, in their home country

Presence of natural persons – Unbound, except as indicated in Horizontal Commitments

---

h. Medical and dental services (CPC 9312)

China commitments
(any limitations/requirements or offers for services supplied in different modes)

Limitations on market access

Cross-border supply – None

Consumption abroad – None

Commercial presence – Foreign service suppliers are permitted to establish joint venture hospitals or clinics with Chinese partners with quantitative limitations in line with China's needs, with foreign majority ownership permitted.

Presence of natural persons – Unbound, except as indicated in Horizontal Commitments and as follows:

Foreign doctors with professional certificates issued by their home country shall be permitted to provide short-term medical services in China after they obtain licenses from the Ministry of Public Health. The term of service is six months and may extend to one year.

Limitation on national treatment

Cross-border supply – None

Consumption abroad – None

Commercial presence – The majority of doctors and medical personnel of the joint venture hospital and clinics shall be of Chinese nationality.

Presence of natural persons – Unbound, except as indicated in Horizontal Commitments.

B. Sub-sector: Computer and Related Services

a. Consultancy services related to the installation of computer hardware (CPC 841)

China commitments (any limitations/requirements or offers for services supplied in different modes)

Limitations on market access

Cross-border supply – None

Consumption abroad – None

Commercial presence – None

Presence of natural persons – Unbound except as indicated in Horizontal Commitments.

Limitation on national treatment

Cross-border supply – None

Consumption abroad – None

Commercial presence – None

Presence of natural persons – Qualifications are as follows: certified engineers, or personnel with Bachelor's degree (or above) and three years of experience in these fields.

b. Software implementation services (CPC 842)

– **Systems and software consulting services (CPC 8421)**
– **Systems analysis services (CPC 8422)**
– **Systems design services (CPC 8423)**
– **Programming services (CPC 8424)**
– **Systems maintenance services (CPC 8425)**

c. Data processing services (CPC 843)

– **Input preparation services (CPC 8431)**

China commitments (any limitations/requirements or offers for services supplied in different modes)
Limitations on market access
Cross-border supply – None
Consumption abroad – None
Commercial presence – Only in the form of joint ventures, with foreign majority ownership permitted.
Presence of natural persons – Unbound except as indicated in Horizontal Commitments.
Limitation on national treatment
Cross-border supply – None
Consumption abroad – None
Commercial presence – None
Presence of natural persons – Qualifications are as follows: certified engineers, or personnel with Bachelor's degree (or above) and three years of experience in these fields.

– **Data processing and tabulation services (CPC 8432)**
– **Time-sharing services (CPC 8433)**

China commitments (any limitations/requirements or offers for services supplied in different modes)
Limitations on market access
Cross-border supply – None
Consumption abroad – None
Commercial presence – None
Presence of natural persons – Unbound except as indicated in Horizontal Commitments.
Limitation on national treatment
Cross-border supply – None
Consumption abroad – None
Commercial presence – None
Presence of natural persons – Qualifications are as follows: certified engineers, or personnel with Bachelor's degree (or above) and three years of experience in these fields.

D. Sub-sector: Real Estate Services

a. Real estate services involving own or leased property (CPC 821)

China commitments (any limitations/requirements or offers for services supplied in different modes)
Limitations on market access
Cross-border supply – None
Consumption abroad – None
Commercial Presence – None except for the following: Wholly foreign-owned enterprises are not permitted for high standard real estate projects[6], such as apartments and office buildings, but excluding luxury hotels.
Presence of natural persons – Unbound except as indicated in Horizontal Commitments.
Limitation on national treatment
Cross-border supply – None

---

[6]High standard real estate projects refer to the real estate projects with construction costs per unit two times more than the average construction costs per unit in the same city.

Consumption abroad – None

Commercial presence – None

Presence of natural persons – Unbound except as indicated in Horizontal Commitments.

b. Real estate services on a fee or contract basis (CPC 822)

China commitments
(any limitations/requirements or offers for services supplied in different modes)

Limitations on market access

Cross-border supply – None

Consumption abroad – None

Commercial Presence – Only in the form of joint ventures, with foreign majority ownership permitted.

Presence of natural persons – Unbound except as indicated in Horizontal Commitments.

Limitation on national treatment

Cross-border supply – None

Consumption abroad – None

Commercial presence – None

Presence of natural persons – Unbound except as indicated in Horizontal Commitments.

F. Sub-sector: Other Business Services

a. Advertising Services (CPC 871)

China commitments
(any limitations/requirements or offers for services supplied in different modes)

Limitations on market access

Cross-border supply – Only through advertising agents registered in China who have the right to provide foreign advertising services.

Consumption abroad – Only through advertising agents registered in China who have the right to provide foreign advertising services.

Commercial presence – Foreign service suppliers are permitted to establish advertising enterprises in China only in the form of joint ventures with foreign investment no more than 49 per cent. Within two years after China's accession, foreign majority ownership will be permitted and within four years after China's accession, wholly foreign-owned subsidiaries will be permitted.

Presence of natural persons – Unbound except as indicated in Horizontal Commitments.

Limitation on national treatment

Cross-border supply – None

Consumption abroad – None

Commercial presence – None

Presence of natural persons – Unbound except as indicated in Horizontal Commitments.

c. **Management Consulting services (CPC 865)**

China commitments
(any limitations/requirements or offers for services supplied in different modes)

Limitations on market access

Cross-border supply – None

Consumption abroad – None

Commercial presence – Only in the form of joint ventures, with foreign majority ownership permitted. None, within six years of China's accession, foreign firms will be permitted to establish wholly foreign-owned subsidiaries.

Presence of natural persons – Unbound except as indicated in Horizontal Commitments.

Limitation on national treatment

Cross-border supply – None

Consumption abroad – None

Commercial presence – None

Presence of natural persons – Unbound except as indicated in Horizontal Commitments.

e. **Technical testing and analysis services (CPC 8676) and freight inspection covered by CPC 749, excluding statutory inspection services for freight inspection services**

China commitments
(any limitations/requirements or offers for services supplied in different modes)

Limitations on market access

Cross-border supply – None

Consumption abroad – None

Commercial presence – Foreign services suppliers which have been engaged in inspection services in their home countries for more than three years are permitted to establish joint venture technical testing, analysis and freight inspection companies with no less than US$ 350,000 in registered capital. Within two years after China's accession, foreign majority ownership will be permitted and within four years after China's accession, wholly foreign-owned subsidiaries will be permitted.

Presence of natural persons – Unbound except as indicated in Horizontal Commitments.

Limitation on national treatment

Cross-border supply – None

Consumption abroad – None

Commercial presence – None

Presence of natural persons – Unbound except as indicated in Horizontal Commitments.

---

f.   Services incidental to agriculture, forestry, hunting and fishing (CPC 881, 882)
m. Related scientific technical consulting services (CPC 8675)

China commitments
(any limitations/requirements or offers for services supplied in different modes)

Limitations on market access

Cross-border supply – None

Consumption abroad – None

Commercial presence – Only in the form of joint ventures, with foreign majority ownership permitted.

Presence of natural persons – Unbound except as indicated in Horizontal Commitments.

Limitation on national treatment

Cross-border supply – None

Consumption abroad – None

Commercial presence – None

Presence of natural persons – Unbound except as indicated in Horizontal Commitments.

– **Offshore oil-field services geological, geophysical and other scientific prospecting services (CPC 86751); Sub-surface surveying services (CPC 86752)**

China commitments
(any limitations/requirements or offers for services supplied in different modes)

Limitations on market access

Cross-border supply – None

Consumption abroad – None

Commercial presence – Only in the form of petroleum exploitation in cooperation with Chinese partners

Presence of natural persons – Unbound except as indicated in Horizontal Commitments.

Limitation on national treatment

Cross-border supply – None

Consumption abroad – None

Commercial presence – None

Presence of natural persons – Unbound except as indicated in Horizontal Commitments.

– **Onshore oil-field services**

China commitments
(any limitations/requirements or offers for services supplied in different modes)

Limitations on market access

Cross-border supply – None

Consumption abroad – None

Commercial presence – Only in the form of petroleum exploitation in cooperation with China National Petroleum Corp. (CNPC) in the designated areas approved by the Chinese government.

In order to carry out the petroleum contract, the foreign service supplier shall establish a branch, subsidiary or representative office within the territory of the People's Republic of China and go through registration formalities in accordance with the laws. The domiciles of the said offices shall be determined through consultation with CNPC.

The foreign service supplier shall open its bank account with a bank approved by the Chinese authorities to engage in foreign exchange business within the Chinese territory.

Presence of natural persons – Unbound except as indicated in Horizontal Commitments.

Limitation on national treatment

Cross-border supply – None

Consumption abroad – None

Commercial presence – The foreign service supplier shall furnish CNPC accurately and promptly with the reports on the petroleum operations, and shall submit to CNPC the data and samples as well as various technological, economic, accounting and administrative reports related to petroleum operations.

CNPC shall have the ownership of all of the data records, samples, vouchers and other original information acquired during the implementation of the petroleum operations. The investment of foreign service suppliers shall be made in US dollars or other hard currencies.

Presence of natural persons – Unbound except as indicated in Horizontal Commitments.

p. Photographic services (CPC 875)

China commitments (any limitations/requirements or offers for services supplied in different modes)

Limitations on market access

Cross-border supply – None

Consumption abroad – None

Commercial presence – Only in the form of joint ventures, with foreign majority ownership permitted

Presence of natural persons – Unbound except as indicated in Horizontal Commitments.

Limitation on national treatment
Cross-border supply – None
Consumption abroad – None
Commercial presence – None
Presence of natural persons – Unbound except as indicated in Horizontal Commitments.

q. Packaging services (CPC 876)

China commitments (any limitations/requirements or offers for services supplied in different modes)
Limitations on market access
Cross-border supply – None
Consumption abroad – None
Commercial presence – Foreign services suppliers will be permitted to establish joint venture in China. Within one year after China's accession, foreign majority ownership will be permitted. Within three years after China's accession, foreign service suppliers will be permitted to establish wholly foreign-owned subsidiaries.
Presence of natural persons – Unbound, except as indicated in Horizontal Commitments.
Limitation on national treatment
Cross-border supply – None
Consumption abroad – None
Commercial presence – None
Presence of natural persons – Unbound except as indicated in Horizontal Commitments.

s. Convention services (CPC 87909)

China commitments (any limitations/requirements or offers for services supplied in different modes)
Limitations on market access
Cross-border supply – None

Consumption abroad – None

Commercial presence – Only in the form of joint ventures, with foreign majority ownership permitted.

Presence of natural persons – Unbound except as indicated in Horizontal Commitments.

Limitation on national treatment

Cross-border supply – None

Consumption abroad – None

Commercial presence – None

Presence of natural persons – Unbound except as indicated in Horizontal Commitments.

t. Translation and interpretation services (CPC 87905)

China commitments (any limitations/requirements or offers for services supplied in different modes)

Limitations on market access

Cross-border supply – None

Consumption abroad – None

Commercial presence – Only in the form of joint ventures, with foreign majority ownership permitted

Presence of natural persons – Unbound except as indicated in Horizontal Commitments.

Limitation on national treatment

Cross-border supply – None

Consumption abroad – None

Commercial presence – None

Presence of natural persons – Qualifications are as follows: three years of experience in translation or interpretation and a good command of the working language(s).

– **Maintenance and repair services (CPC 63, 6112 and 6122)**
– **Maintenance and repair services of office machinery and equipment including Computers (CPC 845 and 886)**
– **Rental and leasing services (CPC 831, 832 excluding CPC 83202)**

China commitments (any limitations/requirements or offers for services supplied in different modes)
Limitations on market access
Cross-border supply – None
Consumption abroad – None
Commercial presence – Only in the form of joint ventures. Within one year after China's accession, foreign majority ownership will be permitted.
Within three years after China's accession, wholly foreign-owned subsidiaries will be permitted. For Rental and Leasing services, service suppliers will have global assets of US$ 5 million.
Presence of natural persons – Unbound, except as indicated in Horizontal Commitments.
Limitation on national treatment
Cross-border supply – None
Consumption abroad – None
Commercial presence – None
Presence of natural persons – Unbound, except as indicated in Horizontal Commitments.

2. SECTOR: COMMUNICATION SERVICES

B. Sub-sector: Courier Services (CPC 75121, except for those currently specifically reserved to Chinese postal authorities by law)

China commitments (any limitations/requirements or offers for services supplied in different modes)
Limitations on market access
Cross-border supply – None
Consumption abroad – None
Commercial presence – Upon accession, foreign service suppliers will be permitted to establish joint ventures with foreign investment not exceeding 49 per cent.
Within one year after China's accession, foreign majority ownership will be permitted.

Within four years after China's accession, foreign service suppliers will be permitted to establish wholly foreign-owned subsidiaries.

Presence of natural persons – Unbound, except as indicated in Horizontal Commitments.

Limitation on national treatment

Cross-border supply – None

Consumption abroad – None

Commercial presence – None

Presence of natural persons – Unbound, except as indicated in Horizontal Commitments.

C. Sub-sector: Telecommunication Services[7]
Value-added Services

Including the following sub-sectors "h" through "n":
Electronic mail; Voice Mail; On-line information and database retrieval;
Electronic data interchange; Enhance/Value-added facsimile services (including store and forward, store and retrieved); Code and protocol conversion; On-line information and/or data processing (including transaction processing).

China commitments
(any limitations/requirements or offers for services supplied in different modes)

Limitations on market access

Cross-border supply – See "Commercial Presence"

Consumption abroad – None

Commercial presence – Foreign service suppliers will be permitted to establish joint venture value-added telecommunication enterprises, without quantitative restrictions, and provide services in the cities of Shanghai, Guangzhou and Beijing. Foreign investment in joint venture shall be no more than 30 per cent.

---

[7]China's commitments are scheduled in accordance with the following: Notes for Scheduling Basic Telecom Services Commitments (S/GBT/W/2/REV/1) and Market Access Limitations on Spectrum Availability (S/GBT/W/3) attached hereto.

All international telecommunications services shall go through gateways established with the approval of China's telecommunications authorities, which will act as an independent regulatory authority in accordance with the principles of paragraph 5 of the Reference Paper. [Ed. see Annex 1 to this schedule]

Further liberalization of this sector, including with respect to the level of equity participation permitted, will be discussed in the services negotiations during the new round of trade talks.

Within one year after China's accession, the areas will be expanded to include Chengdu, Chongqing, Dalian, Fuzhou, Hangzhou, Nanjing, Ningbo, Qingdao, Shenyang, Shenzhen, Xiamen, Xi'an, Taiyuan and Wuhan and foreign investment shall be no more than 49 per cent.

Within two years after China's accession, there will be no geographic restriction and foreign investment shall be no more than 50 per cent.

Presence of natural persons - Unbound except as indicated in Horizontal Commitments.

Limitation on national treatment

Cross-border supply – None

Consumption abroad – None

Commercial presence – None

Presence of natural persons – Unbound except as indicated in Horizontal Commitments.

Additional Commitments

China undertakes the obligations contained in the Reference Paper in Annex I attached hereto.

Basic Telecommunication Services
— Paging Services

China commitments (any limitations/requirements or offers for services supplied in different modes)

Limitations on market access

Cross-border supply – See "Commercial presence"

Consumption abroad – None

Commercial Presence – Foreign service suppliers will be permitted to establish joint venture enterprises, without quantitative restrictions, and provide services in and between the cities of Shanghai, Guangzhou and Beijing. Foreign investment in joint venture shall be no more than 30 per cent. Within one year after China's accession, the areas will be expanded to include services in and between Chengdu, Chongqing, Dalian, Fuzhou, Hangzhou, Nanjing, Ningbo, Qingdao, Shenyang, Shenzhen, Xiamen, Xi'an, Taiyuan and Wuhan and foreign investment shall be no more than 49 per cent.

Within two years after China's accession, there will be no geographic restriction and foreign investment shall be no more than 50 per cent.

Presence of natural persons – Unbound except as indicated in Horizontal Commitments.

Limitation on national treatment

Cross-border supply – None

Consumption abroad – None

Commercial presence – None

Presence of natural persons – Unbound except as indicated in Horizontal Commitments.

Additional Commitments

China undertakes the obligations contained in the Reference Paper in Annex I attached hereto.

Mobile Voice and Data Services:
— **Analogue/Digital/Cellular Services**
— **Personal Communication Services**

China commitments (any limitations/requirements or offers for services supplied in different modes)

Limitations on market access

Cross-border supply – See "Commercial Presence"

Consumption abroad – None

Commercial presence – Upon China's accession, foreign service suppliers will be permitted to establish joint venture enterprises, without quantitative restrictions, and provide services in and between the cities of Shanghai, Guangzhou and Beijing. Foreign investment in the joint venture shall be no more than 25 per cent.

Within one year after accession, the areas will be expanded to include services in and between Chengdu, Chongqing, Dalian, Fuzhou, Hangzhou, Nanjing, Ningbo, Qingdao, Shenyang, Shenzhen, Xiamen, Xi'an, Taiyuan and Wuhan and foreign investment shall be no more than 35 per cent.

Within three years after accession, foreign investment shall be no more than 49 per cent.

Within five years after accession, there will be no geographic restriction.

Presence of natural persons – Unbound except as indicated in Horizontal Commitments.

> **Limitation on national treatment**
>
> **Cross-border supply** – None
>
> **Consumption abroad** – None
>
> **Commercial presence** – None
>
> **Presence of natural persons** – Unbound except as indicated in Horizontal Commitments.

— **Domestic Services:**
  - a. **Voice services**
  - b. **Packet-switched data transmission services**
  - c. **Circuit-switched data transmission services**
  - f. **Facsimile services**
  - g. **Domestic private leased circuit services**

— **International Service:**
  - a. **Voice services**
  - b. **Packet-switched data transmission services**
  - c. **Circuit-switched data transmission services**
  - f. **Facsimile services**
  - g. **International closed user group voice and data services (use of private leased circuit service is permitted)**

> ## China commitments
> ### (any limitations/requirements or offers for services supplied in different modes)
>
> **Limitations on market access**
>
> **Cross-border supply** – See "Commercial Presence"
>
> **Consumption abroad** – None
>
> **Commercial presence** – Within three years after China's accession, foreign service suppliers will be permitted to establish joint venture enterprises, without quantitative restrictions, and provide services in and between the cities of Shanghai, Guangzhou and Beijing. Foreign investment in the joint venture shall be no more than 25 per cent.
>
> Within five years after accession, the areas will be expanded to include services in and between Chengdu, Chongqing, Dalian, Fuzhou, Hangzhou, Nanjing, Ningbo, Qingdao, Shenyang, Shenzhen, Xiamen, Xi'an, Taiyuan and Wuhan. And foreign investment shall be no more than 35 per cent.

Within six years after accession, there will be no geographic restriction and foreign investment shall be no more than 49 per cent.

Presence of natural persons – Unbound except as indicated in Horizontal Commitments.

| Limitation on national treatment |

Cross-border supply – None

Consumption abroad – None

Commercial presence – None

Presence of natural persons – Unbound except as indicated in Horizontal Commitments.

D. Sub-sector: Audiovisual Services
— **Videos, including entertainment software and (CPC 83202), distribution services**
— **Sound recording distribution services**

| China commitments
(any limitations/requirements or offers for services supplied in different modes) |

| Limitations on market access |

Cross-border supply – None

Consumption abroad – None

Commercial presence – Upon accession, foreign services suppliers will be permitted to establish contractual joint ventures with Chinese partners to engage in the distribution of audiovisual products, excluding motion pictures, without prejudice to China's right to examine the content of audio and video products (see footnote 5).

Presence of natural persons - Unbound, except as indicated in Horizontal Commitments.

Limitation on national treatment

Cross-border supply – None

Consumption abroad – None

Commercial presence – None

presence of natural persons – Unbound, except as indicated in Horizontal Commitments.

Additional Commitments
Without prejudice to compliance with China's regulations on the administration of films, upon accession, China will allow the importation of motion pictures for theatrical release on a revenue-sharing basis and the number of such imports shall be 20 on an annual basis.

— Cinema Theatre Services

China commitments (any limitations/requirements or offers for services supplied in different modes)
Limitations on market access
Cross-border supply – None
Consumption abroad – None
Commercial presence – Upon accession, foreign services suppliers will be permitted to construct and/or renovate cinema theatres, with foreign investment no more than 49 per cent.
Presence of natural persons – Unbound, except as indicated in Horizontal Commitments.
Limitation on national treatment
Cross-border supply – None
Consumption abroad – None
Commercial presence – None
Presence of natural persons – Unbound, except as indicated in Horizontal Commitments.

3. SECTOR: CONSTRUCTION AND RELATED ENGINEERING SERVICES

Sub-sectors:
[A. General construction work for buildings] (CPC 512)
[B. General construction work for civil engineering] (CPC 513[8])
[C. Installation and assembly work] (CPC 514, 516)
[D. Building completion and finishing work] (CPC 517)
[E. Other] (CPC 511, 515, 518[9])

---

[8]Including dredging services relating to infrastructure construction.
[9]Coverage of CPC 518 is limited only to the rental and leasing services of construction and/or demolition machines with operator which are owned and used by foreign construction enterprises in their supply of services.

China commitments
(any limitations/requirements or offers for services supplied in different modes)

Limitations on market access

Cross-border supply – Unbound*

Consumption abroad – None

Commercial presence – Only in the form of joint ventures, with foreign majority ownership permitted. Within three years after China's accession to the WTO, wholly foreign-owned enterprises will be permitted. Wholly foreign-owned enterprises can only undertake the following four types of construction projects.

1. Construction projects wholly financed by foreign investment and/or grants.
2. Construction projects financed by loans of international financial institutions and awarded through international tendering according to the terms of loans.
3. Chinese-foreign jointly constructed projects with foreign investment equal to or more than 50 per cent; and Chinese-foreign jointly constructed projects with foreign investment less than 50 per cent but technically difficult to be implemented by Chinese construction enterprises alone.
4. Chinese invested construction projects which are difficult to be implemented by Chinese construction enterprises alone can be jointly undertaken by Chinese and foreign construction enterprises with the approval of provincial government.

Presence of natural persons – Unbound except as indicated in Horizontal Commitments.

Limitation on national treatment

Cross-border supply – Unbound*

Consumption abroad – None

Commercial presence – None except for the following:

(a) The existing registered capital requirements for joint venture construction enterprises are slightly different from those of the domestic enterprises.
(b) Joint venture construction enterprises have the obligation to undertake foreign-invested construction projects.

Within three years after China's accession to the WTO, none.

Presence of natural persons – Unbound except as indicated in Horizontal Commitments.

---

*Unbound due to lack of technical feasibility.

4. SECTOR: DISTRIBUTION SERVICES (as defined in Annex 2 to this Schedule[10])

A. Sub-sector: Commission Agents' Services (excluding salt, tobacco)
B. Sub-sector: Wholesale Trade Services[11] (excluding salt, tobacco)

China commitments (any limitations/requirements or offers for services supplied in different modes)

Limitations on market access

Cross-border supply – Unbound

Consumption abroad – None

Commercial presence – Within one year after China's accession to the WTO, foreign service suppliers may establish joint ventures to engage in the commission agents' business and wholesale business of all imported and domestically produced products, except those products that immediately follow. For these products, foreign service suppliers will be permitted to engage in the distribution of books, newspapers, magazines, pharmaceutical products, pesticides and mulching films within three years after China's accession, and to engage in the distribution of chemical fertilizers, processed oil and crude oil within five years after China's accession.

Within two years after China's accession to the WTO, foreign majority ownership will be permitted and no geographic or quantitative restrictions will apply.

None, within three years after accession, except for chemical fertilizers, processed oil and crude oil within five years after accession.

Presence of natural persons – Unbound except as indicated in Horizontal Commitments.

Limitation on national treatment

Cross-border supply – Unbound

Consumption abroad – None

Commercial presence – None

Presence of natural persons – Unbound except as indicated in Horizontal Commitments.

---

[10][Ed.] which gives the full definition of "Distribution Services"

[11]The restriction on mode 1 shall not undermine the rights of WTO Members to the right to trade as stipulated in Chapter 5 of China's Protocol of accession to the WTO.

Additional Commitments

Foreign-invested enterprises are permitted to distribute their products manufactured in China, including the products listed in the market access or sector or sub-sector column, and provide subordinate services as defined in Annex 2.

Foreign service suppliers are permitted to provide the full range of related subordinate services, including after sales services, as defined in Annex 2, for the products they distribute.

C. Sub-sector: Retailing Services (excluding tobacco)

China commitments
(any limitations/requirements or offers for services supplied in different modes)

Limitations on market access

Cross-border supply – Unbound except for mail order.

Consumption abroad – None

Commercial presence – Foreign service suppliers may supply services only in forms of joint ventures in five Special Economic Zones (Shenzhen, Zhuhai, Shantou, Xiamen and Hainan) and six cities (Beijing, Shanghai, Tianjin, Guangzhou, Dalian and Qingdao). In Beijing and Shanghai, a total of no more than four joint venture retailing enterprises are permitted respectively. In each of the other cities, no more than two joint venture retailing enterprises will be permitted. Two joint venture retailing enterprises among the four to be established in Beijing may set up their branches in the same city (i.e. Beijing).

Upon China's accession to the WTO, Zhengzhou and Wuhan will be immediately open to joint venture retailing enterprises. Within two years after China's accession to the WTO, foreign majority control will be permitted in joint venture retailing enterprises and all provincial capitals, Chongqing and Ningbo will be open to joint venture retailing enterprises.

Foreign service suppliers will be permitted to engage in the retailing of all products, except for the retailing of books, newspapers and magazines within one year after accession, the retailing of pharmaceutical products, pesticides, mulching films and processed oil within three years after accession and retailing of chemical fertilizers within five years after accession.

None, within three years after accession, except for:

- retailing of chemical fertilizers, within five years after accession; and- those chain stores which sell products of different types and brands from multiple suppliers with more than 30 outlets. For such chains stores with more than 30 outlets, foreign majority ownership will not be permitted if those chain stores distribute any of the following products: motor vehicles (for a period of five years after accession at which time the equity limitation will have been eliminated), and products listed above and in Annex 2a of the Protocol of China's WTO Accession. The foreign chain store operators will have the freedom of choice of any partner, legally established in China according to China's laws and regulations.

Presence of natural persons – Unbound except as indicated in Horizontal Commitments.

Limitation on national treatment

Cross-border supply – Unbound except for mail order.

Consumption abroad – None

Commercial presence – None

Presence of natural persons – Unbound except as indicated in Horizontal Commitments.

Additional Commitments
Foreign-invested enterprises may distribute their products manufactured in China, including those excepted products as listed in the market access or sector or sub-sector column, and provide subordinate services as defined in Annex 2. Foreign service suppliers are permitted to provide full range of related subordinate services, including after sales services, as defined in Annex 2, for the products they distribute.

D. Sub-sector: Franchising

China Commitments (any limitations/requirements or offers for services supplied in different modes)

Limitations on market access

Cross-border supply – None

Consumption abroad – None

Commercial presence – Within three years after China's accession to the WTO, none.

Presence of natural persons – Unbound except as indicated in Horizontal Commitments.

Limitation on national treatment

Cross-border supply – None

Consumption abroad – None

> **Commercial presence** – Within three years after China's accession to the WTO, none.
>
> **Presence of natural persons** – Unbound except as indicated in Horizontal Commitments.

E. Sub-sector: Wholesale or retail trade services away from a fixed location.

> **China commitments**
> **(any limitations/requirements or offers for services supplied in different modes)**
>
> **Limitations on market access**
>
> **Cross-border supply** – None
>
> **Consumption abroad** – None
>
> **Commercial Presence** – Within three years after China's accession to the WTO, none[12].
>
> **Presence of natural persons** – Unbound except as indicated in Horizontal Commitments.
>
> **Limitation on national treatment**
>
> **Cross-border supply** – None
>
> **Consumption abroad** – None
>
> **Commercial presence** – Within three years after China's accession to the WTO, none.
>
> **Presence of natural persons** – Unbound except as indicated in Horizontal Commitments.

5. SECTOR: EDUCATIONAL SERVICES

(Excluding special education services e.g. military, police, political and party school education)

Sub-sectors:

A. Primary education services (CPC 921, excluding national compulsory education in CPC 92190)
B. Secondary education services (CPC 922, excluding national compulsory education In CPC 92210)
C. Higher education services (CPC 923)
D. Adult education services (CPC 924)
E. Other education services (CPC 929, including English language training)

---

[12]See paragraph 309 of the Working Party Report.

China Commitments
(any limitations/requirements or offers for services supplied in different modes)

Limitations on market access

Cross-border supply – Unbound

Consumption abroad – None

Commercial presence – Joint schools will be established, with foreign majority ownership permitted.

Presence of natural persons – Unbound except as indicated in Horizontal Commitments and the following: foreign individual education service suppliers may enter into China to provide education services when invited or employed by Chinese schools and other education institutions.

Limitation on national treatment

Cross-border supply – Unbound

Consumption abroad – None

Commercial presence – Unbound

Presence of natural persons – Qualifications are as follows: possession of Bachelor's degree or above; and an appropriate professional title or certificate, with two years' professional experiences.

---

6. SECTOR: ENVIRONMENTAL SERVICES
(excluding environmental quality monitoring and pollution source inspection)

Sub-sectors:

A. Sewage Services (CPC 9401)
B. Solid Waste Disposal Services (CPC 9402)
C. Cleaning Services of Exhaust Gases (CPC 9404)
D. Noise Abatement Services (CPC 9405)
E. Nature and Landscape Protection Services (CPC 9406)
F. Other Environmental Protection Services (CPC 9409)
G. Sanitation Services (CPC 9403)

China commitments
(any limitations/requirements or offers for services supplied in different modes)

Limitations on market access

Cross-border supply – Unbound except for environmental consultation services.

Consumption abroad – None

Commercial presence – Foreign services suppliers engaged in environmental services are permitted to provide services only in the form of joint ventures, with foreign majority ownership permitted.

Presence of natural persons – Unbound except as indicated in Horizontal Commitments.

Limitation on national treatment

Cross-border supply – None

Consumption abroad – None

Commercial presence – None

Presence of natural persons – Unbound except as indicated in Horizontal Commitments

7. SECTOR: FINANCIAL SERVICES[13]

A. Sub-sector: All Insurance and Insurance-Related Services[14]
a. Life, health and pension/annuities insurance
b. Non-life insurance
c. Reinsurance
d. Services auxiliary to insurance

China commitments
(any limitations/requirements or offers for services supplied in different modes)

Limitations on market access

Cross-border supply – Unbound except for:

a) reinsurance;
b) international marine, aviation, and transport insurance; and
c) brokerage for large scale commercial risks, international marine, aviation and transport insurance, and reinsurance.

---

[13][Ed.] Apart from *GATS*, other WTO agreements relative to financial services sectors include: *GATS' Annex on Financial Services* and *Understanding on Commitments in Financial Services ("the Understanding")*; subject to the terms under *the Understanding*, the *Understanding* provides to participants in the Uruguay Round with an alternative approach to take on specific commitments with respect to financial services other than that covered by Part III of *GATS*.

[14]Any further authorization provided to foreign insurers after accession under more favourable conditions than those contained in this schedule (including the extension of grandfathered investments through branching, sub-branching or any other legal form), will be made available to other foreign service suppliers which so requested.

Consumption abroad – Unbound for brokerage. Other, none.

Commercial presence –

A. <u>Form of establishment</u>

Foreign non-life insurers will be permitted to establish as a branch or as a joint venture with 51 per cent foreign ownership.

Within two years after China's accession, foreign non-life insurers will be permitted to establish as a wholly-owned subsidiary; i.e., with no form of establishment restrictions.

Upon accession, foreign life insurers will be permitted 50 per cent foreign ownership in a joint venture with the partner of their choice.

The joint venture partners can freely agree the terms of their engagement, provided they remain within the limits of the commitments contained in this schedule.

For brokerage for insurance of large scale commercial risks and brokerage for reinsurance and brokerage for international marine, aviation, and transport insurance and reinsurance: upon accession, joint venture with foreign equity no more than 50 per cent will be permitted; within three years after China's accession, foreign equity share shall be increased to 51 per cent; within five years after China's accession, wholly foreign owned subsidiary will be permitted. For other brokerage services: Unbound. Internal branching for an insurance firm will be permitted consistent with the phase out of geographic restrictions.

B. <u>Geographic Coverage</u>

Upon accession, foreign life and non-life insurers, and insurance brokers will be permitted to provide services in Shanghai, Guangzhou, Dalian, Shenzhen and Foshan. Within two years after China's accession, foreign life and non-life insurers, and insurance brokers will be permitted to provide services in the following cities: Beijing, Chengdu, Chongqing, Fuzhou, Suzhou, Xiamen, Ningbo, Shenyang, Wuhan and Tianjin. Within three years after China's accession, there will be no geographic restrictions.

C. <u>Business Scope</u>

Upon accession, foreign non-life insurers will be permitted to provide "master policy" insurance/insurance of large scale commercial risks, which has no geographic restrictions. In accordance with national treatment, foreign insurance brokers will be permitted to provide "Master policy" no later than Chinese brokers, under conditions no less favourable.

Foreign non-life insurers are permitted to provide insurance of enterprises abroad as well as property insurance, related liability insurance and credit insurance of foreign-invested enterprises in China upon accession. Within 2 years after China's accession, foreign non-life insurers will be permitted to provide the full range of non-life insurance services to both foreign and domestic clients.

Foreign insurers are permitted to provide individual (not group) insurance to foreigners and Chinese citizens; within three years after accession, foreign insurers will be permitted to provide health insurance, group insurance and pension/annuities insurance to foreigners and Chinese.

Upon accession, foreign insurers will be permitted to provide reinsurance services for life and non-life insurance as a branch, joint venture, or wholly foreign-owned subsidiary, without geographic or quantitative restrictions on the number of licenses issued.

D. Licenses

Upon accession, licenses will be issued with no economic needs test or quantitative limits on licenses. Qualifications for establishing a foreign insurance institution are as follows:

- the investor shall be a foreign insurance company with more than 30 years of establishment experience in a WTO member;
- it shall have a representative office for two consecutive years in China;
- it shall have total assets of more than US $5 billion at the end of the year prior to application, except for insurance brokers.

Insurance brokers shall have total assets of more than US$ 500 million. Within one year after accession, they shall have total assets of more than US$ 400 million. Within two years after accession, they shall have total assets of more than US$ 300 million. Within four years after accession, they shall have total assets of more than US$ 200 million.

Presence of natural persons – Unbound except as indicated in Horizontal Commitments.

Limitation on national treatment

Cross-border supply – None

Consumption abroad – None

Commercial presence – None, except for:

- Foreign insurance institutions shall not be engage in the statutory insurance business.

- Upon accession, a 20 per cent cession of all lines of the primary risks for non-life, personal accident and health insurance business with an appointed Chinese Reinsurance Company shall be required; one year after accession, 15 per cent shall be required; two years after accession, ten per cent shall be required; and three years after accession, five per cent shall be required; and four years after accession, no compulsory cession shall be required.

Presence of natural persons – Unbound except as indicated in Horizontal Commitments.

B. Sub-sector: Banking and Other financial Services (excluding insurance and Securities)[15]

Bank Services as listed below:

a. **Acceptance of deposits and other repayable funds from the public;**

b. **Lending of all types, including consumer credit, mortgage credit, factoring and financing of commercial transaction;**

c. **Financial leasing;**

d. **All payment and money transmission services, including credit, charge and debit cards, travellers cheques and bankers drafts (including import and export settlement):**

e. **Guarantees and commitments;**

f. **Trading for own account or for account of customers: foreign exchange**

China commitments (any limitations/requirements or offers for services supplied in different modes)
Limitations on market access
Cross-border supply – Unbound except for the following: – Provision and transfer of financial information, and financial data processing and related software by suppliers of other financial services; – Advisory, intermediation and other auxiliary financial services on all activities listed in subparagraphs (a) through (k), including credit reference and analysis, investment and

---

[15][Ed.] *See The Regulations of the People's Republic of China on Administration of Foreign-Invested Financial Institutions* adopted by the State Council on 12 December 2001 and promulgated on 20 December 2001 and came into effect on 1 February 2002. The minimum registered capital for wholly foreign-owned banks and joint venture banks is the equivalent of RMB 300 million in a freely convertible currency. The minimum registered capital for wholly foreign-owned finance companies and joint venture finance companies is the equivalent of RMB 200 million. The head office of a foreign bank branch must allocate operating funds to the branch of an amount not less than the equivalent of RMB 100 million in a freely convertible currency.

The total assets of a party applying to establish a wholly foreign-owned bank or wholly foreign-owned finance company must not be less than US\$ 10 billion at the end of the year preceding the application. The total assets of a party that applies to establish a foreign bank branch must be at least US\$ 20 billion at the end of the year preceding the application. The total assets of a foreign joint venture partner applying to establish a joint venture bank or joint venture finance company must be US\$ 10 billion at the end of the year preceding the application. The Regulations provide that a foreign-invested financial institution must meet the following requirements in order to carry on Renminbi business: It must have carried on business in China at least three years before the application. It must have made a profit in the two successive years preceding the application. It must meet other prudential requirements stipulated by the People's Bank of China.

Also see The Announcement of the People's Bank of China on Market Access for Foreign-Invested Financial Institutions issued on 9 December 2001. The Announcement states that beginning from 11 December 2001, restrictions on the customers to whom foreign-invested financial institutions may provide foreign exchange services will be lifted. The range of customers may be expanded to include all units and individuals in China. Beginning from 11 December 2001, foreign-invested financial institutions established in Shanghai and Shenzhen may formally carry on Renminbi business. Foreign-invested financial institutions established in Tianjin and Dalian may apply to carry on Renminbi business. The Announcement also contains provisions on improving market access for the provision of motor vehicle financing and financial leasing services. *Website of China Legal Change www.chinalegalchange.com*

portfolio research and advice, advice on acquisitions and on corporate restructuring and strategy.

Consumption abroad – None

Commercial presence –

A. <u>Geographic coverage</u>

For foreign currency business, there will be no geographic restriction upon accession. For local currency business, the geographic restriction will be phased out as follows: Upon accession, Shanghai, Shenzhen, Tianjin and Dalian; Within one year after accession, Guangzhou, Zhuhai, Qingdao, Nanjing and Wuhan; within two years after accession, Jinan, Fuzhou, Chengdu and Chongqing; within three years after accession, Kunming, Beijing and Xiamen. Within four years after accession, Shantou, Ningbo, Shenyang and Xi'an. Within five years after accession, all geographic restrictions will be removed.

B. <u>Clients</u>

For foreign currency business, foreign financial institutions will be permitted to provide services in China without restriction as to clients upon accession.

For local currency business, within two years after accession, foreign financial institutions will be permitted to provide services to Chinese enterprises. Within five years after accession, foreign financial institutions will be permitted to provide services to all Chinese clients. Foreign financial institutions licensed for local currency business in one region of China may service clients in any other region that has been opened for such business.

C. <u>Licensing</u>

Criteria for authorization to deal in China's financial services sector are solely prudential (i.e., contain no economic needs test or quantitative limits on licenses). Within five years after accession, any existing non-prudential measures restricting ownership, operation, and juridical form of foreign financial institutions, including on internal branching and licenses, shall be eliminated.

Foreign financial institutions who meet the following condition are permitted to establish a subsidiary of a foreign bank or a foreign finance company in China:

– total assets of more than the US $10 billion at the end of the year prior to filing the application.

Foreign financial institutions who meet the following condition are permitted to establish a branch of a foreign bank in China:

– total assets of more than US $20 billion at the end of the year prior to filing the application.

Foreign financial institutions who meet the following condition are permitted to establish a Chinese-foreign joint bank or a Chinese-foreign joint finance company in China:

– total assets of more than US $10 billion at the end of the year prior to filing the application.

Qualifications for foreign financial institutions to engage in local currency business are as follows:

– three years business operation in China and being profitable for two consecutive years prior to the application, otherwise, none.

Presence of natural persons – Unbound except as indicated in Horizontal Commitments.

| Limitation on national treatment |

Cross-border supply – None

Consumption abroad – None

Commercial presence – Except for geographic restrictions and client limitations on local currency business (listed in "market access"), foreign financial institution may do business, without restrictions or need for case-by-case approval, with foreign invested enterprises, non-Chinese natural persons, Chinese natural persons and Chinese enterprises. Otherwise, none.

Presence of natural persons – Unbound except as indicated in Horizontal Commitments.

Additional Commitments

For financial leasing services, foreign financial leasing corporations will be permitted to provide financial leasing services at the same time as domestic corporations.

—Motor vehicle financing by non-bank financial institutions

China commitments
(any limitations/requirements or offers for services supplied in different modes)

| Limitations on market access |

Cross-border supply – Unbound except for the following:

– Provision and transfer of financial information, and financial data processing and related software by suppliers of other financial services;
– Advisory, intermediation and other auxiliary financial services on all activities listed in subparagraphs (a) through (k), including credit reference and analysis, investment and

portfolio research and advice, advice on acquisitions and on corporate restructuring and strategy.

Consumption abroad – None

Commercial presence – None

Presence of natural persons – Unbound except as indicated in Horizontal Commitments.

Limitation on national treatment

Cross-border supply supply – Unbound

Consumption abroad – None

Commercial presence – None

Presence of natural persons – Unbound except as indicated in Horizontal Commitments.

— **Other financial services as listed below:**

K. **Provision and transfer of financial information, and financial data processing and related software by supplier of other financial services;**

I. **Advisory, inter-mediation and other auxiliary financial services on all activities listed in subparagraphs (a) through (k)[16], including credit reference and analysis, investment and portfolio research and advice, advice on acquisitions and on corporate restructuring and strategy.**

China commitments
(any limitations/requirements or offers for services supplied in different modes)

Limitations on market access

Cross-border supply – None

Consumption abroad – None

Commercial presence – None (Criteria for authorization to deal in China's financial services sector are solely prudential (i.e., contain no economic needs test or quantitative limits on licenses). Branches of foreign institutions are permitted.

Presence of natural persons – Unbound except as indicated in Horizontal Commitments.

---

[16][Ed.] Subparagraphs (a) through (k) under Article 1B of MTN.TNC/W/50 (CPC 8131, 8133) pursuant to *GATT* Secretariat's classification list ('the GNS/120 list'— *see Provisional Central Product Classification, UN Statistics Division* web-address http://esa.un.org/unsd/cr/family2.asp?CI=9)

Limitation on national treatment
Cross-border supply – None
Consumption abroad – None
Commercial presence – None
Presence of natural persons – Unbound except as indicated in Horizontal Commitments.

— Securities

China commitments **(any limitation/requirements or offers for services supplied in different modes)**
Limitations on market access
Cross-border supply – Unbound except for the following:
– Foreign securities institutions may engage directly (without Chinese intermediary) in B share business.
Consumption abroad – None
Commercial presence –
a. Unbound, except for the following:
– Upon accession, representative offices in China of foreign securities institutions may become Special Members of all Chinese stock exchanges.
– Upon accession, foreign service suppliers will be permitted to establish joint ventures with foreign investment up to 33 per cent to conduct domestic securities investment fund management business. Within three years after China's accession, foreign investment shall be increased to 49 per cent. Within three years after accession, foreign securities institutions will be permitted to establish joint ventures, with foreign minority ownership not exceeding 1/3, to engage (without Chinese intermediary) in underwriting A shares and in underwriting and trading of B and H shares as well as government and corporate debts, launching of funds.
b. Criteria for authorization to deal in China's financial industry are solely prudential (i.e., contain no economic needs test or quantitative limits on licenses).
Presence of natural persons – Unbound except as indicated in Horizontal Commitments.
Limitation on national treatment
Cross-border supply – None

China commitments (any limitations/requirements or offers for services supplied in different modes)

Consumption abroad – None

Commercial presence – None

Presence of natural persons – Unbound except as indicated in Horizontal Commitments.

9. SECTOR: TOURISM AND TRAVEL RELATED SERVICES

A. Sub-sector: Hotels (including apartment buildings) and Restaurants (CPC 641–643)

China commitments (any limitations/requirements or offers for services supplied in different modes)

Limitations on market access

Cross-border supply – None

Consumption abroad – None

Commercial presence – Foreign services suppliers may construct, renovate and operate hotel and restaurant establishments in China in the form of joint ventures with foreign majority ownership permitted.

None, within four years after accession, wholly foreign-owned subsidiaries will be permitted.

Presence of natural persons – Unbound, except as indicated in Horizontal Commitments and as follows: Foreign managers, specialists including chefs and senior executives who have signed contracts with joint venture hotels and restaurants in China shall be permitted to provide services in China.

Limitation on national treatment

Cross-border supply – None

Consumption abroad – None

Commercial presence – None

Presence of natural persons – Unbound, except as indicated in Horizontal Commitments.

B. Sub-Sector: Travel Agency and Tour Operator (CPC 7471)

China commitments (any limitations/requirements or offers for services supplied in different modes)

Limitations on market access

Cross-border supply – None

Consumption abroad – None

Commercial presence – Foreign service suppliers who meet the following conditions are permitted to provide services in the form of joint venture travel agencies and tour operators in the holiday resorts designated by the Chinese government and in the cities of Beijing, Shanghai, Guangzhou and Xi'an upon accession:

a) a travel agency and tour operator mainly engaged in travel business;
b) Annual world-wide turnover exceeds US$ 40 million. The registered capital of joint venture travel agency/tour operator shall be no less than RMB 4 million.

Within three years after China's accession, the registered capital shall be no less than RMB 2.5 million. Within three years after accession foreign majority ownership will be permitted.

Within six years after accession, wholly foreign-owned subsidiaries will be permitted and geographic restrictions will be removed. The business scope of the travel agency/tour operator is as follows:

a) travel and hotel accommodation services for foreign travellers which can be made directly with transportation and hotel operators in China covering such operations;
b) travel services and hotel accommodation services for domestic travellers which can be made directly with transportation and hotel operators in China covering such operations;
c) conducting of tours within China for both domestic and foreign travellers, and
d) travellers check cashing services within China.

None within six years after accession, there will be no restriction on the establishment of branches of the joint venture travel agency/tour operator and the requirement on registered capital of foreign-invested travel agency/tour operator will be the same as that of Chinese travel agency/tour operator.

Presence of natural persons – Unbound, except as indicated in Horizontal Commitments.

Limitation on national treatment

Cross-border supply – None

Consumption abroad – None

Commercial presence – None except that joint ventures or wholly-owned travel agencies and tour operators are not permitted to engage in the activities of Chinese travelling abroad and to Hong Kong China, Macao China and Chinese Taipei.

Presence of natural persons – Unbound, except as indicated in Horizontal Commitments

11. SECTOR: TRANSPORT SERVICES

A. Sub-sector: Maritime Transport Services

— **International transport (freight and passengers) (CPC 7211 and 7212 less cabotage transport services)**

China commitments
(any limitations/requirements or offers for services supplied in different modes)

Limitations on market access

Cross-border supply –

a) Liner shipping (including passenger transportation): None
b) Bulk, tramp and other international shipping (including passenger transportation): None

Consumption abroad – None

Commercial presence –

(a) Establishment of registered companies for the purpose of operating a fleet under the national flag of the People's Republic of China:

- – Foreign service suppliers are permitted to establish joint venture shipping companies.
- – Foreign investment shall not exceed 49 per cent of the total registered capital of the joint venture
- – The chairman of board of directors and the general manager of the joint venture shall be appointed by the Chinese side.

(b) Other forms of commercial presence for the supply of international maritime transport services: Unbound

Presence of natural persons –

(a) Ship's crew: Unbound except as indicated in Horizontal Commitments.
(b) Key personnel employed by Commercial Presence as defined under mode of "Commercial presence – (b)" above: Unbound except as indicated in Horizontal Commitments.

Limitation on national treatment

Cross-border supply – (a) for liner shipping (including passenger transportation): None
(b) for bulk, tramp and other international shipping (including passenger transportation): None

Consumption abroad – None

---

*Unbound due to lack of technical feasibility.

Commercial presence –

(a) for establishment of registered companies for the purpose of operating a fleet under the national flag of the People's Republic of China: None

(b) for other forms of commercial presence for the supply of international maritime transport services: unbound

Presence of natural persons –

(a) Ship's crew: Unbound except as indicated in Horizontal Commitments.

(b) Key personnel employed by Commercial Presence as defined under (b) of Commercial Presence above: Unbound except as indicated in Horizontal Commitments.

Additional Commitments
The following services at the port are made available to international maritime transport suppliers on reasonable and non-discriminatory terms and conditions: 1. Pilotage 2. Towing and tug assistance 3. Provisioning, fuelling and watering 4. Garbage collection and ballast waste disposal 5. Port Captain's services 6. Navigation aids 7. Shore-based operational services essential to ship operations, including communications, water and electrical suppliers 8. Emergency repair facilities 9. Anchorage, berth and berthing services.

H. Sub-sector: Auxiliary Services

a. Maritime cargo-handling services (CPC 741)

c. Customs clearance services for maritime transport

China commitments (any limitations/requirements or offers for services supplied in different modes)
Limitations on market access **Cross-border supply** – Unbound*

---

*Unbound due to lack of technical feasibility.

Consumption abroad – None

Commercial presence – Only in the form of joint ventures, with foreign majority ownership permitted.

Presence of natural persons - Unbound except as indicated in Horizontal Commitments.

Limitation on national treatment

Cross-border supply – Unbound*

Consumption abroad – None

Commercial presence – None

Presence of natural persons – Unbound except as indicated in Horizontal Commitments.

d. Container station and depot services

China commitments (any limitations/requirements or offers for services supplied in different modes)
Limitations on market access
Cross-border supply – Unbound*
Consumption abroad – None
Commercial presence – Only in forms of joint ventures, with foreign majority ownership permitted.
Presence of natural persons – Unbound except as indicated in Horizontal Commitments.
Limitation on national treatment
Cross-border supply – Unbound*
Consumption abroad – None
Commercial presence – None
Presence of natural persons – Unbound except as indicated in Horizontal Commitments.

e. Maritime agency services

China commitments (any limitations/requirements or offers for services supplied in different modes)
Limitations on market access

*Unbound due to lack of technical feasibility.

Cross-border supply – None

Consumption abroad – None

Commercial presence – Only in forms of joint ventures, with foreign equity share no more than 49 per cent.

Presence of natural persons – Unbound except as indicated in Horizontal Commitments.

Limitation on national treatment

Cross-border supply – None

Consumption abroad – None

Commercial presence – None

Presence of natural persons – Unbound except as indicated in Horizontal Commitments.

B. Sub-Sector: Internal Waterways Transport

b. Freight Transport (CPC 7222)

China commitments
(any limitations/requirements or offers for services supplied in different modes)

Limitations on market access

Cross-border supply – Only international shipping in ports open to foreign vessels shall be permitted.

Consumption abroad – None

Commercial presence – Unbound

Presence of natural persons – Unbound except as indicated in Horizontal Commitments.

Limitation on national treatment

Cross-border supply – Limitations as indicated under "market access".

Consumption abroad – None

Commercial presence – Unbound

Presence of natural persons – Unbound except as indicated in Horizontal Commitments

---

C. Sub-sector: Air Transport Services
d. Aircraft repair and maintenance services (CPC 8868)

China commitments
(any limitations/requirements or offers for services supplied in different modes)

| Limitations on market access |

Cross-border supply – Unbound*

Consumption abroad – None

Commercial presence – Foreign service suppliers are permitted to establish joint venture aircraft repair and maintenance enterprises in China. The Chinese side shall hold controlling shares or be in a dominant position in the joint ventures. Licenses for the establishments of joint ventures are subject to economic needs test.

Presence of natural persons – Unbound except as indicated in Horizontal Commitments.

| Limitation on national treatment |

Cross-border supply – Unbound*

Consumption abroad – None

Commercial presence – The joint ventures have the obligation to undertake business in the international market.

Presence of natural persons – Unbound except as indicated in Horizontal Commitments.

— **Computer Reservation System (CRS) services**

China commitments
(any limitations/requirements or offers for services supplied in different modes)

| Limitations on market access |

Cross-border supply –

---

*Unbound due to lack of technical feasibility.

A. Foreign Computer Reservation System, when having agreements with Chinese aviation enterprises and Chinese Computer Reservation System, may provide services to Chinese aviation enterprises and Chinese aviation agents by connecting with Chinese Computer Reservation System.

B. Foreign Computer Reservation System may provide services to representative offices and sales offices established in the destination cities in China by foreign aviation enterprises which have the right to engage in business according to the bilateral aviation agreements.

C. Direct access to and use of foreign Computer Reservation System by Chinese aviation enterprises and agents of foreign aviation enterprises are subject to approval of the General Administration of Civil Aviation of China (CAAC).

Consumption abroad – None

Commercial presence – Unbound

Presence of natural persons – Unbound except as indicated in Horizontal Commitments.

Limitation on national treatment

Cross-border supply – None

Consumption abroad – None

Commercial presence – Unbound

Presence of natural persons – Unbound except as indicated in Horizontal Commitments.

E. Sub-sector: Rail Transport Services
F. Sub-sector: Road Transport Services
- **Freight transportation by rail (CPC 7112)**
- **Freight transportation by road in trucks or cars (CPC 7123)**

China commitments (any limitations/requirements or offers for services supplied in different modes)
Limitations on market access
Cross-border supply – None
Consumption abroad – None
Commercial presence – Only in the form of joint ventures, with foreign investment not to exceed 49 per cent.

For rail transport, within three years after China's accession, foreign majority ownership will be permitted and within six years after China's accession, wholly foreign-owned subsidiaries will be permitted.

For road transport, within one year after China's accession, foreign majority ownership will be permitted, within three years after China's accession, wholly foreign-owned subsidiaries will be permitted.

Presence of natural persons – Unbound except as indicated in Horizontal Commitments.

Limitation on national treatment

Cross-border supply – None

Consumption abroad – None

Commercial presence – None

Presence of natural persons – Unbound except as indicated in Horizontal Commitments.

H. Sub-sector: Services Auxiliary to all Modes of Transport — Storage and warehousing services (CPC 742)

China commitments (any limitations/requirements or offers for services supplied in different modes)

Limitations on market access

Cross-border supply – Unbound

Consumption abroad – None

Commercial presence – Upon accession, only in the form of joint ventures, with foreign investment not to exceed 49 per cent. Within one year after China's accession, foreign majority ownership will be permitted.

None within three years of China's accession, wholly foreign-owned subsidiaries will be permitted.

Presence of natural persons – Unbound except as indicated in Horizontal Commitments.

Limitation on national treatment

Cross-border supply – Unbound

414

> **Consumption abroad** – None
>
> **Commercial presence** – None
>
> **Presence of natural persons** – Unbound except as indicated in Horizontal Commitments.

— Freight forwarding agency services (CPC 748 and 749 excluding freight inspection)

> ### China commitments
> ### (any limitations/requirements or offers for services supplied in different modes)
>
> **Limitations on market access**
>
> **Cross-border supply** – None
>
> **Consumption abroad** – None
>
> **Commercial presence** – Upon accession, foreign freight forwarding agencies which have at least three consecutive years experience are permitted to set up freight forwarding agency joint ventures in China, with foreign investment not to exceed 50 per cent; within one year after China's accession, foreign majority ownership will be permitted.
>
> Within four years after China's accession, wholly foreign-owned subsidiaries will be permitted.
>
> The minimum registered capital of the joint venture shall be no less than US$ 1 million. Within four years after accession, national treatment will be accorded in this respect. Operation term of the joint ventures shall not exceed 20 years.
>
> After one year operating in China, the joint venture can set up branches when the registered capital of both sides has been provided. Another US$ 120,000 shall be added to the original registered capital of the joint venture for the set-up of each branch. Within two years after China's accession to the WTO, this additional registered capital requirement will be implemented on the national treatment basis.
>
> A foreign freight forwarding agency may set up a second joint venture after its first joint venture has been in operation for five years. Within two years after China's accession to WTO, this requirement will be reduced to two years.
>
> **Presence of natural persons** – Unbound except as indicated in Horizontal Commitments.

Limitation on national treatment

Cross-border supply supply – None

Consumption abroad – None

Commercial presence – None

Presence of natural persons – Unbound except as indicated in Horizontal Commitments.

416

LIST OF ARTICLE II EXEMPTIONS FOR CHINA

LIST OF ARTICLE II EXEMPTIONS[17] FOR CHINA

SECTOR OR SUB-SECTORS:

Maritime Transport
International Transport
Freight and Passengers

Description of Measures Indicating its Inconsistency with Article II	Countries to Which the Measures Applies	Intended Duration	Conditions Creating the Need for the Exemption
The parties concerned may, through bilateral agreement, establish entities to engage in usual business in China either as joint ventures or wholly-owned subsidiaries subject to the Chinese laws on joint ventures and on foreign capital enterprises for ships owned or operated by carriers of the parties concerned.	Unspecified.	Unforeseeable.	According to present state of trade between signatories.
Agreements of cargo sharing	Algeria, Argentina, Bangladesh, Brazil, Thailand, USA, Zaire.	Subject to the effective duration of the agreements concerned.	According to present state of trade between signatories.

---

[17][Ed.] Exemptions to Most-favoured nations treatment permissible under Article II of the *GATS*

Annex 1

REFERENCE PAPER

Scope

The following are definitions and principles on the regulatory framework for the basic telecommunications services.

Definitions

<u>Users</u> mean service consumers and service suppliers.

<u>Essential facilities</u> mean facilities of a public telecommunications transport network or service that

(a) are exclusively or predominantly provided by a single or limited number of suppliers; and

(b) cannot feasibly be economically or technically substituted in order to provide a service.

<u>A major supplier</u> is a supplier which has the ability to materially affect the terms of participation (having regard to price and supply) in the relevant market for basic telecommunications services as a result of:

(a) control over essential facilities; or

(b) use of its position in the market.

1. Competitive safeguards

1.1 Prevention of anti-competitive practices in telecommunications

Appropriate measures shall be maintained for the purpose of preventing suppliers who, alone or together, are a major supplier from engaging in or continuing anti-competitive practices.

417

1.2 Safeguards

The anti-competitive practices referred to above shall include in particular:

(a) engaging in anti-competitive cross-subsidization;
(b) using information obtained from competitors with anti-competitive results; and
(c) not making available to other services suppliers on a timely basis technical information about essential facilities and commercially relevant information which are necessary for them to provide services.

2. Interconnection

2.1 This section applies to linking with suppliers providing public telecommunications transport networks or services in order to allow the users of one supplier to communicate with users of another supplier and to access services provided by another supplier, where specific commitments are undertaken.

2.2 Interconnection to be ensured

Interconnection with a major supplier will be ensured at any technically feasible point in the network. Such interconnection is provided.

(a)   under non-discriminatory terms, conditions (including technical standards and specifications) and rates and of a quality no less favourable than that provided for its own like services or for like services of non-affiliated service suppliers or for its subsidiaries or other affiliates;

(b)   in a timely fashion, on terms, conditions (including technical standards and specifications) and cost-oriented rates that are transport, reasonable, having regard to economic feasibility, and sufficiently unbundled so that the supplier need not pay for network components or facilities that it does not require for the service to be provided; and

(c)   upon request, at points in addition to the network termination points offered to the majority of users, subject to charges that reflect the cost of construction of necessary additional facilities.

2.3 Public availability of the procedures for interconnection negotiations

The procedures applicable for interconnection to a major supplier will be made publicly available.

2.4 Transparency of interconnection arrangements

It is ensured that a major supplier will make publicly available either its interconnection agreements or a reference interconnection offer.

2.5 Interconnection: dispute settlement

A service supplier requesting interconnection with a major supplier will have recourse, either:

(a) at any time; or
(b) after a reasonable period of time which has been made publicly known

to an independent domestic body, which may be regulatory body as referred to in paragraph 5 below, to resolve disputes regarding appropriate terms, conditions and rates for interconnection within a reasonable period of time, to the extent that these have not been established previously.

3. Universal service

Any Member has right to define the kind of universal service obligation it wishes to maintain. Such obligations will not be regarded as anti-competitive *per se*, provided they are administered in a transparent, non-discriminatory and competitively neutral manner and are not more burdensome than necessary for the kind of universal service defined by the Member.

4. Public availability of licensing criteria

Where a licence is required, the following will be made publicly available:

(a) all the licensing criteria and the period of time normally required to reach a decision concerning an application for a licence; and
(b) the terms and conditions of individual licences.

The reasons for the denial of a licence will be made known to the applicant upon request.

5. Independent regulators

The regulatory body is separate from, and not accountable to, any supplier of basic telecommunications services. The decisions of and the procedures used by regulators shall be impartial with respect to all market participants.

6. Allocation and use of scarce resources

Any procedures for the allocation and use of scarce resources, including frequencies, numbers and rights of way, will be carried out in an objective, timely, transparent and non-discriminatory manner. The current state of allocated frequency bands will be made publicly available, but detailed identification of frequencies allocated for specific government uses is not required.

WORLD TRADE S/GBT/W/2/Rev.1
ORGANIZATION

16 January 1997

(97-0173)

Group on Basic Telecommunications

<u>Note by the Chairman</u>

<u>Revision</u>

It has been suggested by a number of delegations that it might be helpful to produce a brief and simple note on assumptions applicable to the scheduling of commitments in basic telecoms. The purpose of the attached note is to assist delegations in ensuring the transparency of their commitments and to promote a better understanding of the meaning of commitments. This note is not intended to have or acquire any binding legal status.

NOTES FOR SCHEDULING BASIC TELECOM SERVICES COMMITMENTS

1. Unless otherwise noted in the sector column, any basic telecom service listed in the sector column:

(a) encompasses local, long distance and international services for public and non-public use;

(b) may be provided on a facilities-basis or by resale; and

(c) may be provided through any means of technology (e.g., cable[18], wireless, satellites).

2. Subsection (g) – private leased circuit services – involves the ability of service suppliers to sell or lease any type of network capacity for the supply of services listed in any other basic telecom service subsector unless otherwise noted in the sector column. This would include capacity via cable, satellite and wireless network.

3. In view of points 1 and 2 above, it should not be necessary to list cellular or mobile services as a separate subsector. However, a number of Members have done so, and a number of offers have commitments only in these subsectors. Therefore, in order to avoid extensive changes in schedules, it would seem appropriate for Members to maintain separate entries for these subsectors.

---

[18]Including all types of cable.

WORLD TRADE S/GBT/W/3/
ORGANIZATION

3 February 1997

(97-0415)

original-English

Group on Basic Telecommunications

CHAIRMAN'S NOTE

Market Access Limitations on Spectrum Availability

Many Members have entries in the market access column of their schedules indicating that commitments are "subject to availability of spectrum/frequency" or similar wording. In light of the physical nature of spectrum and the constraints inherent in its use, it is understandable that Members may have sought to rely on these words to adequately protect legitimate spectrum management policies. There is, however, doubt that words such as "subject to availability of spectrum/frequency" as listed in the market access column of many Members' schedules achieve that objective.

Spectrum/frequency management is not, *per se*, a measure which needs to be listed under Article XVI, Furthermore under the GATS each Member has the right to exercise spectrum/frequency management, which may affect the number of service suppliers, provided that this is done in accordance with Article VI and other relevant provisions of the GATS. This includes the ability to allocate frequency bands taking into account existing and future needs. Also, Members which have made additional commitment in line with the Reference Paper on regulatory principles are bound by its paragraph 6.

Therefore, words such as "subject to availability of spectrum/frequency" are unnecessary and should be deleted from Members' schedules.

Annex 2

DISTRIBUTION SERVICES

Distribution trade services are comprised of four main sub-sectors:

— commission agents services
— wholesaling;
— retailing; and
— franchising.

The principal services rendered in each subsector can be characterized as reselling merchandise, accompanied by a variety of related subordinated services, including inventory management; assembly, sorting and grading of bulk lots; breaking bulk lots and redistributing into smaller lots; delivery services; refrigeration, storage, warehousing and garage services; sales promotion, marketing and advertising, installation and after sales services including maintenance and repair and training services. Distribution services are generally covered by CPC 61, 62, 63 and 8929.

Commission Agents' Services consist of sales on a fee or contract basis by an agent, broker or auctioneer or other wholesalers of goods/merchandise and related subordinated services.

Wholesaling consist of the sale of goods/merchandise to retailers to industrial, commercial, institutional, or other professional business users, or to other wholesalers and related subordinated services.

Retailing services consist of the sale of goods/merchandise for personal or household consumption either from a fixed location (e.g., store, kiosk, etc.) or away from a fixed location and related subordinated services.

Franchising services consist of the sale of the use of a produce, trade name or particular business format system in exchange for fees or royalties. Product and trade name franchising involves the use of a trade name in exchange for fees or royalties and may include an obligation for exclusive sale of trade name products. Business format franchising involves the use of an entire business concept in exchange for fees and royalties, and may include the use of a trade name, business plan, and training materials and related subordinated services.

Annex 3

INSURANCE: DEFINITION OF "MASTER POLICY"

Master policy is the policy that provides blanket coverage for the same legal person's property and liabilities located in different places. Master policy may only be issued by the business department of an insurer's head office or that of its authorized province-level branch offices. Other branches are not allowed to issue master policy.

Master policy business with the state key construction projects as its subject-matter insured. If investors on the state key construction projects (i.e., projects that are so listed and annually announced by the State Development and Planning Commission) meet either of the following requirements, they may purchase master policy from insurers that are located in the same place as the investors' legal persons do.

The investment on the subject-matter insured is all from China (including the reinvestment from the foreign-invested enterprises in China), and the sum of investment of the investor accounts for over 15 per cent of the total investment.

The investment is partially from abroad, and partially from China (including the reinvestment from the foreign-invested enterprises in China), and the sum of investment of the Chinese investor accounts for over 15 per cent for the total domestic investment.

For those projects that draw investment all from abroad, every insurer may provide coverage in the form of master policies.

Master policy covering different subjects-matter insured of the same legal person. For those subjects-matter insured located in different places and owned by the same legal person (excluding financial, railway, and post and telecommunications industries and enterprises), master policy may be issued on the basis of either of the following conditions.

For the sake of payment of premium tax, insurance companies incorporated where the legal person or accounting unit of the insurance applicant is located are allowed to issue master policy.

If over 50 per cent of insurance amount of the subject-matter insured is from a larger or medium sized city, then insurers in that city are allowed to issue master policy, no matter whether the insurance applicant's legal person or accounting unit is located in the city.

Motor insurance, credit insurance, employer liabilities insurance, statutory insurance, and other insurance business excluded by the CIRC can not be underwritten or co-insured by insurers located other than where the subject-insured are located, or covered under a master policy.

Source: www.chinawto.gov.cn

Appendix 4

GATS Services Sectoral Classification GNS/W/120
(This appendix is attached to facilitate readers to check whether their professions are included in Chinese commitments. Further breakdown of sub-sector services in CPC (provisional version) is available on the web page of UN Classification Registry, web site: (http://unstats.un.org/unsd/cr/registry/regcst.asp?CI=9&Lg=1)).

Sectors and sub-sectors	Corresponding provisional CPC[1]
1. Business services	
A. Professional services	
a. Legal services	861
b. Accounting, auditing and book keeping services	862
c. Taxation services	863
d. Architectural services	8671
e. Engineering services	8672
f. Integrated engineering services	8673
g. Urban planning and landscape architectural services	8674
h. Medical and dental services	9312
i. Veterinary services	932
j. Services provided by midwives, nurses, physiotherapists and para-medical personnel	93191
k. Other	
B. Computer and related services	
a. Consultancy services related to the installation of computer hardware	841

---

[1]The United Nations Statistics Division maintains a draft correspondence table between GNS/W/120, the Provisional *CPC*, and *CPC* version 1.0, available at http://www.un.org/depts/unsd/class/class1.htm. These correspondences may be useful for statistical monitoring of trade in services agreements.

Sectors and sub-sectors	Corresponding provisional CPC
b. Software implementation services	842
c. Data processing services	843
d. Data base services	844
e. Other	845+849

C. Research and development services

a. R&D services on natural sciences	851
b. R&D services on social sciences and humanities	852
c. Interdisciplinary R&D services	853

D. Real estate services

a. Involving own or leased property	821
b. On a fee or contract basis	822

E. Rental/leasing services without operators

a. Relating to ships	83103
b. Relating to aircraft	83104
c. Relating to other transport equipment	83101+83102+83105
d. Relating to other machinery and equipment	83106–83109
e. Other	832

F. Other business services

a. Advertising services	871
b. Market research and public opinion polling services	864
c. Management consulting service	865
d. Services related to man consulting	866
e. Technical testing and analysis services	8676
f. Services incidental to agriculture, hunting and forestry	881
g. Services incidental to fishing	882
h. Services incidental to mining	883+5115
i. Services incidental to manufacturing	884+855 (except for 88442)
j. Services incidental to energy distribution	887
k. Placement and supply services of Personnel	872
l. Investigation and security	873

Sectors and sub-sectors	Corresponding provisional CPC
m. Related scientific and technical consulting services	8675
n. Maintenance and repair of equipment (not including maritime vessels, aircraft or other transport equipment)	633+8861–8866
o. Building-cleaning services	874
p. Photographic services	875
q. Packaging services	876
r. Printing, publishing	88442
s. Convention services	87909*
t. Other	8790

2. Communication services

A. *Postal services*	7511
B. *Courier services*	7512

C. *Telecommunication services*

a. Voice telephone services	7521
b. Packet-switched data transmission services	7523**
c. Circuit-switched data transmission services	7523**
d. Telex services	7523**
e. Telegraph services	7522
f. Facsimile services	7521**+7529**
g. Private leased circuit services	7522**+7523**
h. Electronic mail	7523**
i. Voice mail	7523**
j. On-line information and data base retrieval	7523**
k. Electronic data interchange (EDI)	7523**
l. Enhanced/value added facsimile services, incl. store and forward, store and retrieve	7523**
m. Code and protocol conversion	n.a
n. On-line information and/or data processing (including transaction processing)	843**
o. Other	

D. *Audiovisual services*

a. Motion picture and video tape production and distribution services	9611
b. Motion picture projection service	9612

Sectors and sub-sectors	Corresponding provisional CPC
c. Radio and television services	9613
d. Radio and television transmission services	7524
e. Sound recording	n.a.
f. Other	

E. Other

3. Construction and related engineering services

A. *General construction work for buildings*	512
B. *General construction work for civil engineering*	513
C. *Installation and assembly work*	514+516
D. *Building completion and finishing work*	517
E. *Other*	511+515+518

4. Distribution services

A. *Commission agents' services*	621
B. *Wholesale trade services*	622
C. *Retailing services*	631+632+6111+6113+6121
D. *Franchising*	8929
E. *Other*	

5. Educational services

A. *Primary education services*	921
B. *Secondary education services*	922
C. *Higher education services*	923
D. *Adult education*	924
E. *Other education services*	929

6. Environmental services

A. *Sewage services*	9401
B. *Refuse disposal services*	9402
C. *Sanitation and similar services*	9403
D. *Other*	

7. Financial services

A. *All insurance and insurance-related services*	812**
a. Life, accident and health insurance services	8121
b. Non-life insurance services	8129
c. Reinsurance and retrocession	81299*

Sectors and sub-sectors	Corresponding provisional CPC

d. Services auxiliary to insurance (including broking and agency services) — 8140

B. *Banking and other financial services (excluding insurance)*

a. Acceptance of deposits and other repayable funds from the public — 81115–81119

b. Lending of all types, incl., <u>inter alia</u>, consumer credit, mortgage credit, factoring and financing of commercial transaction — 8113

c. Financial leasing — 8112

d. All payment and money transmission services — 81339**

e. Guarantees and commitments — 81199**

f. Trading for own account or for account of customers, whether on an exchange, in an over-the-counter market or otherwise, the following:
— money market instruments (cheques, bills certificate of deposits, etc.) — 81339**
— foreign exchange — 81333
— derivative products incl., but not limited to, futures and options — 81339**
— exchange rate and interest rate instruments, including products such as swaps, forward rate agreements, etc. — 81339**
— transferable securities — 81321*
— other negotiable instruments and financial assets, incl. bullion — 81339**

g. Participation in issues of all kinds of securities, incl. under-writing and placement as agent (whether publicly or privately) and provision of service related to such issues — 8132

h. Money broking — 81339**

i. Asset management, such as cash or portfolio management, all forms of collective investment management, pension fund management, custodial depository and trust services — 8119+** / 81323*

j. Settlement and clearing services for financial assets, incl. securities, derivative products, and other negotiable instruments — 81339**or / 81319**

k. Advisory and other auxiliary financial services on all the activities listed in Article 1B of MTN.TNC/W/50, incl. credit reference and analysis, investment and portfolio research and advice, advice on acquisitions and on corporate restructuring and strategy — 8131 / or 8133

Sectors and sub-sectors	Corresponding provisional CPC
1. Provision and transfer of financial information, and financial data processing and related software by providers of other financial services	8131

C. *Other*

8. Health related and social services
(other than those listed under 1.A.h-j.)

A. *Hospital services*	9311
B. *Other human health services*	9319 (other than 93191)
C. *Social services*	933
D. *Other*	

9. Tourism and travel related services

A. *Hotels and restaurants (incl. catering)*	641–643
B. *Travel agencies and tour operators services*	7471
C. *Tourist guides services*	7472
D. *Other*	

10. Recreational, cultural and sporting services
(other than audiovisual services)

A. *Entertainment services (including theatre, live bands and circus services)*	9619
B. *News agency services*	962
C. *Libraries, archives, museums and other cultural services*	963
D. *Sporting and other recreational services*	964
E. *Other*	

11. Transport services

A. *Maritime transport services*

a. Passenger transportation	7211
b. Freight transportation	7212
c. Rental of vessels with crew	7213
d. Maintenance and repair of vessels	8868**
e. Pushing and towing services	7214
f. Supporting services for maritime transport	745**

Sectors and sub-sectors	Corresponding provisional CPC

B. Internal waterways transport

a. Passenger transportation	7221
b. Freight transportation	7222
c. Rental of vessels with crew	7223
d. Maintenance of repair of vessels	8868**
e. Pushing and towing services	7224
f. Supporting services for internal waterways transport	745**

C. Air transport services

a. Passenger transportation	731
b. Freight transportation	732
c. Rental of aircraft with crew	734
d. Maintenance and repair of aircraft	8868**
e. Supporting services for air transport	746

D. Space transport   733

E. Rail transport services

a. Passenger transportation	7111
b. Freight transportation	7112
c. Pushing and towing services	7113
d. Maintenance and repair of rail transport equipment	8868**
e. Supporting services for rail transport services	743

F. Road transport services

a. Passenger transportation	7121+7122
b. Freight transportation	7123
c. Rental of commercial vehicles with operator	7124
d. Maintenance and repair of road transport equipment	6112+8867
e. Supporting services for road transport services	744

G. Pipeline transport

a. Transportation of fuels	7131
b. Transportation of other goods	7139

H. Services auxiliary to all modes of transport

a. Cargo-handling services   741
b. Storage and warehouse services   742
c. Freight transport agency services   748
d. Other   749

I. Other transport services

12. Other services not included elsewhere   95+97+98+99

The (*) indicates that the service specified is a component of a more aggregated CPC item specified elsewhere in this classification list.
The (**) indicates that the service specified constitutes only a part of the total range of activities covered by the CPC concordance (e.g. voice mail is only a component of CPC item 7523).
Further subdivided into: (i) passenger: (ii) freight; and (iii) supporting, auxiliary and other services.

Source: Annex VII to *MANUAL on STATISTICS of INTERNATIONAL TRADE in SERVICES* compiled by UN Statistical Division [Final draft 6 September 2001], p221–226. It is being edited by the United Nations Statistical Division for a joint publication by the six organisations: European Commission, International Monetary Fund, Organisation for Economic Co-operation and Development, United Nations, United Nations Conference on Trade and Development, World Trade Organization (http://unstats.un.org/unsd/tradeserv/docs/msits_unedited010906.pdf)

Detailed structure and explanatory notes

CPCprov

Click on any code to see more detail.

- 0 – Agriculture, forestry and fishery products
  - 01 – Products of agriculture, horticulture and market gardening
  - 02 – Live animals and animal products
  - 03 – Forestry and logging products
  - 04 – Fish and other fishing products
- 1 – Ores and minerals; electricity, gas and water
  - 11 – Coal and lignite; peat
  - 12 – Crude petroleum and natural gas
  - 13 – Uranium and thorium ores

- 14 – Metal ores
- 15 – Stone, sand and clay
- 16 – Other minerals
- 17 – Electricity, town gas, steam and hot water
- 18 – Water

- 2 – Food products, beverages and tobacco; textiles, apparel and leather products

  - 21 – Meat, fish, fruit, vegetables, oils and fats
  - 22 – Dairy products
  - 23 – Grain mill products, starches and starch products; other food products
  - 24 – Beverages
  - 25 – Tobacco products
  - 26 – Yarn and thread; woven and tufted textile fabrics
  - 27 – Textile articles other than apparel
  - 28 – Knitted or crocheted fabrics; wearing apparel
  - 29 – Leather and leather products; footwear

- 3 – Other transportable goods, except metal products, machinery and equipment

  - 31 – Products of wood, cork, straw and plaiting materials
  - 32 – Pulp, paper and paper products; printed matter and related articles
  - 33 – Coke oven products; refined petroleum products; nuclear fuel
  - 34 – Basic chemicals
  - 35 – Other chemical products; man-made fibres
  - 36 – Rubber and plastics products
  - 37 – Glass and glass products and other non-metallic products n.e.c.
  - 38 – Furniture; other transportable goods n.e.c.
  - 39 – Wastes or scraps

- 4 – Metal products, machinery and equipment

  - 41 – Basic metals
  - 42 – Fabricated metal products, except machinery and equipment
  - 43 – General purpose machinery
  - 44 – Special purpose machinery
  - 45 – Office, accounting and computing machinery
  - 46 – Electrical machinery and apparatus
  - 47 – Radio, television and communication equipment and apparatus
  - 48 – Medical appliances, precision and optical instruments, watches and clocks
  - 49 – Transport equipment

- 5 – Construction work and constructions; land

  - 51 – Construction work
  - 52 – Constructions
  - 53 – Land

- 6 – Trade services; hotel and restaurant services
  - 61 – Sale, maintenance and repair services of motor vehicles and motorcycles
  - 62 – Commission agents' and wholesale trade services, except of motor vehicles and motorcycles
  - 63 – Retail trade services; repair services of personal and household goods
  - 64 – Hotel and restaurant services
- 7 – Transport, storage and communications services
  - 71 – Land transport services
  - 72 – Water transport services
  - 73 – Air transport services
  - 74 – Supporting and auxiliary transport services
  - 75 – Post and telecommunications services
- 8 – Business services; agricultural, mining and manufacturing services
  - 81 – Financial intermediation services and auxiliary services therefor
  - 82 – Real estate services
  - 83 – Leasing or rental services without operator
  - 84 – Computer and related services
  - 85 – Research and development services
  - 86 – Legal, accounting, auditing and book-keeping services; taxation services; market research and public opinion polling services; management and consulting services; architectural, engineering and other technical services
  - 87 – Business services n.e.c.
  - 88 – Agricultural, mining and manufacturing services
  - 89 – Intangible assets
- 9 – Community, social and personal services
  - 91 – Public administration and other services to the community as a whole; compulsory social security services
  - 92 – Education services
  - 93 – Health and social services
  - 94 – Sewage and refuse disposal, sanitation and other environmental protection services
  - 95 – Services of membership organizations
  - 96 – Recreational, cultural and sporting services
  - 97 – Other services
  - 98 – Private households with employed persons
  - 99 – Services provided by extraterritorial organizations and bodies

Source : first page, CPC Provisional Version, 1989, UN Classification Registry, United Nations Statistics Division,
http://unstats.un.org/unsd/cr/registry/regcst.asp?Cl=9&Lg=1

General Keywords Index

China Laws Index

See also laws and regulations quoted in *Chapter 4*, *Part II* under "recent modifications to IP regime", and all rules and laws under *Section "E"*.

WTO Rules Index

Important Disclaimer

The texts quoted in this book in respect of WTO provisions or China accession documents do not have the legal standing of the originals of full texts which are entrusted to and kept at the WTO secretariat at Geneva. Any interpretation of such provisions shall be based on the official interpretation of the WTO at the point of time the source is cited.

Likewise, for Chinese legal provisions, the official web sites of the Chinese government shall be consulted for the full text and English translation thereof. For the articles or other documents quoted in this book, the originals of their full text, contents or data shall be consulted from the sources or web sites indicated for interpretation and accuracy.

While every effort has been made to contact the publishers of cited materials prior to publication, we have not been successful in some cases. Where we could not contact the publishers, we have acknowledged the source of the material.

Neither the editors nor the publishers are liable for any errors or actions taken in reliance thereon.